Renovating
Old Houses

A post-1850s farmhouse in Garfield, Vt.

Renovating Old Houses

George Nash

The Taunton Press

Taunton

BOOKS & VIDEOS

for fellow enthusiasts

© 1992 by The Taunton Press, Inc.
All rights reserved.

First printing (soft cover): 1996
Printed in the United States of America

A FINE HOMEBUILDING Book

FINE HOMEBUILDING® is a trademark of The Taunton Press, Inc., registered in the U.S. Patent and Trademark Office.

The Taunton Press, 63 South Main Street, Box 5506, Newtown, CT 06470-5506

Library of Congress Cataloging-in-Publication Data

Nash, George, 1949-
    Renovating old houses / George Nash.
        p.   cm.
    "A Fine homebuilding book"—T.p. verso.
    Includes bibliographical references and index.
    ISBN 0-942391-65-9 hard cover
    ISBN 1-56158-128-3 soft cover
    1. Dwellings—Maintenance and repair.   I. Title.
TH4817.N38   1996
643'.7—dc20   95-44407
                                               CIP

To all of us who just can't help it, who would still rather live in an old house even after fixing one up, remember the words of the poet:

He who loves an old house
never loves in vain.

—Isabel La Howe Conant, "Old House"

Acknowledgments

First, I'd like to thank all of you who sent letters and called to ask where you could find a copy of my out-of-print book *Old Houses: A Rebuilder's Manual*. It was this need that inspired me to pursue the idea of an updated and improved version of the original. I'd also like to express my appreciation to the people at The Taunton Press for their cooperation and support, especially Paul Bertorelli, who launched the project, and Kevin Ireton, who put in a good word for me. I am also grateful to all those who let me into their homes to take pictures, especially Kevin and Becky Walters, Peter and Rebecca Whitmore and Eric and Lester Adams. Thanks also to the crew at Blush Hill Real Estate, and all the other contractors who worked under the eye of my telephoto lens. I'd also like to thank Steve Marlens for his constructive criticism and philosophical counterpoint, and all those whose ideas I have borrowed or built upon—learning the craft of renovation is a lifelong enterprise, and it helps to have good advice along the way. And, of course, I thank everybody in my family, who had to put up with me slipping off for weeks at a time into that twilight zone inhabited by writers—the late suppers out of cans, the dirty dishes piling up and the fabric of daily life unkempt. We're all relieved now that it's over. Finally, I thank my editor, Laura Tringali, for her insight, tight reins and those damn queries. It's a much better book because of her. I enjoyed the partnership and also appreciated the encouragement (sometimes bordering on outright threat) that forced me to pull together all the loose ends of this project under pressure of a tight deadline.

Contents

Introduction   2

Structural and Financial Evaluation   14

Making an External Examination   16
Foundation problems • Insect problems
Structural decay • The chimney • The roof
Walls and windows • Exterior attachments

Making an Internal Examination   27
The cellar • Waste disposal • The plumbing system
Water supply • The heating system • The electrical system
Bulkhead and cellar windows • The attic • The rest of the house

Preserving Historically Significant Features   38

Financial and Legal Considerations   39

Organizing Priorities   44

Developing the Design   46
Attic conversion • Radical changes

Approaches to Renovation   55
The blitzkrieg approach • The caterpillar approach

How to Rebuild and Stay Sane   57

Hiring a Contractor   60
Types of contracts

Architects and Designers   63

Foundations   64

Water-Infiltration Problems   66

Installing an Exterior Drainage System   68

Repairing and Replacing Foundation Walls   70

Raising the House   73
Where to lift • Jacking equipment • Safety considerations

The New Foundation   86
Laying out the footings
Building the foundation wall • Working with concrete
Waterproofing and insulating the foundation wall

Adding a Cellar   95

Pouring a Concrete Floor   98

The House Frame   102

Types of House Frames   103
Timber frames • Balloon frames • Platform frames

Replacing Rotted Sills   109

Repairing Rotted Posts   115

Repairing Sagging Floors   116
Raising a sagging girder • Stiffening a sagging girder
Repairing floor joists

Repairing Other Structural Elements   121
Using steel repair plates • Joinery for beam repair

Truing Up the House Frame   125
Correcting leaning walls and swayback roofs

The Roof   130

Roofing Materials   131
Wood • Slate • Metal • Cement-asbestos shingles
Asbestos-free cement roofing and tile roofing • Asphalt roofing
Roll roofing • Asphalt-composition shingles

Roofing Repairs   137
Finding a leak • Causes of leaks
Repairing built-up roofing • Replacing asphalt shingles
Repairing slate roofing • Repairing cement-asbestos and tile roofing
Replacing wood shingles • Repairing metal roofing • The roofer's panacea

Reroofing with Asphalt Shingles   144
Laying new shingles over old • Stripping the roof

Installing Asphalt Shingles   152
Estimating materials • Vertical layout • Horizontal layout
Application techniques • Ridge-cap shingles • Valley installation
Installing other kinds of asphalt roofing

Reroofing with Wood Shingles   159

Reroofing with Steel Sheets   160

Eave Protection   164

Eavestroughs and Downspouts   165
Yankee gutters • Repairing built-in gutters
Replacing wood gutters • Metal and plastic gutters

The Cold Roof   171

Windows, Doors, Siding and Trim   172

Infiltration and Heat Loss: Tightening Up the House   173
Caulking • Weatherstripping

Windows   177
Storm windows • Rebuilding a double-hung window
Replacing rotted windowsills • Reinstalling crooked windows
Adding and subtracting windows

Doors   184
Replacing a threshold • Taking care of doors
A shortcut to successful door hanging • Storm doors

Exterior Siding and Trim 189

Getting under the house's skin • Repairing and replacing exterior trim
Retrofitting soffit vents • Installing clapboards
Wood-shingle siding • Some other siding choices

Painting Protocol 202

Paint problems • Stripping exterior paint
Latex vs. oil • Stain • Cleaning brickwork

Attachments, Additions and Alterations 206

Porches and Verandas 207

Common problems and repairs • Stoops

Sheds and Garages 214

Radical Changes: Attic and Roof Retrofits 215

Removing the roof

Walls, Ceilings and Floors 220

What to do about Plaster 221

Plaster repairs • Gutting the plaster
Plaster walls and insulation • Alternatives to plaster

Inside the Walls: Insulation Theory and Practice 227

R-values • Installing insulation

Interior Partitions: Moving Walls 234

Removing nonbearing walls • Removing load-bearing walls
Adding straight walls to crooked houses

Building and Repairing Stairs 241

Rise and run • Framing the stairwell • Laying out the stairs
Installing the stairs • Stair repair

Interior Wall Finishes 245

Installing drywall • Taping drywall • Wood paneling

Ceiling Treatments 252

Ceilings with exposed beams • Covered ceilings
High vs. low ceilings

A Note on Trim 257

Finished at Last: The Floors 258

Repairing floors • Refinishing floors

The Electrical System 262

Basic Electrical Theory 263

Alternating current

Evaluating Your Electrical System 264

Types of wiring systems

Designing a Circuit 267

Rewiring an Old House 268

Tools for rewiring • Surface-mounted wiring systems
Wiring within the walls • Adding a switch
Wiring between floors • Other wiring solutions

Making the Right Connection 276

Household Plumbing 280

Plumbing Materials and Theory 281
Pipe systems

Springs and Wells 283
Problems at the source

Water Pumps 285
Pumping systems • Pump problems

An Old-House Plumbing System 288
The supply system • The drainage system

On-Site Sewage Disposal 290
Septic-tank problems

Plumbing Problems 292
Supply-line repair • Copper-pipe repair
Drain-line repair • A cautionary tale

Plumbing and Structural Changes 303

Home Heating Systems 306

Hot-Air Systems 307

Steam-Heating Systems 308
Venting • Maintenance and operation

Hot-Water Heating Systems 314
Forced-flow systems • Maintenance and operation
Adding and removing radiators

Alternative Heating Systems 319
Wood-burning stoves • Passive solar heating

Repairing and Restoring Chimneys 323
Relining a chimney • Repointing a chimney
Rebuilding a chimney • Flashing a chimney • Chimney draw

A Few Thoughts about Fireplaces 330

Afterword 332

Bibliography 334

Index 339

Introduction

*…this square home, as it stands in unshadowed earth
between the winding years of heaven, is, not to me, but of itself,
one among the serene and final uncapturable beauties of existence:
that this beauty is made between hurt but invincible nature and the
plainest cruelties and needs of human existence.*

—James Agee and Walker Evans, *Let Us Now Praise Famous Men; Three Tenant Families* (Boston: Houghton Mifflin, 1960).

*In northern Vermont, a house does not remain vacant very many winters before it begins to sag, slip and
ease itself back into the soil from which it was so laboriously raised.*

Why buy an old house?

What is it about old houses? What strange spells do they cast, so that otherwise perfectly rational human beings are compelled against all sanity and sense to commit large amounts of energy, money and time to their rebuilding?

Is it economics? In an era of inflated real-estate prices, fewer and fewer people can afford the up-front costs of a new or completely remodeled house. The "handyman's special" (real-estate agent's euphemism for crumbling disaster) ostensibly offers first-time buyers home ownership on a limited budget, or enterprising individuals a chance to make a good return on an investment. Of course, the low purchase price will be offset by the cost of remodeling, but this can theoretically be spread out over a long time—ideally, cash flow will keep pace with repairs. But even with that low purchase price, an old house, when all the costs of remodeling are finally tallied, will typically cost as much as, if not more than, a comparable new house.

Is it then a matter of aesthetics, the charm of a bygone style? Form and function do seem to complement each other in old houses, whether grandiose mansions or austere farmhouses, with a depth and beauty that has been left behind by our heedless rush into modernity. But although the contrast between a hand-built old house and the developer-assembled "product" of today is obvious, it is not fundamental. The success of present-day custom builders proves that pride in workmanship is still economically viable. Traditional houses can be built, complete to the last details of the woodwork, without the shortcomings of plumbing, wiring and comfort that plague their prototypes.

People who work with and live in old houses use fuzzy words like "feel," "aura" and "essence" to justify their obsession. These are aesthetic categories that attempt to describe the perception of beauty, the way that so many old houses almost seem to live a life of their own, breathing in slow, subtle rhythms of shifting lines and weathering wood. As do all living things, a house achieves a delicate equilibrium, a precariously maintained and constantly changing relationship to time, the seasons and its people. It responds to the care given it—growing, changing, adding windows and doors, sprouting porches and sheds in season. And when its people depart, a house begins to die. The process occurs with a grace, beauty and terrible simplicity. The tilt and sag of the walls, the weathered shades of clapboard and peeling paint, the tired angles of the roof, all give mute expression to the ebb and flow of the lives once harbored within. Like woodsmoke from the cooking fire that has been absorbed into the plaster, the rooms and walls of old houses are suffused with the spirits of former inhabitants. All old houses are full of ghosts.

For me, it is this spiritual dimension, above all, that makes the renovation of old houses so deeply satisfying. To bring back a house to useful life, immersing oneself in the grain and texture of an earlier way of living in the process, is ultimately an act of resurrection of both the house and its owners.

Although the old-house restorer may undertake a profoundly spiritual journey, the path is full of physical details. Like all heroic quests, it is fraught with pitfalls and perils, both real and imagined. On the mundane level, this translates into lots of work, time and money. Because purchase price is obviously a function of the neighborhood and the condition of the house, determining how much work the house needs and how to go about doing it is the crux of the matter. No matter how astutely you may have examined the structure for defects, others are guaranteed to appear. It's quite likely you'll discover not only rotted beams but also windowsills eaten away clear through the sheathing boards, a roof as watertight as an old bucket used for target practice and a torrent deep enough to float a river raft pouring through the foundation wall every time it rains. You will soon find that as bad as you thought the place might be, the reality is actually much worse. Your original estimate of time and money needed to restore the house to bare livability will increase by a factor of three. This money will disappear into largely invisible, and therefore ungratifying, structural repairs. And winter will be coming on early this year.

You probably knew all this at the outset, knew that the place really was in terrible shape even as you were poking your finger through the dry-rotted beams and telling yourself, yes, there will have to be some minor repairs here, and yes, perhaps the cracks in the foundation need some patching, or is it pointing? And of course that ghastly linoleum on the floors will have to go, but the plaster seems sound enough, just a coat of spackle ought to fix it up fine. So potent is the spell of the old place that you simply ignore your reservations and common sense even as the real-estate agent is thanking the stars for city slickers. And so you proceed to sign not only a mortgage, but body and soul, spouse and children, over to an idea that will soon become a joy and a burden, a monster that devours every molecule of your time, money and spirit. Yet even when you discover that the only thing keeping the place from blowing away is the holes in the walls and the weight of the mouse droppings in the attic, you wouldn't have it any other way. If this is the case, you might be one of those old-house people, a peculiar kind of maniac who is one part ability, one part inventiveness, two parts determination, three parts romanticism and six parts damn foolishness.

Conscious Renovation: Philosophies Defined

Given that the renovation of old houses deals with psychic as well as physical matters, it's hardly surprising that the field has its ideologues and iconoclasts who wage polemical jihads in the pages of journals and at professional conferences. Because of the fierceness of these passions, it's almost impossible to define terms, make recommendations or locate oneself in a niche without arousing accusations of heresy from adherents of a different persuasion.

There are basically three approaches to working with old houses: preservation, renovation and remodeling (or "remuddling"). These are distinguished by the degree of alteration (or violence) to the existing structure considered permissible and the amount of importance attached to historical fidelity.

Preservation

The umbrella of preservation, encompassing both restoration and conservation, covers the most conservative (some might argue sensitive) end of the spectrum. Preservationists believe that there are thousands of old houses that have a far more enduring importance to society as educational examples and tools than they do as dwelling places for any one family or as investments for any one group or individual at any one time. Since so few of these historically important houses can be protected through outright acquisition by preservation societies, preservationists argue that the lack of a legal mandate to preserve old houses does not absolve private home owners of their moral responsibility to do so.

The number of surviving American homes built before 1850 in original (or even "modernized") condition is dwin-

This abandoned house clearly needs a lot of work, yet its undeniable character and a location both secluded and accessible to a ski area might justify the expense of major renovation.

dling much faster than the realization is dawning of how much important historical and social information is bound up in them. Through the process of "seriation" (the correspondence of particular details and structures to a specific chronological period), architectural historians are just starting to trace the evolution of specific features and construction techniques. To do this effectively requires a large stock of original unaltered old houses. In this light, even seemingly minor details of fairly ordinary old houses could be historically significant. Thus, if the owners of an architecturally important house make an irreversible change to suit their personal needs or tastes, they will destroy the opportunity for anyone else to learn from that house. They could even permanently erase information considered important by future scholars.

Personally, I think the concept "old house" is too slippery to assign the cut-off date of 1850. The shingle-style houses built in the 1930s in Berkeley, California, are now "old," and architecturally significant. The day will doubtless come when preservationists decry the desecration of historically important examples of Southern California tract houses. Accordingly, the most important test for any proposed change to a pre-1850 house is *reversibility*. If the change cannot be undone later, it should be avoided. If this is impractical, the original features and changes should be documented on film and/or videotape, with measured drawings and written or taped descriptions: Documentary overkill is an invaluable aid to future researchers.

Ultimately, preservationists hold that if a prospective buyer finds a particular old house absolutely charming in its ambience but feels that it needs drastic changes in floor plan, window size and interior finishes to make it "livable," he or she has an obligation to history and society not to buy it. They argue that it is immoral to impose irreversibly one's personal tastes and needs on the shrinking fabric of history. Such people should seek a house more suited to their sensibilities, or build a new "old" home instead.

The round tower and curved porches make this Antrim, N.H., house a worthy candidate for preservation. The private owner is struggling to keep it off the market.

Evidence of an architectural 'missing link': an unusual mortise-and-tenon joint used to secure the ceiling joists to the wall studs of this c. 1850s farmhouse in Stowe, Vt. Features such as these are important examples of the evolution of framing techniques.

Within the preservationist camp there are some nuances of methodology that are confusing enough to merit further discussion. Although it can be argued that in a strict technical sense preservation can be distinguished from conservation, the difference is so subtle that the terms can be used almost interchangeably. At most it's a distinction of fine degree: Just as conserves are a jam made from whole fruit and preserves are a jam made from mashed fruit, a conservationist is perhaps more insistent on leaving the existing structure intact than a preservationist, whose primary interest is in historical continuity. Whereas a preservationist might paint over existing trimwork with modern latex paint, nevertheless preserving the underlying paint strata, a conservationist would be more likely to oppose the use of any but the traditional calcimine or whitewash formulas.

Restoration, however, is in no way synonymous with either preservation or conservation. It refers instead to the historical investigation and precise technical processes by which a structure is stripped of all later additions and returned to its original condition. Thus, restoring an early 18th-century village home would require the removal of its 19th-century porch, no matter how well that addition harmonized with the core house. Likewise, continuing the earlier example, the restorationist would carefully remove each layer of paint down to the earliest, and would repair or replace any damaged surfaces with materials and methods duplicating the originals.

Generic 19th-century farmhouses, such as this central Vermont 'joint house' (a complex of connected house, sheds and barns), seldom have historically significant features and are excellent candidates for renovation.

This most conservative and demanding branch of preservation is usually reserved for historically significant, museum-quality examples of a particular architectural style, and has little impact on the average home owner. If you are confronted with the purchase of a truly important old house, a specimen of a rare and perhaps endangered species, you should recognize your responsibility at least to preserve (if you cannot afford to restore) it for future generations. If you cannot be comfortable within the confines of this trusteeship, be reasonable and don't buy the house. There is no shortage of quaint, charming, generic antebellum farmhouses and late colonials perfectly ripe for renovating without destroying an irreplaceable heirloom.

Chances are good that your house may contain some historically important features, so take the time to inform yourself about their value through research and reading, or better yet, by hiring a professional conservationist or architectural historian, before making any but the most superficial changes. You can also contact your state's historical preservation office for advice on how to proceed, or refer to the technical preservation bulletins issued by the National Park Service, which can be obtained from their regional offices.

Renovation

Because renovation presupposes the idea that one is free to adapt the old to the new, to preserve or uncover the spirit while changing the form to suit personal needs, the mere mention of the word is enough to raise the hackles of preservationists. Living in a restored house is a little like collecting antiques or old bottles, which, whatever its merits, can be carried to extremes. It's a question of personality, I suppose, whether one wishes to live in a museum. The restored house ignores those elements of antique design that may be impractical or unsuitable to modern living. For example, even though an earthen cellar floor may be historically important, it is a prime cause of excessive household

This brick Georgian Revival in McIndoe Falls, Vt., would benefit architecturally from the removal of the attached nondescript wood ell.

Only routine maintenance is needed to keep this beautifully preserved late 19th-century farmhouse intact.

humidity and structural rot. Likewise, few people would be willing to sacrifice the comfort and convenience of central heating, adequate insulation or modern electrical systems for historical authenticity. In the same vein, how does one live with authentic "Indian blinds" (the wood panels used to cover the window sashes of circa-1800 country houses, which disappear into uninsulated pockets in the jambs) in an age of high heating costs? One can also argue that to be successful (if success is a felicitous marriage of form and function), the design of a house must derive from the needs of its occupants. We are not 18th-century pioneers or Jeffersonian gentry, and it seems to me that antiques have real value only if they are useful as well as beautiful.

So renovators are not afraid to make changes. Where a preservationist might insist that broad expanses of decayed original plaster be repaired or restored with new material mixed and applied according to traditional recipes and finishes, a renovator would more likely remove the plaster entirely, replacing it with modern materials that would more or less duplicate the original texture. Likewise, a renovator would suffer no qualms over installing thermally efficient modern windows (as long as they duplicated the look or feel of the original sashes), or over sanding and refinishing old floorboards with polyure-

thane varnish instead of the original shellac. Removing interior walls to open up a cramped, confining floor plan or adding a dormer to a low attic ceiling would not automatically be problematic. For a renovator, a house is never a monument, never fixed in time. In this respect, at least, the modern owner is carrying on the tradition of the previous owners who, adding and subtracting new wings, porches, walls and windows, worked to adapt the house to their needs and circumstances.

The difference between renovation and preservation and the root of much internecine conflict is that the latter is precise, a science, if you will, while the former is poetic—and dangerously indeterminate. Since preservationists must observe the canons of historical fidelity, stylistic options, and the very real potential for historical home-icide, are limited. But the problem with renovation is that it's one thing to admonish a home owner not to do violence to the spirit of an old house in the rush to change it, and another to define exactly what that means and how to accomplish it. How does one divine the spirit of a place before disturbing its bones? How do the new owners listen to the heartbeat of the house and match their own to it? The very vagueness of the words renovators use to describe their approach is infuriating. They are mean-

8

This 19th-century village home has already been disastrously compromised by remodeling. The new windows are inappropriate.

Renovation or remuddling? It's a judgment call for this c. 1870 Vermont farmhouse. The large area of south-facing glass brings light into the main living area at the expense of a traditional facade.

A clear case of remuddling here: The original panel door was replaced with a steel door blank and an inappropriate stoop, destroying the facade of the house.

ingless to anyone who isn't already receptive to such a way of thinking, to those who don't already speak the language.

The most instructive examples of sensitive renovation are necessarily negative. Somehow, examples of what one shouldn't do seem better able to suggest what one should do. The *Old-House Journal* (see the Bibliography on pp. 334-338), which I recommend for its information on all aspects of renovation and restoration, features monthly photos of outrageous "remuddling," which are especially egregious examples of insensitive and clumsy architectural faux pas. Replacement windows that don't match the historical style of the original house are a common offender. Additions and deletions to the main house are another frequently bungled area. Vinyl siding does not mate well with Federalist brick. Porches, not decks, belong on the front of farmhouses; if you must have a deck, put it on the back of the house where it can't be seen from the road. Although solariums and greenhouses were a common feature of elegant Victorian mansions, adding a contemporary sunspace to an old house without having it appearing tacked on is not easy.

Matching the trimwork is a key element of success for any addition. Even without the full-blown gingerbread fretwork of the high Victorian or Gothic style, the cornices of a simple rustic farmhouse are much more complex than anything modern style dictates. Nevertheless, failure to carry existing detailing over to new work because it costs too much guarantees an aesthetic abomination. Developers who convert old houses into commercial and apartment complexes by tacking low-rise brick or vinyl-clad boxes onto elegant Fed-

The narrow line of vinyl-clad replacement windows does violence to the original trimwork. This white vinyl cannot be painted to blend in.

eralist townhouses, replete with exposed cinder-block firewalls, are some of the worst offenders in this area.

Rehabilitation, which is the adaptation of a structure for a purpose (typically commercial) different from that for which it was originally intended, is the radical wing of renovation. It's also an excellent example of recycling. Buildings that otherwise would be economically unusable and slated for demolition can be put to other profitable and even pleasing uses. A dilapidated factory block becomes a key element in a revitalized city core when it is reincarnated as a shopping mall or low- or middle-income housing.

Remodeling

To my mind, renovation is to preservation as the Unitarians are to mainstream Protestants. Extending the metaphor, remodelers are the atheists or, since that persuasion presupposes intellectual awareness, perhaps the berserkers on the continuum. Remodelers don't believe in ghosts. Depending on their sensitivity, or lack of it, remodelers will not hesitate to gut the entire house at the first sign of a bulge in the ceiling and wrap every available surface in drywall and texture paint. Since

the object is to standardize materials and methods, maximize profit and eliminate variables, a remodeler's tool of choice is invariably the wrecking bar. Remodelers are served by (and beholden to) the advertising industry, which markets the images that fuel the successive waves of modernization that have caused the literal vandalization of countless old homes. Like most products of mass culture, the fashions of remodeling have proved ephemeral. Who today would panel their "rec" rooms with knotty pine? Does anyone still cover the insides of their houses with barnboards?

I confess my sympathies lie somewhere between liberal preservation and conservative renovation. Except for those few houses where a plaster ceiling is distinguished by ornamental medallions and cornice castings of historical value, which are worthy of professional restoration, my feeling about plaster, for example, is to get rid of it rather than to repair it, and to replace it with new, modern plaster (but not drywall). Although I agree with the need for preserving truly historical houses both

'Camps' are the second homes of the working class, typically built with the cheapest materials and shoddiest methods; they are usually uninsulated and lack any real foundations. This row of generic camps cannot be hurt by extensive remodeling, and is a good example of how a handyman's special can form the nucleus of a sound house.

out of simple respect for the past and as objects of study, how many of them are needed is an open question. There are many places (such as Colonial Williamsburg) that provide living examples of the evolution of public and domestic buildings. Every town has a historical society that encourages the recognition and preservation of old houses. Special zoning designations also can prevent the depletion of traditional styles, at least for exterior facades. All these preservation and rehabilitationist trends should be nourished, if only for the sake of raising general historical awareness.

But people need places to live. And, as they have always done, people will change their houses as they live in them. Outside of a costume party or stage play, we don't wear whalebone corsets or waistcoats anymore. Likewise, I don't think we should be forced to fit into houses that no longer suit the modes of a less formal age. Eric Sloane may be thinking of such people when he cautions us in *An Age of Barns* (New York: Ballantine Books, 1967) that "the only thing about age is that it affords time for learning and for good deeds. If you do not learn or do good works, old age will do for you what it does for a dead

fish, but slower." Perhaps this means a smaller stock of museum-quality examples in the public domain. This is certainly a rationale for increased scholarship before it is too late. Fortunately, the availability of sophisticated documentary techniques allows a smaller pool for study. Once a feature is thoroughly recorded, its alteration or loss is less disastrous. And, as with the great private collections of art, those who can afford it and to whom it is important will pay for the restoration of their old houses. That is what keeps conservation consultants in business. Education (and tax incentives) can play a role in increasing the preservation consciousness.

Like it or not, it's not possible to legislate good taste or mandate that only appropriately sensitive individuals be entrusted with the ownership of historic homes. A pluralistic and highly commercialized society shares no cultural consensus on what a house should look like, or even more important, on the value of the past and the desirability of preserving its vessels. There is some consolation in the fact that at least older houses are being recycled rather than left to fall down, uninhabited and pristine examples of historical architecture.

A Manufacturer's Warning and Limited Warranty

Some people might feel that this is a dangerous book. The information it contains is powerful stuff. It's possible that someone not in tune with a preservation or sensitive renovation philosophy, following the letter of the methods but ignoring the spirit, could damage some significant part of our architectural heritage. Although my book will help professionals and amateurs alike decide what, when and how to deal with the many problems unique to preserving or renovating an old house, it can't do anything more than try to make

Better that this unusual Colonial revival had fallen into the hands of a remodeler than succumb to neglect.

people aware of the special responsibilities that come with old-house ownership. I believe that a course of sensitive renovation offers the least harmful and most economical and emotionally satisfying cure for the ills of most old houses, most of the time. I hope the cautions expressed here and in the following chapters will alert the reader to those cases when heroic measures are needed. Please, before you pick up the wrecking bar, take the time to research the history of your house or hire a professional to do it for you. You'll want your ghosts to join comfortably with the community that stays behind after you pass through.

The information presented in this book is also powerful because it is specific to old houses. There are guidebooks on every aspect of the building trade, but there is very little actual crossover between the methodology and mind-set of new construction and that of renovation. Most standard instruction is predicated upon ideal situations, where wood is uniform in thickness, walls are square, doors plumb and foundations firm. This may not seem all that important until you try to fit a rectangular sheet of plywood into a trapezoidal corner.

In new work, the craftsperson proceeds in logical and rectilinear order. The actual work is relatively simple and even resembles the clear line drawings in the textbooks. The order of an old house is not that simple or coherent. Not only must you deal with someone else's mistakes, but you'll confront large imponderables and unsolvable dilemmas as well. Houses a century or more old typically feature a heavy-timber post-and-beam framework that is as individual and arbitrary as its builders. Beyond that, an old house settles and shifts through years of use, and often abuse, into a totally idiosyncratic entity. Walls lean, floors sag, major beams are rotted or missing. Any existing mechanical systems or insulation are at best inadequate. There may be a logic underlying the

Renovation is often a matter of dealing with someone else's mistakes. There are certainly plenty of them showing on the outside of this old farmhouse.

carpenter's nightmare of crumbling walls and patchwork roofing, but it has to be teased out.

Fortunately, you don't have to be a structural detective or an accomplished carpenter to rebuild your old house. With a little help from an occasional professional and a lot of reading, you can learn as you go, matching your skills to the job, stretching your abilities to the task. I do presuppose a familiarity with tools and a working knowledge of basic carpentry. I also presuppose that you have the determination to tackle some difficult and tedious jobs for the simple satisfaction of their completion. Renovation demands inordinate amounts of perseverance for what may seem to be nebulous rewards. It's a good thing that we seldom realize just how difficult the job can be; otherwise we might prudently turn aside and thereby miss the opportunity to test our mettle. For these reasons, I'll also attempt to chart the psychic waters of the renovation process, waters that are seldom clear or calm. Many a marriage, many a self-image, have run aground on the rocks of rebuilding. All too often home owners are caught in a whirlpool of obsession, and the work at hand becomes more important than the reason it is being done. You'll have to keep a firm hand on the tiller of self as you run this passage.

Although the information in this book is based upon my experiences in rural northern New England, it is nevertheless applicable to older houses in just about any region of the country. The rural focus is not meant to be exclusive. Indeed, in many areas, since the available stock of classic farmhouses is just about used up, what's left tends to be expensive. Fortunately, not everyone wants to live back in the "puckerbush," so village and suburban homes are increasingly attractive candidates for renovation. One thing is certain —existing houses get older every year.

Wood-frame structures also comprise a large part of the housing stock in smaller cities. Here, formerly blighted urban zones are rapidly being converted into fashionable neighborhoods. Without becoming embroiled in the politics of gentrification, I would say that these areas offer great opportunities to the potential renovator, especially one who buys before the development wave gathers momentum. But those who are rebuilding houses in the cities or suburbs may have to contend with problems of a bureaucratic nature that we rustics are not yet cursed with. In fact, local ordinances or mortgage lenders may prevent anyone but a licensed professional from doing any renovation work at all. In

such cases, the information in this book will at least allow you to evaluate a prospective purchase, outline the scope of the work and help you communicate with your contractor.

In all modesty, even this book won't answer all your questions. It's fortunate that there is a large body of knowledge that is part of the oral and manual tradition, learned by, and passed on through, generations of carpenters. A goodly part of it is totally contradictory, being based on the personal experience of whomever you might be talking to at the moment. Each situation requires its own strategy. This is particularly true in rural areas where old houses have been continually propped up and patched together by their inhabitants, who are often making do with the place their great-grandfather's father hewed the beams for. Just about any old country carpenter knows something about the problems of preserving houses and barns from the ravages of difficult weather and hard years; he's had to do it on his own place or the neighbor's. That this pool of knowledge has remained largely inaccessible to the novice builder is no surprise; it is unknown to more than a few modern trade-school carpenters as well. These old-timers are still very much alive, working back in the hills where time shambles along like a tired horse on a dusty summer road. By asking around, you might find someone who's done it before, or has a fair idea of how to go about doing whatever it is that needs to be done.

I know a fellow who is a bridge between two cultures, a dairy farmer starved out of farming who turned to carpentry, father of eight children, who in his own words was "born too late for a big family and too early for birth control." As a young man he owned 500 acres of prime farmland. Now he owns six. The rest he sold off to a succession of wealthy newcomers from downcountry, whose houses he built. What makes him so special is his keen awareness of what he has lost. It is a thing you can almost touch, an aura that pro-

Wood-frame houses are often prime candidates for affordable renovation in small cities.

vides an eerie counterpoint to the humor with which he customarily faces the world about him.

We were wondering once how things had come to such a state, and he told me how in his father's time people got by. They didn't have much, but they didn't need much, either. They always seemed to have enough. But when the boys came back from the wars, they brought with them the itch to have some of those things they had seen out there. It was easy to sell a few cows and make a payment on the new pickup truck, the television set. The things his father had valued just didn't seem that important anymore. One by one, they left the farm for the big money and easy life in construction. Once they got a taste of it, by God, they were bound and determined to spend it. What they couldn't see was that they were spending their heritage, their spiritual capital, as well. Once started, things seemed to run in one direction only. More and more, the old ways were tossed aside and simply forgotten, like the rubbish heap at the edge of the sugar woods.

Old houses are a bit like my old friend, tossed aside and forgotten. They are a bridge between the ways of a slower and more harmonious time and our own shallow frenzy. In some ways, too, I hope this book is a bridge between these cultures. The renovation of old houses is more than an investment, more than a handyman's challenge or a shortcut to home ownership. It is a spiritual undertaking as well.

In closing, I offer a thought from John F. Kelly's classic treatise, *Early Domestic Architecture of Connecticut,* as one answer to the question that opened this book.

Consciously or unconsciously, man looks with satisfaction upon that which is substantially and enduringly built. It is primarily, or at least largely, this sense of sheer structural value which makes us admire the pyramids, the temples of Greece, the mighty cathedrals of the thirteenth century. The same instinct infal-

The sensitive renovator will always strive to preserve the hard-won character of an old house while balancing the need for changes that will ensure its habitability for future generations. (Photo by Joe English.)

libly communicates to every observer, even the most casual, the bluff and rugged strength of our old houses; and he who knows these ancient dwellings more intimately, perhaps through having been fortunate enough to live in one of them, is keenly and sensitively responsive to the security, the abundance of strength which they embody. Their mighty frames of oaken timbers — which measure sixteen and even eighteen inches — have stood unshaken for two centuries or more. By comparison, the frame house of today, built as it is of 2x4 studs which must be sheathed with inch boards to impart to the framework the practicable modicum of rigidity, seems pathetically, not to say ludicrously, frail. He who warms as he ought to the spirit of these old houses must revel in the well-nigh barbaric massiveness of their framing.

Structural and Financial Evaluation

*"Do you see, Pooh? Do you see, Piglet?
Brains first and then Hard Work. Look at it!
That's the way to build a house," said Eeyore proudly.*

—A.A. Milne, *The House at Pooh Corner*

The art of structural evaluation requires an ability to 'read' the lines of a building. Here, the sag in the roofline is a sign of structural trouble, while the plastic swathing the first floor indicates cold, drafty and probably poorly insulated walls and ill-fitting windows.

I remember quite well that leaden April morning, the front end of our ancient van clanking in protest as we climbed the steep washboard road through the forest, where stale snow still clung to the dark places, climbed to where the woods shrank back from the dull, matted fields to reveal the ridges rolling away to the mountains at the end of the valley, like some moldering purple blanket that had lain out by the garden all winter. And there it sat, at the end of a sparsely graveled drive, dwarfed by a pair of towering cottonwoods. The clapboards had weathered to a delicate filigree of grain and fissure, which to us seemed the purest distillation of poetry. The front of the house leaned opposite of the back, the dormer slouched, and even from a distance we could see the chimney was crumbled. The porch quivered uneasily underfoot as we pushed our way into the kitchen, where plaster hung from the ceiling in leprous patches of decay. The floors tilted through so many planes, we began to feel seasick. There was at least 2 ft. of water in the basement, and a portion of the foundation wall (made of loose stones) had tumbled inward. We bought the house that very day, for what seemed to us quite a bargain price—the very first place we saw, the very first day we went looking. And 15 years and many thousands of dollars later, I'm quite sure it could happen again. But this time, I'd know better what price to offer the real-estate agent.

Some places are just *there*. In all of the universe, at that moment this is your particular place. No amount of rational temporizing will change the destiny that has already begun to unfold. There is some deep congruence between your innermost self and the molecules of the old house. You have no choice but to buy the place. You were meant for each other. This description is not in the least facetious. The experience is very real. On the surface of your mind, you tell yourself the obvious, that the place is in terrible shape, that only a fool would buy it, while within,

you are already setting out the window boxes on the sills, and the tea kettle is singing on the stove.

Just about any old house has the power to perturb the spirit, but not always on your personal frequency. You'll need some sort of filtering device to weed out all but the strongest vibrations. It's a commonplace that a marriage needs more than the first flush of passion to sustain itself. Likewise, even if it's love at first sight, you shouldn't buy an old house without conducting a thorough investigation into even its most uninviting corners. At least then you'll know the extent of the work that lies ahead and whether it's an ordeal you wish to undertake. But how do you do this?

Most books about buying old houses advocate a checklist of some sort to determine whether a house is worth buying. If enough items appear on the wrong side of the list, you are advised to look for another place. Such checklists are undeniably useful (I offer one myself at the end of this chapter). But it seems that according to most of these systems, a house with major structural defects, such as a cracked or heaved-in foundation, rotted sills or leaning and bowed walls, is immediately disqualified from further consideration. Although it's true that these kinds of defects call for expensive and time-consuming repairs, I don't agree that they necessarily rule out purchase. Instead, they might serve as a bargaining chip when negotiating the price.

Except in very unusual cases, most structural defects are not life-threatening, nor do they rule out interim habitation until repairs are complete. After all, another family had been living in the place before you showed up. Problems that are immediately obvious even to the untrained eye are the raison d'être of the "handyman's special." With the information and the checklist in this book you'll be able to expose the less obvious but often even more significant defects, and perhaps exert enough downward pressure on the price to bring it into the realm of affordability; by studying the subsequent chapters, you'll gain enough knowledge to make the necessary repairs. Finally, by learning how to separate the merely cosmetic from the truly structural problems, you'll be able to decide whether your infatuation with this particular house has a chance of maturing into a successful and satisfying long-term relationship.

The dip in the line of the attached shed shows foundation settlement.

The curve of this hip rafter is hardly intentional; the roof framing is too light and the pitch too low to carry the heavy snow loads of Vermont winters safely.

What should you look for? How do you decide? What are the symptoms of an unsound structure?

Anything can be fixed if you spend enough time and money, but unless you are one of those people who have more dollars than sense, you should know how to discriminate between problems so bad they make renovation unfeasible and problems that are formidable but worth the effort.

The great divide of structural evaluation falls on the line between the absolute and the optional; the distinction between structural repairs that must be done to preserve the integrity of the house or, indeed, make it minimally habitable, and those cosmetic renovations that can be done as circumstances permit. But there are degrees of urgency even within this absolute category. For example, you could live with a poor foundation or rotting sills for several years, but a defunct furnace, inadequate water system or badly leaking roof all require immediate attention.

Making an External Examination

Your evaluation should always begin with the exterior of the house. Stand back some distance and look at its shape. Sight along the ridgeline of the roof. Does it sag noticeably in the middle or is it straight? Do the eaves hump upward or curve outward? Look at the walls. Do they bow outward, inward or sag? Do the end walls lean, or the corners appear to tilt? These defects may not be obvious at first glance. The subtle warnings of bows and sags are sometimes ignored in the excitement of an initial favorable impression.

A house is a physics equation writ large in a script of stone and wood. Essentially, its frame is a series of interwoven triangles. The stability of the house structure depends on maintaining the integrity of each corner angle. In structural terms, this translates into proper bracing and uniform transfer of internal and external stresses. The triangle of the roof is lifted above the earth by walls that are joined to it through the foundation. But because the frame is not seamless, being broken by joints and fasteners, and the forces that operate upon it are, stresses can concentrate at any number of structurally weak points. These places act as hinges, causing failure. Deformation of the frame, either through settlement or failure of individual framing members, disrupts the balance and causes the house to lean, bend or tilt. If the cause is not corrected, the static equilibrium of the structure will continue to decay, and the condition will gradually worsen.

As the house inexorably moves from the vertical toward the horizontal, a critical point is reached, and the triumph of gravity is realized in a moment of sudden collapse. Your house is likely to be some-where along this curve of accelerating decay. Reversing the direction is a question of knowing at which end to push.

The drawing below shows how the forces operating on a house can lead to its collapse. The point is, a square house is a sound house: The roofline should be level, the corners should appear to line up with each other and look vertical when you sight down along the walls. The walls themselves should inhabit a single plane; bows, sags and other free-form curves are sure signs of structural failure. Since clapboards were originally installed level, their present orientation clearly reveals hidden problem areas. The lines can also reveal a history of structural changes. For example, when a window appears level but is not parallel with the clapboards, it has to be a later addition, installed after that section of the building settled.

A Square House is a Sound House

A house frame is made of triangles. No triangle leg can lengthen or shorten unless another breaks.

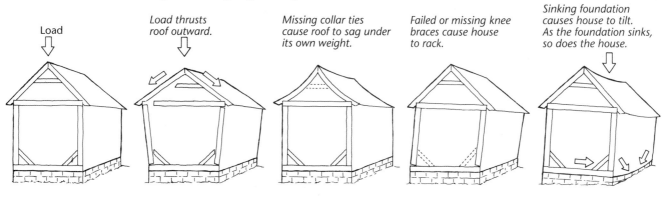

Load

Load thrusts roof outward.

Missing collar ties cause roof to sag under its own weight.

Failed or missing knee braces cause house to rack.

Sinking foundation causes house to tilt. As the foundation sinks, so does the house.

Reading Clapboards

These ripples hint at structural problems, confirmed when rotted sills and wall framing are revealed beneath them.

A gap between the house and ell is a sign of foundation settlement. Note also that the window and roof are not parallel. Determining whether the fault was arrested or is still active requires further inspection.

The vertical joint line suggests that something was either added or taken away. In this case, it is reasonable to suspect that the original cellar bulkhead may have been protected by some sort of roofed structure that was later removed.

What hidden problems do these tilting clapboards, leaning walls and sagging rooflines manifest? As mentioned earlier, something has to give before things start to move. Because there is a fair amount of play in a braced timber frame (not all timber frames were built by master craftsmen), over a long enough time such houses tend to lean away from the direction of the prevailing winds. Sometimes major structural timbers were cut or even removed during a bout of careless earlier remodeling. Water from a chronic leaky roof can rot the heavy beams that support the roof—when these pull apart, the entire house is twisted by the misplaced load. Sometimes the framing is simply not strong enough to withstand the weight of the years. As timbers bend or crack and joints separate, the walls follow the line of least resistance.

Foundation problems

In an old house with structural abnormalities, foundation settlement is the most likely culprit. When a section of wall gives way or sinks, the frame has no choice but to follow. The effect is amplified throughout the structure as unbalanced loads try to reestablish a new equilibrium. Rotted sill beams have the same effect as settled foundations.

Can your budget accommodate a foundation replacement? Since every foundation is different, it's impossible to estimate costs by any running-foot rule of thumb, but, in my experience, hiring a contractor to jack up a typical 24-ft. by 32-ft. farmhouse, remove the existing wall and replace it with a poured-concrete foundation will cost anywhere between $14,000 and $20,000, or more, especially if replacement of rotted sills is involved. Concrete subcontractors charge a premium for work under existing structures, since it's much more awkward and slower—as much as double their standard cubic-yard-in-place rate. Since labor is the main component of any foundation/sill repair job, doing it yourself can save a significant part of that cost. If neither your budget nor your confidence are up to the job, you should consider another property.

Although final confirmation must wait until you inspect the cellar, now is a good time to check the exposed part of the foundation wall for cracks and other signs of settlement. The wall should not bow outward or inward from the line of the building. Bulkheads or cellar entries are a common trouble spot. Unless care was taken to prevent frost damage, these walls can push the main foundation wall in. Dry-laid or mortared stone walls should be sound, with no obvious gaps or loose stones. The ground should slope away from the walls. If it doesn't, surface runoff will flow back against the foundation and into the cellar. Minor regrading can be done with a shovel and wheelbarrow, but anything more calls for a bulldozer. Examine the window wells: They shouldn't let water pond up against the foundation. The cellar vent windows, framed before the availability of preservative-treated wood, will be at some stage of decay and will probably need replacement.

An earlier attempt to shore up a heaving foundation without correcting the cause of the problem only makes the job more difficult when it's your turn.

Loose and crumbling stone foundations are almost always in need of replacement; buttress walls (see p. 21) were poured against a wall like this to stop wind infiltration and falling stones.

A leak left unfixed allowed a major structural joint to rot away. As a result, the back wall of the house is pulling away from the gable wall in response to foundation settlement.

Water pouring into the cellar through a window well helped destroy this foundation. As the wall heaved, the unsupported sill settled, pulling away from the studs and floor. Note the bricks filling the wall cavities —an early form of insulation.

Insect problems

If you live in the northern tier or Rocky Mountain states, termite infestation will not be a problem, but in most other areas of the country these insects are a structural hazard. Examine the sills carefully for evidence of either a termite shield (a metal collar between foundation wall and wood) or the characteristic earthen tubes that these insects build from the soil up the foundation walls to edible wood. The actual infestation will be hidden within the walls, safe from casual detection. Unlike the common subterranean termite, which nests in the soil and only forages in your woodwork, the drywood termite, a species native to the Gulf and southern and western coastal areas, both nests and feeds in wood, and so leaves no telltale soil tube. Instead look for piles and pellets of partially digested wood and entrance holes covered by a thin brownish seal.

Ask for a certificate (if applicable) of termite inspection before you sign any sales agreement. Since the chemicals traditionally used to control termites pose severe environmental and health hazards for years after their application, even when used by reputable professional exterminators, buying a termite-infested house is a poor idea. Making sure that no wooden part of the house is in direct contact with the soil is helpful, but by no means foolproof.

A sill peppered with the emergence holes of wood-boring beetles.

Northerners are not entirely secure from the threat of wood-chewing insects. Carpenter ants belie their name; they excavate long galleries and nests along the grain of wood sills and joists. These large black ants (½ in. to ¾ in. long) need moist wood to survive, so infestations are likely wherever water is held against a wall, as for example, under a porch pillar, behind a ledger or where wood is in direct contact with earth. Since moisture also tends to collect in cracks where several timbers join together, ant nests are often found in these hard-to-repair places. The ants can usually be seen entering and leaving their tunnels on foraging expeditions. Deposits of coarse sawdust are also a sign of their handiwork. On the other hand, piles of fine, powdery sawdust indicate an infestation by the larvae of any of a number of species of wood-boring beetles grouped under the name powderpost beetles. It is rare to find a sill or floor joist unmarred by a peppering of their characteristic ¹⁄₁₆-in. to ⅛-in. holes (see the photo below).

Although carpenter ants and wood-boring beetles can cause severe damage, professional eradication is much easier and more successful than for termites. Most infestations can be arrested by promoting good ventilation to reduce moisture content of wood framing, especially in dank cellars. Stripping off the bark commonly left on half-round log floor joists will also deprive borers of their shelter. If you see obvious and widespread signs of insect activity, find another house or at least have a professional pest inspection done to determine the severity of the problem before you sign a sales contract.

Structural decay

Much more than insects, wood-digesting fungi are responsible for structural decay in every area of the country. Unfortunately, rotted beams or sills aren't normally visible from the outside of the house. Decaying exterior siding is a danger sign; there's a good chance that the sheathing underneath and the sills are at least partially affected. If there is enough sound wood left to support the framing above (when less than half the thickness of a sill has rotted) the damaged portions can be dug out and filled in with new wood. Where sections have collapsed or crumbled away, causing settlement of the structure above, sill replacement is a must. Sills under thresholds are especially prone to rot. So are sections of wall behind steps, or any other places where water or snow can sit. Fortunately, repairing such localized decay, although tedious, does not require a great outlay of materials and is not especially difficult.

In an attempt to shore up a heaved wall or to prevent surface water and wind infiltration, builders of an earlier generation would often pour a sloped concrete wall directly against the old stone foundation (see the middle photo at right). Since these "buttress" walls seldom extended more than a few inches below grade, they usually were pushed up by frost action, taking the wall stones with them. Even worse, the concrete was typically poured right up against the siding. A more ideal incubator for rot than the unprotected joint between mortar and wood is hard to imagine. Any foundation featuring this kind of wall is immediately suspect. Probe the siding boards with an ice pick to test for soundness. If the pick penetrates the boards easily, sill replacement is almost guaranteed.

The chimney

If the lines of the house appear straight, the sills intact and the foundation solid, the house is probably structurally sound. The chimney is the only other significant (translation: expensive) structural problem you are likely to encounter. A telephoto lens or binoculars will enable you to examine the chimney without clambering onto the roof.

Look for the obvious signs of decay; large cracks, missing bricks, crumbly mortar and spaces where mortar has fallen out. The portion of the chimney exposed to the weather above the roofline usually falls

Rotted sills are not usually exposed to view from outside. Here, the bottom siding courses have been removed to reveal the extent of the damage.

Even when properly flashed, buttress walls can cause trouble. Since they rarely extend below grade, they will not prevent water infiltration.

Seen through a telephoto lens, this chimney is in pretty bad shape.

apart long before the rest. Sometimes the entire chimney will be unsafe. Look also for a tile flue liner; it should project an inch or two above the mortar or brickwork cap. The size of the chimney is a good indication of the presence of a liner. A four-brick or six-brick chimney is unlined. More than six bricks per course indicates multiple flues or a large single flue. As a rule, older chimneys were unlined, which is why so many old houses burned down because of chimney fires. A slightly less expensive and certainly more convenient alternative to tearing down and rebuilding an unlined masonry chimney is to install a metal or special concrete flue liner.

The roof

While looking up at the chimney, note the condition of the roof. First, ascertain the type of roofing material and try to count how many layers of old roofing the deck is carrying. If there is only one, it may be possible to lay new roofing directly atop the old. But adding another layer of shingles to a roof already carrying two or three layers of asphalt could severely overload the rafters and cause the roof to sag. Asphalt roofing has a relatively short life, particularly under harsh climatic conditions; 20 to 25 years is considered normal. Signs of a roof that has outlived its useful life span (not counting leaks, of course) include shingles worn so thin they've lost their protective mineral surface, wood or tar paper showing between the cutouts, areas of cracked and buckled shingles, or numerous patches and tarred-over spots. Unless the previous owner has replaced the shingles within the last 15 years, you can expect to do so within the next few. Stripping and replacing an asphalt-shingle roof is not a difficult job. The materials themselves are relatively inexpensive (about $40 per 100 sq. ft. of coverage).

Cedar shingles and shakes in need of replacement will appear crumbly, with many splits in individual shingles. In shady areas under tree canopies, colonies of moss and lichen on wood shingles hold water and promote decay. The only difference between replacement of wood and asphalt shingles is that wood shingles are much more expensive and require much more labor to apply.

Although slate roofing lasts a very long time, the slates eventually erode (acid rain hastens the process). But individual slates fall off or break long before the entire roof requires replacement. Also, unless the roofers used copper or lead, flashing metal (like galvanized steel) decays much faster than slate. Repair of slate roofing, although a bit tricky, is not so difficult as to be beyond the skills of the home owner.

If the roof is covered with corrugated steel sheets instead of shingles, it's likely the nails that secure the seams will need tightening down. Because of its constant contraction and expansion, metal roofing works loose over the years. If the metal is rusted but still sound, it can be restored to years of useful life by a coat of asphalt- or metallic-based roof coating. Paint or asphalt roof coating can also revitalize a rusted, but not yet disintegrated, standing-seam or soldered flat-seam metal roof. Unfortunately, replacement of these metal roofing systems is expensive and beyond the abilities of most nonprofessionals.

Walls and windows

While inspecting the outside of the house, bear in mind that a fresh coat of paint is a notorious technique for boosting the selling price of a house while avoiding basic repairs. It's something like an undertaker's cosmetic act. I know of just such a place: Viewed from the roadside, its neat white clapboards and trim black shutters are the perfect image of a quaint country house. Underneath that new paint, the foundation walls and sills are suffused with rot.

The condition of older paint (paint that has had a chance to ripen, as it were) can tell you something about the insulation, or lack thereof, in the wall cavities. For reasons that we will explore in detail on pp. 227-229, moisture must either be prevented from entering the wall or be vented to the outside. Water vapor migrating through an improperly insulated wall eventually loosens the bond between the

The erosion of the cutouts and the rounded edges show that these shingles have outlived their usefulness.

These badly decayed wood shingles should be replaced before they cause serious structural harm.

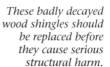

Evidence of repairs: The original galvanized metal flashing of this valley has corroded. Note the slates on the lower section, which were damaged in the repair attempt. Instead of patching the damaged area, the entire valley should have been relined.

When nails work loose, the seams of corrugated steel roofing can open up, allowing water to penetrate the roof, especially under windy conditions.

paint film and the exterior siding, causing the paint to blister. Repainting will not solve the problem.

The presence of small round plastic plugs inserted in the siding at regular intervals indicates that the wall cavities have been filled with cellulose or fiberglass insulation, blown in from the outside. This method is not completely efficacious, since it's almost impossible to find and fill every cavity between the wall studs, particularly with erratically framed old houses. Moisture buildup in the walls is sometimes a problem with blown-in insulation.

*These clapboards are beyond repair.
The house needs residing.*

A hidden treasure revealed: Perfectly sound clapboards were covered over with ugly asphalt composition siding.

out escalating damage to the remaining material. Asphalt composition siding or cement-asbestos shingles may mask a hidden treasure (see the bottom photo at left). These materials were usually applied directly over the original clapboard siding, which, other than requiring a new coat of paint, might still be quite sound. Removal of cement-asbestos composition siding or roofing shingles (they are heavy, brittle, grey, ¼-in. thick tiles) is a potentially hazardous undertaking. Check with local health or environmental protection officers about protective measures and recommended disposal methods. Usually, special bags and protective clothing are necessary to prevent the release of asbestos fibers into the environment and your lungs.

The various elements of decorative trimwork at the edges of the roof that comprise the cornice serve as more than mere embellishment. The eave (bottom edge of the roof) and the rake overhangs (side of the roof at the gable walls) help channel water from the roof surface away from the walls and foundation. Thus, badly deteriorated exterior trim can let water work into the walls and lead to structural rot. Squirrels, birds, bats and wasps can gain access to the interior of the attic through holes in rotted trim. Reconstructing a cornice, especially at the return (over the corner trim) is a demanding and finicky job that requires high-grade, expensive lumber. All too often, original exterior trimwork has been partly or even entirely replaced with a bastardized and slapdash version by insensitive (or insolvent) remodelers.

While you're still poking around the outside of the house, scrutinize the windows. The glass more than likely will need reglazing, a tedious but inexpensive job. If the putty between the glass and the sash (the wood frame) has dried out and cracked, water and wind can infiltrate. Sashes left unpainted for too long will typically rot at their bottom corners and where they rest on the windowsill. The joints between the windowsill and the side casings also create a rot-prone water trap. If not too

Note the condition of the exterior siding. Clapboards or wood shingles so badly split and warped that they reveal the underlying sheathing have outlived their usefulness. It's almost impossible to remove a section of deteriorated wood siding with-

Rotted cornice returns are a common vector for vermin and water damage.

Years of neglect and half-hearted attempts at repair have rendered this window almost inoperable. Unless a sill is kept well painted, it will absorb water and soon rot.

severe, the rot can be dug out and filled with patching putty and painted over. Often, water will seep behind the sill and into the sheathing boards, or especially behind an improperly flashed drip cap at the top of the window. The accumulated effect of this water can cause considerable damage to the sheathing and even rot the framing and sills behind the sheathing, necessitating extensive reframing and rebuilding of the windows. Since old double-hung windows are anything but airtight and aluminum storm windows sacrifice beauty for effectiveness, it may make sense to consider installing new energy-efficient replacement units. Fortunately (the units are not cheap), the old windows can be replaced piecemeal, as budget permits.

What is true of windows applies also to doors. Because thresholds are even more exposed to wear and weather than windowsills, they are one of the most common vectors of rot-producing fungal infection. Furthermore, a door that has a warped frame or split panels is no longer weathertight. Unless an old door is an architectural treasure, restoration may be more trouble than replacement. Consider using relatively inexpensive but very energy-efficient steel doors for utility entries, and reserve the expensive, finely crafted wood door for the main entry.

Anatomy of Window Trouble

Unless kept well painted, windows rot wherever wood contacts wood on a surface that can hold water.

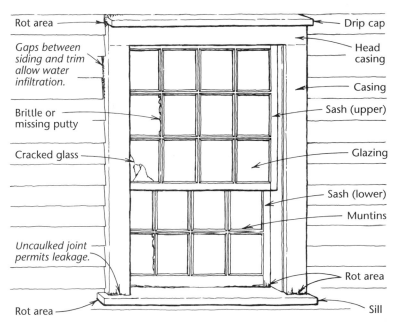

Rot area — Drip cap

Gaps between siding and trim allow water infiltration. — Head casing

Brittle or missing putty — Casing

Cracked glass — Sash (upper)

Glazing

Sash (lower)

Muntins

Uncaulked joint permits leakage.

Rot area

Rot area — Sill

26

The dipping ridgeline of this handyman's special suggests insurmountable problems. In addition, the attached shed has no real foundation and has pulled away from the main house. It will have to be torn down along with the rest of the place.

Exterior attachments

Finally, evaluate any attached sheds or porches. These were often tacked onto the main structure at a later date in a lackadaisical manner or built with inferior materials. In any case, they are more likely to be rotted or resting on heaved and makeshift foundations. Note the junction between the addition and the house proper. A noticeable gap between the two indicates settlement. The junction between the addition roof and the side walls of the house is also a possible source of leakage and hidden structural rot, which will often show

The unevenness of this porch girder suggests problems with the foundation.

up as a sagging porch roof. Since porch floors are exposed directly to the weather, the framing that supports them will often be rotten. Porch columns, posts and railings are especially prone to deterioration. Repair or replacement is compounded by the difficulty and expense of duplicating or locating the often unique patterns of the original woodwork.

Making an Internal Examination

If the external examination of the house has failed to daunt your spirits or reveal any terminal defects, proceed to an internal inspection. Don't let the refinished wide floorboards, the delightful reproduction wallpaper and all the other details the real-estate agent will be pointing out deter you from the object of your quest: Ask to be shown to the basement.

The cellar

In the cellar, more than anywhere else, the true condition of the house is revealed. As you descend the stairwell, note its condition: Are the treads sound? Do the stringers rest on solid rock or disappear into muck and mold? Are the stairs steep and narrow, do they tremble with each queasy step? Can you negotiate them without striking your head on a beam? Is there room to rebuild them?

The cellar of an old house is the place of childhood terrors—of damp, nameless dread, of vermin and mold. Bring a flashlight; most old houses lack adequate or even working subterranean lighting. You will need it to examine the sills and joists in any case. First, can you find the floor or is it underwater? If it is, go no further. Look for another place unless you are prepared literally to sink your money into a new foundation and perimeter footing drainage. Water in the cellar is almost always a sign of serious foundation trouble. At the very least, it can be caused when runoff from a heavy rainstorm saturates the soil outside the foundation wall and works through into the cellar. Sometimes, regrad-

ing to direct water away from the house and installing subsurface drainage pipes can alleviate the problem. Despite promotional claims to the contrary, I have little faith in the long-term efficacy of hydraulic-cement compounds and basement sealers, which claim to stop basement water infiltration from the inside. If the water is coming from outside the wall, the remedy must be applied from the outside.

For reasons that are explained in detail on pp. 66-68, water (or rather, drainage) problems are the main cause of foundation failure. Examine the foundation walls. Do they appear sound? If masonry or concrete, are they free from extensive cracks, which might indicate settlement? If there are cracks, have sections of the walls bowed or tilted? If the walls are stone, have they collapsed in sections or parts? Is the mortar (if any) still solid or crumbly? Infiltration sites will show as outwashes of earth between the stones.

Sometimes what looks from inside the basement like a smoothly faced mortared stone wall neatly capped with brickwork is only the facade of a double-wall foundation. This is likely where brick or stonework runs up to the floorboards in between the floor joists and no sill beam is visible. A foundation showing stone on the outside and brick on the inside is another tip-off. In such cases, the load-bearing foundation is an ordinary rough stone wall and the smooth inside wall is primarily cosmetic, although the above-grade brickwork does keep out the wind. Less frequently, the sills are also doubled, the inside one carrying the floor joists, the exterior sill bearing the wall studs and roof load. When the outside sill rots away, the shell of the house sinks below the floors.

Unfortunately, a double-laid wall is no more watertight than a single wall. Because the cellar face of such walls is evenly laid up, it's often mistakenly assumed that water infiltration can be cured by pouring a new face wall against the exterior side. But excavation of the foundation perimeter usually uncovers a haphazardly laid

Problems in the Cellar

Persistent flooding
has scoured these
stones clean.

This wall cracked
because the section
to the right contained
a door opening that
was not footed below
the frost line.

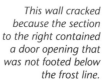

The poor fit of this
door confirms a problem
with chronic foundation
movement.

Water draining into the cellar through the
window opening is the obvious cause of this
problem. The solution is to slope the
outside grade away from the wall.

stone wall with several sections on the verge of collapse, which is almost impossible to hose clean for a good bond to concrete without increasing the risk of collapse. It's much better to plan on removing such a wall right from the beginning than to base your cost estimate on saving it. Then, if it so happens that the outside wall is relatively even, the surprise will be a pleasant one.

The usual remedy for a collapsed or leaking stone foundation in the days before backhoes and portable concrete forms was to pour a massive hand-mixed concrete wall against the inside of the failed stone wall. But if nothing is done about the exterior drainage of the foundation wall, poured walls are about as effective as the aforementioned hydraulic-cement basement sealers. Worse, they will eventually crack and heave, and so become just more rubble to dig out when the foundation is finally—and inevitably—replaced.

If you do your househunting in the spring, when the underground water table is at its peak level, any seasonal infiltration problems will be obvious. Although standing water usually disappears after a spell of dry weather, basement water problems always leave telltale signs. A concrete floor will show dark stains from chronic water infiltration. A musty odor is another giveaway.

An earth-floored cellar is likely to be damp in the spring in any case, and there is not much you can do about it other than laying down a vapor barrier and covering it with either crushed stone or concrete. As long as adequate ventilation is provided during the summer months and the foundation walls are watertight, earth-floored cellars are not necessarily a problem. Look for water stains or mineral deposits on the walls if actual dampness or trickles are not evident. Cellar posts will often show high-water marks or even rot (especially if they are in direct contact with bare earth) in an otherwise dry cellar. An earth floor that has been underwater will appear something like a mudflat after

At first glance, this cellar wall appears to be solid and stable mortared stone with a brick cap. But the cross section of a previously repaired section shows the wall to be of double-faced construction, with smooth nonbearing material on the cellar side and ragged stone on the exterior load-bearing side. Excavation clearly reveals the cross section.

the tide has gone out; smoothed over, but with grainy deposits. If you leave footprints behind as you cross, you've got water problems.

Here is where the demon must be squarely faced. How badly do you want this particular house? Can you find or afford another? Will you have the time and money for the repairs? Although you won't have to fix the foundation immediately, you will have to fix it eventually. And this work must be done before any other work can begin.

Replacing a foundation wall by yourself is hard, dirty work that consumes a great deal of time with very little visible reward for your labors. Hiring outside help is expensive. No contractor in his right mind will give a firm or low bid, because the variables are too unpredictable. For example, a determined but inexperienced home owner sought my advice for a do-it-yourself foundation repair. The original idea was to replace only two walls. Alas, the perimeter excavation revealed that the other two, which had appeared solid from the cellar side, were completely decrepit on the outside. Two walls became four and costs doubled.

Later, as he was jacking the sills up, he noticed an ominous bulge in the second-story wall above. Stripping the clapboards revealed that the connection between the plank wall and the beam that carried the second-floor joists had rotted away and that the wall was actually moving past the second floor as he jacked. For me, this was another one of those interesting surprises that make remodeling so enjoyable. For my client, it was a budget meltdown.

If it appears that the foundation, or lack thereof, has been accounted for by a corresponding reduction in selling price, then by all means continue on to check the sills for soundness, insect damage and rot. So-called "dry rot" is actually caused by a fungus nourished by exposure to moisture and lack of ventilation. If unchecked, the soft dark streaks that are the first signs of infection eventually progress to a crumbly reddish charcoal. Besides the exterior face, the underside of the sills where they rest on the foundation wall are most vulnerable to decay. Use an ice pick or carpenter's awl to probe the depth of the damage.

Replacing a sill is not as expensive or difficult as replacing a foundation, but it's nothing you'd want to do for a hobby either. Examine the floor joists, girders and the underside of the floorboards. If these too are substantially rotted, it makes more sense to look for another house than to rebuild the floor framing. But don't worry too much about settled or rotted cellar posts and the sagging floors they usually cause. Replacing cellar posts and straightening sagging floors are not difficult or expensive jobs.

Waste disposal

The cellar is also the best place to evaluate the household mechanical systems. As you grope about in the murk, look for a waste drain, typically a 4-in. to 6-in. dia. cast-iron pipe that runs through the foundation wall or floor to the sewer or septic tank. Sometimes the grey water (drainage from sinks and laundry) and the black water (drainage from the toilets) will use separate lines, with grey water routed into a drywell or convenient ditch. Somewhere before the sewer line exits the basement, a clean-out trap should be evident. Sometimes these are installed in a well under the floor, or even completely covered over with concrete. If the clean-out trap is inaccessible, or even absent, unclogging a plugged sewer line becomes a lot more complicated.

Usually, the realtor's property description will indicate whether the house is connected to a municipal sewer and water system or if it has on-site disposal and supply. If the information is not listed, ask the realtor to find out for you. Don't settle for "I think so." Although a water meter is an obvious sign of municipal supply, its presence doesn't preclude connection to an on-site waste-disposal system.

Septic systems, when properly constructed and maintained, are a safe, reliable, inexpensive and ecologically sound means of waste disposal (much more so than municipal sewers and treatment plants). Does the house have a septic tank and leach field? It's still possible to find houses that simply dump their raw sewage into a stone-filled pit in the ground (drywell) or an open or covered lagoon (cesspool). In most cases, these unhealthful and inadequate systems exist only because they were "grandfathered" in under newly

Hidden Infection Comes to a Head

2. Pushed by the weight of the second floor, the totally decayed end girt slipped down behind the ends of the first-floor wall planks, causing the wall to bulge outward. When that end of the house was raised level on its new foundation, the bulge swelled ominously, prompting an investigation.

1. Over the years, water leaking into the wall at the cornice return caused serious hidden structural damage that was only discovered during a foundation repair. Leakage through uncaulked casing joints and unkempt windowsills also contributed to the decay.

3. From the inside: Beneath the water stain on the ceiling, insulation held moisture like a sponge, rotting the corner post and part of the plate beam.

4. The decay of this three-way joint between corner post, end girt and wall plate beam leaves the entire end wall of the house essentially free-floating.

5. Protected by a polyethylene sheet, the full extent of the decay is exposed for repair.

Old houses offer some truly bizarre examples of creative plumbing, such as this drainage connection with the sewer line. (Photo by Joe English.)

adopted health codes with the requirement that they be replaced by systems meeting the new regulations if the property changed hands or was renovated.

What do the codes in your area specify? If you find that a new septic system is needed, the sales agreement should be contingent upon the owner's furnishing a permit for an on-site sewage-disposal system or a favorable soil percolation test report (usually referred to as a "perc" test) by a licensed engineer accompanied by an approved system design. Ideally, the costs of engineering, testing and permits should be borne by the owners, but these are sometimes items for negotiation.

Whatever you do, don't rely on some vague notion about an alternative waterless composting toilet to solve perc problems. Most of these systems demand too much involvement and thoughtfulness on the part of the user to suit the average lifestyle, and, even more important, health codes still mandate a suitable septic system for household grey water.

If there is an existing septic system, is the tank steel or concrete? Steel tanks don't last as long and can collapse. What is the tank's capacity? A 1,000-gal. tank is standard for a typical household. For in-

sink garbage disposals, the tank and field size must be at least 50% greater. Where is the tank and leach field? If you are excavating a foundation or moving heavy equipment around the property, you don't want to sever the sewer pipe, collapse a tank or compact the leach field.

If, during your exterior inspection, you happened to notice a wet area with lush vegetation and the odor of sewage, you have septic-tank problems. Usually, too much water is entering the tank. Check capacity—sometimes roof drains are connected to the house drain. Dumping chemicals such as drain cleaners, paint thinner and photographic wastes down the drain wreak havoc with the bacterial populations in the septic tank; waste will then pass undigested into the leach field and plug up the absorption beds, eventually causing the sewer to drain slowly or back up. If the problem is not traceable to blockage in the sewer line before the tank, or to a tank filled with indigestible grease and cooking oils, and pumping the tank does not improve the symptoms, you'll probably have to dig up and replace a clogged leach field. Since septic tanks should be pumped out at least once every two to five years as part of routine maintenance to prevent clogging, try to find out when this service was last performed and where the tank is located.

The plumbing system

Since plumbers deviate from code compliance at the peril of losing their licenses, there shouldn't be any problems with a professionally plumbed old house per se. Properly installed cast-iron or copper drain lines are, except for clogging, maintenance free, and for all practical purposes, eternal. Water-supply lines are another story. The galvanized-iron pipe used before copper became widely available in the 1950s can corrode, and inevitably suffers from atherosclerosis caused by mineral deposits on its walls. Depending on the age of the plumbing and the hardness of the water, much or all of the iron pipe may have to be replaced. The buildup is much slower with copper pipe. But copper tubing is much more vulnerable to freezing. If the water supply is not currently in use, look for bulges, splits or soldered joints that have pulled apart.

Usually, the worst plumbing problems are caused by ignorant and substandard owner modifications and additions. Rather than trying to unravel a tangle of hybrid pipes, iron wedded piecemeal to copper and plastics, fixtures added without proper venting, improperly sized pipes and appliances lacking shutoff or drain valves, complete replumbing may be the most economical solution.

Water supply

The property description should also indicate the water source. Drilled deep wells are usually the most reliable, whereas springs can be questionable both in terms of safety and reliability. In some areas of the country, the water must pass a health test before the house can be occupied or sold. In other areas, the seller must only report whether or not the water was tested and if it passed. For drilled wells, find out when the well was installed, by whom and its rate of flow. Depending on depth, 3 gal. to 8 gal./min. should be adequate. Well drillers have the information on file if the owner doesn't know or remember.

For shallow wells and springs, look at the source. Is the spring lined with concrete tiles or just a wooden box or stone-lined pit? Is the supply pipe to the house buried deep enough not to freeze? Is it galvanized iron or noncorrosive polyethylene? Is there a shutoff on the line where it enters the cellar?

The pump for a dug or shallow (25 ft. deep or less) well is usually located in the basement. Is it corroded, showing signs of leakage, or does it appear in good working order? Have someone open a tap (if the water is turned on) long enough to start the pump while you watch the pressure gauge. If the pump runs for a long time before operating pressure is reached, or

runs every time a tap is opened, the piston washers could need replacement, the check valve at the pump or the foot valve at the bottom of the well may be stuck open, or, most likely, the pressure tank may be waterlogged. These problems are all owner-fixable and relatively minor. A burned-out or frozen pump is not.

Open a tap yourself and note the flow for amount, color, odor and taste after you let it run for a while. If you have any doubts about potability, obtain a sample bottle from the town health officer and have the water tested. A water purifier (a tank similar to a welding gas cylinder) connected to the pump indicates water-quality problems (hardness and/or excessive iron or sulfur levels among other things). The purifier element must be properly maintained and replaced at regular intervals if it is to work at all.

Water for some households flows by gravity from the spring to the cellar. Unless the source is high enough above the point of use, the pressure may be too low to run a dishwasher or washing machine, or provide a comfortable shower on the second floor. If it hasn't already been done, you'll have to add a pump to boost the pressure. Naturally pressurized (artesian) wells and some springs are so prolific that they have a constant overflow. If this is allowed to drain across the floor (as was often done in old dirt-floored cellars), the moisture buildup will encourage mildew and rot. At the other extreme, a basement cistern (a large, covered concrete or stone tank) is sometimes used as a reservoir for

This mongrel 'system' mates polyethylene tubing with corroded galvanized-iron supply lines and cast-iron drainpipe with ABS and CPVC plastics, lead pipe and brass fittings. Note the burlap wrapping the drain to the crawl space, a sure sign of freezing problems. (Photo by Joe English.)

springs with low recovery rates. These are more commonly employed in arid regions to store rainwater collected by a system of downspouts from the roof. Water from such systems should not be used for drinking without treatment.

Heat tapes and insulation wrapped around water pipes in the cellar, or daylight visible through or insulation stuffed into the cracks between stones, under sills and around windows, are sure signs of a very cold basement, a hard-to-heat house and the nagging danger of freeze-up.

The heating system

As you examine the plumbing, note the condition of the furnace (if there is one). Attached somewhere should be a tag or placard that shows the serviceman's name, date of the last servicing and furnace efficiency. If this information is not on the premises, get the name of the fuel dealer from the real-estate agent's listing or from the owner, and inquire about the condition of the heating system. The fuel cost for the previous season is usually included in the property description, and some owners furnish copies of the heating bills. Old furnaces are not necessarily troublesome, but they are usually much more expensive to operate than modern units, especially furnaces converted from coal to oil. A comparison of furnace efficiencies and fuel costs may suggest replacing an antique unit.

Other than seeing if the furnace runs and the heat rises to the radiators or floor registers, there is little a nonprofessional can tell about the condition of a heating system, at least on an initial inspection. If the house is being shown in the winter, the furnace will be running anyway (unless you are looking at an abandoned property). During warm weather you can turn the thermostat way up and see if the furnace responds.

If the furnace or boiler does not provide hot water directly, then locate and inspect the water heater. Try to find out when it was installed. Water heaters are considered to have a service life of seven to ten years, depending on the type of liner and the hardness of the water. Stone-lined tanks (read the label) are the longest lasting. Glass-lined tanks are better than galvanized steel, which will barely last five years. If the heater runs on LP gas, check the flue pipe for corrosion.

The electrical system

Before you leave the cellar, find the electrical service entrance panel. This grey steel box is the heart of the electrical system. It's possible, however, that you'll find instead a conglomeration of fuse blocks, secondary boxes and disconnect switches added piecemeal as the original main fuse panel became too small to handle the increasing electrical loads of modern living.

Although there is no legal obligation to bring your old wiring up to date, any electrical work you do must conform to the requirements of the National Electrical Code (NEC). In rural areas, you are usually allowed to do your own residential wiring, although your work may be subject to inspection for code conformance. In cities, all work must be done under the supervision of a licensed electrician. Since replacement of the service entrance requires working with potentially dangerous power levels and is subject to a host of code conditions, many home owners prefer to leave this part of the renovation to a professional, and wire only the individual room circuits themselves.

Open the entrance box (or main fuse panel) and find its maximum rating, which will be imprinted somewhere on the main breaker, disconnect switch or fuse block. A 100-amp service is the bare minimum for today's electrical needs. If you find a 60-amp service, the entire service entrance will need replacement, most likely beginning with the power drop at the transformer on the utility pole. This is also a good time to replace an old fuse panel with circuit breakers.

Determine the type of electrical cable that feeds your circuits. The oldest systems employed rubber-coated wires strung on porcelain insulators. Most surviving knob-and-tube circuits are seldom active or their use is restricted to attic or cellar lighting circuits where the conductors are accessible and uncovered by insulation and wall finishes. You're more likely to find cable containing two rubber-coated conductors wrapped in black or aluminum-colored cloth (a later version). It's a good idea to replace these types of early cable, since the rubber tends to become brittle with age and mice often chew the cloth, which can create a serious fire hazard.

Although the NEC does not require existing two-wire circuits to be replaced by circuits with a continuous ground conductor, you may want to do this for the added safety and convenience, especially if you plan to gut the interior walls anyway. The earliest forms of plastic-jacketed cable (Romex®) typically have only two conductors. Look for the imprint on the jacket: 12-2 (or 14-2) WG (with ground) is used for new work. Chances are good that the cellar won't be well lighted. Plan on adding a circuit there. In the meantime, don't forget to bring along the house inspector's number-two tool—a flashlight (your ice pick or awl is number one).

Bulkhead and cellar windows
Finally, before you leave the cellar, inspect the bulkhead (the exit from the cellar to the outside). Unless the entry walls have pushed in the foundation walls, repairs should be simple. Expect the wooden door frame, door and steps to be rotten. The same is true for any cellar windows. Replace these with new window units that can be easily opened for cross-ventilation during summer months. Set them into a pressure-treated wood frame.

The corrosion at the bottom of this LP gas water heater is probably attributable to the dampness of the earthen floor, and presages impending tank failure. Note also the undersized water-supply pipe connected to the pump, and the standard hodgepodge of waterline miscegenation.

This old 60-amp entrance panel has room for only four 15-amp circuits, far too little capacity for the electrical demand of a modern home. A subfeed tap running to a distribution box adds a few more circuits.

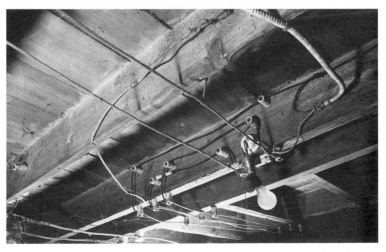

Despite a dangerously frayed bare spot visible in the upper part of this photo, this ancient knob-and-tube wiring is still in use. Because of the likelihood of dangerous corrosion, electrical codes no longer permit steel-jacketed cable in damp locations (like a moldy cellar).

By now you will have garnered enough information to make a structural assessment. Added to a decayed foundation and sills, the weight of any other defects, although fairly negligible in themselves, may sink your proposed renovation project. If the wiring, plumbing and heating systems also need replacement, the prudent buyer would look for a better place. Prudence, however, is often overwhelmed by romance, especially when the magic is sweetened by an affordable selling price. If you find yourself already caught up in the spell of the old place, at least use your evaluation to bargain down the price.

The attic

There are a few more items to inspect before you get carried away and sign a sales contract. Proceed to the attic. Is it accessible by a stairwell or just a hatch in the ceiling? Converting an unfinished attic is just about the most economical way to gain extra living space, even if you have to restructure hallways and rooms to include a set of stairs. In any case, be sure to poke your head up through the hatch (if you don't have a stepladder, use a chair, crates or shoulders of a friend). Shine your light on the underside of the roof boards. If you can see metal roofing or asphalt shingles between roughly spaced boards, count on removing the roofing and resheathing. Note the thickness and spacings of the rafters. Pole rafters and hewn or sawn timber rafters should be at least 6 in. in diameter or cross section when spaced 4 ft. on center. Ordinary 2x dimension lumber should be spaced no less than 2 ft. on center. Sagging rafters must be stiffened by jacking new timbers into place alongside the old or adding extra rafters in between the spans. Check for signs of leakage—daylight showing through the roof is one of the more obvious.

The attic should also have a gable louver or window at each end for ventilation. Is the attic floored or capped with insulation? How much insulation and of what type? Attic floorboards, since they are the same age as the rest of the house and often unnailed to the joists, make perfect replacement boards for floors throughout the rest of the house.

Chances are good that the fiberglass batt or loose-fill insulation laid between the floor joists won't be thick enough. In the North, 12 in. of fiberglass (R-30) is the minimum. The fill or batts should not block the roof overhangs either. If there's no insulation in the attic, either in the floor or ceiling, there probably isn't any in the walls either, since the attic is the easiest and most cost-efficient part of the house to insulate.

Also look for water stains on the underside of the roofing, and for rot and fungus growing on any beams and rafters. Does the chimney appear sound below the roof or is it a candidate for demolition?

The rest of the house

Now you can look around the rest of the house. As you came up the stairs, were they narrow and steep, with turns and landings? Can you imagine moving a chest of drawers or your antique bed frame up them? Is there a way to improve on them without tearing the entire house apart?

Note the condition of the wall and ceiling finishes. When you push on the plaster it shouldn't move. Sometimes faded wallpaper is all that keeps the plaster stuck to the wall. Small, isolated cracks and crumbled areas can be patched, but if the walls are a continuous landscape of decrepitude, complete removal is the only sensible approach, especially if insulation and rewiring are needed anyway.

At this point it's too early to see things architecturally. The rooms can be unscrambled later. For now, simply catalog the condition of the surfaces and components. Are the original floorboards exposed or, more likely, buried under strata of linoleum and hardwood strip flooring? Hardwood flooring must be applied over a solid subfloor, typically the original wideboard old-growth softwood boards. Upstairs, these same boards are normally disguised by an iron-tough layer of grey or dark red paint. Your rescue efforts will release the warm glow of time-burnished wood unmatched by new material.

Look for chimneys that don't run all the way down to the basement. These seldom-used half-chimneys are usually supported by stout vertical planks in the corners of upstairs bedrooms. At one time, stovepipes from below heated the rooms

Wall and Ceiling Problems

Peeling paint is caused by excessive moisture in an unvented bathroom.

The gap at the top of the door and the cracked plaster are signs of floor settlement. Additional cellar posts may be needed.

Small areas of falling plaster can be repaired. But when entire ceilings are falling down, the plaster is best replaced with drywall or new plaster.

The foundation under this wall began settling before the window was installed. Otherwise, the window would be parallel to the floor. The recent crack shows that the movement is continuing.

as the pipes came through the floor and into the chimney. These old chimneys leak creosote in and warm air out. Their weight also tends to bow floors and roof beams over time, which is a good argument for removal of half-chimneys.

Finally, note the existence (or lack) and condition of kitchen and bath fixtures. Are there any good or restorable antique fixtures? The original faucets and fittings,

This stovepipe is much too close to the ceiling for safe operation.

Although the bathroom they inhabit is fairly bleak, these antique fixtures are irreplaceable treasures and should not be thrown out with the bathwater. For comfort and roominess, you can't beat an old clawfoot tub.

hardware, doorknobs, switch plates, light or gas fixtures, woodwork, stair parts, raised panel doors, bathtubs, water closets, woodstoves—all irreplaceable functional treasures—are too often thrown out with hasty renovations.

Preserving Historically Significant Features

As I mentioned in the introduction, strict preservationists believe that anyone who owns or is contemplating buying a pre-1850 house is obligated to preserve historically significant features. This obligation will necessarily determine the nature of proposed renovations and perhaps severely limit any design options. My own belief is that although historical integrity is important, comfort and suitability to one's own lifestyle are equally important. Nevertheless, in the interest of fairness, I offer here some specific guidelines endorsed by strict preservationists.

First, maintain the overall floor plan of all early or original rooms so that their relationship to each other is identifiable. Likewise, don't disturb the layout or character of original windows, doors or stairs, or add new ones.

Because of the possibility that the earth under and around a pre-1800 house contains valuable historic artifacts or archaeological information, consider hiring a specialist to inventory the area before it is disturbed by extensive excavations. For the same reason, do not disturb earthen cellar floors or crawl spaces. This is especially true for urban houses, which were frequently built upon the ruins of much earlier structures.

Preserve intact all original or early masonry. Since it's more important to preserve examples of materials and construction details of early brick and mortar than to have a working fireplace or chimney, if the original cannot be strengthened or made safe by the addition of a flue liner or made to work without reconstruction that changes the outside appearance, leave the chimney and fireplace unused.

Leave the original plaster on the walls and ceilings. Special plaster washers can be used to repair plaster keys that have failed (see p. 222). If most of the plaster has already fallen off or is beyond repair, at least retain the original lath when replastering or installing drywall.

Continuing with the principle of leaving as much of the original materials and structure intact as possible, do not remove early floorboards. If they are unusable in their present condition, cover them over with new flooring, shimming as necessary between layers. Don't sand the floors or stairs; to do so will erase the record of use patterns and wear. After all, part of the charm of old houses is in their time-softened edges. Accordingly, don't try to level sloping walls and straighten skewed walls unless the house is in danger of structural failure, or induces unmanageable vertigo in its occupants. The weak rafters or joists that typically underlie those picturesque ridges and valleys should be left intact with new wood "sistered" onto them for strength (see p. 118). When structural timbers or other materials have failed and must be replaced, use similar materials of similar size. Save labeled samples of the originals and document their location.

Rather than disturb the original configuration of the rooms by attempting to retrofit modern plumbing fixtures or a kitchen where they are lacking, install these amenities in an addition. When adding such a space to the house, the connection should be superficial rather than structural, that is, the new addition should only abut the original part.

Since the installation of ductwork and vents required for modern central heating will destroy significant parts of the original fabric of the house, use room-by-room woodstoves or other stoves that can vent into the original chimneys if possible. (These may have to be relined for fire safety, as discussed on pp. 323-325.) Electric baseboard heat is also an acceptable, albeit expensive, alternative to wholesale destruction. Installing or modernizing an electrical system will also damage the walls and ceilings. Use a preservation consultant to help you and the electrician design surface-mounted electrical raceways that leave them intact.

Never strip, sand or scrape early wood, plaster or painted surfaces of a pre-1850 house. Instead, paint over the earlier layers, adding to the historic record rather than subtracting from it. The original color can be determined by paint analysis and a modern equivalent formulated.

Many well-intentioned home owners, under the mistaken assumption that preservation means going back to the "original" condition, have removed and discarded later coverings in the attempt to "restore" an old house. But except in the few instances where museum specimens are involved, going back only destroys the continuity of the historical record. Because our knowledge of how things were actually done in the past is speculative, these reconstructed "original" features are of dubious historical value and authenticity. Leaving later coverings intact serves to protect the underlying earlier features. If you must add new or new "old" material to an early house, don't try to mimic or reproduce the originals. Instead, contribute to the ongoing historical record by using materials typical of our time. Carve or write your initials and date on them.

To sum up, the guiding principle of the preservation approach is: Don't cause any more damage to the original fabric than has already been wrought by the hands of earlier tenants. As long as you hew to this course, you are free to upgrade and renovate as you please.

Financial and Legal Considerations

Often, despite its defects, the asking price of a run-down old house may not be much less than that of renovated houses in the neighborhood. The sellers, especially when the property is first placed on the market, may just be fishing for the highest offer. After too many prospective buyers are frightened off by the prospect of major repairs, they might consider an offer that allows for the estimated cost, especially if the market is flat. In some areas, older houses don't compete well against an oversupply of newer ones. If the price has already been discounted, or the sellers don't feel any great compulsion to bargain, at least you'll know how much more to borrow up front or squeeze out of the budget for repairs, or whether to look for another place.

For example, you look at an antique farmhouse with an asking price of $205,000. Your offer of $160,000 is based on the fact that besides the usual cosmetic remodeling, it needs a complete foundation, new water system, plumbing and insulation, to the tune of $45,000, before it can be comfortably considered habitable. Four months after the owners dismiss your offer as not serious, the real-estate agent calls back to say that they're willing to go with it. Although you'll still have to take out a mortgage for $184,500 (assuming a 10% down payment), you'll pay yourself to do the repairs, and end up with a structurally sound house for the same amount of money. Since the estimated repair cost is based on hiring outside contractors, there should be money left over for the cosmetic renovations as well. With an estimated market value of $265,000 for the fully renovated house, you'll stand to gain a fair amount of equity, which certainly adds to the viability of the project, at least from a bank's point of view.

You can't know if a property is over- or under-priced until you gain a feel for the local market. This takes research and time. First, collect all the listings, catalogs and brochures you can from local real-estate agents. As you look through their Multiple Listing Service (MLS) catalogs, note the difference between the asking price and the actual selling price of properties listed as sold. This will give you some idea of whether you are in a buyer's or seller's market. Read the real-estate classifieds in the local papers. By the time

you're ready to draw up a list of potential candidates for inspection, you should know what your money can buy.

Spend the next several weekends looking at houses, and use the information in this book to make a list of their problems and defects. Eventually, you'll narrow the field down to one or two contenders. At this point, I suggest you hire a local renovator to take a look at the place, review your checklist and give you a ballpark estimate of the repair cost. This is also a good time to enlist the services of an architectural historian or conservation consultant to determine whether the house has any important features whose preservation could either limit the scope or increase the cost of renovations. Consultations such as these typically run $100 to $300. If they help you negotiate a lower selling price, prevent you from buying a property you can't afford, getting mired in a project beyond your abilities or destroying a historically important house, the money will be well spent. (Whatever you do, please don't take advantage of a contractor by asking for a free estimate on a job you have no intention of letting out to bid.)

The total of the asking price and the cost of repairs (include your labor at full value) represents the true purchase price and furnishes a basis for evaluating the reasonableness of the deal and any potential return on your investment. If this figure is substantially lower than the asking price for comparable completely renovated properties, and you have the resources to undertake the work (or plan to do it slowly over time while living in the house), it's certain to be a good investment. If the total is only slightly less or about the same as the prevailing market prices, you can gamble on profits from an expected future increase in property values in excess of inflation. If the market has already peaked, or is even declining, this strategy will prove disastrous. Once again, location and timing are the key to making money at fixing up old houses. By the time most people catch on, the wave is already passing.

Can you make money fixing up old houses? Maybe. The difference between an investment and a disaster may not be as much a function of one's financial acumen, remodeling skills and capital resources as it is of sheer luck; just happening to be in the right place at the right time. Back in 1984, we had to relocate so my wife could attend graduate school. After several discouraging weekends of looking at expensive redecorated but unrenovated farmhouses (new wallpaper, refinished floors, rotted sills, waterlogged basements), we chanced upon a remodeler's dream: a structurally sound, but cosmetically uninviting, 80-year-old home on the shores of a neighborhood lapped by the rising tide of gentrification. A year later, after a facelift that cost $4,500 in materials and 450 hours of not-so-spare-time labor, we sold the house for $19,000 more than we'd paid for it, two weeks after it was listed.

Subtracting the realtor's commission and other expenses of sale, our venture netted a $10,800 profit. Even after adding in my labor at $10 per hour (my hourly wage as a carpenter back then) instead of considering it as devotion to a somewhat demanding hobby, $6,300 represents a 24% return on the original investment (down payment and expenses of $13,100 plus costs of sale and renovation). Had we held on to the place for another year, I'm sure the yield would have been even better.

The question here is not so much can you make money, but what does it cost you to do it? What kind of a life do you want to live while you're doing it? It's possible to buy a place, live in it as you fix it, sell it, reinvest the profits into another place, fix that one up, and so on, constantly pyramiding your capital. Ideally, you'll eventually build up a working-capital fund that frees you from reliance upon bank loans. Otherwise, using borrowed money puts you in the unenviable position of having to finish the project and sell it before interest and other carrying costs eat into profits; a strong argument for living in the place while you complete it. Also, if

the house you are working on is your primary residence and the profits of sale are plowed back into buying your next home within a year, you may be able to take advantage of a capital gains tax break. But one of the rewards of home ownership is the sense of fulfillment derived from the gradual fusion of structure and self as the house becomes a home. This, and the refuge from the cares of the workplace that a home offers will be denied to those forced to inhabit a succession of short-term "investments." Like shooting an overlong series of rapids, eventually the exhilaration fades, and only the grueling struggle to make it through remains.

Do-it-yourself property renovation is no longer as secure an investment as the real-estate brokers would have you believe. Timing and location are much more critical than ever before. I heard a horror story about a builder who paid a bargain price of $200,000 for a "handyman's special" in a New Jersey neighborhood where comparable homes in good condition were selling for $400,000 or more. He put $100,000 into renovations, only to watch as his profits were siphoned off at the rate of $2,600 a month in carrying costs while the property sat unsold, a victim of a suddenly collapsed market.

There's also the fellow who bought an abandoned church for its appraised market value of $25,000. The structure, although quite sound and ripe for renovation, was blessed with an altogether too intimate view of an abandoned house trailer and some sorely dilapidated houses on the adjoining lots. The bank turned down his request for a remodeling loan on the grounds that the general condition of the neighborhood would drag the market value of his property down below the worth of the mortgage. Of course, if one of those neighboring eyesores were bought and fixed up by some newcomer from downcountry, the terms of the equation would be completely different. Like the first settlers, real-estate pioneers must be self-sufficient. Bank loans are written against present value, not future potential.

I certainly have no objection to realizing a good return on the value created by a long-term labor of love. But there is something sleazy and unethical, to me at least, about the buying and fixing up of old houses solely for profit. Real-estate development is a subtle and possibly pernicious form of social disruption; its agents tend, like the carpetbaggers of the Reconstruction era, to be a peculiar species of parasite. So for the remainder of this book, I'll assume that you're fixing up an old house because you intend to make it your home. Although future appreciation in value is always important (the increased equity can be regarded as a kind of do-it-yourself pension fund), it seems to me that such considerations could be secondary to the rewards of householding and home-making in the here and now.

The last consideration, the most pertinent perhaps, to which all the structural criteria are appended is, can you afford it? What terms are available? Will the owner finance all or part? Or will you have to convince strangers at a bank that you are in fact a decent, hardworking, reliable credit risk? Are the monthly payments bearable? You'll need to pay yourself a living wage while working on the house or borrow additional funds to cover renovation costs.

Ultimately, the condition of an old house seems to vary in inverse proportion to the financial liquidity of its prospective buyers. Even though it may categorically fail every structural requirement mentioned above, it may also be all you can afford to buy. Whatever the disadvantages, at least you can move in and begin acquiring equity rather than paying rent. Don't delude yourself into thinking that house renovation is cheap or easy. It's a bigger, messier and costlier job than you can imagine.

If you decide to take the plunge, set up an appointment for the closing with a local lawyer. Then go and visit the place again. Walk around and look at it. Sit under a tall tree and try to feel it as your place. Does it fit? Visit with the house. Sit in the front room and listen, try to hear its quiet talk of groans and rumbles, let the emptiness fill you, the dust of the world dancing before your eyes in the clear light of the afternoon.

That night read through a copy of Les Scher's *Finding and Buying Your Place in the Country* (see the Bibliography on pp. 334-338), to prime yourself for the lawyer. He or she should make certain that there is a clear title—no undischarged mortgages, liens or attachments, or rights-of-way that could in any way hinder the sale or your enjoyment of the property. A policy of title insurance or an abstract should be furnished. Find out if the land has been surveyed, and if not, who bears the cost. Don't make the mistake of thinking that a survey is not all that necessary. A deed generally specifies X acres "more or less," to cover any margin of error. That very same clause was in the deed of my own property, which had remained an undivided parcel described as "100 acres, more or less." The survey, done just before I acquired it, showed 68½ acres "more or less." As the former owner, who had been paying taxes on those 100 elastic acres remarked, "There warn't no rebate on the taxes neither."

Now you're ready for the checklist promised at the beginning of this chapter. Besides comparing properties, this checklist (shown on the facing page) is useful for organizing renovation priorities once you have bought the right house. The categories are arranged in order of decreasing importance and expense. The topmost items are most influential in determining the reasonableness of the project. Since the degree of difficulty diminishes from left to right, a cluster of checks in the "poor" column is probably good grounds to rule out a prospective property.

Renovation Checklist

Item	Poor	Passable	Good
Purchase price (high, manageable, a real bargain)			
Historic significance, preservation considerations			
Foundation (cracks, settlement, leaks)			
Cellar floor (type, water present)			
Sills (rot, insect damage)			
Structural timbers, joists, visible framing (rot, insect damage)			
Walls and roof (bows, sags, indicating failure)			
Water supply (source, reliability, potability)			
On-site sewage disposal (existing or required? perc test?)			
Plumbing system (waste and supply lines)			
Heating system			
Electrical system (service entrance capacity, circuit wiring condition, number of outlets and fixtures)			
Roofing (type, condition, rot in deck)			
Exterior siding (type, condition)			

Item	Poor	Passable	Good
Exterior trim, paint			
Windows and doors (repair or replace)			
Chimney and flues			
Attachments (porches, sheds, decks)			
Insulation (type, quantity)			
Interior plaster (and other wall and ceiling finishes)			
Woodwork			
Flooring			
Stairs			
Kitchen (cabinetry, appliances)			
Bathroom fixtures			
Water heater			
Outbuildings			
Landscaping, grading, rubbish on site			
Land, acreage, features, general neighborhood			
Public highway access, driveway condition (maintained by town or owner?)			
Legal (title, survey, zoning)			
Does it feel right?			

KEY:
Poor (needs major work now)
Passable (needs work, but can wait)
Good (does not require any work)

Organizing Priorities

Managing the logistics of a major renovation means juggling time, materials and money. Concentration, experience and a calm temperament coupled with a sense of humor are required for success and sanity.

A New York lawyer busy with the many chores in closing his place for the winter interrupted his work to say goodbye to his neighbor at a time he thought appropriate for the farmer's schedule. It turned out, as it sometimes does with supposedly taciturn denizens of the hill country, that his neighbor wanted to talk, and after some exchange the lawyer said, "I'm sorry but I've got to go along. Have a hundred things to do."
"You've got a hundred things to do?"
"Well, perhaps not quite," the New Yorker replied, "but it seems that many."
"Let me give you a piece of advice," said the Vermonter, "Do 'em one at a time."

—Allen R. Foley, *What the Old-Timer Said* (Brattleboro, Vt.: Stephen Greene Press, 1971)

Rescuing an old house from decay can seem like an overwhelming job. So many disasters clamor for your attention that it's difficult to decide which can safely be ignored and which cannot. Like the hospital emergency room, a renovation needs a triage system to make those necessary choices.

As you worked through the renovation checklist on p. 43, you probably noticed that the work arranges itself into two major categories: structural work, which must be done immediately, and cosmetic work, which can be done as time and money allow. Which work fits into which category is frequently self-evident.

I remember a day in June…the grass, deep and golden green, parted to let our van up the drive. Like an ark wallowing in the waves, we rolled to a stop. Tired motor hissing, we stretched cramped arms and legs in the warm sunlight. The cicada's song filled the silence shimmering around us. In this strong light, the weathered grey clapboards revealed their subtle depths, the feathers of some huge dull bird. Key in hand, I removed the rusted padlock from the back door—no need, it wasn't hitched to the latch. We were home.

Later, while cooking dinner on a Coleman stove perched on an orange crate in the middle of the bare linoleum floor, we tried to list our priorities—where and how to begin the metamorphosis of house into home. That night, as the rain poured through the ceiling, overflowing our supply of pots and pans, we moved our sleeping bags to the highest corner of the floor. I began to get the idea…fixing the roof was in the structural category. So was plugging the hole in the foundation wall through which the runoff cascaded into the cellar. The plaster dripping from the ceiling was only a cosmetic defect.

The point is that structural work is the first link in a logical chain. You can't do any interior or finish work until you've dealt with the foundation, roof and structural timbers. If you aren't able to tackle major structural repairs right off, you could do all the interior demolition, rewiring and whatever plumbing, heating and insulation are absolutely necessary for health and habitability. But beware of going overboard: Changing the foundation can result in cracked wall finishes, doors and windows that stick open or closed, and partitions and floors that are out of plumb and out of level.

Since many structural repairs will expose the vitals of the house to the elements for some length of time, arrange your work schedule so that you perform repairs in warm, dry weather. Nothing is more conducive to an ulcer, frostbitten fingers and skyrocketing costs than a house jacked up on timbers in November in a place like Vermont or Minnesota. The messiest jobs, the ones that make the house absolutely unfit for living, should coincide with those times when you are free to set up temporary quarters outside, or to leave on vacation while the hired help tears the place apart. Allow plenty of time for structural work; it always seems to take longer than estimated, since the links in the chain are never clear as the metaphor. One muddy timber doesn't always connect to another. If you intend to replace a foundation working nights and weekends, plan on spending an entire summer in mud and dust.

Except for redoing the exterior siding and trim, most cosmetic work is interior. Save the least disruptive work for winter months, after the house has been footed and roofed. Painting, staining and roofing, which require warm weather, are ideal summer projects.

Obviously, the border between structural and cosmetic work is not very precise. Nor does the work always fit the ideal season. Renovation projects have a way of unraveling slightly faster than you can knit them together. Schedules are torn apart in the tug-of-war between what should happen and what did happen. Come Septem-

Common Exterior Repairs

Rebuild chimney to roofline; reflash.

Replace chimney cap.

Replace finial.

Replace missing brackets; renail loose trim; caulk joints.

Scrape all loose paint; prime with oil-based primer.

Replace missing shingles and renail loose ones.

Replace rotted trim.

Weatherstrip doors and windows.

Repair or replace rotted window sills.

Caulk around casing.

Install storm windows.

Reputty sash.

Replace flashing.

Caulk seams between siding and cornerboard.

Repair gutter; replace leader.

Renail loose siding; replace rotted boards.

Install splash blocks.

Correct grade for proper drainage.

Rebuild bulging area.

Replace crumbling brick.

Remove vegetation close to foundation wall.

Repoint mortar.

Peeling paint indicates possible interior condensation problem.

Repair splits in door.

Repair or rebuild stairs.

Replace rotted decking.

Replace rotted parts and missing balusters.

Caulk at sill connection.

Replace rotted lattice.

ber, I'm usually just about caught up with my June work. But it helps to visualize the scope of the work on a sliding scale, with a chart such as the one shown on the facing page, which correlates projects to the seasons, time available and estimated costs.

Developing the Design

There is one more step before you pick up shovel and screw jacks. Your schedule of renovations must be supplemented by, or more precisely, informed by, a master design plan. This design plan will enable you

Planning the Work—Structural and Cosmetic

Priority	Scheme	Item	Estimated Cost	Estimated Time	Season
NOW	STRUCTURAL	1. foundation 2. sills 3. roof repair 4. chimney repair			SPRING

SOON		5. sheathing
		   (if rotten, otherwise
		   leave till later)
		6. windows and doors
		7. gutting interior
		8. rewiring
					SUMMER

LATER	COSMETIC	9. replumbing 10. insulation 11. heating system			FALL
		12. interior changes 13. interior walls 14. cabinets, fixtures 15. floor refinishing			WINTER
		16. grading, seeding 17. siding 18. outbuildings, porches 19. painting 20. everything else			NEXT YEAR

Note: When an item takes up the entire seasonal cycle, all the others merely shift into the next rotation, ad infinitum. Here, the time scheme might be best listed as "mañana."

to meet the challenge of reshaping the house to your needs without doing violence to its structural and spiritual integrity. I am, of course, presupposing that you would not consider "updating" a historic treasure. In that case, design changes are not an option unless they fit within the preservation guidelines outlined on pp. 38-39. If you can't comfortably live in lots of tiny rooms with no closets, don't buy a historic house.

In the best of all possible worlds, you'd have spent the winter before renovation drawing up the master design plan. Develop lists and rough sketches of each inhabitant's wants, needs and fantasies. Then measure every room and passageway, and with an architect's ruler and graph paper,

make a scale drawing of the existing floor plan. It doesn't have to be (nor will it be) perfectly accurate. But it should show the location of windows, fixed items such as sewer vent stacks and chimneys, the swing of doors, and the run of floor joists and major support beams. Make scaled cutouts of major appliances and furniture pieces, and place them in various combinations on the floor plan. Use tracing-paper overlays to project changes onto the existing floor plan.

Because there are likely to be things you have overlooked or hidden problems, it's a good idea to have these drawings evaluated and refined by an architect or designer, or a friend in the building business. Although time for leisurely reflection may be a luxury, a well-thought-out design is a necessity. Better to take a week thinking about the changes you'd like to make both in the present and over the long term than to find out later that your renovation needs remodeling. It's a lot easier to correct mistakes with an eraser than with a sledgehammer.

A house is a tool for living. And since living is, above all, a personal art, the tool should be shaped to the hand of the user. An ill-fitting house, like a poor hammer, causes psychic blisters. Think of house design in systematic and functional terms. Living is an energy flow, and the layout of a house can influence the current of this flow, alternating between spillways and dams, locks and waterfalls.

As architects will tell you, houses organize themselves into three distinct kinds of space, which are defined by the activities that take place within them. The inner, or private, space encompasses such things as sleeping, lovemaking and bodily care. Family and social activities such as food preparation, dining and entertaining take place in the outer, public space. Finally, there is the middle space, the transition zone between public and private spaces, indoors and outside. This space includes laundry rooms, mudrooms, porches, hallways and playrooms.

These design concepts can also relate to the cycles of the seasons. As one moves through the year, one moves through space as well. In winter the family draws together, gathering around the hearth or stove, thinking deep thoughts, sleeping late. In summer the family wakes early, and expands onto porches and lawns. One continually moves from the inner spaces to the outer ones within the sphere of the house itself. A well-designed house will allow graceful transitions, and balance the often conflicting feelings of each member of the household about their needs for public and private space.

Both graceful transitions and good design can be a hard act to pull off within the confines of an existing structure. The harmonious mating of old and new is one of the most difficult challenges in renova-

A New Hampshire joint house arranged around a courtyard.

Restoration to its original shape would only rob this house of its rather odd charm.

tion. Chances are good that the necessary additions were already added sometime over the last century or so when the former occupants extended the original core house to meet the needs of expanding family or farming operations, or to reflect growing prosperity.

The connected farm buildings of New England, also known as "New Hampshire joint houses," whose construction often stretched over decades, are an example of successfully integrated additions (see the photos on the facing page and on p. 6). The verse, "big house, little house, back house, barn," recited by 19th-century children at play, describes their organization. As agriculture declined in the first years of the 20th century, joint-house complexes tended to fall into ruin inversely, starting with the barn, through the woodsheds and carriage barns, to the kitchen ell. Unfortunately for present-day owners, much of the outermost sections are unsalvageable. The woodshed and kitchen ell, however, can usually be rescued.

Because zoning regulations mandate specific setbacks, a collapsed structure may prove valuable, since you can rebuild within the original "footprint" of a building even if it overshoots setback requirements. The house in the photo story on pp. 50-52, which was targeted to be converted into offices, did not conform to minimum property-line setback requirements. The new building could not extend beyond the original footprint, nor could the old building be torn down. The high cost of commercial real estate in the rapidly growing area justified the expense of a renovation that left only the barest portion of the original structure intact.

If you do decide an addition is needed, check with the zoning board before you get too involved in your design. If it's in a village, the present structure probably crowds the lot lines already. One of the benefits of rural living is the relative freedom from such bureaucratic annoyances.

Sometimes a house benefits more from subtraction than addition, especially when restoration is a priority. Removing later accretions of inferior workmanship or conflicting styles can do a lot to upgrade and harmonize the appearance of an otherwise unremarkable or ugly house. I don't think one should be fanatical about architectural purity, though. Sometimes the charm of a particular house is its unique style of crazy-quilt patchwork.

The Importance of a House's Footprint

2. Since the attached shed at the rear of the house had no real foundation, it was removed and a new cellar poured in the original footprint.

1. The rotted porch deck and its supports were removed, exposing the crumbling brick-cap wall, which rested on the solid concrete foundation, a legacy of an earlier foundation repair.

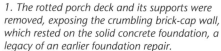

4. Rotted sills were replaced with new timber. For most of their length, the new sills were supported by concrete blocks laid over the old concrete wall just below grade.

3. The brick face wall was pulled out to reveal parts of an old stone foundation interspersed with sections of concrete.

5. Detail of new sill and cap wall. Old studs were sawn off and nailed into the timber sill.

6. Since this section of the former porch was to be incorporated into the new building line, the new sill would become a girder spanning a heated crawl space.

7. Here the formwork for the frost wall is in place.

8. To create an open floor plan, the original side wall was replaced with a carrying beam.

9. In preparation for the new roof framing and its junction with the rear addition, most of the old gable wall was removed.

10. The previous bay window had been hung from the wall. The new one would be two stories high and rest on a solid foundation.

11. The original footprint would soon be the only part of the bay window left intact.

12. In addition to the changes in floor plan and bearing walls, extensive structural changes were needed to make the building solid and safe, including a section of new floor and beefed-up ceiling framing.

The Importance of a House's Footprint

13. *The last of the original wall framing separating the old from the new section was removed.*

14. *Only a shadow of the original building is left.*

15. *A rehabilitation Cinderella story: The finished project seems strangely familiar, as if the original rather dowdy house had somehow been decked out in elegant formal attire.*

Attic conversion

As a family settles and grows, its needs blossom into possessions, like lush new growth in the orchard (attic cleanings are but the pruning of wild growth). Growth is the natural expression of life, and families sometimes outgrow their houses. As the nautilus adds another chamber to its shell, we add to our houses to make the space for our burgeoning needs and desires. Attic conversions are the most economical additions you can buy—all you need is insulation, mechanical systems and finish work.

But not all attic spaces are adequate. As the top drawing on the facing page shows, under a traditional 12/12-pitch gable roof the effective living area is about half the floor space. Living space increases slightly with a 3-ft. or 4-ft. high kneewall and decreases as the pitch lowers—the space under a 6/12-pitch roof is useful only for storing unwanted things. Adding a shed or gable dormer will increase the usable space quite dramatically. Consider this option before you reshingle or rebuild the roof deck. Let your needs guide your imagination when planning a dormer. The cost differential between the various options will not be so great as to make any one choice more attractive than another.

Dormers preserve the integrity of a steeply pitched roof while creating usable space. On the other hand, skylight windows, contrary to the impression conveyed by the sales brochures, offer only a psychological increase in space; the usable floor area remains unchanged. Although they are simply and quickly installed, in my opinion, skylights, like decks, seem ill-suited to old houses. If you insist on using them, put them on the back side of the house, and avoid buying cheap units, which can leak or fall apart.

The bottom drawing on the facing page suggests some dormer possibilities. Gable dormers are the most traditional and arguably the best-looking option, although they are more difficult to frame and yield less usable living space than

Roof Pitch and Living Space

Living space decreases as pitch lowers. (Shaded area represents living space.)

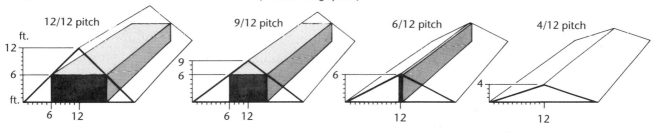

Dormer Options

When traditional gable dormers are added to a Cape-style house, they are best aligned directly over the windows of the lower story. The width of the dormer windows should match that of the lower units.

Traditionally, the eave cornice is left intact.

By eliminating the continuous eave cornice overhang, European-style dormers merge with the front wall. These are usually tall and narrow.

A shed dormer is easier to frame and offers more usable living space, but is not as elegant in appearance.

Except for the projecting rakes and eaves, this shed dormer includes the entire roof.

The next step in the progression is to eliminate the rake and eave overhangs, which creates the saltbox style.

When dormers are extended to share a common roofline, they form a gable roof.

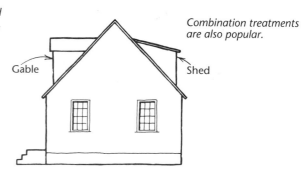

Combination treatments are also popular.

Although undersized, this dormer doesn't detract from the appearance of the house. Unfortunately, the modern skylights strike a confusing and discordant note. Notice the poor workmanship in fitting together the shingles at the 'woven' valley.

shed dormers. Amateur remodelers should probably hire an experienced carpenter rather than attempt the job on their own. Size and proportion are critical to the successful integration of a dormer into the roofline. A common mistake is to make them too small—it takes very little additional time or money to build a usefully sized dormer. But size should defer to harmonious proportion. For some reason, shed dormers always seem awkward unless they are very small or very large.

Radical changes

If the roof deck and rafters are rotted beyond reasonable repair or the pitch is too low to allow use of the attic, consider removing the roof entirely and framing a new one (see pp. 216-219). But even with steep-pitched roofs, kneewall spaces (the area at the bottom of the triangle formed by the roof and floor deck) are limited to use as out-of-the-way storage areas. Raising the height of the side walls can solve this problem. Many old houses were framed with 10-ft. or 12-ft. walls for just this reason. Any kneewall added to the floor platform should be at least 3 ft. to 4 ft. tall. Shorter walls will be unstable; even a 4-ft. wall will have to be braced with diagonals let into interior partitions.

You might even consider adding an entire second story. But here again, proportion is important: The extra height may present too severe a facade, especially for a narrow house. A two-story house with a steep roof, set in the middle of an open field, will look like Aunt Em's Kansas house in *The Wizard of Oz*. Surrounded by tall trees, it may seem homier and less imposing. The vertical lines of the facade can be offset to some degree by a lower roof pitch, the addition of porches or the use of horizontal siding and shingles without cutouts.

Rebuilding the roof is an opportunity to correct any mistakes in the original construction. Of course, before you go live on your former ceiling, you should determine whether its timbers will support your weight in their new capacity as floor joists. A fellow I know not only reframed his roof but added an entire set of new joists to carry the attic-floor-turned-living-space, which previously had been supported by 2x4s. This particular case was a bit extreme—the house was only a temporary shelter, a wood-framed tent to keep out the weather while he rebuilt his real house inside. Like the larvae of those strange wasps that lay their eggs inside a living host, he slowly and methodically devoured the original house from the inside out, until all that remained was an empty husk, a few warped and shattered boards piled in the dooryard as kindling.

This man was a beacon of inspiration, a true champion rebuilder. A decade later, his original $2,000 hunting camp had metamorphosed under its cocoon into a country cottage that he sold for $115,000. Considering that it was raised off its shaky, rotting, post foundation, a cellar dug almost entirely by hand out of the hardpan, the entire back wall removed, porches torn off and rebuilt, the roof raised, dormers and gables framed, new walls, sheathing, ceilings, floors, windows, doors, plumbing, wiring and heating systems added, he probably doesn't feel overpaid for his efforts. I'm told there is a small relic of the original house preserved in a glass case on the living-room wall. The triumph of this man's folly (some might same mania) has a moral: However bad it seems, someone has been there and back already.

Adding a Second Floor

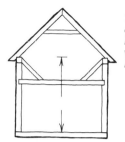

To gain extra ceiling height, old houses were framed with 10-ft. or 12-ft. high walls.

Because the framing can act like a hinge, adding too short a kneewall (less than 4 ft.) can cause structural problems.

When adding kneewalls to raise a roof, plan interior partitions to add diagonal bracing for resistance to racking.

I used to tease that same friend about his lack of running water. His spring had dried up, and his new plumbing languished unused for lack of time to dig a new one. I was building my own place at the time, and although I had cold running water to the kitchen sink, the plumbing was not yet finished. A case of cold beer was riding on which of us would get to have a shower first. The night after his roof was torn off, I was at home, listening to the rain gently falling when the phone rang. It was my friend. All he said was, "I prefer dark beer."

Radical surgery is also an option to be considered at the nether end of the house. If a pier or crawl-space foundation must be replaced anyway, consider digging a full basement instead. See pp. 95-98 for details. Sometimes bold solutions are the simplest. For example, instead of replacing a foundation under the house, you might be able to move the house onto a new foundation built alongside the old one.

Approaches to Renovation

Short of tearing the place down to the ground and starting from scratch, what is the best way to untangle this Gordian knot masquerading as a house? What is most efficient is not always the most practical. Rebuilding an old house can be a form of economic strangulation, even suicide; it can also be the only chance you will ever get to have a house of your own. You can work on your house piecemeal while you live in it (the caterpillar ap-

proach), or you may want to move out for a while and do the work all at once (the blitzkrieg approach).

The blitzkrieg approach

If you choose the blitzkrieg approach, consider living in temporary quarters like a tent, an old house trailer, a camper or minimally converted outbuilding or garage while rebuilding; house trailers have the advantage of being resalable when the house is ready. I know of a couple who spent their first summer converting a tool-shed into a small but serviceable house. Free from the pressure of having to get it all done under a seasonal deadline, they renovated their charming but unlivable farmhouse as time and money allowed. Five years later they moved into the big house and rented out the former shed.

Living in a temporary shelter while rebuilding your dream house goes a long way toward relieving the tensions that inevitably arise during the dust and rubble of renovation. It also is a sensible strategy for using spare time and financial windfalls, and allows for wholesale (and therefore more efficient) demolition, especially if the entire house has to be gutted. Interior walls can be removed, wiring and plumbing exposed, and structural weak points repaired as needed. Dormers can be framed in or sections of roof removed without fear of damage to household goods.

Whatever is rotten can be replaced while the structure is exposed. Excavation and foundation repair can be done at any time during and after the stripping process. A timber frame will be much easier to straighten if the interior or exterior wall coverings and partitions have been removed—assuming of course that they are in need of removal. Each added layer of board or finish, every partition, adds stiffness that must be overcome if the frame is to move. Exposing the house's skeleton also makes it easier to decide where to begin, and lightens the loads that must be lifted when foundations and sills are replaced. Drafty old sheathing boards can be replaced or covered with modern anti-infiltration barriers. In effect, a new house can be hung on the old framework of hand-hewn beams, which in some cases is the only part of the house worth saving.

This blitzkrieg approach to renovation offers the advantage of quick results. Most important, the work can proceed in logical order. Unhampered by having to live around your work or work around your life, by having to redo work you did the month or season before as a temporary expedient, you can do it right the first time.

The disadvantage of this approach is that you are not allowed much time for reflection. Your idea of what you require for living space will change and evolve as you live in the house. What seemed like a good idea at the time may prove to be unworkable. A kitchen that seemed large to an ex-apartment dweller might be far too small to handle the harvest of a neo-rustic. The arrival of children certainly requires a complete reorganization. Former urbanites a few seasons removed to the country discover a whole new crop of needs rising to replace those they had plowed under. Previously important functions and their attendant spaces may well rest unused: The study and TV room may be collecting dust as occupants look in vain for a place to store the growing stock of tools or hang wet laundry in winter. And, of course, the all-out assault presupposes adequate reserves of time and money, which may effectively rule it out.

The caterpillar approach

The caterpillar approach—living in the house and restoring it over a period of years—is the solution to the dilemma. Since fewer and fewer people have the financial assets to build or buy a new house, fixing up as you go may be your only choice.

Unfortunately, this approach is the most expensive and demanding way to renovate. Doing a job rapidly and right the first time is inherently more efficient. As a caterpillar, too much of your time will be spent cleaning up the mess as the house reverts from renovation project to residence at the end of each workday. To maintain even the barest simulacrum of domesticity, the work must be organized by zones that can be quarantined from the flow of family life rather than by job description. For example, you rebuild the back bedroom, gutting the walls, running new wiring down into the cellar, hanging new drywall, painting and finishing the entire room, and so on, before moving on to the next room and repeating the process. It would be far more economical (especially of time) to gut the entire house all at once, and make and clean up a huge mess only once. You could also hire a drywall subcontractor to hang, tape and finish all the walls within a few days (most won't do just a single room), instead of laboriously botching the job yourself.

If each zone corresponds to a different level of the house, you may be able to increase efficiency and also coordinate the work more easily with the seasons. Start at the top: Rip out the upstairs walls, the plaster and lath, and clean up. Then patch the roof, reshingle it, and frame and close in a dormer. Cover the window rough openings with plastic until you can afford to pay for the new window units. Leave the final finish to next year. Then start on the foundation. Work on what has rotted until the nights grow crisp. Now is the time to rebuild the chimney. After the new foundation is backfilled, insulate the attic before cold weather sets in. During the winter months, you can finish the upstairs rooms while living on the first level. The following year, you can move upstairs into finished quarters while renovating the first floor.

This house-within-a house concept, the movable feast, allows you to live and work under the same leaky roof with the least amount of disruption. Plan the work in different stages or modules, try to leave blocks of time open for major jobs (these used to be called vacations) and always leave a refuge or sanctuary, some small undisturbed or finished corner of the house that will allow you to escape from the grime and noise.

The caterpillar approach is probably best suited to self-employed individuals or couples, who will find it somewhat easier to arrange their schedules to accommodate jobs that refuse to fit into weekends, or to set aside larger chunks of time without jeopardizing their employment. The temptation is to spread yourself too thin, to commit to a large project and then spend all of your time working to pay for it while you try to sandwich the actual work into weekends and nights. But you can easily get caught on a dizzying seesaw of working on the place until the bills are too large to ignore and then working elsewhere until you have enough to go back into debt. In the meantime, you'll never get a chance to live in the house.

And so it goes for as long as it must, a rhythm of seasonal breaths, in and out, in and out, until one day the burden of "things to be done" is suddenly very light. Like a bucket that has sprung a leak, there is not much more to carry. You feel empty, strange. Suddenly, work is no longer a reflex; you have to ask yourself, what am I going to do this weekend? What needs to be done? The days have expanded, your evenings are your own. Your legs spongy, you move with an unaccustomed lightness of purpose.

As trying as the process will be, there are some compensations to living in the house while renovating it. You'll be able to reflect on the progress, and to adapt to circumstances as they arise. For example, you may have planned to panel the bedroom walls with plasterboard when you got around to it next winter, only to come across a great deal on pine boards that fall. You might decide to add an attached woodshed after a winter spent chipping frozen logs out of a snowbank. In a sense, rebuilding an old house is too great an undertaking to be digested whole. It must be thoroughly chewed. The objective is chopped like spaghetti for a two-year-old into small, manageable bites. Focusing on limited goals helps maintain a sense of proportion—you are not so likely to be overwhelmed and swallowed by The Goal. The reason for enduring this ordeal is easier to keep in sight. Enjoy and savor the process in and of itself, as a vehicle for self-discovery, not as an accounting of steps taken to reach the horizon.

Once, an old-timer I used to work with was watching me slam and jam a block of wood into a space too small for it. I was determined to stretch that opening rather than recut the block. I guess he finally lost patience because he turned to me and said, "What's your hurry? You'll be doing this for the rest of your life. You might's well slow down and enjoy it, you damn fool!"

How to Rebuild and Stay Sane

The table on p. 47 suggests a correspondence: The ratio of input to output, or effort to satisfaction, is generally greater at the cosmetic end of the scale. The importance of this psychological factor cannot be underestimated. An unwholesome amount of simple drudge labor and great sums of money can be poured into a mud-filled foundation hole. When the job is finished and the hole backfilled after weeks of hard work, nothing has visibly changed. The satisfaction of knowing that at least your house will stand safely and that whatever else you do rests on a firm footing simply isn't dramatic enough.

The reward of hard labor comes in the satisfaction of being able to stand back and see the results. There is a revitalization of the spirit that allows you to tackle the next incredibly tedious job with renewed energy. As these largely invisible repairs eat up more and more time and money, you will begin to feel the gnawing of despair and exhaustion. It will seem as if nothing has been accomplished. It's then that you need to stop a while and perhaps plant a flower garden, build a doghouse, tear down a rotted porch. Take a few days to clean up the rubbish pile out back. Changing the subject can give you much-needed psychic refreshment.

A house cannot be experienced apart from its householders. You can contract out the entire renovation but you're still involved, even if only ceremonially. You still make decisions, you still react to each new change with trembling and joy. At first this deep involvement is a welcome thing. Full of energy and enthusiasm, you embrace the work, constantly measuring in your mind's eye where the curtains are to hang, where the bookshelves will go, the color of the braided rugs by the new hearth. As the days wane and the nights grow sharp and clear, your horizons begin to shrink. Getting the place closed in for winter becomes a consuming passion. You sit down at the breakfast table and eat insulation. A rainy day is a personal insult from a malevolent god. At night, lying in bed, your head is in the cellar jacking up a sagging beam, your spouse wondering where you are and why you never sent a postcard.

This obsession has a tendency to destroy family and interpersonal relationships. Whatever tensions already exist are exacerbated, like the scab on your knuckle that is constantly sloughed off every time you pick up a tool. Life becomes an incubator for a host of new and increasingly virulent strains of discord between you and your loved ones.

Although cultural patterns are changing, many of us are still the products of our upbringing. We tend to fall back into role stereotypes when the pressure is on. Many men still assume, consciously or not, that women are tailored for the role of household manager. And, equally important, many women are conditioned to expect men to know all about hardware. He fixes a leaky faucet, she fixes dinner.

According to the standard pattern, the woman is expected to provide the emotional and logistical support system, taking care of domestic chores, cooking meals and tending children, so that her mate can pursue the "important" work of renovating their house. This dynamic can even overcome the good intentions of couples who consciously strive to avoid it. The subversion begins when "efficiency" is invoked as a necessary evil. Because the male is so often stronger and more skilled with tools, and because there is simply so much to be done, he's the one who runs the chainsaw while she stacks the firewood. He measures and cuts the boards and nails them into place. She pulls nails from old boards, piles up the rubbish and moves stacks of building materials. He does the skilled labor, she does the gofer work. It doesn't take too long before expediency becomes expectation. These tasks are just added to the list of her "inconsequential" domestic duties. And hardly is there time taken to say thank you.

As the work increases and the days shorten, so do resentments and tempers. The couple that starts off equally unskilled is at an advantage here. Both can learn to use tools with equal skill. Brute strength is not the main component of intelligent carpentry. I know of one woman who wired and plumbed the entire house while her husband's job paid for the materials. They cooked supper together, a welcome break from the daily routine and the start of their evenings together.

Most couples are not that well balanced. Child care complicates the equation. In most cases, the man is the one with the skills and the woman the one with the children. It's also a simple fact that moms have to spend a lot of time with their babies. It really is more efficient for him to do the work while she does dinner. But ask yourself, what is more important, efficiency or your marriage?

The conflict between the need to make a living and the demands of do-it-yourself renovation also feeds the interpersonal polarization. Striking the proper balance requires saintlike patience. You must immerse yourself in the here and now, striving to enjoy the process in and of itself rather than as a means toward a goal, no matter how important that goal, how near the first frost. For no matter how fast and how hard you work, there will always be more to do. When getting it done becomes your only motivation, you will get done in.

When this happens, arguments degenerate into a vicious cycle. He has no time for his mate, her needs are an annoying interference with his important work. If she speaks to him about his mania or acts upset, she is immature or emotional, an additional weight on his already overburdened back. The same is true for his family. The conflict accelerates, the fights grow in frequency and intensity, a snappish remark touches off a flood of anger and invective. More than one relationship has been the casualty of a renovation project. How do you avoid getting caught in this vise? The advice is easy enough to give but hard to implement. You can read the writing on the wall, but not always know what it says.

You could begin by trying to state clearly what you expect of each other, to define responsibilities, to create a job description of your lives for the next few months, with the provision that the terms be subject to review and renegotiation after each phase. Remember that a house is not rebuilt in a vacuum of time and space. The chores and needs of daily life are not suspended during renovation. Those chores are every bit as important as moving walls or nailing boards. My wife and I both started out with the idea that we could share the building and the housework. I could be up on the scaffolding nailing on the siding. She could be on the ground, cutting it to length. After a half-dozen attempts at forcing boards to fit the measurement, I found my patience wearing thin, and she found that carpentry wasn't really all that interesting. We were both frustrated by our impatience. She'd eventually learn how to use a saw; I only had a seven-year head start on her. She went and made dinner, I cut and nailed the boards myself. Later that evening (after I'd done the dishes) we talked about it and decided that the content was more important than the form. What she wanted was not to be necessarily equal on the job (which was rather unrealistic) but included in my life as a priority at least equal to, if not more important than, my work. She wanted to feel that I wouldn't make plans without consulting her, that just once in a while her needs might override the demands of the renovation.

It's a good place to start. But it won't carry you all that far. Constant vigilance will be needed to keep from backsliding into those old roles. You'll know you are succeeding when your complacency is disturbed, when you feel tongue-bound and uncomfortable. Talk about things before they go much further. Don't bottle up frustrations or let too much slide, hoping your partner hasn't noticed or that it will go away. Learning when to let up or lean a little harder is a skill that furthers your relationship.

Touch home base. Remember that the house is a means, not the end. There are times when you should put the hammer down, say "to hell with it" and go out to dinner. Listen to your partner. Keep your sense of humor well oiled. Listen to yourself, know when you need to stop. And stop. Do not ignore this advice. There is nothing sadder than a house that has de-voured the souls of its people, or than the emptiness of waking up at night and see-ing a stranger lying beside you.

Better is a handful of quietness than two hands full of toil and a striving after wind. (Ecclesiastes 4:6)

Hiring A Contractor

Should you hire a contractor? For many home owners, by reason of temperament, skill or economy, the answer is an obvious "no." But others, especially those with limited skills, confidence or experience, might feel certain jobs are best left to pro-fessionals. You might, for example, hire out the heaviest, dirtiest work and reserve the more pleasurable projects for yourself. Since time and money exist in a rough equilibrium, paying for work with your outside income may be more economical than staying home and blundering through it yourself.

Suppose you desire to take an active role in the renovation of your house and, mindful of potential savings, are thinking about being your own contractor. Just as no professional contractor makes a com-mitment without an accurate estimate of labor and materials, you must make an equally precise estimate of your available resources. Ask yourself:

1. How much time can you allow for the job?

2. When can you spare it?

3. What technical skills and general building skills do you have?

4. What tools and equipment do you have/need?

5. How well can you communicate with tradespeople?

6. How much do you know about renovation, and how much do you want to learn?

A contractor is someone who is paid to stay awake at night and worry about the job. How much is this worth to you? Con-tractors are often little more than errand-runners, checking off endless lists of

things to do, problems to solve, kinks to straighten, within a tight financial and temporal framework. How obsessive are you? Experience is what enables a good contractor to make informed choices, and the lack of it is perhaps the greatest stum-bling block to successful do-it-yourself contracting. A beginner is at a disadvan-tage evaluating job progress or anticipat-ing the next unforeseen problem. Learning from your mistakes is effective, but it is also expensive. The skills and techniques may not be very complicated, but the translation from reading about a task to doing it is not always a direct or simple affair—books don't leak, pipes do.

Finally, a contractor has the time to do the job. And supervising a large-scale ren-ovation is a full-time job, not a sideline that can be crammed into a few hours before work, an odd afternoon, weekends or nights (those moments should be re-served for the rest of life). It's the contrac-tor who has to smooth things out when the plumber gets mad about the drywallers and the carpenters can't stand the way the owner is always hanging around asking questions. It's the contractor's job to work as late as necessary to finish drawing a cor-nice detail, to listen to the weather fore-cast to see if frost will hamper a morning concrete pour. Do you have the time to do all this? Can you afford not to?

Types of contracts

If you decide to go the contractor route, do your homework on how to select and work with one. (Check the Bibliography on pp. 334-338 for some good sources of information.) Pay particular attention to the type of contract offered. The fixed price, or "lump-sum," contract is most familiar, but it is least suited to renova-tion. Here, the contractor simply agrees to perform the specified work for a fixed amount—period, no surprises. If costs run over, the contractor eats them; if they come in under his estimate, he pockets the windfall. Caught between the rock of fixed costs and the hard place of fixed price, there is a built-in incentive to push productivity and keep costs low to increase profits. Ideally this contract should benefit the client. But since there is no way to recoup costs of oversights, mistakes or unforeseen events (all of which characterize renovation work), the slush factor in the fixed price must be quite large if the temptation to cut corners, pad changes and squeeze extras to make up the losses is to be avoided. Because of this, lump-sum contracts must be especially clear as to what is included and what is an extra.

In theory, the cost-plus contract offers the lowest price. The contractor's percentage for profit and overhead, as agreed upon in advance, is added to the sum of the invoiced charges for materials, subcontractors and labor. The contractor, assured of a reasonable profit, does not have to finagle the price to cover surprises and run-of-the-mill disasters. However, our national experience with defense contractors reveals the flaw in this arrangement—the temptation to milk the job for more time than it's worth is hard to resist. Although it leaves a lot to trust and good will, this type of contract is well suited to reconstruction of rotten sills and walls, where there are often too many variables to allow a meaningful bid.

I've found that a combination of the preceding contracts—the cost-plus-not-to-exceed contract—works best. Here the contractor bills for the actual cost of the work plus a percentage for overhead/profit up to a maximum figure, at which the price becomes fixed. Should the total costs be less than the maximum, the customer saves the difference. Should they exceed it, the contractor absorbs the overrun. Of course, an opportunistic contractor can inflate the not-to-exceed figure and then milk the job or fudge labor costs to push against the limits. Here's where competitive bidding—submitting plans and specs to several contractors for their bids—limits dishonesty to tolerable levels.

If you decide to hire labor by the hour, you are no longer legally a contractor, but an employer, and as such are subject to various federal and state regulations. See an accountant for advice; you could also pose your hypothetical case to your state Department of Employment before proceeding. Becoming a short-term employer could turn out to be a great deal of trouble and expense. It's a lot easier to find a hungry general contractor willing to work for an hourly wage and perhaps a small percentage to cover wear and tear on tools and equipment. Whoever you hire, he or she should expect to furnish you with a Certificate of Insurance to protect you from liability suits. If you hire individual carpenters instead of a subcontractor with crew, each carpenter should furnish proof of insurance.

Despite any impressions to the contrary, carpentry is an inexact art. No one builds perfectly, at least not anyone you can afford to hire. Mistakes are a given. The best builders make precious few and know how to fix them when they do. Every job has a built-in allowance for "fudge," for covering over or correcting mistakes. My experience indicates that about 2% of the total labor cost is part of that recipe. With a fixed-price contract, the contractor eats it all. If you are paying cost-plus or hiring help by the hour, you can expect a taste, too. But you shouldn't have to pay for a three-course meal. Unless caused by poor planning or changes after the fact on your part, major errors should be repaired by the builder at his own expense, not yours. If it's the contractor's fault, it's the contractor's obligation to make it right. An honest builder will absorb the damage without even mentioning it, and simply deduct the time spent straightening things out from the time you are billed. This situation presupposes that you know what the contractor isn't doing right.

Once the work is underway, keep in touch. But don't be obtrusive. Carpenters and other craftspeople tend to get nervous when the owner is standing around. Sometimes they become so self-conscious about making a mistake and try so hard to avoid one that they make mistakes. And the contractor or foreman is loath to draw attention by correcting someone in front of the owner. A proven means of winning worker confidence is to show up on Friday afternoon with the paychecks and beer. But even if you do bring the doughnuts, don't visit during coffee break except on rare occasions. Workers instinctively react with resentment to this intrusion into their most intimate territory. There's a substratum of awkwardness in the hierarchy of worker and worked-for that can never be resolved, no matter how nice a person you are.

You have to trust your contractor's experience, but you shouldn't be a victim of his malfeasance. If you sense a problem developing, talk about it, after hours or aside from the crew. If something they're doing doesn't make sense, ask about it. If the answer rings false, ask someone else. It could be that you misjudged and picked the wrong contractor. If this is so, stop and clear the matter up. And if you feel justified in so doing, don't hesitate to let the idiot go, right then and there. The situation will only get messier if you let things continue askew.

Many owners, some motivated by a desire to save money, and others by a wish for greater involvement in, and simple fascination with, the building of their homes, will ask to help out or work along with the crew. Since the owners rarely have the skill or time to mesh with the builder's timetables or quality standards, their participation is seldom a good idea.

There are cases, however, where an owner might be a tradesperson or sufficiently skilled to undertake an area of the job that would otherwise be subcontracted out. This can be specified as "by owner" in the contract and an allowance factored into the bid. But such cases are rare. More often than not, the owners will ask how much they can save if they do the painting or staining. The wise contractor will answer "nothing," and explain that since it is his name that will be on the finished product, he would prefer having control of the outcome. Or he may allow the owner to perform these functions so long as the contract specifies his right to complete or continue them at cost-plus if they are not completed within the necessary time frame.

This is tricky stuff. Usually, only good friends or builders working for other builders will have the necessary rapport to pull it off. Scheduling can be difficult. For example, weekends or long summer evenings are the best time for the owners to stain clapboards, pick up rubbish, stack lumber or fetch materials to the job site for the next day's work. A fair contractor should compensate for the value of this behind-the-scenes, after-hours help by generosity in the client's favor when figuring up the allowances for job overruns and extras.

Owners on the job site during the workday are a distraction at best. Never try to borrow a carpenter's tools for any reason, unless specifically invited to do so. Carpenters are scrupulously careful about the protocols of such things among themselves—it's one of the ways harmony is maintained. It can cost you dearly to interfere with it.

Hiring a contractor should be no more difficult than hiring a lawyer, accountant or any other professional. Like them, a good contractor has spent 10 or more years learning the trade and survived in an intensely competitive environment. A solid reputation takes years to cultivate. Only a fool would destroy it for a quick buck at a client's expense. Only fools believe their misdeeds will escape unnoticed. Most successful contractors survive because, given enough time, honesty and competence do go hand in hand. But perhaps because people entrust their deepest and most personal dreams to their contractor's care, they are so often quick to shout "thief" when something is lost in the translation.

Architects and Designers

If you're capable of doing your own renovation work, chances are you won't need to hire an architect or a designer. Here's the difference between them: Architects are licensed professionals who have completed a course of graduate study and real-life apprenticeship before passing their certification exam. A designer is anyone who can translate ideas into drawings or models, and does not necessarily have any particular training. Designers do the same thing as architects, but they are less expensive since they don't have licenses or know how to build skyscrapers and post offices. Consulting with either a designer or an architect may be invaluable before or during your renovation. These people can spot serious structural problems in your plans before they become a reality. By simply reviewing your rough sketches, a designer or architect can make recommendations that could save you hundreds of dollars or dramatically affect the comfort and utility of your home.

But if you've hired a contractor, do you also need to hire an architect to supervise your contractor? Or should you hire a contractor who can also furnish you with designs? There are arguments in favor of both options. With the power of creative vision, the architect is supposed to transmute your wishes into a work of art written in the language of builders (plans and specs), while acting as your agent to ensure the contractor's compliance with the contract terms. The unspoken assumption is that contractors are in need of supervision to secure their honesty or enforce their competence.

Although it is true that there are still contractors who are as aesthetically aware as a mudpuddle (as there are designers and architects who wouldn't recognize a hammer if it was thrown at them), the separation between white and blue collars is no longer clear-cut. Today most renovators also offer some level of design services. For most residential projects smaller in scale than an opera house, the designer/builder is probably the most economical alternative to the traditional client/architect/contractor triad. Just like an architect, a good designer/builder will have the communication skills and insight to interpret your ideas and translate them into a plan that reconciles budget and dreams. The emphasis is on translation, not adulteration (architects are sometimes suspected of forgetting that they work for the client and not vice versa). Unlike most architects, the designer/builder will have solid hands-on experience with how to implement those plans. And since the person using the drawings is the one who drew them, there's one less level of potential misunderstanding between the client and contractor, and one less professional to pay.

Foundations

A Vermonter had bought an old, run-down farm and had worked very hard getting it back in good operating condition. When it was back in pretty good working shape, the local minister happened to stop by for a call. He congratulated the farmer on the result of his labors, remarking that it was wonderful what God and man could do when working together.
"Ayeh," allowed the farmer, "p'raps it is. But you should have seen this place when God was running it alone."

—Allen R. Foley, *What the Old-Timer Said* (Brattleboro, Vt.: Stephen Greene Press, 1971)

This shaky stone foundation capped by a buttress wall is badly in need of replacement.

*T*he foundation is a link, the anchor that binds the house frame to earth. Unlike modern light framing, which must be mechanically secured to the foundation wall, an old-fashioned timber frame with its continuous sill beams and great weight required no supplemental fasteners. Despite this aura of invincible durability, untreated wood given over to the moist embrace of earth will soon rot, returning to the ground from which it sprang. Holding wood and earth apart, a foundation serves to postpone this inevitable reunion.

Under the right conditions, water can easily destroy a foundation. Depending on their porosity, soils are saturated to varying degrees with subsurface water. This "water table" fluctuates seasonally in response to variations in precipitation. Especially during spring, cellars can lie beneath the crest of the water table. The situation is complicated by surface water (rainwater or snowmelt). As it pours off the eaves or drains toward the house along the ground, water will saturate the soil around the house and eventually run down the foundation wall.

Whether from surface runoff, a high water table or both, water that ponds up against a cellar wall exerts a force (hydrostatic pressure) strong enough to push the water through microscopic pores in solid concrete, causing a damp basement, or, under extreme circumstances, the buckling of the wall. Think about it: Water weighs 62.4 lb. per cu. ft. This may not seem like much, since concrete can withstand pressures of several thousand lb./sq. in. But hydrostatic pressure is exerted laterally as well as vertically, which means that if the soil surrounding a cellar is typically saturated over a large enough region, the actual pressure against a wall can easily exceed the elastic limit of poured concrete.

With foundations, the best protection is prevention. The ground next to the house (the grade) should be sloped away from the house. Gutters and downspouts should be installed to collect roof runoff and divert it away from the foundation. In new construction, the foundation is waterproofed on the outside, a perforated drainpipe is laid along the base of the foundation wall and the excavation is filled with porous material that allows water to drain away, preventing any buildup of hydrostatic pressure on the wall. In effect, the water table can never rise above the level of the drain tile.

Unfortunately, most old houses don't have monolithic poured concrete foundations or foundation drains. In cold regions, frozen water trapped in poorly drained clay or silty soils causes the soil to expand, which exerts tremendous pressure in all directions, like millions of tiny screw jacks. Obviously any foundation that doesn't extend below the frost line (the depth of average maximum frost penetration) will rise and fall on the swells of frost heave. Even when deep enough, a foundation lacking proper drainage is vulnerable to the equally destructive lateral pressure. No mere concrete wall can withstand the onslaught; it is only a matter of time before the foundation will buckle, shift and fall in. Stone foundations have little resistance to the effects of frost heave.

Vitrified clay drain tiles were in use as far back as the first quarter of the 19th century, but the labor involved in hand or horse-powered excavation and hauling of materials was formidable, so it's not surprising few houses were equipped with drains, or that the trenches around the cellar were backfilled with native soil rather than more porous gravel drawn in from off-site. One might then wonder, in the absence of well-drained soils or adequate foundation drainage systems, why any old houses still stand at all. Fortunately for both preservationists and old-home aficionados, houses in cold climates had some built-in protection. Heat escaping through the cellar walls kept adjacent soil thawed, while the heavy snow cover typical of most Northern winters created an insulating blanket that restricted downward frost penetration.

In less rigorous climates, old foundations didn't succumb to waterlogged soils because the joints between their stones allowed water to enter, reducing hydrostatic pressure to a greater or lesser degree. Over time, these foundations would shift as water undermined parts of the wall or loosened stones. In those cases, the best prescription for disaster was pouring concrete against the inside of the cellar to block seepage. Like modern block, brick and poured concrete walls, these simply gave way faster. Of course, even in somewhat drier or more stable soils, the build-up of moisture in an unventilated cellar promotes the growth of wood-attacking fungi and insects, which cause structural rot. Whatever the condition or the climate, it's the rare old house that doesn't exhibit some sign of foundation damage or the kinds of water problems that will eventually cause foundation trouble.

Water-Infiltration Problems

It's important to distinguish between problems caused by surface runoff as opposed to problems caused by a high water table. The former can often be cured easily while the latter are seldom resolved without resort to heroic (and expensive) measures. As mentioned previously, when the ground doesn't slope away from the foundation on all sides, surface water flows toward the house. Likewise, roof runoff works down along the foundation wall and through any cracks or pores into the cellar. So-called "dry walls" of unmortared stones will usually start to weep after a heavy rain. Rivulets are often visible at the height of the downpour. The mortar joints of concrete block walls are very susceptible to this sort of infiltration; even poured concrete walls are not impervious.

If enough surface water percolates down to the bottom of the foundation, water will ooze up between the wall and floor slab, and puddles will form on the cellar floor. If you were to walk around the exterior perimeter of such a house, you'd

Water in the Cellar: Problems and Remedies

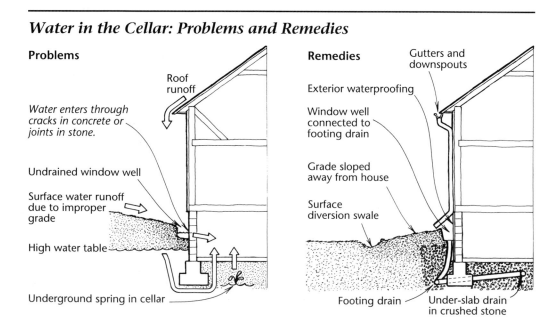

Problems

Roof runoff

Water enters through cracks in concrete or joints in stone.

Undrained window well

Surface water runoff due to improper grade

High water table

Underground spring in cellar

Remedies

Gutters and downspouts

Exterior waterproofing

Window well connected to footing drain

Grade sloped away from house

Surface diversion swale

Footing drain

Under-slab drain in crushed stone

notice sunken areas and what appear to be small tunnels formed where the surface water has seeped through the foundation wall. A few wheelbarrow loads of clay soil spread over these spots and compacted will build up the grade and allow runoff to flow away from the house. If the grade pitches toward the foundation, a swale (a grassed-in shallow trough) should be cut into the slope. The swale itself must be pitched to channel water away from the house. Because of the sheer volume of material to be redistributed, this is bull-dozer work.

Gutters (or eavestroughs, as they are somewhat more mellifluously called) and downspouts can help prevent water infil-tration by catching roof runoff and divert-ing it away from the house. But in the far North, these tend to fill up with ice, which splits the gutter seams or backs up under the shingles or wall covering causing leaks.

Window wells were often used in the foundations of old houses to admit light (but not ventilation) into the cellar through fixed glass panes set in wooden frames. Rare is the window unit that has not rot-ted away, providing an entrance for water, insects and rodents. The only quick fix is to dig out the bottom of the window well by hand and extend a shallow trench the length of a drain tile (or more) out from the wall (see the drawing at right). Lay a solid drainpipe in this trench, connected at its far end to a short length of perforat-ed pipe and teed into another perforated pipe at the well end (all ends should be capped). Cover this end and the bottom of the window well with crushed stone, and backfill. This "mini-drywell" will diffuse runoff into the soil at a safe distance from the wall.

Below-grade windows are probably best blocked in and replaced with a venti-lating louver. Remove the remains of the window with a hammer and prybar, scrub the stone clean with a wire brush, then moisten and fill in the opening with con-crete block and bricks as needed. Set a screened aluminum louver made to fit

Quick Fix to Improve Window-Well Drainage

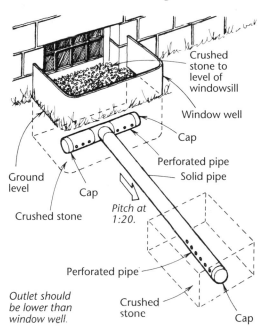

Crushed stone to level of windowsill

Window well

Cap

Perforated pipe

Solid pipe

Ground level

Cap

Crushed stone

Pitch at 1:20.

Perforated pipe

Outlet should be lower than window well.

Crushed stone

Cap

into the space of a standard concrete block in the mortar. If possible, provide at least two vents along each wall for cross venti-lation. In winter close the vents and stuff a piece of rigid foam or fiberglass insulation against them. Although simple to install, these louvers don't provide natural light and are best suited to walls under porches where light wouldn't penetrate anyway, or where there is not sufficient clearance above grade to install a proper foundation window. Modern insulated glass cellar windows are designed to open and admit both light and air. Unless they are vinyl or metal-framed, the units should be set in a framework of pressure-treated lumber se-cured to the masonry.

The cellars of some old houses were deliberately dug over a spring to guaran-tee a year-round water supply without the need for burying the expensive pipe that would connect an outside source to the cellar. In theory, any overflow (some springs flow continuously) will run into a drain and through the wall to an outlet away from the house. But sometimes the overflow pipe is clogged, rotted or missing and the water just trickles out into the cellar. A new overflow pipe, routed through the cellar wall to an existing or retrofitted foundation drain or into a cellar sump pit, will dry up this quagmire.

Hydraulic cements and various cement-based waterproofing paints applied to the inside of the foundation walls can sometimes cure occasional seepage caused by surface runoff. If the joints between dry-laid stones are first stuffed with mortar (the technique is called "pointing" or "tuck-pointing") and large-scale irregularities smoothed over, it may even be possible to stop further leakage by sealing the stones and mortar with a thin stucco of hydraulic cement. Since all hydraulic cements differ, be sure to read the manufacturer's recommendations carefully and select a product intended for your specific need. Although these cements are up to ten times more costly than ordinary mortar, they're still cheaper than excavating and sealing the wall from the outside.

When water is squeezing between the base of the foundation wall and a floor slab, a stucco coat alone won't stop the leak. Cut a ¾-in. deep channel into the floor slab where it joins the wall to anchor the cement. Ideally, for greater bond strength, its profile should form a keyway wider at the bottom than the top, but since the concrete chips out in irregular chunks, this is seldom possible. Renting a hammer drill with a chisel blade will make this tedious job a lot easier.

When standing water in the cellar lingers throughout the year, disappearing only after a prolonged dry spell, the infiltration is most likely caused by ponding from a high water table and an inadequate or nonexistent foundation drain. Houses built on small and/or level lots don't offer enough slope for the foundation drain's outlet to be below the footing level, so water typically drains into a municipal sewer or a drywell (stone-filled pit) located somewhere on the property. Occasionally, a wet cellar can be traced to a blocked or broken drain tile or silted-in dry well; dead animals and tree roots are also a source of blockage. Unfortunately, since foundation drains are seldom accessible to a mechanical cleaner, the cause can only be discovered by excavation. I remember one particularly stubborn case of floor seepage that was cured only when exposure of the foundation-drain outlet pipe revealed a high spot that forced subsurface water to flow back into the cellar. Our only clue was the suspiciously small trickle of water that flowed from the drain's outlet.

Installing an Exterior Drainage System

Interior basement waterproofers, no matter how aggressively marketed, are seldom a cure-all for a serious water-infiltration problem. Even when they do help, they hasten the emergence of long-range problems by permitting the buildup of exterior hydrostatic pressure. Correcting the grade, fixing window wells or adding gutters, if not coupled with good foundation drainage, does not address the underlying cause of chronic water buildup either. This can only be cured by waterproofing the exterior of the wall and installing a proper drainage system.

In theory, a foundation wall is made impermeable to moisture infiltration by an exterior coating of asphalt-based stucco or other waterproofing material. These are easily applied to new concrete walls, but they cannot be used to seal an old stone wall. Even if you could clean all the dirt from the joints of the stones and fill them full of mortar (you can't), the irregular contours of the stones are just about impossible to cover. If the wall is structurally sound, it makes more sense to scrub and spray the loose dirt from the stones as best you can (soil prevents a good concrete bond) and then pour a 4-in. thick buttress wall against them (see the top drawing on the facing page). Although it's possible to form the sloped cap with the pour, it's a lot easier to shape it from mortar with a trowel after the concrete has set and the forms have been stripped. Since the new wall sticks out beyond the siding, you'll have to install a strip of flashing under the first course of siding and seal it to the outside of the concrete. Otherwise water can collect on top of the buttress wall and rot the sills.

Waterproof this new concrete wall (and any foundation wall) before you lay your drain tile (the tar splatters over everything). Apply asphalt flashing cement to seal any voids left by form ties before waterproofing. For drainpipes, 4-in. dia. perforated PVC pipe is most common— it's light, strong, easily installed and inexpensive. The "Orangeburg" asphalt-fiber, cement-asbestos and clay drainpipes formerly used for footing drains are no longer widely available. Flexible ABS corrugated plastic pipe, sold in 250-ft. coils, is used for draining fields and roadways and is not suited for footing drainage.

With a square-edged shovel, scrape smooth and level the excavation beside the footings and lay perforated pipe, its holes facing sideways, along the footings at their bottom edge (never on top). Some builders recommend sloping the perforated pipe 1 in. per 20 ft. (½ in. per pipe length) all the way around the building. This might make sense in theory, but in reality it means you'll have to run drain outlets from each corner of the building or else dig down by hand 5 in. or 6 in. alongside the footing by the time you come to the outlet of a 120-ft. long perimeter. By laying the pipe level with the bottom of the footing, water will move into it and flow toward the outlet following the path of least resistance, preventing hydrostatic pressure from building up against the wall. Solid pipe is teed in at a convenient point and pitched slightly downward toward an outlet some distance from the foundation.

Cover the pipe with at least 6 in. of 2-in. crushed coarse "chestnut" stone; apply a layer of straw or building paper (not tar paper) or filter fabric (much more expensive) over the stone to prevent silting-in while the soil settles. Backfill the trench

Buttressing a Stone Foundation Wall

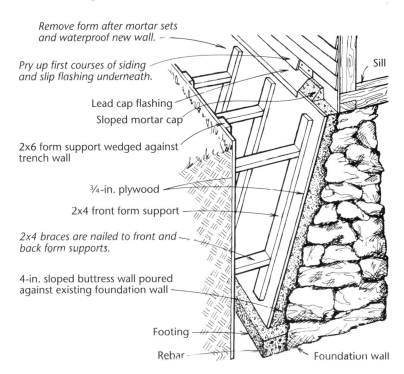

Remove form after mortar sets and waterproof new wall.

Pry up first courses of siding and slip flashing underneath.

Lead cap flashing

Sloped mortar cap

2x6 form support wedged against trench wall

¾-in. plywood

2x4 front form support

2x4 braces are nailed to front and back form supports.

4-in. sloped buttress wall poured against existing foundation wall

Footing

Rebar

Sill

Foundation wall

Foundation Drainage

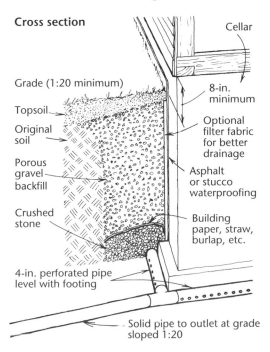

Cross section

Cellar

Grade (1:20 minimum)

8-in. minimum

Topsoil

Original soil

Optional filter fabric for better drainage

Porous gravel backfill

Asphalt or stucco waterproofing

Crushed stone

Building paper, straw, burlap, etc.

4-in. perforated pipe level with footing

Solid pipe to outlet at grade sloped 1:20

with gravel or sand to a few inches above finished grade. Porous backfill material is necessary to conduct both runoff and sub-surface water into the drain tiles and elim-inate pressure on the wall; the large spaces between gravel particles also provide plen-ty of room for ice crystals to expand with-out creating frost heave. Finally, spread and grade topsoil after the new material has settled (it usually takes a heavy rain) and seed. Seal the outlet of the drainpipe with a ½-in. mesh wire screen ("hardware cloth") to keep rodents out.

Good perimeter drainage is the only sure-fire cure for a chronic leaky founda-tion, but chances are that water infiltra-tion will be the least of your worries if your foundation has suffered from poor drainage. Typically, sections of wall will have heaved, cracked, settled or caved in, calling for whole or partial foundation replacement. Thus, excavation solely for the installation of perimeter drainage sys-tems is rather rare—dry-laid stone or brick walls in light, sandy soils are probably the only exception. If the stonework is fairly regular it can be stuccoed ("parged") and then waterproofed. Deep joints should be pointed with mortar. Sometimes fingers seem to work better than a pointing trow-el, especially for novice masons, but wear rubber gloves because the lime in fresh mortar will erode your fingertips. Moisten the fissures before pointing the mortar to prevent overly rapid absorption of water from the mortar by the stone or bricks, which weakens its bonding strength. Ob-serve this precaution whenever you bond new work to old.

Repairing and Replacing Foundation Walls

Hairline cracks in concrete walls are usual-ly the result of too-rapid curing, improper concrete mixing or placement, or minor settling. As long as the crack does not ap-pear to be increasing in length or width, it can be repaired with a quick patch of hy-draulic cement. To determine whether a crack is active, tape one side of a piece of paper across the crack and mark the edges of the opening on it. Check before and during winter, in spring and in late sum-mer to see if and how much the edges of the crack have moved relative to the gauge marks. If the movement is greater than $\frac{1}{16}$ in., you have a problem crack.

Assuming that good drainage exists (or will be provided by you), these and much larger cracks in the wall can still be patched. Trench the outside of the foun-dation wall at least 4 ft. to each side of the crack to relieve inward pressure. There's no exact rule: The greater the displace-ment of the wall sections, the greater the required wall exposure. This done, it's pos-sible, by means of steel jack posts or sec-tions of timber and screw jacks, to move the damaged sections back into their orig-inal position, thereby closing the cracks. (Note: Most ordinary hydraulic jacks will not work in the horizontal position—an exception is the hydraulic ram jack, like the kind used for heavy-duty auto-body work and frame straightening.)

Prepare the cellar side of the crack for patching with hydraulic cement by cut-ting a keyway into it with a cold chisel. Seal the immediate area of the crack on the outside with flashing-grade asphalt cement and then coat with foundation coating to match the existing coating. As long as no additional water presses against it, the repair will remain perfectly stable once the jacks are released. (If not, keep the jacks in place until after backfilling.) Of course, these repairs work only when the walls are still relatively intact and the damage not too extensive. They also work best for poured concrete or concrete-block

Repairing a Cracked Foundation Wall

Position jacks. Use screw jacks or hydraulic ram jacks (which can be used in horizontal position, unlike ordinary hydraulic jacks).

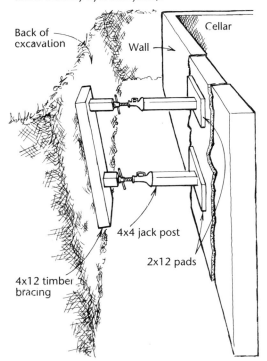

Back of excavation

Wall

Cellar

4x4 jack post

2x12 pads

4x12 timber bracing

Chisel 1-in. deep (minimum) groove in crack faces for keyway. Trowel in hydraulic patching cement. Coat exterior face of crack with asphalt flashing cement before waterproofing.

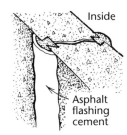

Inside

Asphalt flashing cement

For brick or block walls, use jack box to distribute pushing force over damaged area. Work carefully.

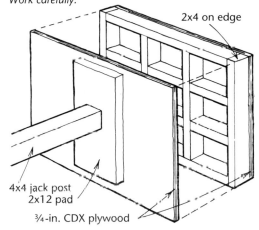

2x4 on edge

4x4 jack post
2x12 pad

¾-in. CDX plywood

walls. Brick walls are too flexible and fieldstone (as opposed to cut stone) walls too irregular. Here, the weight of the house above could actually cause the wall to collapse as you tried to move it. There's usually no choice but to jack up the house and replace the wall. A small section of bowed brick or concrete block could safely be realigned by use of a "jack box," as shown in the drawing above.

Before replacing a foundation wall, dig a 3-ft. wide work trench on the outside of the wall—slope the sides if the soil is not firm enough. If all the walls are to be replaced, trench the entire perimeter. The trench should extend to the bottom of the existing footing, or to where there seems to be more earth than stone for unfooted

dry-laid walls. Even if the foundation doesn't go deeper than the frost line, the trench should. Always provide an outlet to grade—otherwise, even the slightest rainfall will turn the trench into a moat. Not only will this hamper your movement, but there is also a good chance of losing the wall (and the house) as its earthen bulwarks turn to mud soup.

Even under the best of circumstances, digging against a foundation wall is ticklish work. Hire the best backhoe operator you can find—it's not a job to cut your teeth on. Not only will most excavators not guarantee against cave-in, they might even ask you to sign a release holding them free from liability if the wall or house does give. Take heart, this seldom

The below-grade portion of a dry-laid stone wall is most often irregular, partially collapsed and potentially dangerous to excavate. Leave extra earth to help brace the wall.

happens with a good operator, one for whom that cumbersome shovel is a surgically precise extension of hand and mind. Some operators can perform tricks with their machines that would confound a circus elephant. Trust your operator, and listen to his advice.

Just the same, it's ultimately you (or your contractor) calling the shots. If you say go, he goes, and if the wall goes with him, well he just works here, mister. If you don't have confidence in your judgment (or in the machine operator's) then hire someone who does to supervise this job. Although failures occur often enough so that you should be aware of the possibility, they generally result from foolhardiness and rushing the job. If you proceed slowly and cautiously, you shouldn't fail to detect a potentially serious problem before it happens. Nothing really happens without warning. You learn to listen and feel for the signs. In time you can feel timbers strain as easily as you feel the muscles in your own arms.

Dig as close to the wall as you can. With a poured-concrete wall this means tight against it. Don't let the bucket get too close to a block, brick or stone wall: These can buckle when pushed. Instead, work alongside the hoe with your hand shovel, pulling the earth that clings to the stones into the ditch for the machine to remove. Don't worry about losing small sections of loose walls. If the sill above is solid it will span the opening and carry the weight. Simply remove the collapsed wall along with the rest of the rubble.

Dry-stone walls require the most caution. Often the only thing holding them up is the earth you're removing. These walls are pyramidal, with much wider, larger stones at the base. It's easy to mistake an outcrop of the wall for a boulder, and pull the whole thing apart before you know what you're doing.

Another precaution: Locate water and sewer lines, phone and electric cables before you dig. Measure from a fixed point, like the bottom of the sill and an inside corner or doorway, to find the center of each penetration inside the cellar. Drive stakes along the foundation to mark these points. When the machine has dug to within a foot or so of the expected pipe or line, locate and expose it by hand so the machine can clear around it. Experience has taught me to include an assortment of plumbing and electrical couplers and splicing kits in my foundation-job toolkit.

Raising the House

With the trench finished and the wall exposed in all its sad glory, you'll have to decide which of the many ways to lift a house off its foundation and support it safely until the walls are replaced is best suited to your particular case. The choice depends upon the structural configuration and integrity of the frame and foundation, the equipment and funds on hand, and your own design requirements.

Ultimately, all foundation repairs fall into one of two basic categories: holding the house or raising it. "Holding," or, more accurately, lifting the load-bearing sill beams just enough to relieve their bearing on the foundation wall (about ½ in. to 1 in. is usually enough), allows the old foundation to be removed and replaced, usually a wall at a time, leaving the remaining walls to stabilize the house.

Because it can be done piecemeal, with a lot less equipment and a greater margin of error, the holding method is ideally suited to the weekend contractor. But it also takes more time, complicates the concrete work and precludes any major corrections in house level. If you simply hold the house at its existing level, it's unlikely that a full-sized 8-ft. concrete form panel will fit under the sills. Even if it could, there wouldn't be enough clearance between the top of the panel and the underside of the sills to pour and work the concrete into the forms. Instead, the foundation wall must be formed with a 6-ft. panel and topped with two or three courses of 8-in. concrete block. Furthermore, because machines are repeatedly moved onto and off the site, excavation costs could be considerably higher.

Since all the walls are removed at the same time, "raising" the house (anywhere from 1 ft. to a full story) makes the most efficient use of expensive excavation subcontractors. The same is true of concrete work. Money is saved when enough headroom is gained to form and pour a full-height wall without hindrance, especially if the entire foundation can be set up and

poured at once. Raising the house and removing the old foundation (or adding to an existing one) is also one way to increase the depth of a low-ceilinged cellar or crawl space. It's the only way a house can be prepared for moving onto an adjacent foundation.

But there are two considerable drawbacks to this method, which might make the inexperienced housemover consider hiring an experienced contractor. When a house has no connection to its foundation, it can move quite easily, like a boat drifting on its moorings. A strong gust of wind could push it out of alignment, or careless jacking could cause it to slide off its supports. Believe me, there's nothing quite like the thrill of working under a house and feeling it shift sideways as you adjust the jacks.

Thus, if you raise the house, you must take extreme care that it rests on very stable cribbing. Lifting a house requires a lot more timber than holding it does. Setting up these supports calls for some experience or, at the very least, a good understanding of how the weight of the house is carried by its frame. If you don't have either of these but are still determined to tackle the job yourself, hire an experienced contractor as a consultant to recommend the best and safest approach, and perhaps review your progress at appropriate intervals. Unless required by local codes, hiring a structural engineer is expensive overkill. In rural areas, you may be able to enlist the guidance of a neighborhood old-timer just for "consideration and a handshake" and the joy of having his knowledge valued.

Raising a house calls for disconnecting and lengthening a formidable number of pipes, ducts and wires, which involves no small inconvenience for those trying to live in the house while repairing it. If you have a hot-water heating system, for example, every riser and return line to and from the radiators must be cut and lengthened. Sewer lines, water supplies, drains, electrical feeds, all must be spliced or rerouted to accommodate the change in height, which could add thousands of dollars to the job in plumber's and electrician's bills. (This won't be an issue with a house where the plumbing and wiring are so rudimentary or decrepit that cutting them is the first step toward their replacement.)

An alternative to raising the house in order to gain a cellar is to dig a deeper cellar under the house. Since digging deeper is not always practical or advisable (for example, where there are ledge outcroppings or a high water table), sometimes it makes more sense to raise the house a foot or two at the same time the cellar is undermined. I once had to lower a house off concrete piers onto a new wall.

All things considered, in my opinion, the combination of a 6-ft. poured concrete wall and two courses of concrete block on top is still the most practical and economical do-it-yourself foundation repair. The poured wall gives maximum strength below grade, where it is most needed, and requires you to pour almost one-third less concrete. Laying two courses of concrete block is not very difficult. Unlike poured concrete walls, where support timbers that run under sills must coincide with future window openings, concrete blocks can simply be left out and the opening filled in after the frame is lowered onto the new foundation and the timbers removed.

Where to lift

The structural configuration of the house frame determines where to place the jacks and support timbers for lifting. With timber frames, the weight of the walls, roof and upper floors is transferred by braced vertical posts onto continuous sill beams (typically 8x8s, although 8x12 and larger timbers are not uncommon) that span the length and breadth of the foundation wall in one or two pieces. Heavy timber girders (also known as girts, or carrying beams) mortised into the sills and posted at midspan carry the squared timber or half-round log joists that support the floorboards and interior partitions. The girts are sometimes

parallel to the length of the house, sometimes perpendicular to it. Interior posts under ceiling girts also distribute weight onto the cellar girts. Other than this concentrated loading, the floor plan of a stud-frame house follows the same basic layout of the heavy-timbered house, substituting lighter framing members. And joists are nailed, rather than notched into the sills.

A basic principle for safe house lifting is to provide support directly under a concentrated load, or as near it as possible. This is what posts do. Thus, your temporary supports should shoulder the load carried by the posts. Supporting a sill at midspan, where there may be no significant load, causes the weight carried by a corner or chimney post to put undue strain on the timber.

Sometimes the cellar girts carry part of the wall weight where they are mortised into the sill. Since there are usually vertical posts in the wall above such points, these are good places to lift and support the frame. A jack placed within a foot or two of the actual joint is usually sufficient. For example, you may find that a timber placed under the floor joists just inside the sill, when lifted, will raise the sill off the foundation wall; or you may find that only the joists move, taking the floorboards with them. This is most likely to happen when the sills are pinned down by posts supporting girders that carry the floor and roof loads from above. Here, lifting the girders and floor joists simultaneously usually brings the sill up with them.

Unless they include support girders and posts as described above, the gable ends of the house don't carry any great weight and can be raised by lifting the floor joists if they run perpendicular to the gable sill. You may find, especially with stud-framed houses, that the entire gable foundation wall can be removed without any more support needed than the stiffness provided by the curtain of wall sheathing and framing. Since the upper floor framing is usually laid out in the same manner, study the run of cellar floor fram-

Typical Traditional Braced Timber Frame, 1½- to 2-Story House

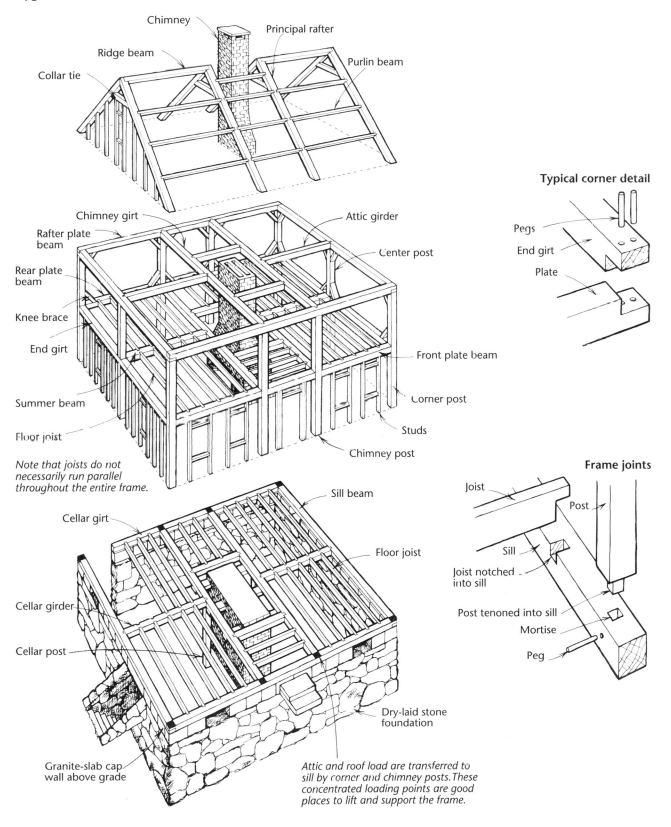

Chimney

Principal rafter

Ridge beam

Purlin beam

Collar tie

Typical corner detail

Pegs

End girt

Plate

Chimney girt

Attic girder

Rafter plate beam

Center post

Rear plate beam

Knee brace

End girt

Front plate beam

Summer beam

Corner post

Floor joist

Studs

Chimney post

Note that joists do not necessarily run parallel throughout the entire frame.

Frame joints

Joist

Post

Sill

Joist notched into sill

Post tenoned into sill

Mortise

Peg

Sill beam

Cellar girt

Floor joist

Cellar girder

Cellar post

Dry-laid stone foundation

Granite-slab cap wall above grade

Attic and roof load are transferred to sill by corner and chimney posts. These concentrated loading points are good places to lift and support the frame.

76

Most of the time, even a rotted sill is strong enough to hold up the house, especially the gable end, so that a wall can be replaced first.

ing members to determine the best places to support the most weight with the least amount of timberwork and jacks. The less clutter in your foundation trench, the easier it is to replace the wall.

Even for experts, determining the best place to support the frame is something of a matter of trial and error. Fortunately, there's plenty of opportunity to find out if it's going to work before you risk any serious damage. Although it's possible, beams seldom break instantaneously, especially if you don't leave long spans unsupported. The loads typical of residential construction are not that great. Groans, sags, twisting and joints pulling apart are plaintive calls for more support.

The goal is to support the sills and any major carrying beams, which then theoretically support the house. Structural integrity is a consideration when the sills themselves are too rotted to support anything. With solid and sound sills, it makes almost no difference where you place your support timbers, so long as they are distributed at reasonable intervals (within 2 ft. to 3 ft. of a major intermediate or corner post load, or 8 ft. to 12 ft. apart with unconcentrated loads) under the perimeter of the frame.

As you might infer, when sills are rotted, the floor platform and the loads of the upper stories and roof must be supported independently to relieve the load on the sills. This can get cumbersome. Some of these strategies of last resort are detailed on pp. 109-115. When both foundation walls and sills need replacement, it's best to replace the wall first and then fix the sill. Most of the time, enough of the sill is relatively intact to afford some purchase for jacking. Since sills typically rot from the outside face inward, the cellar face, into which the floor joists are notched, is probably strong enough to withstand jacking if probing with your awl finds that at least a third to half the sill is still solid. In extreme cases, you may have to replace sections of the sill with new material before you can lift the house and remove the foundation walls.

Operation Rescue — Replacing a Foundation

1. Time and previous owners had not been kind to this pre-1850 farmhouse in Fairfax, Vt. Attempts to arrest the chronic foundation movement had been limited to replacement and buttressing of the above-grade sections. Here the owner is digging up her daylilies prior to the arrival of the heavy equipment. The disposition of foundation plantings is a consideration often overlooked in contracts or by insensitive excavators.

2. Seen from inside the cellar, the bulkhead, unprotected from frost heave, was the obvious engine of destruction, while water infiltrating through the loose stone wall was fostering dry rot in the damp cellar.

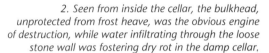

3. The major carrying beams and their floor joists were supported by jacking timbers placed in the cellar, and the house was lifted enough to relieve the load on the bulkhead and rear walls. Lifting only a wall or two at a time lets the unlifted parts anchor the house, allowing the use of economical screw-jack posts and a lot less cribbing without sacrificing stability.

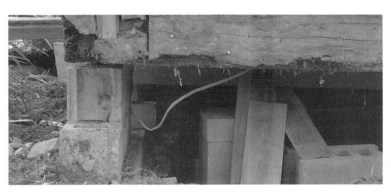

4. With the front wall left intact, the badly cracked concrete-block cap wall is removed in sections. Because most of the weight is carried on the cellar girders, additional support posts under the sill are not needed at this point. Although badly rotted along its face, the oversize sill timber is still sound enough to span almost the entire length of the wall.

5. The weakest section of the sill is carried by a timber cantilevered out from a beam running diagonally under the corner to leave the wall area unobstructed.

Operation Rescue—Replacing a Foundation

6. Two walls have been removed and the trench has been excavated. The footings are lower than the existing cellar floor to facilitate drainage. The string stretched along the sill will guide layout of the new footings.

7. Closeup of corner support. Note the water line running across the trench. Care must be taken during excavation not to damage utility lines. The steel jack posts will eventually rest on concrete pads and can be incorporated into the new footings and wall.

8. By augmenting the existing cellar posts with a single jacking timber, shimmed under each floor joist, it was possible to support almost a quarter of the floor area.

9. The front wall was trenched to grade for an outlet in case of rain. The wall was left intact to help anchor the house, but a heavy rain caused part of the loose stone wall to fall into the ditch. Fortunately, the rest of the house didn't follow. It took a lot of frantic and muddy shovel work to break up the dam.

10. The owners poured the footings themselves. By taking care to make the footings level, a reference point is established for truing up the house. The jog is for the new bulkhead. Lines chalked on the footings simplify the layout of the form panels, which are tacked to 2x4s nailed directly into the edge of the footing.

11. Because of the labor and specialized materials involved, it's usually easier to subcontract concrete work out than do it yourself, especially when time is a factor. A professional crew set up and poured the two walls in a single day.

12. Room enough for two courses of concrete block and a 2x10 pressure-treated mudsill is left between the top of the concrete wall and the bottom of the sills. This height represents an average, since some parts of the house needed to be lifted and others lowered.

13. The new sill is installed under the gable wall. The top of the concrete wall is used as a reference for leveling the sills. Note the bulkhead foundation, which will be covered with a steel hatch.

14. New sills are spliced in with sound old sections.

15. As concrete blocks are dry-stacked between them, sections of cribbing are removed. Note the overhanging pressure-treated mudsill, which provides a stop for the installation of rigid foam perimeter insulation. Allowance is also made for cellar vent window openings.

Operation Rescue — Replacing a Foundation

16. Tapered shims fur the canted sill flush with the finish wall face.

17. The block is coated on both faces with a fiberglass-reinforced stucco that eliminates the need for mortar between courses. The concrete is waterproofed below grade, rigid foam insulation applied and footing drains laid, in preparation for backfilling. Although it's tempting to backfill directly from the spoils of the old foundation, porous gravel must be laid against the wall first. This not only enhances drainage, but also protects the wall from damage by the many frost-propelled stones that pepper the bank.

18. Old meets new at this corner, where the new sill abuts the sound original sill. Note the protective stucco over the face of the foam insulation.

19. Supported by timbers under the joists and carrying beams, with steel jack posts as needed, the remaining two walls are removed. An advantage of this approach is that many of the posts and timbers can be reused. The cribbing is short timber blocks on a base of concrete blocks.

20. The excess material is spread around the site to restructure the contour for an attractive and well-drained grade. The rocks and rubble will be covered with finer fill and topsoil.

Timber cribbing supports a system of steel beams used to lift and reposition this building.

21. Home free! The finish grade is ready for seeding, winter is still a few months away and the foundation is solid and watertight.

Jacking equipment

It takes a lot of timber and other equipment to raise a house. Some ways are easier and more elegant than others. They may also be more expensive. Professional housemovers and jackers use steel beams and short lengths of heavy timber "cribbing" (also called "cobbing"). In a typical application, steel beams, spaced 4 ft. to 12 ft. apart (depending on load, location of supporting posts and girders, and soundness of sills), are inserted under the sills across the width of the house. These beams are then supported by two larger beams run perpendicularly. Alternating between jacks set on four timber cribs under these steel rails, the entire house is lifted, a few inches at a time.

If the house is to be raised beyond the range of the jacks, a second set of cribbing is constructed alongside the first to support the beams while the first set is raised higher. By switching jacks between cribbings and constantly adding more timbers, it's possible to raise the house to any desired height. Since the entire house is supported on only four pillars, all well within the cellar area, the work zone around the foundation wall remains uncluttered. Because steel is so much stronger and stiffer than wood, the cribbing can even be placed well outside the foundation perimeter to support longer beams, which would allow unhampered access to both the trench and the cellar. But this kind of convenience is expensive and often beyond the budget of the home owner.

Although a farm tractor equipped with a bucket loader is more than adequate to maneuver them about, obtaining steel beams in the first place is apt to be the biggest challenge. Because they cost so much, you wouldn't want to buy them (unless you were planning on building an industrial warehouse). You can sometimes rent them from a commercial contractor. If you do, arrange to have them delivered and returned as part of the rental—they don't fit into the average pickup. Nevertheless, since housemoving is very labor intensive, there's still a long way to go before you reach the point of diminishing returns that justifies the hiring of professionals.

As a specialist in foundation repairs, I've found wood timbers easier and more adaptable to work with than steel beams, especially in crowded conditions—try trimming a steel beam with a chainsaw and you'll see what I mean. Although you'll need more cribbing and have to use shorter support timbers, wood beams are always reusable—if only for firewood—and relatively inexpensive. They're also easier to borrow and transport. There is really no other practical choice for do-it-yourself foundation repair.

You'll need at least a truckload of cribbing. These short lengths of timber (2-ft., 3-ft. and 4-ft. pieces are best) are used to build the platforms on which the jacks are placed. If you plan to lift the entire house at once you may need a dumptruck load. Finding the odd pieces of 6x6, 8x8, 2x8 and 4x12 can be a challenge. Contractors often keep a pile of odd timbers around that you may be able to borrow. Sawmills use a lot of the stuff for lumber storage bunks. You might pick up damaged or off-length pieces at a nominal cost or even

free for the hauling. Steel fabricators and heavy construction yards are another possible source.

Jacking timbers may prove even harder to locate than cribbing. Although you may know someone with a barn full of old 8x8s, I'd hesitate to borrow them for two reasons. First, hand-hewn timbers are likely to get gouged and muddied by the time you're finished with them, which pretty well ruins their resale value. Second, most old timbers are full of notches that could weaken them enough to break under a concentrated load. Examine them carefully for soundness before use. Avoid rotted beams that have through-cut mortises in the working part of their span. It's a lot less trouble to buy new timbers from the local sawmill, or good-quality used ones from a demolition and salvage yard (the urban equivalent of the sawmill and poor man's building-supply treasury). Eight-by-eight timbers are suitable for jacking; 6x6s can be used for light structures and short spans or for upright posts.

The timbers should be at least as long as the greatest distance you'll need to span, certainly no less than 16 ft. Since green wood is quite heavy, specify spruce; hemlock isn't any stronger and weighs about twice as much. Pine and balsam are too weak, and hardwoods are much too heavy and costly. Timbers should be free from any serious running splits or bad knots, which could weaken them under load. At somewhere between $1.50 and $2.00 a running foot, a load of 8x8s may seem like a hefty investment. But they can always be reused for new sills, and when the house is back on its foundation, as framing for barns, sheds or even a post-and-beam addition. One person I know left the purposely overlong jacking timbers protruding from the wall and built a porch deck over them. You can always resell them at a discount.

House jacks (or screw jacks) are simple machines—a large screw threaded into a sleeve that widens into a base. A hole through the top of the screw accepts a steel turning bar. A flat collar that can rotate on top of the screw provides the lifting surface. The base is sometimes stamped with a number showing how many tons it can lift. Capacity is determined by the thickness and length of the screw threads. A 2-in. thick screw 12 in. long has a safe working strength of 15 tons, which is more than adequate for most housejacking.

Screw jacks lift hard. They turn slowly, and as the height of the lift increases, the force needed to turn the screw does likewise. I find them useful for supporting timbers once they have been lifted to height, but prefer to do the actual lifting with hydraulic jacks whenever possible. These oil-filled pistons can lift more weight much faster with a lot less effort. Opening or closing the valve at the base of the jack body permits it to raise or lower.

When working with hydraulic jacks it's a good idea to stack blocks or cribbing under the timber as you raise it. Then, if the seal should rupture and the jack loose pressure, the timber won't fall very far. Although unlikely, the possibility of failure is real enough that hydraulic jacks should never be left in place under load for any length of time. For added safety, use an oversize jack: I use a 20-ton jack for everything, even where an 8-ton model would be more than adequate. You'll also need a ½-in. steel plate about 6 in. square to place on the head of the jack cylinder. This lifting plate distributes the jacking force, which would otherwise push the cylinder through the timber.

Hydraulic jacks can be rented. But considering that most foundation jobs spread out over a summer of weekends and other free time, it's probably cheaper to buy one 20-ton jack. You can always use it to change a flat tire on a loaded pickup truck or to put a derailed freight car back on the track. Screw jacks are cheaper to rent but harder to find or buy. Sometimes a farmer neighbor will have a pair or two lying around the barn or toolshed that you might be able to borrow. They do show up at auctions and yard sales. Unless you can get them cheap, there's no real reason you'd ever want to own one.

Safety considerations

By now, the huge mounds of earth in your yard all but obscure the house. Trenches encircle it like a moat. Piles of rubble and heavy timbers are strewn about like Paul Bunyan's matchsticks. The maze of beams in the cellar doesn't look anything at all like the drawings in this book. How can you lift the house and keep it all in one piece? It doesn't seem possible such a mass will ever move.

There are at least nine rules for safe and successful housejacking:

1. **Have a solid bearing.** Keep your cribbing as level as you can and distribute the weight over as large an area as feasible. A crib is a pyramid. Use lifting plates or blocks to distribute the force of the jack. Use shims to keep pads level.

2. **Lift straight.** If the jack begins to tilt, lower it and straighten or shim so that it lifts plumb. A weighted jack that slips sideways can kill you.

3. **Block up as you go.** A safety precaution. You can't get hurt if nothing can fall.

4. **Listen and look.** A house will creak and groan as it is raised. Watch for cracks to open. See if the joists move with the sills or stay in place.

5. **Don't lift too much.** You only need to relieve the weight on the foundation wall. In most cases that means an inch or less of lift. Even if you raise the house much higher, do it in small increments. Give the timbers time to settle and adjust to their new positions.

6. **Lift slowly.** Lift evenly. Move from point to point in succession raising each jack an equal amount. Don't hurry. Rapid lifting can stress timbers past their breaking point.

7. **Balance the load.** Keep the cribbing as close as possible to the lifting points. Avoid lifting from the ends of a beam, leaving the middle unsupported. An 8x8 is not a lever.

8. **Know what is above you.** Before you lift, determine where the loads from the upper stories bear on the sills and other timbers in the cellar. Major load-bearing posts often rest above joints between girts and sills or over cellar posts.

9. **Think.** Lifting a house out of a hole is a whole lot harder than putting it in there, especially if you happen to be under it when it falls.

Reduced to its simplest elements, to lift a wall you slide a long jacking timber under the sill. Crib it on both ends and begin lifting with your jacks until that portion of the sill rises from the foundation. Repeat this process at intervals along the wall. Raise girts or other carrying beams as necessary to avoid having the floor sag and stressing the joints. Use an 8x8 post balanced on top of a screw jack and placed alongside the existing support posts. Add appropriate thicknesses of shims or blocking when the beam lifts off the post and release the jack to lower the beam to its new height. Use jacking timbers to support any weak points or intersections that may carry weight from the upper floors. If you cannot support a splice or joint directly, you must lift both sides of it, jacking each side a little at a time to avoid twisting the joint.

It's even possible to combine jacking with wall removal by digging out the wall along with the work trench. Starting at a corner (to provide solid support) the backhoe removes about 12 ft. of wall. This section of sill is held by a timber running perpendicular to it (unless the sill is non-bearing, and can be left to dangle while the floor joists and girts are lifted from within the cellar). Another, even easier, method uses steel jack posts placed directly under the sill. After the supports are firmly in place, the next section of wall and trench is dug and the posting repeated, and so on, around the wall. Initially, the posts bear on blocks of timber set directly on the ground. Later, these are replaced by square concrete pads, which can be incorporated into the footing of the new wall. Then the jack posts are left in place when the new wall is poured, which adds stability and greatly simplifies final adjustment and leveling of the house.

As mentioned above, it's critically important not to remove more than two walls at a time. The remaining two walls must be left to stabilize the house. Jack posts, and even upright timbers, are easily overturned by lateral movement. After the new wall is poured and the house lowered back down onto it, the remaining sections of old wall can be replaced.

Assuming you plan to lift the entire house and not post or crib under the wall as you dig the perimeter trench, how do you slide a jacking timber under the sill when the sill itself is resting firmly on the wall? Pound the rock or concrete with a sledgehammer until you've broken a hole large enough to admit the timber. Even a solid concrete wall will break apart rather easily (if it doesn't, use a rented heavy-duty electric impact hammer). After all the jacking timbers are in place and the house is lifted off the wall, it's a simple matter to push sections of wall (by hand, if need be)

This timber supports a major girder and some floor joists. Note the shims added to the original girder post after the beam was raised slightly, and the diagonal brace between the support post and the girder—a safety feature.

into the trench for removal by backhoe. You may wish to save any especially well-shaped flat stones for reuse in future landscaping or other masonry projects. They've already cost too much to bury.

By spanning the entire width of the work trench with the jacking timbers, you can reduce the number of jacks and the amount of cribbing needed. Use jack posts set in the trench to lift the jacking timber if you cannot fit jacks under the ends of the timber resting on the original grade. You can also dig and level a platform deep enough to admit both jacks and blocking. You must lift upon the relatively compact original grade and not on newly deposited material. You can avoid a lot of hand-shovel work if the backhoe operator places the spoils a few feet back from the edge of the trench.

Let off the jacks to allow the timber to settle the blocking into the earth. Raise it again and add new blocking as needed. Adjust the jack on the cribbing inside the cellar to bring the jacking timber up to level. You can use a hydraulic jack to do all your lifting by blocking up the jacking timbers to the desired height and then removing the jack, but I prefer to leave a screw jack in place under every lift point. Rather than repeatedly moving one jack back and forth between lift points as I level the house, I can raise or lower it in small amounts, which greatly simplifies fine adjustments. Of course, I happen to have a lot of screw jacks.

You can also run jacking timbers diagonally across the corners of the house to lift two walls with one timber, assuming that the joint under the corner post is solid enough for the post to lift with the sills. Usually, the wall sheathing and studs impart enough rigidity to the frame so that the corner post doesn't require any support. If this isn't the case, refer to p. 111 for information on supporting posts.

Frankly, the more the layout of your jacking timbers resembles the professional housemover's steel cradle, the more stable and easy to level the raised house will be.

Methods for Jacking the House

Single timber, two or three jacks

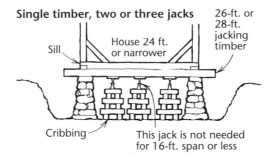

Two timbers with jack under girder

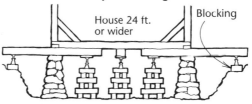

When carrying timbers are thicker than sills, or when joists are irregular in depth, use blocking between carrying timbers and sills to lift everything together.

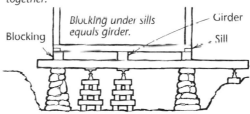

Using less timber to lift more

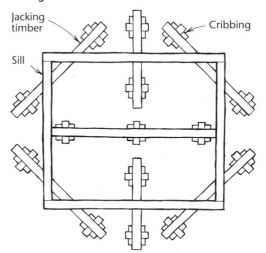

Thus, if you can span the width of the house with four single timbers spaced at even intervals, you will need only 12 cribs (three under each timber) to lift the entire house. Since most houses are at least 24 ft. wide, it takes a 26-ft. to 28-ft. long timber to span the width safely (timbers should project at least a foot beyond the outside walls for stability and safety in case the house slips or slides while jacking). A 26-ft. 8x8 is a hefty stick of wood that takes some levering to get it into place. However, since only a few mills can saw timbers longer than 24 ft., this may prove a moot point (I've used 32-footers). For spanning work trenches, 12- and 16-footers are fine, and they are easily maneuvered in crowded cellars. A 16-ft. 8x8 is about the most that two men can handle without risking their lives.

When carrying timbers or girts are thicker than the sills or when floor joists are irregular in depth, use blocking between the carrying timber and the framing member to lift everything together. This is especially useful when jacking the sills indirectly by lifting from the floor joists or major girts. Remember to strip the bark off any log joists. This deprives borers of their shelter and ensures the longevity of the wood.

The New Foundation

Clear the rubble from under the house and work trench. Throw anything that clutters up the cellar into the trench for the backhoe to scoop away and later bury. Rake the bottom of the trench smooth. If the backhoe operator was worth his pay, the trench bottom should be more or less level. Check the grade with a transit level. If it's within an inch of your benchmark all the way around, you can start to set your footing forms. If there's more of a variation, you'll have to lower the high spots. Even though this might mean a lot of painful hand work, never fill up the low spots, which can cause the footing to crack or settle.

Laying out the footings

As a rule of thumb, footings in normal silty soils should be twice as wide as the width of the wall and as thick as the wall is wide. Standard residential foundation walls are 8 in. wide; standard footings are 16 in. wide by 8 in. thick. In soft clay, increase the footings to 24 in. by 12 in. The bottom of the footing should always be below maximum frost penetration — 4 ft. is considered standard in the North, although bare ground can easily freeze 5 ft. or 6 ft. deep, especially under compacted soils like roadways.

To align the footings with the sills above, drop a line with a plumb bob (or level and straightedge) from the outside corners of the sill. Mark the corner points with a large spike driven into the ground. Measure 4 in. beyond these spikes (half the width of the wall) and drive another set. Stretch a string between these outside points to find the outside edge of the footing (and the inside edge of the form board for that footing).

Laying out the Footings

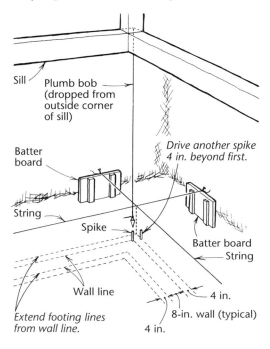

Sill

Plumb bob (dropped from outside corner of sill)

Batter board

Drive another spike 4 in. beyond first.

String

Spike

Batter board String

Wall line

4 in.

8-in. wall (typical)

Extend footing lines from wall line.

4 in.

Setting the form boards to a string makes for straight footings. Unfortunately, the wall of the old house above is not necessarily straight. It may have more curves than a giant slalom. Small bows are best ignored, especially when it's the house wall that overhangs the new foundation. But bends much greater than 1½ in. are hard to hide, especially if it's the new wall that sticks out beyond the old house.

It's possible to pull the house frame and sills back toward straightness with a come-along and chain (see pp. 125-126). Try this first, while the sills can slide across the jacking timbers. Of course, there's also an inch or two of slack that can be taken up in the difference between the footing and wall width. But the new wall will have to follow a major bow that refuses to straighten. Plumb down from the trouble spot, mark the deviation with another spike and set the footing to the adjusted line. Rectilinear perfection is not generally an attribute of the renovated house. Thus footings are aligned with the actual corners of the house rather than squared to themselves. To do otherwise runs the risk of the wall missing a footing entirely.

Footing forms are constructed in the usual way. Lay out 2x8 form boards along the string stretched between batter boards. Drive a 2x4 stake along the outside of the form board at one end. Fasten the stake to the board with a double-headed form nail. Drive another stake near the opposite end of the board, level the board between the stakes and secure. Drive a second nail through each stake to keep it from shifting. Secure additional stakes at 4-ft. to 6-ft. intervals along the form board or wherever it bows off the line. Repeat this procedure, adding form boards until you complete the outside perimeter of the footing form. Nail short lengths of 2x8 stock over each butted joint. When ordering footing boards, remember that the outside dimension of a footing is at least 11 in. longer than the wall (4 in. of footing each end plus two thicknesses of lumber); thus footing forms for a 24-ft. wall require a 12-footer and a 14-footer.

After the perimeter is formed, check the boards for level once again. I always use a transit level, as slight humps in 16-ft. long planks can give a false reading with a 4-ft. level. By the time you go around 128 ft. or so of perimeter, these little discrepancies can add up to forms an inch or more off level. Since all subsequent measurements will be taken from the footings, it's very important that they be level. Some concrete contractors don't pay any attention to the footings and figure to make up level with the wall forms. This is an unnecessarily sleazy way to build a foundation.

Cut a 16-in. length of 2x4 as a spreader guide and use it to space off the inside footing form boards. Repeat the staking and leveling process, this time leveling across from the outside form to the inside. Check the finished forms for level a final time. Use the claw of your hammer to scrape out any high spots under the form boards, and make your downward adjustments with a sledgehammer. Upward adjustments are achieved with a lever and rock shims. Bank the outside with loose dirt to anchor the forms and fill any gaps under their bottom edges. Trim the tops of the stakes level with the forms. Nail 1x4 spreaders at 6-ft. intervals across the forms to prevent the wet concrete from pushing out the tops. Provide a collar through the bottom of the footing for your cellar drain outlet. Add any reinforcing steel (rebar) that local codes may require.

Screed off the top of the fresh pour with a length of 2x4. Don't worry about getting it perfectly smooth — the roughness will ensure a better bond. Before the concrete has set completely, stick 4-ft. lengths of rebar vertically into the footing to strengthen the connection with the wall. Most reference manuals suggest that you press 2x2 lengths of wood into the center of the footing to form a keyway, but I've never seen anyone do this. Leave the forms in place the next day while you lay out the wall, to protect the soft concrete from damage. Remove them after three days.

Now you have a choice. You can:

1. Hire a concrete contractor to pour the walls. You might also consider having him do the footings. He has all the forms and is good at it. But because he will be working under an existing building, which cramps his style and takes more time, the cost per in-place yard is likely to be more than for standard work. In any case, the cost of the concrete is somewhere near half of the contract price.

2. Rent forms yourself, which is not always possible and not always cheap.

3. Build the forms you need, which takes time. Unless you have a use for cement-stained plywood and odd lengths of 2x4s, it is also costly.

4. Build a block wall. The materials are cheap and the wall can be done a little at a time to suit your schedule. But the work demands some skill and the finished wall is nowhere near as strong as poured concrete.

That familiar time/money equation determines your choice. Which do you have more of and which do you value more? Personally, I subcontract out concrete work whenever I can. I don't much care for it. I don't much care for laying block either; at least when I'm spending someone else's money. (I did build a block foundation when renovating my own house.)

But lack of experience alone should not be the reason to avoid a project. The concentration with which a novice belabors a task often brings about first-quality results. When you don't know what you're getting into, you don't know any shortcuts but the long way through.

Building the foundation wall

Whatever method you opt for, the original plumb line that marked the outside corners of the building is dropped onto the footing. A chalkline snapped between these corner points marks the edge of the wall itself. If the sill projects over the wall an inch or so, the discrepancy can be ignored. But if the sill sits inside of the new wall, water will sit on the shelf and rot the sill. Follow the sill with the wall. Metal flashing inserted under the siding and down over the concrete is an alternative solution.

When holding, rather than lifting, the house, allow at least 18 in. (the thickness of two courses of 8-in. concrete block plus finger space to slide the last block into

Although each manufactured concrete form system has its advantages and drawbacks, these have more influence on a contractor's decision of which system to buy than on the outcome of the finished wall. With a competent crew, any form system gives good results. The modular panels of the one shown can be set horizontally or vertically. The system uses 2x4 'whalers' to straighten the top of the wall and screw-jack braces to plumb and hold the corners.

place). A couple more inches makes it easier to fill that course with insulation or concrete. I prefer to fill the cores of all foundation blockwork with hand-mixed concrete for extra strength, rather than opt for a small decrease in heat loss by filling with vermiculite insulation. Galvanized steel strap sill anchors (you'll probably have to special-order them) inserted into the concrete-filled cores tie the foundation to a 2x8 or 2x10 pressure-treated wood mudsill (see the drawing at right). Apply a bead of construction adhesive to help seal the wood to the masonry.

I also insert a layer of sill-seal insulation or ½-in. rigid foam between the mudsill and the old sills. When the house is let back down onto the new foundation, the insulation compresses, forming a tight gasket that seals cracks too small to fill with regular insulation or spray foam. Where termite infestation is endemic, install an aluminum termite shield between the sill and the new wall. This is nothing more than a width of flashing metal projecting out beyond the face of the wall, bent downward, making it impossible for termites to crawl up the wall.

Let the wall sit for three to four days after it is finished and the forms are stripped before easing the house down onto it. Concrete reaches most of its strength in about a week. Setting a house down onto a "green" foundation (new concrete actually does look green until it cures) can cause it to crumble like a dry cookie.

A fast and simple alternative to mortaring concrete blocks together is to coat dry-laid block with a fiberglass-reinforced bonding cement (see photo 17 on p. 80). Sliding blocks into tight spaces under a sill is much easier with block-bonding: There's no mortar to knock off the joint as you fit the block. The finished wall is just as strong as the traditional mortared wall and more water-resistant. But the labor savings are offset by the expense of the bonding compound. I'd also leave 4-in. rebar pins sticking out of the poured wall

Pouring this frost wall to within 2 in. of the existing sill took time, but eliminated blockwork between the concrete wall and the new pressure-treated mudsill.

Capping a Concrete Wall with Block

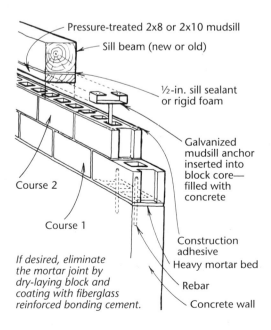

Pressure-treated 2x8 or 2x10 mudsill

Sill beam (new or old)

½-in. sill sealant or rigid foam

Galvanized mudsill anchor inserted into block core—filled with concrete

Course 2

Course 1

Construction adhesive

Heavy mortar bed

Rebar

Concrete wall

If desired, eliminate the mortar joint by dry-laying block and coating with fiberglass reinforced bonding cement.

Site-Built Forms for Replacing a Sill

1. Replacing this short section of sill and wall did not require elaborate forms or jacking—2x4s, nailed to the floor joists and wedged to the footing, supported the inside wall form (and held up the front wall).

2. Half-inch threaded rods with washers and nuts were used for form ties and spacers.

3. Minimal bracing was needed for the outside form. Unlike a full-sized wall, small amounts of concrete can be hand-shoveled into the form efficiently.

4. The finished wall, with new sill in place.

to help anchor the blockwork if it will be below grade. The block cores can be sliced to fit around any pins that are in the way.

Building wall forms from ¾-in. plywood or 1-in. tongue-and-groove boards is a lot of work. But site-built forms are the only practical option when replacing short sections of wall. There are several commercially available form-tying systems. These "snap-ties" are easier to install and align, and make a stronger form, than the old-fashioned hand-wired forms. Your local supplier can usually help you adapt your form design to the particular system he sells. Consult a handbook for details before building any forms. Audel's *Masons and Builders Library* and Willis H. Wagner's *Modern Carpentry* (see the Bibliography on pp. 334-338) are both excellent sources in this regard.

Working with concrete

Ready-mix concrete has pretty much eliminated hand-mixed concrete for all but jobs requiring under 1 cubic yd. If you try mixing and placing a few yards of concrete by hand, you'll understand why. Concrete is sold and ordered by the cubic yard. To calculate the amount required, multiply the length of the wall by its width and height (in feet), and divide the total by 27. Round up to the nearest ¼ yd. For example, 128 ft. of 8-in. wall that is 6 ft. high would require 19 yd. (128 x ⅔ x 6 = 512 ÷ 27 = 19). It's better to have a few wheelbarrow loads left over than be a pailful short. Shovel the extra concrete into 16-in. square by 8-in. deep wood forms for later use as post footings when you fix the cellar floor or porch supports.

Residential concrete is available in two strengths. Standard 2,500-psi concrete is used for walls and footings; 3,000-psi concrete is specified for slabs, basement and garage floors, heavy-duty footings and retaining walls. Some suppliers ask you to specify the mix by proportion rather than test strength. Standard concrete is a 5-bag mix; 3,000-psi concrete is a 6-bag mix. This means at least 5 sacks of cement per cubic yard with a maximum of 7 gal. of water per sack, or 6 sacks with a maximum of 6 gal. per sack. In cold weather, you'll have to ask for hot water as well, to keep the concrete from freezing before it sets up.

The most important part of working with ready-mix is to be prepared before the truck arrives. Drivers are on a schedule, and only so much time per yard is allowed before you are charged an overtime penalty. Concrete should be placed near the wall forms where it will set, so that the mix does not have to be dragged or run over long distances, which might lead to the separation of the large aggregates from the cement paste. You may have to hire a bulldozer to push back the rubble from the edges of your foundation trench and smooth off an access ramp for the concrete truck. This is another advantage to replacing the wall in sections: You can backfill the trench on one side of the house to help gain access to the next pour.

Concrete trucks can get into some pretty amazing places, but they can also get very stuck, especially if you back one over soft clay soil after a couple of days of rain. Once the truck leaves the curbside, you are responsible for damages or towing charges. Never allow a loaded truck to drive over a septic tank, drywell or leach field—it takes a mighty big tow truck to winch a concrete truck out of a collapsed septic tank. If the truck can reach the middle of a wall, extension chutes and a knowledgeable driver usually succeed in minimizing the amount of concrete you'll have to drag. This is especially critical when working under an existing building, since space to maneuver a shovel inside the wall forms is limited.

It's tempting to add enough water to the concrete to make it flow readily. But this not only weakens the cured wall, it increases hydrostatic pressure against the forms enough to risk a "blowout," especially with high walls. There's no sound more disheartening than the musical ping of form ties snapping in rapid succession seconds before the forms burst apart. Stiff mixes are more coherent and exert less

Since most of this new wall is single-faced, that is, poured against an existing wall, a veritable forest of bracing is needed to resist the outward thrust in the sections where there are no wire ties to an inside form. Nevertheless, the near-blowout bulge visible in the photo below shows that the form-builders underestimated the amount of bracing needed.

pressure on the forms, but they're harder to place. A conscientious truck driver is usually happy to suggest the optimum mix to the inexperienced customer (off the record, of course). The ideal mix should settle toward level as you work your shovel or a 1x3 stick up and down within it. Agitating the concrete in this manner consolidates the concrete and brings the finer grains toward the face, which results in a

Two Types of Bulkhead Walls

A. Cellar bulkhead treatment

Pressure-treated 2x4 for door anchor

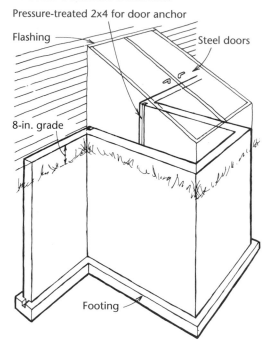

Flashing

Steel doors

8-in. grade

Footing

B. Open end-gable roof bulkhead wall

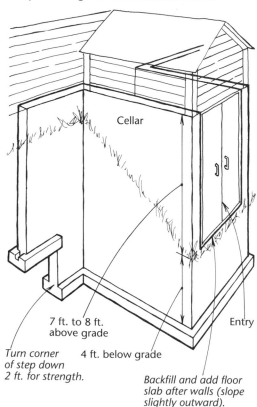

Cellar

7 ft. to 8 ft.
above grade

Entry

*Turn corner
of step down
2 ft. for strength.*

4 ft. below grade

*Backfill and add floor
slab after walls (slope
slightly outward).*

smooth wall free from honeycombing. It also moves the concrete along the form, allowing you to fill large sections without repositioning the truck and chute. Here again, a good driver can be a great help.

Before you form your walls, decide if you wish to add a bulkhead, or ground-level entrance to the cellar. Bulkheads are used when the grade around the house is more or less level. Fitted with a steel hatchway, a set of stairs and a tight-fitting interior door, they are energy-efficient and relatively inexpensive. Set a pressure-treated 2x4 in the corner of the concrete to provide solid fastening for the door unit, as shown at A in the drawing at left. Where the grade drops steeply away from the house, a cellar-floor level entrance (B in the drawing) is preferable. This makes it easy to use the cellar for storage of outdoor equipment like lawn tractors (useful if you don't have a garage) or to bring in firewood. It's absolutely necessary to step the foundation wall down below the frost line where the bulkhead wall turns out from the main wall. Otherwise, frost can lift the bulkhead walls and floor slab, and eventually crack or heave the main foundation walls in.

There's one other detail that should not be overlooked when building forms: Provide sleeves inside the forms to accommodate penetrations through the wall for utilities and the sewer line. A 1-gal. paint can nailed between the walls of the form makes a perfect opening for the cast-iron sewer line. Short lengths of plastic conduit, with a diameter larger than the actual pipe, form sleeves for electric and water lines. These can be left in place or driven out after the forms are stripped. The actual conduits are sealed to the wall with a patching cement.

Block foundation walls are best suited to light sandy soils and relatively frost-free zones. Check with your local building inspector to see if they are allowed in your area. I wouldn't recommend them in heavy soil, since they have so little resistance to lateral pressure. But where feasible, a block wall is inexpensive, and especially well matched to the on-again, off-again time-table of the part-time renovator. For extra strength, consider using 12-in. core block instead of the standard 8-in. block. As mentioned above, filling the cores with concrete strengthens the wall. The concrete mix should be on the watery side so that it can readily fill all the voids between the overlapping block cores. Inserting rebar into the cores also adds strength. Consult a good book for instructions on laying concrete block (see the Bibliography on pp. 334-338).

The working trench can be backfilled as soon as the foundation wall is waterproofed and the perimeter drainage installed (see pp. 68-70). But it's best to postpone backfilling until the house rests on the new wall; the added weight helps the wall resist the inward pressure exerted by the backfill. Use good coarse gravel (not native soil), and place it carefully. If the trenches are fairly wide, the amount of gravel required can be reduced by placing native soil against the bank in steps alternating with the gravel against the wall. Don't allow any boulders to press against the wall.

Waterproofing and insulating the foundation wall

If the weather has turned cold by the time you're ready to waterproof, you'll have to heat the asphalt before applying it. Cover the pail loosely, build a fire under it and bring the coating to a slow boil. Make sure the flames have died down before you move the open pail. Storing the pails in a warm place before use also helps. For a more thorough job, hire a foundation waterproofing contractor to pressure-spray the walls with hot asphalt. The cost is rather nominal compared to the effort of doing it by hand.

Nowadays, it's standard practice to install rigid foam perimeter insulation to reduce heat loss through the foundation wall. There are two methods to use with old houses. If the foundation is to be re-placed, the new wall can be inset 2 in. (the recommended insulation thickness for cold climates) under the sills, as shown at A in the drawing on p. 94. If the sills are too narrow to afford an overhang, butt the insulation against a separate beveled pressure-treated drip cap (ripped from 2x4 stock) nailed to the sill under the first course of siding (B in the drawing) or use preformed metal flashing. Beveling the outside edge of a treated 2x10 mudsill (C in the drawing) kills two birds with one stone (if you have a professional-quality table saw to rip the stock).

If you can afford it, the extruded polystyrene foam panels (blueboard) should cover the wall from the sills to the footing. However, since the stuff isn't cheap and most of the heat loss occurs above grade and within the first few feet of the surface, 4 ft. of below-surface coverage is most cost-effective. You might think the foam would stick to the asphalt coating, but it won't. Adhesives are expensive and not really necessary since the pressure of the backfill will pin the foam to the wall. I use hardened masonry nails driven through roofer's discs ("tins") to hold the panels until backfilling. Protect above-grade insulation from sunlight and damage with fiberglass panels that glue to the foam (which offer the best protection, but are expensive), or stucco the foam with a cement coating made especially for the purpose, sold in kit form along with the insulation panels. Apply the stucco before you backfill.

Perimeter insulation can be retrofitted to protect an old house even when the foundation wall is left intact. Use a backhoe to scoop a 2-ft. deep trench alongside the wall or, if the soil is not too hard, dig by hand. Remove the first course of finish siding (if clapboards) and add a drip cap, as shown at D in the drawing on p. 94. For vertical-board siding and wood shingles, make the drip-edge channel by cutting along a chalkline with your circular saw

Perimeter Insulation for Foundation Walls

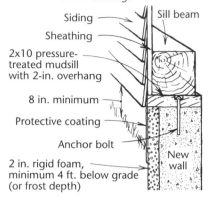

A. Offset foundation wall so insulation is flush with face of building.

- Siding
- Sheathing
- Sill beam
- 2x10 pressure-treated mudsill with 2-in. overhang
- 8 in. minimum
- Protective coating
- Anchor bolt
- 2 in. rigid foam, minimum 4 ft. below grade (or frost depth)
- New wall

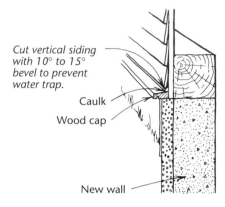

B. Or provide drip cap over insulation.

- Cut vertical siding with 10° to 15° bevel to prevent water trap.
- Caulk
- Wood cap
- New wall

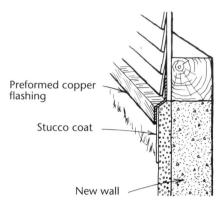

This option eliminates wood cap.

- Preformed copper flashing
- Stucco coat
- New wall

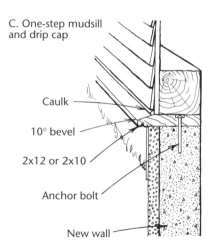

C. One-step mudsill and drip cap

- Caulk
- 10° bevel
- 2x12 or 2x10
- Anchor bolt
- New wall

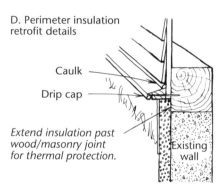
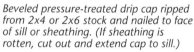

D. Perimeter insulation retrofit details

- Caulk
- Drip cap
- *Extend insulation past wood/masonry joint for thermal protection.*
- Existing wall

Beveled pressure-treated drip cap ripped from 2x4 or 2x6 stock and nailed to face of sill or sheathing. (If sheathing is rotten, cut out and extend cap to sill.)

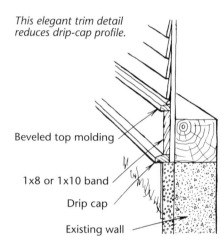

This elegant trim detail reduces drip-cap profile.

- Beveled top molding
- 1x8 or 1x10 band
- Drip cap
- Existing wall

set to shallow depth and a 10° bevel. Seal the joint between the drip cap and the siding with paintable silicone caulk.

Although a backhoe can fill a trench quickly and efficiently, it's not the best tool for finish-grading. Hire a bulldozer to spread the topsoil (which you of course stripped and saved when you began digging) over the fill. A bulldozer can back-drag the surface with its blade, leaving it ready for hand-raking and seeding. If there are a lot of stones in the finish material, a tractor-mounted landscape rake (York rake) will drag them into windrows for removal.

Seed the area and protect it from birds, wind and washout with a sprinkling of mulch hay until the new grass is established.

Every time you hire a piece of heavy equipment, you pay a moving charge that is equal to at least an hour's work. So use the machine to bury stumps, junk or rubble, regrade the driveway or push some boulders out of the field—use that bulldozer every minute it's on your property and keep it for a few extra hours if you can afford it, rather than call it back at a later date for some small job.

Digging a Cellar under an Existing House

1. Excavate work trench to depth of new cellar and run jack timbers under sill.

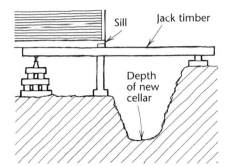

Sill

Jack timber

Depth of new cellar

2. Remove entire length of foundation wall, digging down to new footing depth.

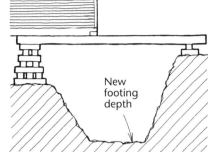

New footing depth

3. Form and pour new footing; pour wall. Remove timbers. Support sills with blocking from new wall. Cap with concrete blocks Repeat for opposite wall and one end wall.

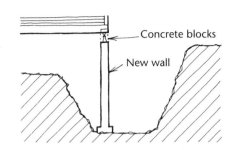

Concrete blocks

New wall

4. Remove last end wall.

8x8 or steel jack post temporarily supports midspan.

5. Excavate gallery on each side of center posts with traxcavator.

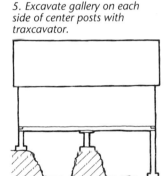

6. Reposition supports to sides of center, remove remaining soil to grade, and replace center post.

7. Spread gravel and install drain tile for slab floor before replacing last end wall and backfilling.

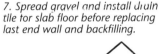
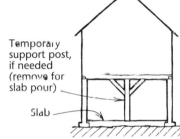

Temporary support post, if needed (remove for slab pour)

Slab

Adding a Cellar

One way to avoid lifting a house and yet increase the headroom in the cellar is to dig the cellar deeper. This approach is recommended for houses that lack true cellars. It's not uncommon for an old house to have a small core cellar, dug at the same time as the original house was built, with crawl spaces of varying heights under later ells and additions. Extending a full basement under the entire house creates a lot of useful space and simplifies heating and plumbing.

The simplest, but most expensive, way to dig a cellar under a house is to span the width of the house with steel beams long enough and stiff enough to be supported on cribbing placed well outside the walls.

For those who cannot afford the services of a professional housemover, working with jacking timbers, although more cluttered and less elegant, is at least accessible to the do-it-yourselfer or small contractor.

First, dig the outside work trench to the depth of the new cellar. Set up the cribbing inside the cellar away from the old wall so that the excavation will not threaten the stability of the cribbing. (Alternatively, use posts instead of cribbing, angle-bracing the posts to the floor joists for stability.) The other end of the jacking timber is supported on the bank of the work trench as usual. Remove and replace the entire length of one long wall. Do the same for the other side of the house and one end wall. With the house resting on

Cellar Retrofit Problems

Changes in wall level

Technique for unstable soil

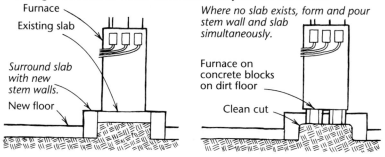

Original house end wall

Slab

Single-faced stem wall poured against stable cut

Straight cut in hard clay

Slab

Old wall

Slab cap

New wall formed at edge of stable cut into soil

Sloped cut

Gravel fill

Unstable soil

Putting a furnace or other immovable objects on an island

Furnace

Existing slab

Surround slab with new stem walls.

New floor

Where no slab exists, form and pour stem wall and slab simultaneously.

Furnace on concrete blocks on dirt floor

Clean cut

three new walls, remove the last end wall. You may find it necessary to support it under the middle of the span with a temporary 8x8 or steel jack post.

A "traxcavator" is a small tracked loader equipped with a digging bucket and sometimes a hoe. It has a low profile that allows it to fit under spaces with low headroom. The traxcavator is the most efficient machine to use for digging a cellar under an existing house. It cuts an access ramp from the end-wall bank and then works its way bite by bite into the cellar floor, digging forward as it lowers the grade. The machine works to one side of the center jack post until the desired grade is reached. The post is then lengthened and moved sideways while the other side of the cellar is

lowered. Interior posts are treated the same way. An aisle is dug down on each side of the center line. Then timbers are used to support the center girder from each side while the center post(s) and remaining material are removed.

What do you do with those parts of the existing cellar that you can't lower or move, such as the chimney or concrete pad already in place under the furnace? Or the change in level between the main cellar and an area that will remain a crawl space? For example, suppose the house's original end wall (which is 4 ft. tall) is now inside an attached garage or woodshed. You can't very well dig down and replace that wall from inside the garage. Here, depending on the stability of the soil, the traxcavator digs down along the cellar face of the short wall to the required depth. In hardpan clay, it's easy to get a clean cut. A new wall is poured against the clay extending above the bottom of the old wall or its footing. Where the soil is too loose to permit such close machine or hand digging, the new wall is formed at the edge of a stable cut and then backfilled with gravel and capped with a concrete slab poured over the footings of the old wall.

The same principles are used to dig around and wall off chimneys and existing slabs that are too much trouble to remove. Unless the furnace is sitting on bare earth, in which case you'll need to disconnect and remove it until a floor is poured, it's a lot simpler and cheaper to leave it in place and pour a stem wall against the existing slab. If it's sitting on concrete blocks and you can pour directly against an earth cut, simply pour a slab around the blocks and under the furnace at the same time you pour the stem walls.

Because the footing for a chimney is not much larger than the chimney itself, it's not safe to dig too close to it by machine, especially in loose soils. Use the same stem wall and slab-capping technique as for pouring a furnace slab. Since all four corners are tied together, the form-

Incorporating an Outside Chimney into the New Cellar and Foundation

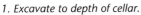

1. Excavate to depth of cellar.

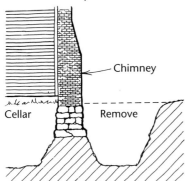

Chimney

Cellar   Remove

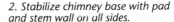

2. Stabilize chimney base with pad and stem wall on all sides.

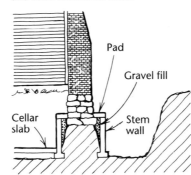

Pad

Gravel fill

Cellar slab

Stem wall

3. Fit wall form panels to chimney support.

Note: Provide openings through wall for cellar flue and/or clean-out door.

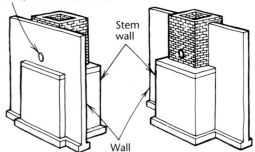

Stem wall

Wall

work is really only a simple column, and no inside form for the wall is needed, even in loose soil.

What happens when the chimney is built against an outside wall? It's not too likely that the foundation form panels will fit alongside the earth left to support the chimney. You may not even be able to undermine the chimney to fit a footing. If the chimney also includes a fireplace, it's probably best to dig down around it first and pour a stabilizing stem wall and then step the foundation forms up to accommodate the new chimney base. If the chimney has only one flue, it can be secured to the wall of the house with 4-in. wide straps of ⅛-in. steel bands bent to the size of the chimney, and lag-bolted into solid wood. Three or four of these straps will hold the chimney securely while you remove the entire below-grade section under the chimney, leaving room for wall forms. The missing portion of the chimney is replaced on a new footing after the wall is poured. Inexperienced housemovers should consult with a mason before attempting this sort of operation.

There is another way to add a cellar under an existing house, which is so radically simple that it's almost never thought of. Instead of going through the trauma of removing the old foundation and undermining the house, consider the possibility of digging a new cellar hole and a new foundation alongside the old one. The house can move on wood or steel rollers inserted between the jacking timbers and a timber rollway constructed between both foundations, or even pulled on greased timbers set into notches in the walls by a bulldozer winch hooked to a chain encircling the sills.

The transfer can be made without resorting to jacks at all. Slide four or more 8x8s under the span of the house (you'll have to use steel if the beams are longer than 24 ft.). These should project 2 ft. to 4 ft. beyond the foundation wall. Place a steel beam or timber perpendicularly under these lifting beams along the outside walls. Hang it with ropes or support with temporary cribbing underneath. Cable slings hooked around these beams will allow a crane to lift and swing the house onto the new foundation. If everything is properly prepared ahead of time, the entire move can be completed in an hour or less. Timing is important, since 40-ton and larger cranes (smaller ones don't have the lift range) are charged out at $600 an hour or more plus moving time. Moving the house onto the foundation rather than putting the foundation under the house may be the logical extreme of foundation repair, but if the house itself is otherwise sound, it might also be the most economical approach.

The moral of this section is, if faith can move mountains, you can move your house. Although it helps, you don't need a great deal of prior experience to do the job. A knowledge of how houses are put together, common sense and patience are prerequisites, but the best insurance is to seek out the advice of those who have the experience. Crane operators, riggers, concrete contractors, masons, renovation specialists, housemovers and even the retired farmer down the road all could contribute suggestions that could ensure the success and reduce the cost of your project.

Pouring a Concrete Floor

In the era before refrigeration and home freezers, an earth floor was beneficial. All summer long the floor would store heat, slowly warming up. Since this temperature rise was so much slower than outdoors, the cellar helped cool the house in the hottest part of the year. During the cold months, the stored heat was released, keeping the cellar from freezing. Because of these relatively moderate temperature fluctuations, the cellar was an ideal storage area for root vegetables, apples, smoked meats, canned items and such household staples as dandelion wine and hard cider. Unfortunately, this moist, cool environment was also an ideal incubator for mold. Insufficient ventilation coupled with water vapor released by the earth fostered the growth of wood-devouring fungi. Any

wooden objects in direct contact with an earth floor would rot. Metal objects rusted, which is why concrete pads were poured under furnaces and water heaters.

For a quick fix to dry out the cellar, lay a 6-mil polyethylene vapor barrier down over the earth. Cover this with 1 in. of sand (to protect the film from punctures) and grade a final 4-in. layer of pea stone over this. This setup can be left permanently or form the base for a future floor slab. Boards laid over 4x4 pressure-treated sleepers set level in the pea stone to leave 1 in. or so of clearance are an inexpensive alternative to a poured concrete floor.

To install a concrete floor, prepare the cellar by first removing whatever is movable. If the furnace and water heater are not already on concrete pads or blocks, lever them up to finished floor height with a crowbar or 2x4 while you slip the right number of bricks or blocks underneath. Lighter utilities like the water pump and pressure tank can be temporarily hung from the ceiling. Unless you use pressure-treated wood, support posts cast in concrete will rot. It's best to set them on precast footings no more than 1 in. below finish floor height. Paint the bottom end and sides of the posts with wood preservative or asphalt cement. You can remove most of the support posts until the concrete sets up—the floors will sag quite a bit, but so long as no one walks on them, they won't collapse. Dig out the floor about 4 in. deeper where the posts will sit. Trim the bottom edges of the stair stringers to fit the new floor height. You'll probably need to rebuild them anyway.

With a rake or coarse broom, pick up all loose material, stones, bark chips and other debris. The floor should be compacted from years of use. Settle any loose areas with a hand tamper, which is nothing more than a heavy cast-iron plate mounted on a handle that you pound up and down. Gas-powered compactors are more effective and faster, but the exhaust fumes are apt to poison you and stink up the house for days even with all the windows open. When the air becomes blue with smoke, it's generally time to take a breather. Lower any noticeably high spots with a shovel, and spread and compact this fill to bring up the low spots.

Spread a 4-in. layer of clean gravel or sand over the earth grade, and compact it. Here you'll have no choice but to choke and suffer with the gas-powered compactor (perhaps someday someone will make an electric one).

Sometimes, especially when digging a cellar deeper than the original crawl space, water will ooze from the earth because of an uncovered spring within the cellar or a high water table. The hydrostatic pressure exerted under the slab acts like water lifting a boat, and water oozes up between the slab and the wall, or the slab itself lifts and breaks. Water problems of this magnitude will be apparent while excavating the cellar or work trenches. As water continues to percolate up into a hardpan clay soil, the compacting action of the traxcavator will turn the floor into a quivering, structurally worthless jellylike mass. It may take several dump-truck loads of coarse stone and boulders treaded into the pudding to stiffen it.

If this is your dilemma, run perforated drain lines 6 ft. to 12 ft. apart (depending on the severity of the hemorrhage) the length of the floor area before pouring the slab, and tee these lines into a line run along the perimeter of the footings. This drain line should exit through the bottom of the footing and connect with the exterior foundation drain system. Cover the pipes and the stabilized floor with 6 in. of chestnut stone. This porous bed will harmlessly and rapidly drain any infiltrating water out of the cellar. Cover the crushed stone with enough gravel to form a protective base for the vapor barrier.

Since a floor slab turns the cellar into a potential swimming pool, it's also a good idea to add a floor drain should your plumbing leak or washing machine overflow. This drain can connect through the footing to the outside foundation drain. Boring a drain line through an existing wall is a lot of work. The alternative is to dig a sump pit. This is simply a concrete-lined box, about 18 in. square and 2 ft. or 3 ft. deep, in which is set a float-actuated electric pump. The outlet for this pump is a hose run through the sill to the outside. A plywood cover notched to fit around the pump shaft sits over the pit. Dig a hole about 1 ft. wider than the finished pit. Form and pour 4-in. thick walls (another use for leftover concrete from wall pours). Backfill with coarse stone and throw a few shovelfuls of stone into the bottom of the pit. Leave the inside forms in place. These should extend to your eventual finish floor height, which will be about 1 in. lower than the surrounding floor for better drainage. Nail 1x1 strips to the top of this form to make the lip that will support the sump cover.

Assuming that all under-slab water problems have been solved, mark a point on the wall 4 in. above the prepared gravel base, which should be nearly flush with the top of the footing. With a transit level, shoot that point around the perimeter and snap a chalkline between the marks. If you're working against an existing stone wall, drive stakes into the floor and stretch a string between them to indicate floor level in front of the wall. With a helper, stretch strings across the cellar from wall to wall and look for any obvious high or low spots under the string that need further leveling. These strings will also help establish grade when working around posts, furnace slabs or any other difficult areas. (The same technique is used to set the slope for a floor drain.)

Screeding a floor slab requires the skill born of experience. If you want a good job, hire a professional.

Lay the vapor barrier over the prepared gravel base. Carefully cut around existing pads or footing blocks if you cannot slip the barrier under them. Following the vapor barrier, lay 6x6 wire reinforcement mesh. Mesh is supposed to be held above the vapor barrier by special steel "chairs," but most contractors simply lift the mesh up as they pour the slab, or support it on small flat stones. The wire is cut with a bolt cutter to fit around posts and other obstructions. Bend the cut ends over to hook around adjoining pieces of mesh. Bend the ends upward to avoid puncturing the vapor barrier.

One problem remains: How to get the concrete into the cellar. Window openings and a bulkhead are the best places to start pouring. If, as is likely, the truck can reach only one end of the cellar, add a temporary chute built from plywood or boards (if it's lined with metal, the concrete will slide a lot easier) and supported on sawhorses to reach the far end. The concrete company will not supply an extension chute unless you ask for one. If the truck cannot reach the cellar, the concrete can be placed with a pumper boom. This raises the cost per yard considerably, but if it's the only alternative to hauling the concrete down a ramp in a wheelbarrow, it might be worth it.

Gather the help and outfit them with rakes and shovels. Pull the concrete from the chute to the farthest corners first. The mix should be on the wet side for easier spreading and a slower setting time. Distribute the concrete evenly, working back toward the truck. As the concrete is placed, lift the mesh to float it in the slab. Wear rubber boots. Concrete contains enough lime to eat away leather soles as well as bare feet.

Begin screeding off the surface before the last of the concrete is placed. Ideally, a screed board (a straight length of 2x4 will do) reaches across the entire width of the area to be leveled, but in a cellar, shorter screeds enable you to work around obstructions. Drive steel stakes around the perimeter and down the middle of the slab, and nail 2x4s at floor height before the pour. The top edges are the bearing surface on which the screed is drawn back and forth. They also guide you in keeping level. After an area is screeded, pull the stakes and smooth the holes over before the concrete sets up. If a perfectly level floor is not important, dispense with the screed guides and eyeball the floor as best you can.

Screeding leaves a slightly ridged finish suitable for a barn floor (better traction for the cows) but hard to keep clean. A "bull float," which is a magnesium plate attached to an adjustable handle (rent one) is used to smooth the ridges left by screeding. When the surface appears frosted (or "sugared") it is ready for floating. The concrete will be hard enough to bear your weight, but still soft enough to take an imprint. Working from 1-ft. square plywood kneeling boards, smooth off any ridges and fill any low spots made by the bull float. The kneelers shouldn't sink any more than ¼ in. into the surface. Otherwise, let the concrete set up a little more.

When the concrete has become hard enough to bear your weight without imprinting, it's ready for steel troweling, which gives a hard, polished finish. Steel troweling by hand is incredibly tedious. And, since concrete gives off enough heat while setting to turn a cellar into a sauna, it's not a job for the faint-hearted. A power trowel does a lot better job with much less

effort. Unfortunately, they run on gas, but in this case I'd either leave the floor with a wood-float finish or brave the fumes.

I remember the day I poured my own cellar floor. By noon the temperature was already in the low 90s, as was the humidity. The job resembled a scene from Dante's *Inferno:* Three near-naked bodies, clad in rubber boots and cut-off shorts, sweating and grunting, tugging at a sluggish puddle with shovels and hoes. The cellar was a Turkish bath, the concrete was setting too fast. My glasses fogged in, the light bulbs glimmered dully through the heavy dew. But there was no stopping, not yet. The concrete was stiffening almost as fast as we could place it. In broad, rough strokes I smoothed the pour with a length of 2x4. "Good enough for a cellar hole, this ain't the Taj Mahal!" And we left it just like that—no screed, no float—and escaped blinking into the shimmering daylight.

The House Frame

And the dust returns to the earth as it was....

—Ecclesiastes 12:7

Although seriously compromised by decay, this 150-year-old hardwood beam is still quite rugged.

A sill is a sermon on paradox. It is the bridge between heaven and earth. It raises the house up from the ground and yet is the path of return. It is the strongest and weakest link in that intricate chain of force and counterforce that is the frame of a house. Because they are at the bottom of the house, sills are closest to the earth and the most vulnerable to decay. Water can work at them from both sides. Season after season, rain ricochets and snow banks against the skirts of the house, leaving tiny capsules of moldy earth to colonize the timbers. Water eases through crevices between eaves and cornerboards and along the borders of windows and drip caps. Wind drives rain deep under door jambs, sills and thresholds, myriad reservoirs collect on the interface of wood and stone, fungus spores swell and are nourished. The tendrils of fungi burrow into the muscle of the wood, devouring its strength. Water kindles the slow fire of decay, flowing down gravity's curve. The cycle completes itself — wood and earth become one.

Wood won't rot unless it is exposed to moisture, and there is no more perfect water trap than the space between the sill and the top of the foundation walls, or the back side of the sheathing boards. Sometimes houses are too close to the ground —although a good 2 ft. is necessary to avoid damage, standard specs allow the sills to lie a mere 8 in. above grade. Here, the bottom-most boards of the siding rot first, acting like sponges, holding moisture against the sills. Condensation created by improperly insulated walls causes water to run down the vertical members and pool on top of the sills. If constantly exposed to moisture, new wood rots in about seven years. Older timbers rot sooner because their natural wood-preserving resins are lost with age. Conversely, when wood is kept dry, it lasts a long time. John Cole and Charles Wing, in *From the Ground Up* (Boston: Atlantic Little, Brown, 1976), observe that wooden doors, frames and furniture buried with their Egyptian owners several thousand years ago are still as strong, functional and lovely as the day the tombs were closed.

A few pages back we suspended our disbelief and raised a house. If we had lifted a rotted sill beam, the jack timber would have cut through the sill like a knife through soft cheese. Over the years, the weight of the house will compress rotted sills like a brick resting on a loaf of white bread. The house begins to tilt, twisting and racking when a sinking sill throws it off balance. If the rot can be arrested in its early stages, major repairs will be avoided later.

Types of House Frames

When you understand where the loads are concentrated in your house and how they are distributed across a span, repair work is a matter of logic instead of luck. Of course you should be familiar with the basic elements of house framing. Several useful books on the subject are listed in the Bibliography on pp. 334-338.

Timber frames

Until the introduction of the circular saw and the availability of cheap machine-made nails just before the middle of the 19th century, houses were framed as they had been for hundreds of years, of heavy timbers held together with pegs and mortise-and-tenon joints. But the popular image of the farmer and his sons hewing out the house frame is a misconception. A settler newly arrived in the vast wilderness of northern New England had enough to do with the business of mere survival. He quickly cut down logs, notched up a rude cabin and got on with the work of clearing and planting. As the farm prospered and the settlement grew, he could afford to hire a master carpenter and crew of framers to cut the joints. Joinery was an art and a science, the secrets of which had been jealously guarded since the guilds of the Middle Ages. After these specialists had cut and joined the beams on the ground, the farmer gathered his neighbors for the traditional house-raising. The carpenters were paid and they departed. The farmer and his sons would then shingle and sheathe the house.

Timber frames tend to follow a set pattern (see the drawing on p. 75). The earliest were centered around a massive central fireplace and chimney—the focal point of life in the house. The chimney was thus an integral part of the frame, limiting the layout of the timbers and defining the design of the house. It's not uncommon for the chimney to support the principal girts. This configuration is typical of house frames built from the earliest colonial period up to the end of the 18th century. The widespread use of the heating stove and the introduction of central furnaces around the beginning of the 19th century made it possible to omit the large central fireplace. With the resulting elimination of chimney girts and summer beams, this frame became the direct ancestor of modern layouts.

A variation that, in a way, recapitulated the fortress-like log cabins of the early settlements, was the plank house. In the days of hand-powered or water-powered sawmills, boards were expensive and difficult to saw. Turning logs into planks saved time and labor. Nails were also costly and usually reserved for fastening hardware and crafting doors. Instead of thin boards nailed to studs, the walls of the aptly named plank house were built with solid vertical planks (usually 2 in. to 3 in. thick by 10 in. to 12 in. wide) mortised into the face of sill and plate beams. The interior paneling or plaster and exterior siding were applied directly to the planks. But despite their superabundance of solid wood, plank houses are less rugged than ordinary timber-frame houses, since they lack the stiffening knee bracing at the corner posts.

In a timber-frame house, the weight of the roof and the second-floor deck is transferred to the sills through the upright posts at very specific points. The sills and horizontal plate beams anchor the critical knee braces that keep the posts plumb and impart rigidity to the frame. Although it does spread some of those substantial vertical point loads to the horizontal, most of the sill doesn't actually bear any weight—sills are more bracing than bearing. Obviously, then, all of the sill between posts could be replaced without any jacking other than that required to support the floor joists.

Despite the march of progress elsewhere, in the rural backwaters of New England the old methods persisted well into the latter half of the 19th century. It was still cheaper and easier to hew heavy tim-

Plank-House Frame

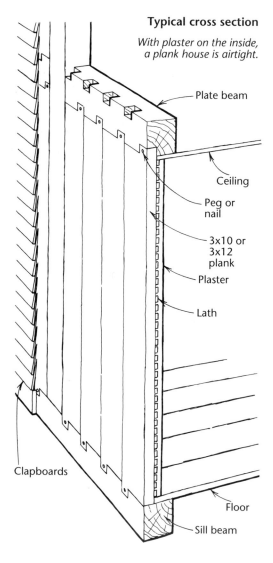

Typical cross section

With plaster on the inside, a plank house is airtight.

Plate beam

Ceiling

Peg or nail

3x10 or 3x12 plank

Plaster

Lath

Clapboards

Floor

Sill beam

This mid-19th century 'hybrid' frame combines a braced heavy-timber plate beam (and sills) with 4x4 studs, built-up corner and balloon-framed gable wall.

Balloon framing for a gable wall is not really load-bearing and can therefore be minimal.

bers over 16 ft. long by hand on site rather than transport them from a distant sawmill. These were mixed with sawn timbers, solid hewn corner posts and heavy dimensioned studding (3x6s set flatwise, for example) in a hybrid framing system that was common through the early years of the present century. Perhaps those builders used heavy timbers as insurance just in case the newfangled sticks didn't work. So, at least in the Northeast, chances are good that a house built before 1860 will have a traditional timber frame. The innovations of mass production did not filter down to rural areas until well into the Victorian era.

Balloon frames

In 1832, a Chicago businessman constructed the first building employing a radically different framing system. It made full use of the accurately sized lumber that was suddenly turned out in great quanti-

ties by rapidly proliferating circular-saw mills. This lumber, cut from the forests of the Great North Woods, was shipped over the newly opened railroad network to build the cities that were dotting the treeless Great Plains.

In the "balloon" frame, studs run continuously from the mudsill to the rafter plate; floor joists are nailed to the face of studs and rest on let-in ledger strips. Despite its fragile appearance, this frame is incredibly strong. The principal difference between stud and timber framing is anatomical. The timber frame is modeled on the human skeleton. The bones are large, heavy members; sheathing (the skin) fills in the spaces between, tacked to whatever odd lumber was left over for studding. The balloon frame is analogous to the hard shell of an insect, which is at once skin and bone. The entire frame would collapse were it not for the bracing afforded by the diagonal sheathing boards. By dispersing great loads over large areas, house design was freed from the rigid requirements of the timber frame. The fanciful confections of the Victorian era were soon forthcoming. The other advantage of balloon framing was that, unlike traditional timber framing, it required no great skill to master and no great time to put together. What more could a burgeoning nation of immigrants ask for?

Platform frames

The balloon frame dominated residential building until after World War II, when it was supplanted by the "platform" or "Western" frame. The main difference between them is that platform framing uses discrete platforms for each story in place of a joist ledger hung from continuous studs. By using shorter studs, entire walls could be framed on the platform, even sheathed, and then tilted up, making for even faster assembly with a minimal sacrifice of strength. Most platform-framed houses aren't yet old enough to require structural repairs, especially since advances in building technology and awareness of moisture problems have tended to reduce the incidence of structural rot.

Stick-frame structures (as both balloon and platform framing are called) distribute loads along the entire length of the foundation. One might suppose that this would complicate sill repair, but since the actual portion of the load at any given point is quite small, large pieces of sill and attached framing can be removed with impunity. The lattice of framing, sheathing, siding and interior walls supports itself as long as some portion of the wall or corner is left to bear on the foundation. An adjacent section of wall will support the corner of the building while the sill directly under the corner is removed, which is not always the case with timber-framed walls. I am continually amazed by how much structure can be removed and how little support is required to maintain the stability of a stick-framed house.

Truing Up the House Frame

1. Under the tutelage of his father, Lester, Eric Adams set about curing the old Knapp house in Stowe, Vt., of its terminal slouch. A leak at the peak of the formerly attached shed (now removed), coupled with a settled and badly cracked foundation, had pulled the corner of the house apart.

2. The value of a drainage swale couldn't be clearer. Groundwater trapped in the heavy clay soil has pushed in more than one foundation wall. A temporary brace keeps the wall from escaping while portions of the foundation are removed.

3. Lifting up on the wall studs inside begins the leveling process. Stone shims serve as cribbing until more elaborate measures are substituted—not particularly elegant, but it works.

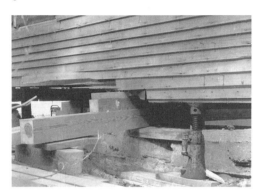

4. Once the corner is lifted free, cribbing and jacks can be inserted under the back wall to raise it off the old foundation.

5. Although the original foundation is badly cracked, parts of it are so massive that it's easier to incorporate them into the footings of the new wall than try to remove them.

6. The flooring along the entire back half of the house is removed to accommodate the cribbing for the beam that will carry the ceiling joists and main girts.

7. An advantage of balloon framing: Since the ceiling joists are pegged into the wall studs, lifting them will raise the entire wall without danger.

Truing Up the House Frame

8. The rear wall hangs like a curtain from the joists as the jacking timber is lifted from the cribbing and the old foundation is removed. With some additional cribbing, the timbers were repositioned so that the rear and end walls were both free-floating. This allowed the complete removal of the worst part of the gable wall and freed up the decayed corner for repair.

9. Formwork for the rear wall is built in place on top of a footing poured over the remains of the old foundation. When the rest of the formwork is finished, the two walls can be poured at once.

10. Matching the formwork to the remaining portion of the rear wall requires some fancy scrollwork. The top of the wall is a fossil imprint of a long-gone sill. Wall forms were built from 1x6 spruce boards with 2x4 'strongbacks.'

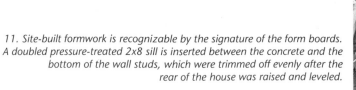

11. Site-built formwork is recognizable by the signature of the form boards. A doubled pressure-treated 2x8 sill is inserted between the concrete and the bottom of the wall studs, which were trimmed off evenly after the rear of the house was raised and leveled.

12. *Because the entire gable was hung from the cribbed-up timber, all but the solid front corner of the foundation was replaced in one easy pour. As soon as the floating corner is anchored to the foundation, the remaining gable wall siding will be stripped off and the wall reframed.*

13. *The plate beam and corner are pulled in with a come-along while pushing on the outside diagonal brace. A let-in 2x6 ties the corner to the wall studs. Plywood sheathing provides even more rigidity.*

Replacing Rotted Sills

The condition of the first course of siding boards offers a clue to the state of the underlying sills. If the sheathing boards under the siding are also crumbly, chances are that the rot has progressed into the sill. The building paper covering the sheathing has wonderful wicklike properties that can draw moisture a long way up the wall and keep it there. Remove as many courses of siding as necessary until the sheathing boards appear sound. The areas under windows often have their own veins of rot, which extend downward to meet the rot working upward from the sills. Take off the rotted sheathing to the nearest sound board and expose the sill. Rotted wood will be soft and crumbly, stained dark red; sound wood is pale and resists a chisel.

Clean out the pockets of rot with a chisel until good solid wood is showing, leaving a rectangular excision in the sill. Coat the exposed new wood with a wood preservative (such as Cuprinol #10®), size a new block of wood to fit the opening and pound it in. When at least half of the old sill is still sound, it's easier to scab new wood onto old than to replace the entire timber, as long as the good part runs vertically through the sill (that is, if it's still capable of bearing a load).

Cut vertical kerfs across the face of the sills with a reciprocating saw or heavy-duty jigsaw. (The foundation wall will interfere with a circular-saw blade—use this tool with the blade set to the depth of the rot to cut horizontal kerfs to simplify removing the rotted wood.) Coat the new wood with preservative and use as many layers of pressure-treated dimension lumber and boards ripped to fit as needed to fill the cavity flush to the original face. ("Dimension" refers to lumber with a nominal thickness of at least 2 in., e.g., 2x4s, 2x6s, etc. "Boards" are lumber less than 2 in. in nominal thickness.)

When decay has eaten into the ends of the floor joists or all the way across the bottom of the sill, there's no choice but to replace the whole piece. Sills do carry the

Supporting Floor Joists While Replacing a Rotted Sill

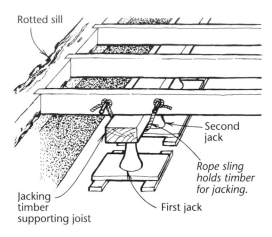

Rotted sill

Second jack

Rope sling holds timber for jacking.

Jacking timber supporting joist

First jack

The half-lap joint under this house is perpendicular to the way it should be. It must be supported when the wall is removed. (Photo by Joe English.)

This is the correct way to lap a sill joint.

ends of the floor joists, but these loads are easily relieved by a jacking timber hung from the joists with a rope sling and then lifted by screw jacks (see the drawing at left). Use vertical 4x4 jack posts under the jacking timber if the distance from the cellar floor to the joists is greater than can be supported with a jacking timber and screw jacks alone.

With a chainsaw or reciprocating saw, cut the remains of the rotted sill into bite-sized portions and pull the pieces free with a prybar. If posts are mortised and pegged into the sill, cut through the joints at the bottom of the studs. Cutting through any nails (use a special nail-cutting blade in your reciprocating saw) before attempting to release the sill will prevent splitting the posts and ease removal. Clean the surface of the old foundation wall. Uneven stones should be capped level with mortar. This is especially necessary when replacing a sill behind a buttress wall, where the face of the wall is actually higher than the bottom of the sill, creating an ideal water trap. Before the cap sets hard, lay a 2x10 pressure-treated mudsill on the mortar bed and anchor it with 20d galvanized spikes driven through the wood into the mortar.

Cut back the rotted ends of the floor joists to solid wood. If the joists aren't resting directly on the sill, they should be secured to the new rim joist or sill beam with metal joist hangers. The local welding shop can fabricate custom hangers for odd-dimensioned joists and timbers. Purists may wish to mortise the new sill to accept the ends of the joists (when sound), but that's a lot of trouble to go through down in the cellar.

The old sill should be cut to accept a half-lap joint where it abuts the new. Nail the ends together with 40d spikes driven at an angle, or pole-barn nails (long, ring-shanked nails used for joining timbers) driven through the top of the splice. This not only ties the sills together, but also allows them to be lifted as a unit should it be necessary to replace the foundation wall. Remove and replace as much sill as you can before repositioning the jacking timbers. Usually, this means a corner and half the length of a wall or to the edge of the first intermediate post.

The situation is a bit more complicated when the sill directly under a post must also be replaced. As is obvious from the discussion of framing, the post must be supported or its load relieved before the sill can be removed. This is often a judgment call. Most of the time (for single-story structures anyway), the post will just dangle from the beam it supports. Removing the sill won't cause even a slight sag, since the sheathing boards and wall studs will spread out the load to the solid sections already replaced.

But sometimes a post really does carry a substantial load. If the rotted sill under a post appears squashed, it's wise to assume that there's some downward pressure; likewise assume this is the case if, when cutting through the tenon or nails at the bottom of the post, the sawblade pinches tight before the cut is finished. The posts of multi-story houses are also much more likely to require support. Relieve the load on the post by lifting the plate beam (the one carried by the post) with a jack placed on the remaining sound sill on either or both sides of the post, or simply make sure that any new sill already installed ends just short of the troublesome post.

Replacing a Rotted Sill

1. The damage caused by an improperly flashed buttress wall is obvious once the siding and sheathing boards are removed. The floor joists are supported by a jacking timber slipped into the cellar, and the sill is sawn into pieces for easy removal.

2. The old stone foundation wall is capped with mortar to bring it level with the lip of the buttress wall.

3. A pressure-treated 2x10 mudsill is set on top of the wall and anchored with 20d galvanized spikes driven into the soft mortar. The rotted ends of the joists and wall studs are cut back to sound wood.

Replacing a Rotted Sill

4. *A band joist is nailed across the face of the floor joists, a treated wood sill built up under it and new sole plates added under the studs. The framing is shimmed out as needed so that the sheathing boards will conform to the irregularities in the existing wall.*

5. *If a face cut is made first with a circular saw, the kerf will guide the reciprocating saw the rest of the way through the stud.*

6. *The framing is added between the new sill and the bottom of the old studs.*

7. *New sheathing in place, the wood is waterproofed with lead flashing sealed to the concrete. The repair is ready for finish siding.*

Three Ways to Brace Above a Post

A braced cradle carries the plate beam and allows a damaged post or sill section to be replaced. Siding must be removed to slide cradle beams through the wall.

Although more cumbersome, this method supports the plate beam with minimal damage to siding and wall finishes.

A timber under adjacent beams can lift a corner post. This method is especially useful where heavy loads are bearing on rotted sills at a corner.

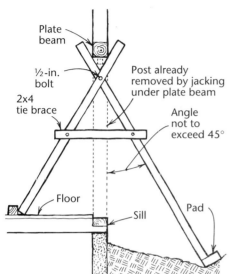

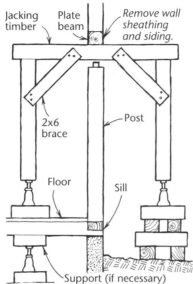

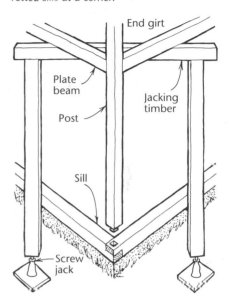

When it's neither practical nor desirable to piece in so many sections of new sill, first lift the post as described on p. 111. Then support the plate beam on a braced cradle, as shown at left in the drawing above, so that you can remove the jack post to permit unhindered replacement of the rotted sill. Sliding such cradles through the wall necessitates the removal of substantial amounts of sheathing and finish siding. Although a jacking timber supported by the floor joists requires more setup (see the middle drawing above), only a narrow band of sheathing must be removed where the timber goes through the wall. But in any case, sheathing boards nailed across both the post or studs and the sill beam should be removed to ease lifting the post. Also, posts will not lift (very far) if they are still secured to the sill by their bottom knee braces. These braces should be cut flush with the sill and later renailed.

Use 4x4 or 6x6 posts for the cradles under the plate beams. Brace them firmly against a bearing block outside the house and a block nailed to the floorboards over a joist on the inside. Crib or post up under the joists to carry the added stress. Using a jacking timber instead of a cradle increases stability and is better suited for repairing heavy buildings. Cribbing can be stacked quite high so long as it is kept level. The more cribbing and the less posting, the greater the stability. Jacking timbers can also be inserted diagonally under a plate beam and end girt to relieve the load on a corner post (as shown at right in the drawing above).

I've used these methods to carry the roof and upper floor loads while removing entire walls together with their sills. Radical surgery of this sort is called for in situations where something has caused large areas of a wall to decay, for example, where

Replacing the Sill of a Stud-Frame Building

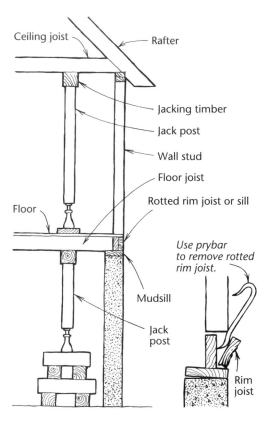

Use prybar to remove rotted rim joist.

Ceiling joist — Rafter

Jacking timber

Jack post

Wall stud

Floor joist

Floor

Rotted rim joist or sill

Mudsill

Jack post

Rim joist

manure was left piled against a barn or snow was trapped between the wall and a steep slope.

Replacement of sills is much easier with stud-frame houses. Sections up to half the length of a wall can typically be removed without any jacking or lifting at all, other than that needed to support the floor or ceiling joists. Since the studs hang from the top plate, which, in turn, is nailed to ceiling joists and/or rafters, an entire wall, sheathing, sills, studs and even foundation can be removed or repaired by supporting the roof and floor loads with jacking timbers installed on the inside of the house, as shown in the drawing above. Here the jack placed in the cellar stiffens the floor, to support the jacks placed under the ceil-

ing joists, which help carry the roof load where they join the rafters on the plate. Where the floor joists are still sound and resting firmly on the foundation wall (and not hung or attached to a decayed sill), the basement jacking can be eliminated. Instead, use a 2x12 plank laid on the floor and under the jacks perpendicular to the run of the floor joists to disperse the lifting force across as many joists as possible. At gable ends, a jacking or supporting timber is not needed, since the floor joists run parallel to the sill and the wall framing can support its own weight.

After exposing the damage, pull the rotted rim joist (which is part of the stud-frame equivalent to a timber sill) free from the floor joists with a prybar or pinchbar. (Prybars are smaller than pinchbars, which are what most people call crowbars. Crowbars are straight, pointed at one end, 5 ft. or 6 ft. long and used for heavy-duty levering. Pinchbars, also known as wrecking bars, are for pulling big spikes and for levering, ripping and tearing. Prybars are for ordinary nail pulling and light-duty levering, as opposed to the smaller cat's-paw, which is for extracting nails just enough so they can be removed with a prybar or hammer claw.)

You'll probably find it a lot easier to remove the rim joist if you saw through the nails that secure it to the floor joists and sole plate first. Likewise, if you loosen and remove any nails that tie the floor joists to the mudsill with a cat's-paw (or saw them through), the bottom edges of the floor joists won't split when the mudsill is ripped out. Cut the mudsill into manageable sections, especially at any sill anchor bolts. Before installing pressure-treated wood replacement framing, brush all sound old surfaces, particularly the end grain, with a wood preservative.

Replacement sills laid straight along a wall may not always line up with the framing above. New sheathing boards and studs aren't likely to match the irregular thicknesses of old ones. Rather than try to curve an 8x8 sill or saw boards to fit, use tapered shims, beveled clapboards or vary-ing layers of that renovator's standby, the cedar shingle, to fur the new work out to the old. These are added vertically and/or horizontally, depending on where cosmet-ic compensation is needed. The object is for the finish siding to approximate a flat plane rather than a topological singulari-ty. How this illusion is created is not criti-cal. When large areas of sheathing boards must be replaced, it's usually quicker to remove all the boards from the entire wall and resheathe with plywood rather than match new boards to old.

With an old house, there's a good chance that you won't be the first to at-tempt repairs. Previous owners may have already shored up a bad foundation or re-placed rotted sills. But although they may have halted the damage, they may not have restored the house to its original level. In other words, you might have a solid house sitting on a tilted foundation. The choice to live with it or correct it de-pends less on structural necessity than on how much your chair and table legs must be sawn off to fit the room. Having estab-lished the highest point of the foundation (which is usually the original level of the house) you may wish to raise up the rest of the house to correspond more or less. Through a combination of lifting floor joists and/or carrying beams, and jacking under corner posts, it's usually possible to align the sills with the rest of the house. Additional concrete can be hand-poured into the gap and later capped off like a buttress wall, or pressure-treated wood shims and planks added as required, de-pending on the regularity of the existing foundation wall.

Repairing Rotted Posts

Rot is hardly confined to sills alone. Corner posts are especially vulnerable to decay, fed by water seeping behind ill-fitting or uncaulked corner trim boards. All posts tend to rot from the bottom up. Although a horizontal sill can suffer a good deal of decay without its function being seriously impaired, a vertical load-bearing post can-not. Despite the very great compressive strength of wood parallel to its grain, a weakened post, because of the weight it carries, is potentially dangerous. A rotted post is similar to a cardboard mailing tube stood on end. It will support a lot of weight if you balance it carefully, but should the balance shift, or the end of the tube dent, the whole thing immediately collapses.

As mentioned earlier, it's usually pos-sible to remove a post without any jacking or lifting of plate beams, since the adjoin-ing wall sheathing and studding provide more than enough support. Simply cut the post free of its knee bracing and pull the nails from the sheathing boards that cover it (this assumes that the interior walls have been removed or at least cut back from the damage zone). Saw through the tenons at top and bottom and lever the post free. If you wish to cut a tenon in the new post to fit the existing plate beam, mortising instead of toenailing it in place, remove the stub of the old tenon by drilling out the wooden pegs ("trenails" or "trunnels") if they won't pull or drive out. Since in-serting a tenoned post requires lifting the plates, I can't imagine anyone but a fanat-ic restorationist going to such lengths.

Complete removal and replacement of posts is seldom called for. Most often, a new post is "scabbed" alongside the old one, on either or both sides, depending on the extent of the rot (after the source of the infection has been found and cured). If 4x4 stock is used for the scab post, it will be hidden inside the wall, leaving the old post cosmetically exposed to the interior. Take care to fit repair posts tightly to any knee braces, as only those surfaces in di-rect contact will actually bear weight.

Post Repair

Support the load by scabbing new wood onto rotted posts (find and fix the source of the rot first).

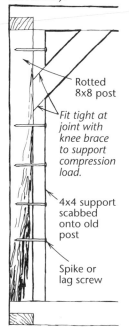

Rotted 8x8 post

Fit tight at joint with knee brace to support compression load.

4x4 support scabbed onto old post

Spike or lag screw

It's also possible to amputate the rotted lower extremity of an otherwise sound post and fill in the gap with a prosthetic section. Where the post must be exposed to view, use a piece of similar salvaged timber, and join it to the remainder with a half-lap joint such as that shown at left in the drawing below. This joint is strong, relatively easy to cut and handsome. It can look structurally deliberate rather than merely necessary. For added interest, the simple half-lap joint can be mitered at a 45° angle, as shown at right in the drawing. Countersink the heads of the through-bolts and plug them with dowel pins.

A single-story post is actually rather uncommon. Most old Cape-style houses were framed story-and-a-half. Posts for these houses extend from the sill to the rafter plate beam, with end-wall girts and floor-joist girts tenoned into them at ceiling level. This complex joint considerably lowers the resistance of the post to outward and downward thrusts and, if inadequately braced or overstressed, can easily fail. If you're lucky, the top portion of the post, having bent outward, will have sheared the tenon pegs, simply pulling the joint apart. This situation is a lot easier to fix than when the post itself snaps off at the pegholes. The walls can be pulled back in (more on this on pp. 125-129) and the joint repegged. A sheared post, however, requires that a new section be scarfed in somewhere well below the break. Depending on the extent of the damage, sections of the intersecting girts may also need replacement. If appearance is not a problem, consider using custom-fabricated steel supports for splicing and strengthening failed joints. These are much less labor-intensive than cutting scarfs and duplicating the old joinery.

Repairing Sagging Floors

With new sills and foundation walls under it, the house will probably not fall down before the next winter. You now can turn your attention to sagging floors and leaning walls. Trusty jack in hand, it's back to the cellar. You've probably come to know every beam and post in that hole by name —some by all kinds of names.

Floors sag because whatever is supposed to be holding them up isn't. Refer back to the framing drawing on p. 75. Joists are the main floor supports. These in turn are carried by girders or (as they are aptly named) carrying timbers, which are themselves held up by posts that ideally rest on rocks or concrete footings on the cellar floor. Because of the structural limitations of wood construction, joists seldom span the entire width of the building; instead, they end over the girders. Even so, settlement and sag at midspan is quite common with floor joists. Girders also will sag or tilt when the support posts beneath them have rotted away or settled into soft earth. Sometimes posts are simply missing. If the load on a girder is too heavy for the number of posts, that is, the span between them is longer than the girder can bridge without sagging, adding extra posts will straighten out the sag.

Two Joints for Repairing Exposed Posts

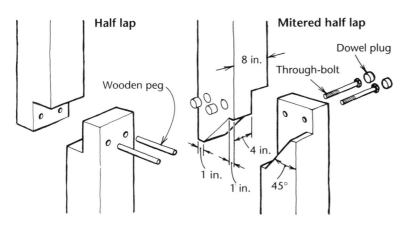

Half lap

Wooden peg

Mitered half lap

8 in.

Dowel plug

Through-bolt

4 in.

1 in.

1 in.

45°

Determining the Sag of a Main Girder

Case 1: Stringing a girder with mortised floor joists

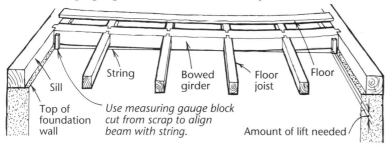

Sill

Top of
foundation
wall

String

*Use measuring gauge block
cut from scrap to align
beam with string.*

Bowed
girder

Floor
joist

Floor

Amount of lift needed

Case 2: Stringing a girder with floor joists carried on top

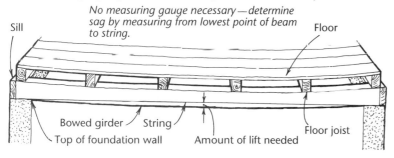

*No measuring gauge necessary—determine
sag by measuring from lowest point of beam
to string.*

Sill

Floor

Bowed girder

String

Top of foundation wall

Amount of lift needed

Floor joist

One of the side benefits of a complete foundation replacement is that the perimeter of the house at the sills is now level, which provides a convenient reference point for leveling the floors. To determine the amount of sagging, stretch a string along the bottom edge of the main girder or carrying beam. The ends should be fixed to blocks nailed at a distance from the bottom of the sills equal to the depth of the maximum sag, as shown in Case 1 in the drawing above. In other words, the string should just touch the lowest point of the girder. The goal is to raise the girder so that the gap between it and the string is constant. Make a measuring gauge from a scrap of board cut to the correct length.

When the bottom of the girder is flush to the bottom of the sills, a string stretched at this level will show the amount of lift required directly against the girder itself, without the need for a gauge block (as shown in Case 2 in the drawing). However, in most cases, joists mortised into the sides of the girder rather than carried on top of it will preclude this somewhat easier method.

The string method works even if the foundation has not been replaced or the sills brought back up to level. It gives a straight, although not necessarily level, line across the span of the house. The floors may tilt in the same plane, but at least they won't sag.

Raising a sagging girder

If the girder needs to be raised up and the existing post has settled but is otherwise sound and solidly footed, simply jack alongside the post using a 6x6 and hydraulic jack (don't forget the steel lifting plate over the jack cylinder head). Once the girder is lifted to the desired height plus a hair or two more to allow for set-

Raising a Sagging Girder

*Use block and shims on a short post
to stiffen a continuous girder.*

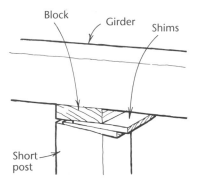

Block   Girder   Shims

Short
post

*Use a pillow block where two girders
butt over a post.*

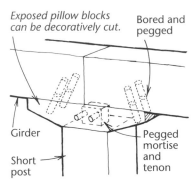

*Exposed pillow blocks
can be decoratively cut.*   Bored and
pegged

Girder

Short
post

Pegged
mortise
and
tenon

thick and 16 in. square. An existing floor
slab will support a post without additional
footings unless it is carrying an unusually
heavy load, in which case it's necessary to
break through the slab and excavate a 1-ft.
deep by 2-ft. square area and fill it with concrete to floor level. Do this where a slab
has cracked and dips noticeably under an
existing post.

Additional posts are frequently needed
to support the dangling ends of joists or
beams that were carelessly cut through for
a stairwell opening, chimney passage or
plumbing drain.

Stiffening a sagging girder

If a forest of posts seems to be growing in
your cellar, an alternative is to stiffen the
girders themselves by "sistering" planks
along their length (see the top drawing on
the facing page). Jack the girder from the
middle of its span past the level line so
that it is crowned. Cut a 2x plank the same
width as the depth of the girder to length,
and nail it flush to the top of the girder
at each end. Use another jack to raise its
middle flush to the crowned edge of the
girder. Then nail the stiffener to the girder
with 16d or 20d spikes driven 16 in. apart
along the length of the girder, three or four
to a row. Repeat on the opposite side of
the girder. When the jacks are released,
the girder should settle to near level. Because it has been prestressed by the crown-
ing, it will resist downward deflection.
Sistering can also be used to rebuild and
strengthen cracked or rotted girders.

Obviously, planks cannot be sistered
to a girder into which floor joists are mortised or nailed. Instead, install an additional timber directly under the sagging girder
and shorten the posts to fit after relocating
them farther apart (see the middle drawing
on the facing page). The girder can usually
be left briefly unsupported while the new
timber is jacked into place. To carry heavy
loads over long spans, add a continuous
girder composed of shorter segments, the
butt ends centered on the posts (see the
bottom drawing on the facing page).

tling, insert an appropriately sized block
between it and the post (as shown in the
drawing above), and back off the jack just
enough to pinch the post. Check for plumb
and make any fine adjustments with a
sledgehammer before completely releasing the jack. Blocks for increasing post
height should be cut from dimensioned
lumber or boards wide enough to cover
the top of the post and the width of the
girder itself. Drive tapered shingle shims
for solid bearing on top of uneven posts or
under a canted beam.

Where two girders butt over a post,
additional support is gained by a "pillow
block," which is a short length of timber
centered over the post and cantilevered
under each side of the splice. Pillow blocks
can stiffen a sagging girder somewhat
by effectively shortening the span. If the
amount of shimming required is more than
a few inches, or if a neat appearance is important, remove the old post and install a
new one cut to the correct length.

Any extra posts added under the girder
must have solid bearing on the cellar floor.
A large, flat stone at least 3 in. thick makes
a fine instant footing. Solid or cored concrete blocks don't, since they crack easily.
Instead, pour a concrete pad at least 8 in.

Repairing floor joists

Floor joists are frequently damaged by dry rot, as often happens when plumbing fixtures above have leaked for years. Carpenter ants and termites seem to favor these timbers. As suggested for the girders, new joists can be sistered onto the old ones and tensioned by jacking after the ends have been nailed. Jacking and sistering may be required in any case to lift a sagging overstressed or undersized joist back to level. Use string and blocks for calibration. The new joists will most likely need metal joist hangers to fasten them to the girder or sill. Where joists cross over the girder instead of running into its face, the added joist must be slipped between the flooring and the girder at a slant and then pounded plumb with a sledgehammer.

Replacement joists running perpendicular to other joists will also need joist hangers. Chances are that the standard sizes (for rough and planed lumber alike) won't fit your particular joists, especially after sistering. Custom hangers fabricated at the local welding shop, while not exactly cheap, are the best alternative. Finished flat black, ¼-in. steel hangers can be a pleasing solution to the problems of repairing or supporting exposed beams in the living areas of the house.

Where joists have rotted completely, leaving the floorboards above nailed to empty spaces, pry the remains of the joist free, clip off the nails flush to the subfloor and insert a new joist. Jack each end tight to the subfloor and install joist hangers. In most cases, if the joists have decayed enough to require replacement, the subfloor boards will also be rotted. You'll have to take up enough finish floor to expose the rotted subfloor. Cut the boards back to sound wood at the edge of the nearest joist. A 2x4 nailer scabbed alongside this joist will carry the new subfloor boards or plywood. Set new floor joists to accommodate any difference in thickness between the old floorboards and the new, especially if you use plywood instead of boards. If the rot is extensive, it's probably easier to

Stiffening a Sagging Girder

How to 'sister' a girder

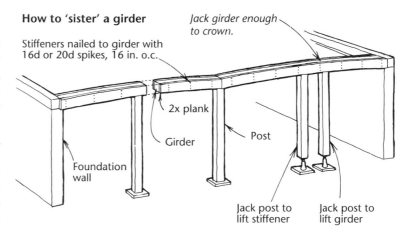

Jack girder enough to crown.

Stiffeners nailed to girder with 16d or 20d spikes, 16 in. o.c.

2x plank

Girder

Post

Foundation wall

Jack post to lift stiffener

Jack post to lift girder

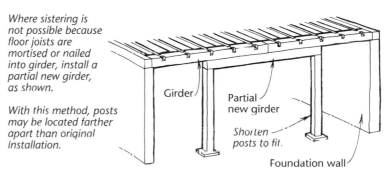

Where sistering is not possible because floor joists are mortised or nailed into girder, install a partial new girder, as shown.

With this method, posts may be located farther apart than original installation.

Girder

Partial new girder

Shorten posts to fit.

Foundation wall

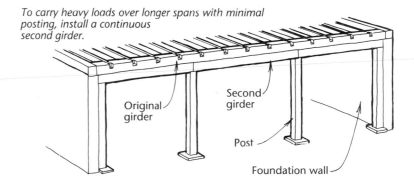

To carry heavy loads over longer spans with minimal posting, install a continuous second girder.

Original girder

Second girder

Post

Foundation wall

Finish floorboards have been removed to expose the decayed subfloor. The easiest way to deal with a severely rotted floor is to take it out and build a new one.

take up the entire floor and reframe it with new joists and a new subfloor rather than attempt piecemeal repairs.

The string technique won't be of much use with half-log joists. The lack of a constant depth eliminates any reference line. Here the leveling will have to be done from above, with strings stretched across the finish floors if possible. Otherwise, make a map of the relative floor heights using a water level to determine the necessary amount of lift at each obvious point. Although dead accurate, this method requires a lot more time and trouble, since the level will have to be rechecked constantly. Dead-level is not really all that important. Chances are, if the floor doesn't look tilted, it probably isn't too far from level. Strings and your trusty eyeball level will give tolerable results. A ball bearing set on the floor is another fairly good indicator of pitch.

Sistering won't save this badly rotted stud, because the floor joist it carries still remains unsupported.

Repairing Split or Sagging Rafters

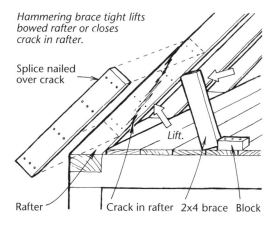

Hammering brace tight lifts bowed rafter or closes crack in rafter.

Splice nailed over crack

Lift.

Rafter   Crack in rafter   2x4 brace   Block

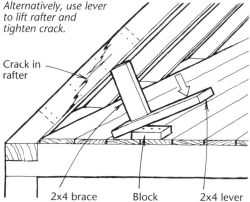

Alternatively, use lever to lift rafter and tighten crack.

Crack in rafter

2x4 brace   Block   2x4 lever

Repairing Other Structural Elements

Sistering can be used to repair sagging ceiling joists and cracked rafters, with or without jacking. A good substitute for a jack where there is no great load to be lifted is a 2x4 jammed at an angle to the timber to be straightened (see the drawing above) As the brace is hammered tight, the bowed framing member is lifted or a crack is closed tight. A lever, substituted for a hammer, gives a compound lift. Once the pieces are correctly realigned, a splice is nailed over the break or a sister is added.

After the plaster and lath are stripped from the ceilings and walls, it's not unusual to discover deep cracks running through the exposed beams. These fissures, called "checks" or "shakes," are caused by uneven drying of the wood and in most cases are not structurally deleterious. Most checks are natural and nothing to worry about, which is a good thing, since there's nothing you can do to prevent them. Timbers soon reach equilibrium and check no further. But sometimes a timber is stressed so much that it begins to check, or a check continues to deepen. This often happens where a portion of a beam has been removed where it is notched into another.

Stress at a Joint

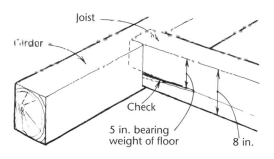

Joist

Girder

Check

5 in. bearing weight of floor

8 in.

A serious crack tends to open along the length of the timber. A tenon weighted from above typically splits apart where it is unsupported. Although, as shown in the drawing above, the joist itself is 8 in. thick, its effective thickness is only that portion actually supported by the girder. The rest of the joist is dead weight and only adds to the stress already on the joint. Thus for an 8-in. beam, only 5 in. actually carries the floors. The crack follows the line of the joint.

Types of Steel Plates Used to Reinforce Timbers

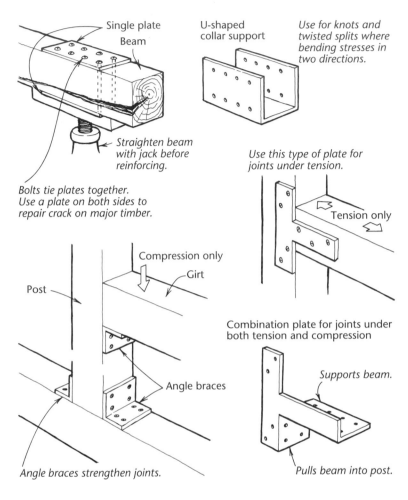

Single plate

Beam

U-shaped collar support

Use for knots and twisted splits where bending stresses in two directions.

Straighten beam with jack before reinforcing.

Use this type of plate for joints under tension.

Bolts tie plates together. Use a plate on both sides to repair crack on major timber.

Tension only

Compression only

Girt

Post

Combination plate for joints under both tension and compression

Angle braces

Supports beam.

Angle braces strengthen joints.

Pulls beam into post.

A steel angle plate secures a pulled corner post (note sistered edge) to the plate beam.

I am of two minds about such cracks. If a 5-in. joist has held up the floor for a century or more, it will probably continue to do so. Timbered houses were often framed with timbers much larger than an engineering analysis would require. On the other hand, the floor above may be stressed by new occupants and new uses with a greater load than it can carry. A piano and several heavy pieces of furniture, or a waterbed or whirlpool bath, could cause structural failure of beams that adequately supported a few bushels of onions or old trunks.

Using steel repair plates

The simplest repair for checks and splits in beams is a well-finished metal joist hanger secured by ¼-in. lag screws after the crack has been jacked closed. Predrill ³⁄₁₆-in. holes for the lags and avoid turning them in too far as the heads can torque off. Lag screws can also be used to draw together splits in other structural beams once they have been jacked closed. Frequently a beam will not draw together appreciably because it has taken so long to get to its present condition that there is no resiliency left. Stable beams are best left alone. Lag screws, though, can prevent further splitting by relieving strain.

Quarter-inch steel splicing plates are useful for repairing cracked timbers or weakened joints. Before fastening a repair plate over a split beam, the crack should, of course, be closed tight and the beam straightened with a jack. Major beams such as rafter plates or girts should have plates on both sides of the crack, tied together with hex bolts. Timbers that have failed at large knots or where the grain twists around can be stiffened with a U-shaped collar support. Angle braces and combination plates add strength to the joints between girts and posts and are useful for fastening new timbers between existing uprights.

Repairing a Damaged Tenon When the Girt or Post Cannot Be Easily Removed

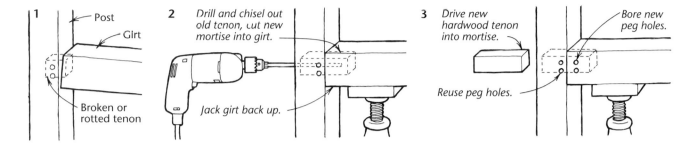

1 Post — Girt — Broken or rotted tenon

2 Drill and chisel out old tenon, cut new mortise into girt. — Jack girt back up.

3 Drive new hardwood tenon into mortise. — Bore new peg holes. — Reuse peg holes.

Joinery for beam repair

When sistering or steel repair plates are not viable because the beams are exposed, a tension scarf joint or a tension/bending scarf joint may be worth the trouble and will certainly add an aesthetic appeal to the repair, especially when the only other alternative is to replace the damaged timber entirely, which involves removing a lot more floor and ceiling. Scarf joints are especially practical if only the last few feet of an otherwise sound long beam are rotted or damaged.

Tension scarfs are used to join beams that must resist pulling forces only, such as an end-wall girt or a rafter collar tie. As shown in the drawing at right, the wooden key locks the joint and prevents it from pulling apart. A scarf designed to resist both pulling and loading (tension and bending stresses) must be cut accurately, which is awkward with an existing beam, even if enough surrounding flooring and ceiling is removed to facilitate access. Make a template to transfer the cut lines of the scarf in the existing beam to the new replacement section.

Scarf joints can also be used to splice a new end onto a rotted girt where it was formerly tenoned into a post. If only the tenon itself has rotted or broken, drill and chisel out the old tenon from the opposite side of the post and drive a new double tenon through it into a mortise also cut

Tension Scarf Joint for Wood Beams

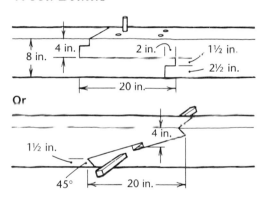

8 in. | 4 in. | 2 in. | 1½ in. | 2½ in. | 20 in.

Or

1½ in. | 4 in. | 45° | 20 in.

Tension/bending scarf

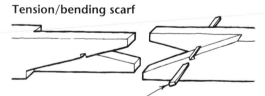

Tapered pegs driven from opposite sides

into the girt. Pin it in place as shown in the drawing at top. Since you probably can't move the post or the girt to the side, cutting this mortise is quite a job. Except where absolutely necessary, I'd try to avoid these kinds of repairs.

Repairing Rotted Rafter-Plate Junction

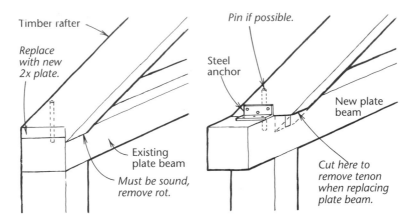

Timber rafter

Replace with new 2x plate.

Existing plate beam

Must be sound, remove rot.

Pin if possible.

Steel anchor

New plate beam

Cut here to remove tenon when replacing plate beam.

The junction of the rafters and the top of the wall (the rafter plate beam) is particularly prone to decay. Water backing up under the shingles from melting ice dams at the eaves, or running down the rafters from leaky roofing materials, pools on top of the beam, especially where the rafters are mortised or nailed to it. As the plate rots away from the rafters, the roof begins to shove out and downward. If the rot is not too severe the rafters can be notched to fit a new 2x plate nailed on top of the existing plate, as shown at left in the drawing above. Because timber rafters are usually notched into a mortise cut into the top face of the plate, the notch to accept the sistered plate need not be very deep, nor will the existing pegs have to be cut or the rafters lifted or moved.

It's another story if the plate has deteriorated beyond this simple repair. To replace the entire plate, the rafters must be supported to relieve the load on the beam. Fortunately, most roofs have collar ties between the upper portions of rafter pairs. It's a simple matter to insert a 6x6 jacking timber under the collar ties and post to the floor.

If collar ties are missing, the rafters can be supported by nailing a 2x4 ledger directly to their underside. Lengths of 2x6 jammed between this ledger and the floor prevent the roof from slipping outward. In either case, once the rafters and roof load are supported, the plate (or the rotted portions of it) are cut into sections between each rafter and pried free of the sheathing boards that are nailed to it. The nails or tenons that join any studs or posts to the underside of the plate are likewise sawn through. The remaining sections of beam actually pinned to the rafters can then be split apart with a chisel and the pegs salvaged for ornamental use.

Take care not to damage the framing for the underside of the cornice boards (the soffit) if it, too, is nailed into the face of the plate. It won't be possible to renail it (there's no room to swing a hammer), but the cornice can be secured by toenails from the outside. Since the new plate must slide straight into place between the tops of the posts and studs and the underside of the rafter, there's no room to lift it up and therefore no reason to cut mortises in the top of the replacement beam. Instead, cut a level seat just as you would for conventional rafters across the bottom of each rafter notch to accept the square edge of the plate. Join the reshaped rafters to the plate with steel framing anchors, as shown at right in the drawing on the facing page.

Truing Up the House Frame

The foundation is firm, the sills are solid and the floors are more or less level, but the roof may still sag and the walls push out into an odd parallelogram. Missing knee braces, broken joints, cracked timbers or inadequate framing will permit the house to rack under its own weight (dead load), the weight of its inhabitants and furnishings (live load), and in reaction to any forces acting upon it, such as wind and snow loads.

Although the visible tilt of the walls may have originated in a settled foundation or sill, it doesn't follow that restoring the base of the house to level will realign the rest of the frame. The pegged mortise-and-tenon joints of a timber frame are much stronger than the nailed joints of a stud frame, but any joint is still the weakest part of the overall structure. As a frame shifts or settles, its joints may be stressed past their strength. This is especially true across the relatively small cross-sectional areas where the knee braces are inserted into girts and sills, or at the corner post/ girt mortise mentioned earlier.

When a knee-brace peg shears under stress, the brace becomes unhinged, allowing the post it anchors to move in reaction to that stress, pulling a part of the house along with it. Braces also pull apart when their ends rot. A leaking roof that has caused a corner post to rot at the plate or girt also causes the walls to lean outward as the house pulls apart under the weight of the roof. Sometimes there simply aren't enough knee braces in the first place. Early housewrights weren't necessarily any more conscientious than contemporary builders. But even the best frames were hard pressed to withstand the "improvements" wrought by subsequent genera-

tions of slipshod, haphazard remodelers. I've seen more than one major girt cut through to house a chimney or stairwell.

Houses tilt in the plane of the gable end, the plane of the roof-bearing walls or in both directions at once. An eyeball level suffices to tell which. The outward lean of a gable wall is almost always attributed to brace failure (as a result of foundation settlement or whatever). But "swayback" (the outward tilt of the roof-bearing walls that pulls the ridgeline down in the center) can occur even without foundation or sill settlement. This usually happens when the collar ties (beams that stiffen the rafters and resist the outward thrust of the roof) are missing or inadequate.

Missing collar ties or undersized rafters are also the reason for dips in the plane of the roof along the run of the rafters. Over time, the downward/outward thrust of the roof can shear the joints between chimney girts and center posts or floor joists and wall studs. Like a pair of dividers, the angle increases with the spread. However charming this swayback ridge may seem, it's a symptom of an ultimately fatal structural defect. If uncorrected, the frame will become so unstable that a heavy snow, a thaw and rain, then more snow, will burst the walls apart, collapsing the house under the weight of its own roof. Straightening the sag in a roof is really no different from leveling a floor. The loads are a little lighter, but the principles are the same.

Correcting leaning walls and swayback roofs

Pulling skewed walls back into true alignment can sometimes be done with the aid of a come-along. The heaviest-duty puller sold in discount and hardware stores is probably rated at 2 tons, which is not usually powerful enough to pull a house together unless it has been stripped down to the bare frame. Much heavier pullers are sometimes available from equipment-rental centers. You might even be able to borrow one from a commercial steel rigger. In addition to the come-along itself,

Pulling Crooked Walls Together

How the come-along pulls the house together

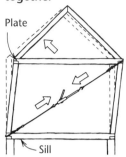

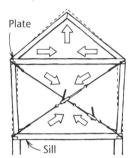

Use two come-alongs if one isn't enough.

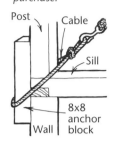

If sill moves before plate, use anchor block to provide more stable purchase.

you'll need lengths of ¼-in. to ½-in. dia. steel cable fitted with thimbles or grab and slip hooks, and an assortment of slings and chains with hooks and shackle bolts to do the actual pulling.

To pull in leaning walls, hook a sling or one end of a cable or chain around the rafter plate alongside a girt. The other end of the cable is hooked to the pulling tool. This in turn is hitched to another length of cable that is attached to a sling hooked around the sill or post. Remove or drill through sheathing boards as needed to allow the cable to pass through the wall. As you begin to pull, the plate may move without the wall following, which means that the post is no longer connected to the beam. In this case, attach a short length of timber over the joint between the plate and post so they both pull together.

As the tension increases, the house should start to pull together with a great groaning and creaking. The roof will rise with a heavy shrug. Or perhaps the come-along will reach its limit without any appreciable movement at all. Rather than risk decapitation from the whiplash of a snapped cable, try pulling with two come-alongs fastened from each plate to the base of the post or sill diagonally opposite. As

you begin pulling, watch to see which moves first, the plate or the sill. If the sill moves, you'll need a more stable purchase, such as an 8x8 timber slipped under the sling against the foundation wall and up over the sill and corner post.

Even the increased leverage of two come-alongs by themselves may not be enough to pull the house together. Lifting the ridge beam while simultaneously pulling in the wall plates will ease the load on the come-alongs. The support for this jacking must be continuous down to the basement. Begin directly over a girder post and install a jack and lifting post between the first floor and the ceiling joists or girt. Then add another jack and lifting post from the attic floor to the underside of the ridge beam. Use a jacking timber under the rafter peaks if a solid ridge beam is lacking. Jacking from the attic floor to the ridge without continuous support down through will only work against the lifting force trying to pull in the walls. Sometimes, jacking the ridge by itself will pull the walls in without further effort, especially with a balloon-framed house. It's also the best way to straighten out a sagging cathedral ceiling.

Handier than a come-along, and capable of immense pulling power, turnbuckles are excellent tools for straightening a leaning frame. Unfortunately, since they aren't commercially available, they'll have to be custom-made at a welding shop, which could be costly. You can order a heavy-duty turnbuckle that will accept ¾-in. or 1-in. dia. threaded steel rods 2 ft. to 3 ft. long with a hook eye or grab hook welded to each end for attaching a pulling chain.

As an alternative to the sling and come-along, use a heavy-duty eyebolt threaded into a nut welded to a flat 8x8 ½-in. steel plate. It's a simple matter of boring a hole through the plate beams to attach a pulling chain and turnbuckle. Take up the slack in the chain or cable, insert a steel bar into the shackle eyes of the turnbuckle ends to prevent the cables from twisting (or use a swivel connector), and with a third bar, begin turning the center of the turnbuckle. Between the jacks lifting the ridge and this turnbuckle pulling in the plates, it's almost impossible not to true up a frame. If you make up four or more turnbuckles, it's possible to pull the whole house in at once, working each turnbuckle gradually tighter.

Turnbuckles can also be used as a permanent repair where girts have pulled apart, or in place of collar beams for cathedral ceilings. Here the rods are threaded at both ends (one end must be reverse-threaded) and made long enough to reach from the turnbuckle itself through the plate beam and the nut of the washer plate. As the walls are drawn together and open joints close, the threaded ends of the rods begin to project past the washer. These can be sawn off with a hacksaw. Turnbuckles such as these are often used to repair or relieve the strain on barn timbers. If attractively finished, they are not an unpleasing design element for open ceiling spaces. They can also be hidden within dummy beams or on top of an existing beam. Turnbuckles will also hold the walls together until a girt beam can be lagged to the posts with angle irons.

A plumb bob hung from a string fastened to the top corner of the outside wall will show how far it needs to move in before it is plumb. So will a 4-ft. level and straightedge placed against the exposed studs or corner posts. After that section of wall is plumbed, nail temporary 2x4 knee braces between the upright posts and the sill, plate and/or girts to help maintain alignment until permanent knee braces are reinstalled, repaired, added, or bolted and nailed securely into place. It's a good idea to pull the walls in just past plumb to counteract their tendency to spring back when the tension is released. Pull along each major girt or wherever there is a serious bow. Leave 2x4 diagonal braces nailed to blocks on the floor if there is no provision for knee braces in the middle of the wall until the house settles into its new alignment. Otherwise, install permanent

Turnbuckles for Wall Pulling

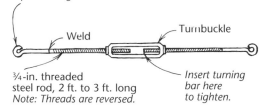

Pulling chain attaches to hook eye with clevis pin, slip hook or grab hook.

Weld — Turnbuckle

¾-in. threaded steel rod, 2 ft. to 3 ft. long
Note: Threads are reversed.

Insert turning bar here to tighten.

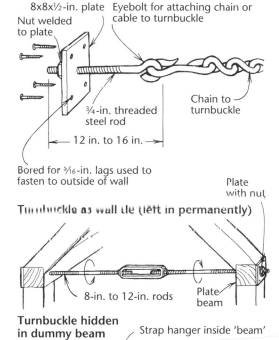

8x8x½-in. plate — Eyebolt for attaching chain or cable to turnbuckle
Nut welded to plate

¾-in. threaded steel rod

Chain to turnbuckle

|— 12 in. to 16 in. —|

Bored for ⁹⁄₁₆-in. lags used to fasten to outside of wall

Turnbuckle as wall tie (left in permanently)

Plate with nut

8-in. to 12-in. rods
Plate beam

Turnbuckle hidden in dummy beam

Strap hanger inside 'beam'

let-in diagonal braces in any interior partitions that abut these long walls. Stairwell walls are a good place to add such bracing. Incorporate some interior partitions into your remodeling if none exist to help brace the frame.

The rafters should be stiffened to relieve their outward thrust on the plates before releasing the come-alongs or turnbuckles. Collar ties are normally nailed

128

These undersized, overspaced rafters were stiffened by sistering and adding plywood gussets at the peak.

Before the collar ties or gussets can be installed, straighten out any sags in the rafters. This may require no more than a length of 2x4 jammed up under the midspan of a dimension-lumber rafter. Or it may call for a jack and post under each side of a timber rafter pair. It's best to support as many rafter pairs as possible with jacking timbers installed under both sides of the roof. Of course, posts and jacks should rest on planks laid perpendicular to the run of the floor joists. Use a string on blocks stretched along the run of each rafter, or even better, across the length of the roof, to find the required amount of lift. Give the rafters a good crown.

Since collar ties by themselves cannot compensate for undersized rafters or over-wide spans, the cure is to sister new, wider rafter stock alongside the old or to add another rafter between the rafters wherever the span is greater than 2 ft. on center. Many old houses were framed with pole rafters set on 32-in. or even 48-in. centers. Adding a rafter in the spans and alongside each irregular pole rafter not only stiffens the roof but also simplifies attic ceiling finish and insulation, should that be part of the plan. An alternative to sistering that will also stiffen sagging rafters is to add a kneewall under the bottom third of the rafter span, thus effectively shortening the total span, before installing the collar ties. The dead space in the triangle behind this wall can be used for storage.

Not all walls lean outward, away from each other. Sometimes rafter walls will lean in the same direction, like a parallelogram. Gable walls can't lean any other way, except if the center of the wall at floor level were to push outward, which could happen in unusual circumstances that cause the end-wall girt to rot out or the summer beams to push apart at the middle of the house. Although it is possible to pull in an outward-leaning wall with a single diagonally installed come-along working inside the house (see p. 126), it's usually much easier to straighten the house from the outside. Gable walls,

across each rafter pair at two-thirds of the distance along the rafter run from plate to peak. These also provide nailers for attaching an attic ceiling. Exposed collar ties should be joined to timber rafters by a half-lap dovetail notch. When the roof pitch is too shallow or the ceiling span too narrow to allow much usable space under standard collar ties, rafter spread can be prevented by installing plywood gussets across the peak of the rafters. Use ¾-in. CDX plywood, fastened with waterproof truss glue and drywall screws on both sides of the rafter pair. Notch the gusset to fit around any ridge beam. Fill the bottom edge of the gap between the gussets with solid wood to provide support for ceiling nailers.

which carry relatively little weight and are perpendicular to the main framing members, should straighten with little difficulty. Rafter-plate walls ordinarily require considerably more persuasion.

Plumbing the wall may require no more effort than installing a jacking post diagonally from the rafter plate to timber pads set against a sloped cut in the earth. Use a screw jack; hydraulic jacks don't work horizontally. Likewise, a come-along chained to the base of a convenient large tree may provide a firm anchor. If there are no suitable trees, a tractor may provide enough pulling power to move the frame. Or, then again, you may only succeed in tilting the tractor or making big ruts in your lawn. Bulldozers or log skidders equipped with winches usually have the horsepower and weight to provide both a firm anchor and a strong pull. Also, the arm of a backhoe can exert a tremendous amount of pushing force, often more than enough to straighten out a leaning frame. Protect the exterior finish by placing a plank between the hoe and the walls.

Pushing is more effective than pulling. In any case, truing up a house frame is easiest when the house has been stripped to the bare frame. If the inside walls are left intact, a lot of plaster will crack when things begin to move, and a lot more inertia will have to be overcome. Whatever method you employ, be careful to push, pull or lift slowly, as chimneys and fireplaces can crack or windows rupture with explosive force if they are subjected to twisting forces or sudden shock. Leveling and truing a house will of course necessitate refitting doors and windows.

One other minor, but not to be ignored, cause of localized ceiling, floor or roof sags is the presence of a half-chimney. Some old houses have more than a few of these, usually on the second floor where they once vented individual bedroom heating stoves or a run of stovepipe from the floors below that was intended to act as a room radiator. The plastered and wall-papered brickwork typically begins on a platform framed of heavy planks just far enough below the ceiling to admit the stovepipe thimble (the space beneath is used for a small closet or shelving) and extends up through the attic and roof. These chimneys invariably leak creosote all over the walls and floors, and, over time, cause the floor under them to sag. The best solution is demolition. Any future chimney should extend all the way to a footing in the basement.

Truing and leveling a house are a great deal of trouble. There is a point of diminishing returns. My advice is, if the walls lean only a few inches, learn to live with them. By all means add braces and collar ties, level or firm up the foundation, but don't try to push too hard. When a timber has been in place for a long time, it has taken on whatever shape it needed to stay there. Like old bones, old timbers don't spring back very well. They may break before they will bend. Sometimes, no amount of lifting or pulling force will persuade a beam to budge. You might move the entire wall in a foot or more and not materially affect the shape of a warped beam. It will stay where it wants to.

I'm not particularly bothered by a house that leans in odd directions. As long as the foundation is solid and the frame well braced, it isn't going anywhere. There is something to be said for the delight of skewed walls and corners that meet in another dimension. It's like living in an M.C. Escher print. Once a house has settled into a comfortable shape, it requires unnatural energy to realign it. Those who feel that the music of the spheres is played on symmetrical strings can pursue the perfection of form and the correction of corners. For myself, I remember the old Chinese saying that only demons travel in straight lines.

The Roof

No roof—no building.

—James H. Acland, *Medieval Structure: The Gothic Vault* (Toronto: University of Toronto Press, 1972)

An asphalt-shingle roof is relatively cheap and easy to install. The band of metal along the eaves prevents water from ice dams from backing up under the lower courses of shingles.

*S*ince the day the first man or woman crawled under an overhanging ledge, creating shelter has entailed the attempt to keep a roof over our heads. Foundation and walls, posts and beams are only the handle of the umbrella.

Roofing Materials

The type of repairs you make to the roof of your old house will depend on the materials that were used to build it and on your knowledge of how to work with them.

Wood

The early colonists soon found that the thatched roofs of their homelands couldn't hold up to the severe storms and heavy snowfalls of North America. Fortunately a superlative substitute was growing in the surrounding forests. Although metal, clay and slate were used successfully in some regions, the wood shingle was by far the most popular roofing material used in the United States until asphalt composition shingles became widely available toward the end of the 19th century.

The earliest shingles were made from bolts split from 2 ft. sections of straight-grained white oak, pine and cedar that were then riven with a mallet and froe into inch-thick shakes. These were held in a combination vise/stool (a "shingle horse" or "shave horse") and tapered with a drawknife to make a shingle. Thus the modern "resawn" wood shingle, made by machine since 1850, is a much more authentic version of early roofing than the hand-split shakes (indigenous only to the Northwest) used by some misguided restorationists attempting to mimic Colonial styles. This is a good thing, since shakes cost a lot more, are harder to install and are more prone to leaks than ordinary wood shingles.

Wood shingles today are manufactured in four grades from Eastern white and Western red cedar, although cypress and red-wood are used where locally plentiful. All these woods have a natural resistance to rot owing to their high resin content, but only the best extra-clear grade is suitable for roofing. When properly applied, wood shingles make a durable, handsome roof. The wood mellows to a soft silver, and as time passes, the roof is adorned with a living tapestry of moss and lichen (these don't affect the tightness of the roof).

The high cost of a wood-shingle roof (four to five times greater than for an asphalt roof), although offset somewhat by its longevity (an average life of 40 years for slopes up to 8-in-12 and 60 years for steeper pitches vs. 20 years for asphalt), contributed to its decline. Because wood shingles are a potential fire hazard, zoning codes in some communities actually prohibit their use; in rural areas, fire-insurance premiums are higher for buildings with wood roofs.

Slate

Slate is fireproof, attractive and durable, capable of lasting for centuries. It was a popular 19th-century roofing material, at least in regions with access to a quarry. Because several colors and patterns could be mixed together, slate roofing complemented the fanciful ornamentation of the Victorian style. But even then, when labor and materials were far less costly than today, a slate roof was an indication of a householder's prosperity. Roofing slates were expensive to quarry, transport and install, and, because of their weight, required heavier roof framing, at least on lower-pitched roofs. Today, thanks to a strong demand for upscale renovation, the almost moribund craft of slating is undergoing a renaissance. It's once again possible to find roofers with the knowledge and skill to repair or install slate. Some quarries have begun producing roofing slate again on a special-order basis. The high price has created a strong demand for the more affordable second-hand slates salvaged from demolished buildings.

Metal

Metal is one of the oldest, most durable roofing materials. The copper and lead roofs of some European buildings are still leak-free after 800 years. But the great expense of these metals confines their use to public buildings and the mansions of the wealthy. The invention of galvanization, which made it possible to protect steel from rust without resorting to expensive alloys, along with the expansion of mass production and distribution systems, made cheap sheet steel an extremely widespread choice for roofing commercial buildings, barns and rural homes from the post-Civil War period up to the present. Metal roofing is economical to ship over large distances. Its light weight and availability in large sheets (which could be laid over open purlins instead of solid decking) made it simple, fast and inexpensive to install, which is perhaps one of the reasons why corrugated steel roofing is characteristic of third-world countries and poor rural housing.

Today, galvanized steel-sheet roofing is manufactured in a wide variety of patterns, none of which is likely to match the style of the old roofing on your house. Fortunately, because of its durability, usable second-hand steel roofing is fairly common and inexpensive in many rural areas. Chances are you'll have no trouble finding a few sheets of a matching pattern for repairing your roof.

New 26-gauge and 28-gauge roofing comes in stock lengths of up to 24 ft., with varying amounts of zinc coating. The more zinc, the longer the life. Two ounces per square foot is considered heavy enough for roofing. But even the best-grade zinc coating wears off in about 30 years, exposing the bare steel, which soon rusts and must be kept painted if it is to last. With proper care, a steel roof can last indefinitely. There is also a premium-grade steel roofing, which features a baked-enamel epoxy finish in a variety of colors. It requires no future painting or upkeep.

Steel roofing is popular in the South because its light weight requires minimal roof framing. In the North, it is preferred for its ability to shed snow. Using steel is also a fast and easy way to reroof over old shingles without adding a lot of weight or disturbing the existing roof. But there are some disadvantages to this seemingly ideal material. Because the long vertical seams tend to siphon water, steel roofing can leak if used on roof pitches shallower than 4-in-12. When used over heated spaces such as a house, special precautions must be taken to prevent condensation of water vapor on the bitter cold underside of the sheets. Since this typically means the installation of a vented roof over solid sheathing, the cost and labor savings are less attractive. The biggest drawback is aesthetic. It's fiendishly difficult to cut steel roofing to fit neatly and tightly to valleys, hips, complex roofs and projections. A casual inspection of some local roofs will verify the truth of this observation. But for simple gable roofs like the Cape-style farmhouse, sheet-steel roofing was and is a good (and authentic) alternative to asphalt shingles.

Terne metal (tin) is another traditional material coming back into vogue. A copper-bearing steel coated with a tin/lead alloy, terne-metal roofing enjoyed a brief but intense popularity in the last 20 years of the 1800s, just before asphalt shingles took hold. Its durability is confirmed by the many tin roofs that have survived to this day. If it is kept painted, a terne-metal roof will easily last a century or more.

Terne metal was used in two different ways. Square sheets, soldered together on all four edges (with hidden nails under the flange of the solder joints), were laid over low-pitched roofs, such as porches, to form an absolutely watertight seal. Because the sheets could be cut to odd angles, this kind of roofing was ideal for protecting the elaborately curved roofs of Victorian verandas. You can find these squares under several layers of asphalt coating on many an old porch roof today.

Terne metal was also used to form the standing-seam roof. In this application, 16-in. wide, 6-ft. long sheets of metal called "pans" were soldered together at top and bottom and joined at their sides by an ingenious waterproof joint (the standing seam). Such roofs, painted red, green, silver or black, are a prominent feature in most small towns and country villages. Because these roofs are completely watertight and very handsome, contemporary architects have begun to specify standing-seam roofs for their clients. This, in turn, has made it easier to find a distributor who carries the material.

Terne metal is sold in various grades according to the weight of the tin-alloy coating. For some reason, the standard measurement is based on a "box" containing 112 pieces of 20-in. by 28-in. sheets (436 sq. ft.) weighing 40 lb. It's also sold in 50-ft. seamless rolls. No matter which weight and grade you select, terne metal is still a very expensive material. And it's not cheap to install either. Because it requires skilled craftsmen who use highly specialized tools, a standing-seam roof is something even most professional roofers leave to experts. A real "tin man," like the slater and plasterer, is a formerly endangered species on the verge of a comeback.

Its distinctive profile, longevity, unsurpassed watertightness and expense puts the standing-seam roof in a class of its own.

Although not widely used for roofing, cement-asbestos shingles were frequently applied over siding in the 1940s.

Cement-asbestos shingles

Cement-asbestos shingles, which are good for 50 or more years, share slate's immunity to rot, decay, fire and weather, at a much more reasonable cost, but they have never gained wide use in roofing. Produced from the turn of the century until the end of World War II, this brittle, dull-grey poor-man's slate was heavier and harder to install than asphalt shingles and lacked the pleasing appearance of its prototype. (This material did achieve some success as a low-maintenance siding installed over old wood clapboards.)

Fortunately, cement-asbestos shingles went out of style long before concern over the toxic effects of asbestos prohibited their use. Many towns rightly require special permits and protective measures for their removal and disposal. If your house has cement-asbestos roofing or siding, check with the local office of the EPA before you renovate.

Asbestos-free cement roofing and tile roofing

Asbestos-free cement roofing came on the market during the 1970s, and is finding a niche in commercial structures and luxury housing. Modern cement roofing tiles are much lighter, more colorful, more pleasingly textured and more durable than their cement-asbestos forebears. These desirable qualities make them a logical alternative to natural slate roofing.

Pitch Limits Choice of Roofing Materials

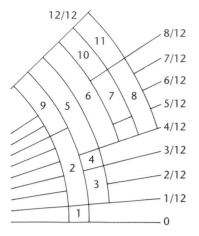

1. Built-up roofing, hot tar
2. Roll roofing
3. Soldered-seam metal
4. Asphalt shingles with waterproof underlayment
5. Standing-seam and corrugated or ribbed metal
6. Asphalt shingles
7. Wood shingles with 5-in. exposure
8. Slate with extra framing
9. Wood shakes with 5-in. exposure, wood shingles with 7-in. exposure
10. Wood shakes with 7-in. exposure
11. Slate with ordinary framing

The same is true for modern ceramic-tile roofing. Although popularly associated with the haciendas of the Spanish Southwest, clay roofing, in both traditional cylindrical and flat tiles, was used throughout this country from the earliest Colonial times up until the 1830s, at which point it went out of style everywhere but in the Sunbelt states. Although lighter and cheaper than slate, its sheer bulkiness may have contributed to its fall from fashion. Traditional tiles appear out of scale on homes less substantial than the fortress-like adobe houses of the Southwest.

Asphalt roofing

Asphalt first made its appearance around the middle of the 19th century as "composition" roofing, a layer of tar-soaked cloth, felt or paper intended as a watertight covering for the flat-roofed urban buildings that were becoming fashionable at that time. A five-layer sandwich of "composition" (tar paper) and hot tar forms the built-up gravel-surfaced membrane still used on flat roofs today. Other than minor repairs, resurfacing such a roof is a job best left to professionals, who have the equipment to boil tar and pump or lift it to the roof.

Roll roofing

During the last quarter of the 19th century, smooth-surfaced (60-lb.) and mineral-surfaced (90-lb.) roll roofing were promoted as modern, convenient, labor- and cost-saving alternatives to traditional wood and slate shingles. Although roll roofing is certainly fast and easy to apply, it also has a short life span (5 to 10 years). It's hard to believe anyone would find it attractive. Fortunately, asphalt-composition shingles were invented before roll roofing caught on. Today, other than for the poorest shacks, sheds and old factory buildings, roll roofing is used almost exclusively as a liner for valleys and for covering low-pitched roofs (slopes between 1-in-12 and 3-in-12) where it won't be seen from the ground. (The drawing at left shows which roofing materials are appropriate for different roof slopes.) "Built-up" roofing, a sandwich of smooth-surfaced roll roofing, asphalt-saturated felts and hot tar, coated with gravel, is used for covering perfectly flat roofs.

Asphalt-composition shingles

As you walk down a city street and look at the roofs of the houses, you will observe a variety of shingle types and patterns. The older-style shingles are getting scarcer by the day as they reach the end of their useful life—very few distributors carry them. There are areas of the country where a particular shingle style may have lingered longer than others. The old mill towns of the industrial Northeast, for example, seem especially rich in unusual shingle styles. Sadly, as roofs wear out, there's seldom any choice but to replace them with standard contemporary styles.

The modern asphalt-composition mineral-surfaced shingle is one of the truly significant contributions of technology to building. Although relatively short-lived (15 to 25 years is the average useful life), the shingles are cheap and simple to install, provide a reasonably tight seal and are available in colors, textures and patterns that can enhance just about any house. The traditionalist may object to asphalt shingles in favor of wood, slate or standing-seam roofing, but for most of us, architectural fidelity must take second place to economic reality. Besides, asphalt shingles have been around long enough to become familiar. They seem at home with just about any architectural style or period.

Today, choice is limited to three basic types. The most common is the three-tab strip shingle. The overlapping cutouts with their vertical accent suggest the slates on which they were modeled. A variation on the three-tab shingle is the random-

Hex-lock shingles are one of the few older shingle styles that seem to be on the verge of a comeback. Since they tend to conceal irregularities in the roof surface, they are well suited for reroofing over existing shingles.

Common and Obsolete Asphalt Roofing Materials

Roll roofing

'Tar paper' (asphalt-saturated felt)	'Smooth' roll (valley and roll underlayment)	Mineral-surfaced roll	'Half-lap' (double-coverage 19-in. selvage roll)	Edge or valley roll (mineral-surfaced)
15 lb. to 30 lb. per 100 sq. ft.	45 lb. to 65 lb. per 100 sq. ft.	90 lb. per 100 sq. ft.	60 lb. per 100 sq. ft.	45 lb. per 100 sq. ft.

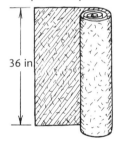
36 in.

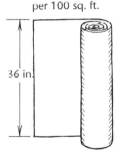
36 in.

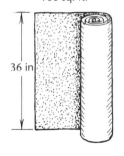
36 in.

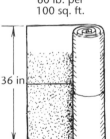
36 in.

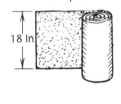
18 in.

Common shingles

3-tab strip shingle	Self-aligning jet shingle	Architect shingle (wood-shake effect)	Lock-tab shingle
235 lb. to 300 lb. per 100 sq. ft.	235 lb. per 100 sq. ft.	325 lb. per 100 sq. ft.	180 lb. to 235 lb. per 100 sq. ft.

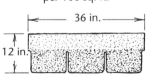
36 in. · 12 in.

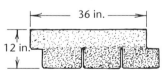
36 in. · 12 in.

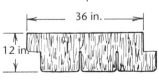
36 in. · 12 in.

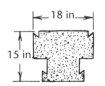
18 in. · 15 in.

Obsolete shingles

Giant individual American	Giant individual Dutch lap	Single-tab hex-lock	3-tab hex-lap
330 lb. per 100 sq. ft.	165 lb. per 100 sq. ft.	145 lb. per 100 sq. ft.	195 lb. per 100 sq. ft.

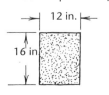
12 in. · 16 in.

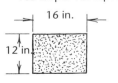
16 in. · 12 in.

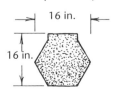
16 in. · 16 in.

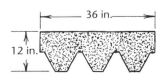
36 in. · 12 in.

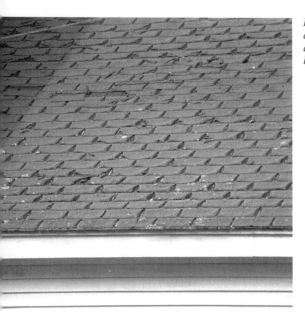

Even without the exaggeration caused by wear, the cutouts of the three-tab asphalt shingle (left) create a strong vertical shadowline. By contrast, because jet asphalt shingles (below) lack any discernible cutout, their lines emphasize the horizontal.

The reinforced corrugated asphalt roofing sheet has not yet gained wide acceptance for residential use.

embossed strip shingle, or jet shingle. Because their self-aligning design allows them to be installed faster than ordinary strip shingles, jet shingles are widely used in new construction. They are stylistically more suitable to ranch-style tract houses than to old houses, as their strong horizontal lines seem to emphasize every hump and sag in the roof deck.

The architect shingle combines the speedy application of jet shingles with the random pattern and raised profile of wood shingles. This premium shingle, which costs about as much as real wood shingles

(although much less labor-intensive to install), is best applied to steep-pitched roofs, where its rich texture can be "read" from the ground to best advantage. Because it consists of two layers at the weather exposure, it has the longest warranty of any asphalt shingle. Three-tab shingles and jet shingles are also available in a heavy-weight grade with a thicker layer of mineral (crushed slate) for longer wear.

All three styles of shingles have a layer of thermoplastic cement on the underside that glues the courses together and greatly increases their resistance to wind. Because ordinary asphalt shingles use an organic (cloth, fiber or felt) base, as the asphalt dries out over time these shingles tend to wick up water and slowly rot. Shingles made with fiberglass mats are impervious to decay and much more fire resistant. They cost a bit more and last about five years longer than comparable organic shingles. They also are extremely brittle in cold weather, which makes them a poor choice for Northern climates.

Except in urban areas, where it is still used, the lock-tab shingle, which once enjoyed great popularity because of its resistance to wind, seems to be in danger of extinction. It was ideally suited for re-

The venerable lock-tab shingle is easy to install, interesting looking and designed for reroofing. Unfortunately, it is no longer available in many parts of the country.

roofing over existing shingles, since the old pattern didn't show through as much as with strip shingles. It's also one of the easiest patterns to apply.

The giant individual and hex-lock shingles are asphalt copies of the slate patterns that they were designed to replace. These shingles were often laid directly over the old slates. Now these formerly ubiquitous styles are fossils, unearthed when stripping off layers of old shingles prior to reroofing. But who knows? A revival of the giant individual Dutch lap shingle may only be waiting for the next wave of gentrification.

Onduline®, a fiber-reinforced corrugated asphalt sheet originally developed for roofing pole barns and industrial structures, is a good alternative to corrugated steel roofing. It is colorful, durable and easy to install.

Roofing Repairs

Because water flows downhill, a roof works like the scales of a fish or the feathers of a bird—in one direction only. If the integrity of the lattice is broken, water can work inward under the shingles, through the sheathing and into the house, where things start to rot.

Finding a leak

Before you can fix a leak, you've got to find it. Obvious leaks can be located by visual inspection if you know where and when to look and what to look for. Water running down the inside of a wall in the winter is usually caused by an ice dam. Water dripping from the soffit boards of a cornice or behind the fascia suggests a problem with the roof overhang or eave. Since the source of the leak may not always be directly above a dripping ceiling or light fixture, the best time to find a leak is during a rainstorm.

Take a flashlight up into the attic. Starting in the general vicinity of the wet spot, see if you can pinpoint the leak. You may have to pull up wet insulation and trace along rafters or sheathing boards to find it. Try to correlate the leak with an established landmark, such as a vent pipe, chimney or dormer wall, so you can locate it on the roof after it has dried off. Don't walk on asphalt roofing in hot weather—the shingles become soft enough to tear or smear under your heel. When walking on slate, tile or cement roofs, prevent cracking by distributing your weight across at least two shingles.

Causes of leaks

Cracked, broken, missing or worn-out shingles are only one of the more unmistakable causes of roof leaks. When any of these conditions exposes the wood decking or the nails and top portions of the underlying shingles, a leak is all but guaranteed. Exposure to the weather will eventually dry out asphalt and tar coatings, causing them to crack, blister and break. In the North, overzealous attempts to remove ice and snow buildup at the eaves with shovels and axes are a common cause of leaks. Shingles are also damaged by storm-tossed branches and unwarranted traffic on the roof.

Heat and cold cause wood framing, metal flashing, caulking, brickwork and roofing materials to expand and contract at different rates. The house settles faster than the chimney. Over the years, all this movement pulls apart joints and cracks seals between walls and roofing, flashing and vents, or chimney and other roof projections. Flashings in particular can prove troublesome. Leaks occur when flashing cement and caulkings crack or dry out around vents and ventilators, chimneys, skylights and end walls. Flashing metal, especially aluminum and galvanized or painted steel, rusts or corrodes in the most awkward places. Metal valleys also have a tendency to split or separate at seams. An often overlooked source of a perplexing leak is a crack in the joint between the flue tile and the chimney cap, or even a crack in the cap itself.

Sometimes leaks occur only when the wind blows from a particular direction or with a special ferocity. This was a persistent problem with three-tab shingles until the invention of the Windseal® shingle. (A thermoplastic cement strip factory-applied across the backs of the shingles glues them together when installed.) The shingle edges would blow upward, allowing water to enter underneath. When this happens with slate and wood shingles or modern wind-resistant asphalt roofing, the problem can usually be traced to faulty workmanship or an inappropriate choice of materials.

Looking back at the drawing on p. 134, you can see that not all roofing materials are suitable for all pitches. Some materials, such as wood and slate, require installation of a layer of asphalt-felt underlayment between courses, which incompetent or unscrupulous roofers may have omitted. Some corner cutters will roof with cheaper wood shingles intended for siding. The exposed knots and weaker grain soon cause these shingles to deform—and leak. Wood

shingles laid directly over a solid roof deck will also rot, because they need good air circulation to dry out between rains. The worst fault a roofer can commit, either through ignorance or greed, is to lay shingles with a greater weather exposure than recommended for the type of material and slope. Insufficient overlap between courses allows wind-driven rain to penetrate under the shingles. The only cure is to tear off the entire roof and reinstall it properly.

Roof repair depends both upon the type of roofing and the kind of damage. Some of the more common problems you might encounter, and their repairs, are described here for each kind of roofing you might expect to find on an old house.

Repairing built-up roofing
The only effective large-scale repair of built-up roofs is total removal and replacement, which is a job best left to professionals. However, it's relatively easy for the amateur roofer to patch small splits and cracks. Built-up roofing most often cracks and leaks at the bend in the roof where it meets the wall flashing. The metal curb flashing also tends to separate from the underlying roofing.

To repair a crack or hole less than 2 in. in diameter, begin by brushing dirt, rocks and gravel away from the damaged area at least 6 in. in all directions. Next, wipe the brushed area clean with a rag soaked in paint thinner or kerosene and allow to dry. Trowel fiber-reinforced asphalt cement ("flashing" cement as distinguished from the lighter, runnier "cold" cement used to glue down roll roofing) into the wound and over the surrounding area at least 3 in. on all sides. (A narrow split of wood shingle trimmed across its end is an ideal applicator.) Then sprinkle gravel and rocks over the surface. If applying cement in cold weather, preheat the can by leaving it in a warm place overnight.

If water has soaked into the wood and roofing material, it may be too wet to bond to the flashing cement. Use a water-

Replacing a Damaged Asphalt Shingle

A broken or missing shingle leaves the unprotected underlying shingle vulnerable to rapid wear and leakage. Shingles are secured by two courses of nails. Use a flat prybar to remove the nails in both courses. Remove damaged shingle.

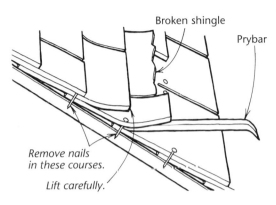

Broken shingle

Prybar

Remove nails in these courses.

Lift carefully.

If you break the tab of a previously undamaged shingle, coat the broken piece with flashing cement and face-nail it to the roof.

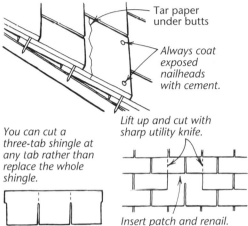

Tar paper under butts

Always coat exposed nailheads with cement.

You can cut a three-tab shingle at any tab rather than replace the whole shingle.

Lift up and cut with sharp utility knife.

Insert patch and renail.

soluble asphalt emulsion instead. This can be applied to wet surfaces, as long as it has 24 hours of dry weather to cure.

Sometimes one area of a built-up roof will be lower than the rest of the roof, causing a chronic puddle and possible leak. To repair the roof, level any depressions with a mixture of equal parts portland cement, water-emulsion asphalt and sand. After the mixture has dried, cover the surface and surrounding edges with flashing cement and embed a layer of 30-lb. tar paper in it. Then coat this layer with cold cement and put down a second layer of 60-lb. smooth-surfaced roofing. Coat this with cold cement and sprinkle gravel over it to complete the patch.

Sometimes, instead of cracking, the tar surface will blister. Some of these air- or water-filled swellings can be the size of pillows. As previously, begin by brushing away the dirt and gravel and cleaning the area with solvent. Then, with a hooked roofing knife, cut through the blisters, draining and wiping them clean. Force flashing cement under the skin of the blis-

ters and press them flat. Nail the edges of the cuts to the deck. Cut a patch of 60-lb. smooth roll roofing large enough to cover the entire area with a 2-in. overlap. Coat the area under the patch with flashing cement, press the patch into the cement and nail off its edges with nails spaced 2 in. apart and 1 in. in from the edges. Cover the nailheads with flashing cement. Then coat the entire patch with cold cement and replace the gravel and rocks.

Replacing asphalt shingles

Just before a roof is ready for replacement, the shingles will become brittle and begin to curl upward. Substantial amounts of the mineral surface will have eroded, exposing the mat below, which soon crumbles. Long before most of the shingles reach this terminal state, individual tabs will begin to crack or break.

In theory, replacing missing asphalt shingles is a fairly easy job. One simply lifts up the tab of the shingle above the missing course, inserts a prybar to loosen and pry out the nailheads, and removes the remains of the damaged shingle, or as many damaged shingles as necessary. The repair is completed by inserting new shingles and nailing them off. At least this is how the process works in the best of all possible worlds. But on real roofs, the old shingles tend to be so brittle that the tabs break into pieces as soon as you try to lift them. Sometimes even stepping on a roof will damage more shingles than you can fix. Contrary to the advice given earlier, it's best to fix old shingles on a hot day when they're more flexible. Most old roofs are too steep to walk on anyway, which means you'll be working from a ladder hooked over the ridge—all the more reason to wait until the shingles soften.

With any luck, the damaged shingles will be old enough to lack the Windseal® cement coating; otherwise, the tabs must be gradually pried apart, lest part of the tab remain stuck to the shingle below as you lift it. In cool weather, the thermoplastic cement will separate easily if given a quick snap, but the shingles tend to break also. If, despite your best efforts, you still break off the tabs of a previously undamaged shingle, don't throw the piece away. You've got to stop somewhere. Spread flashing cement over the exposed area and under the edge of the cracked shingle and bed the broken piece into the cement. If you need to, secure it to the roof with two roofing nails and butter the exposed nailheads with cement.

Replacing damaged ridge-cap shingles involves a similar ordeal. The only difference is that there is no way you can lift one ridge shingle without breaking it. In most cases, the shingles are already cracked along the peak of the ridge and should be coated with flashing cement in lieu of total replacement.

Shingle colors have changed remarkably little over the years. Although many new "earth tones" have been added, the same basic greens, reds, blacks and slate blends have been around forever. If you are lucky enough to discover the manufacturer of the shingles used on your roof (sometimes leftovers are in the attic or garage, or a scrap of old packaging is left under the shingles), the new shingles can, allowing for weathering, come very close to blending in.

Size, however, is a different story. For a few years back in the 1970s and early 1980s, manufacturers decided to switch to metric sizes. Standard three-tab shingles are 12 in. by 36 in. (each tab is thus 1 ft. square), with a 5-in. weather exposure. Not only is it a lot easier to lay out a roof with 1-ft. modules or 5-in. courses, but 39⅜-in. (1-meter) by 13⅛-in. (⅓-meter) shingles with 5⅝-in. (½-meter) exposures simply do not fit into 12-in. by 36-in. spaces. Fortunately, the manufacturers switched back after everyone complained loud enough. Nowadays you can get either kind. Be sure you know which kind you're buying before you start to patch the roof.

Repairing slate roofing
If slate is so durable, you may wonder, then why do so many slate roofs have missing or broken shingles? Why are we even discussing repairs? There are at least three reasons why slate roofs fail. The first has to do with installation. It might seem that installing slate shingles should not be any more difficult than wood shingles. But the difference and the difficulty lie in the fact that slates must be nailed to the roof deck exactly right.

If the nails are driven too tightly, the shingle will break, if not immediately, then at some time in the future when the nails contract with the cold and are pulled down into the slate. If nailed too loosely, the heads stick up and push against the overlying shingles, which eventually crack under the weight of snow and time. The choice of nails is important, too. Ordinary galvanized roofing nails will rust away long before the slate has even begun to weather. Solid copper nails are the only kind that will keep pace with slate. Just the same, the roofers may have used coated or even steel nails, resulting in a lot of loose or missing slates.

The second cause of slate-roof failure has to do with the nature of the material itself. Part of the reason slate roofing became so very expensive was that the highest quality and most easily quarried slate beds were exhausted fairly quickly. Lesser-quality slates tended to absorb water along their grain, which would freeze and thaw and eventually split apart the shingles. They were less dense and more prone to fracture, which made for a less durable roof. When using second-hand replacement slates, test them for soundness by tapping with a hammer. A solid slate will ring true, while a worn-out shingle will sound muted.

Finally, although the shingles themselves may have been perfectly installed and of high quality, the metal flashing used to line the valleys, eaves, ridges and hips might have been less durable. Not everyone could afford copper or lead. Galvanized steel and terne metal were used instead. Owing to the danger and difficulty of reaching often forbiddingly steep roofs, flashings weren't painted as often as they should have been. Once they rusted, water could work under the shingles and rot some of the decking. No longer held tightly by the nails, the shingles would be forced downward by the pressure of snow and wind. If the metal had been replaced at the right time, the shingles would still be intact.

Installing or repairing slate shingles requires several specialized tools. The first, and most important, is fairly easy to find at the local hardware or building-supply store. This is the "slater's hook," or, as it is sometimes called (when used for removing wood shingles) a "shingle thief." It's unlikely you'll find a slate cutter (which is the same as a ceramic-tile cutter, only larger) or a slater's stake, knife or hatchet locally. Fortunately, you can make do without these tools, at least for minor repairs. If you wish to buy them, one mail-order source is John Stortz & Sons, 210 Vine St., Philadelphia, PA 19106.

Replacing a Broken Slate

1. Grab nail with hook, then drive tool downward to cut the nail or pull it out.

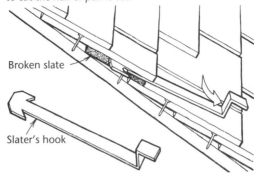

Broken slate

Slater's hook

2. Nail copper repair tab to underlying slate.

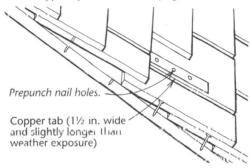

Prepunch nail holes.

Copper tab (1½ in. wide and slightly longer than weather exposure)

3. Slide new slate into place, fold over copper tab to anchor.

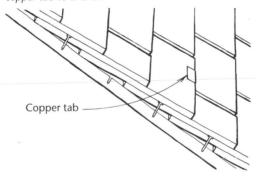

Copper tab

When possible, remove slates from top down before repairing flashings.

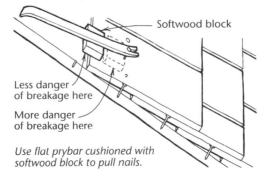

Softwood block

Less danger of breakage here

More danger of breakage here

Use flat prybar cushioned with softwood block to pull nails.

To replace a missing or broken slate, slide the hooked end of the slater's hook up under the remains of the broken shingle and feel around until you find the nail shanks. Slide the hook over the nail and, striking the flat part of the tool with a hammer, drive it downward, severing the nail. Repeat with the other nail. Remove the rest of the shingle and be sure no small chips or nailheads are left underneath. Feel around with the hook. Drive it into the stubs of the nail shanks and remove them. A hacksaw blade inserted flatwise under the shingle will also do the job, albeit a lot more slowly.

Cut a copper repair tab about 1½ in. wide and slightly longer than the weather exposure of the shingles. Nail this to the course under the shingle you are replacing, with a copper nail, so that it will project beyond the bottom edge of the new shingle about ¾ in. Drill or punch (a ⅛-in. nailset works fine) a hole through the slate for the nail. The hole should be countersunk slightly to seat the nailhead. Scrape it with a knife or tapered punch if you don't have a slater's punch. Slide the replacement shingle into place and fold the projecting copper tab up over its edge to anchor it.

Although a fairly large number of slates will have to be removed to replace rusted valleys or other flashings, the basic method is the same as outlined. Start at the top and outside edge of the repair area. Once these shingles are removed, it's easy to take up the freshly exposed shingles below. Use an ordinary flat prybar to pull the now visible nails. Lift or pry gently, so as not to crack the shingle. A piece of softwood board inserted under the prybar will cushion the shingle. Despite your efforts, some slates will break, so you'll need a stock of replacements on hand. If you're lucky, the original roofers anticipated this, and left a few dozen matching slates somewhere down in the cellar or in an odd corner of the garage. Buy some if you have to.

For repeated cuts that can be made all at once, professionals use a tile cutter on the ground. The slater's stake is used when working on the roof. It's really nothing more than a steel bar with a dog that can be driven into a convenient plank or roof board. A scored slate is placed across its edge and tapped with the cutting edge of the slater's hammer until it breaks more or less cleanly. You can achieve the same result by scoring the slate with a cold chisel, holding it over a square-edged hardwood board and repeatedly tapping it with your hammer claw along the score line. Smooth any rough edges with a Surform® block plane fitted with a tungsten-carbide blade. Angled cuts tend to shatter or break irregularly; cut these with a masonry blade in your circular saw. Slate shingles now come predrilled for nails, so the only time you'll need to make new holes is for custom-cut replacement shingles.

Repairing cement-asbestos roofing and tile roofing

Many of the techniques used to repair slate roofs are also applicable to cement-asbestos and tile roofing. For all practical purposes, cement shingles are interchangeable with slate, with one difference: The absence of a directional grain makes them less likely to shatter when scored and snapped to size. Unfortunately, it's the snapping that releases asbestos fibers into the air. If you find yourself having to cut a few shingles in the course of repairs, wear a good dust mask (not the cheap paper ones) and wet the shingle down. Do all your cutting in one area out of the wind, and bury the debris.

Tile roofs can be difficult to repair because it's virtually impossible for the amateur to remove some of the intricately interlocked tiles used in some styles without damage. The French style, in particular, is one of the most fiendish, although Greek and Roman styles can also prove challenging. It's best to make a temporary patch from a piece of asphalt roll roofing until professional help can be obtained.

There are some flat tiles that are fastened exactly like slates and are likewise amenable to the slater's hook and copper-tab technique. The alternating semicylindrical Spanish tiles are another. The intersections of tiles with ridges and hips are fairly complicated, and a number of special pieces are needed for finishing these areas. The gaps between the tile curves and the capping trim pieces must be sealed with mortar. This is skilled work.

Replacing wood shingles

Wood shingles leak because they split, allowing water to work under and between courses. Sometimes they rot, if not properly ventilated. But most of the damage is caused by the drying effect of direct sunlight. Wood shingles that have outlived their usefulness may appear sound, but when touched they fall apart. Dried out or rotted, such shingles must be replaced.

The slater's hook/shingle thief is an indispensable tool for repairing wood shingles. Depending on their condition, wood shingles can be even more infuriating to remove than crumbling asphalt shingles. As a rule of thumb, it seems that you need to pull three shingles for every one you try to replace. You can usually loosen the shingle by gently lifting it with the tapered edge of the hook. This allows you to slip the hook directly under the nailhead and, instead of cutting it, to pull out the entire nail as you drive the tool downward.

The standard approach is to face-nail the replacement shingle, with either unobtrusive galvanized finish nails, sealed with clear caulking, or regular shingle nails. The problem with leaving nails exposed is not so much that they might leak, since that can be prevented with caulk or flashing cement, but that they will eventually cause a surface split that will leak. In *The Old-House Doctor* (see the Bibliography on pp. 334-338), Christopher Evers suggests an elegant solution: The replacement shingle is slipped into place with its butt end projecting 1 in. below the other shingles in the course. Two shingle nails are driven

The Old-House Doctor's *Wood Shingle Trick*

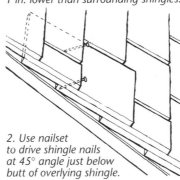
1. Leave butt of replacement shingle 1 in. lower than surrounding shingles.

2. Use nailset to drive shingle nails at 45° angle just below butt of overlying shingle.

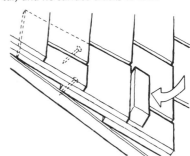
3. As new shingle is driven into line, the nails move under the butt of the covering shingle — no exposed nails to tar, and no surface cracks to leak.

slightly below the surface of the shingle at a 45° angle at the butts of the course above. Then, as you tap the shingle up into line with a wooden block, the angled nails are drawn straight and flush to the surface and hidden about ½ in. under the butts of the overlying shingles.

A quick temporary fix for missing wood shingles is to cut a scrap of asphalt roofing to the same width as the missing shingle, coat it with flashing cement on both sides and slide it up under the edge of the broken shingle.

Repairing metal roofing

The best cure for rusting or decayed metal roofing or flashing is an asphalt coating. Repainting with rust-resistant enamels or fibered asphalt emulsions is also useful. The aluminized coating used for refurbishing mobile-home roofs is much too expensive for an area as large as a house roof.

Small holes in corrugated sheet roofing are easily filled with flashing cement or a clear caulk suited to metal, such as Geocel® acrylic copolymer, available at building-supply centers. Larger holes require reinforcement. Cloth buttered with roofing cement on both sides will work, as will fiberglass mesh designed for patching gutters or automotive bodywork. Follow the same procedure for patching holes in metal valleys or eave flashing. Vertical seams that leak because of a low pitch can be tarred or sealed with Geocel®. Even so, such seams will usually need annual re-coating, as the expansion and contraction of the metal breaks the seal.

This same relentless movement tends to work even the most tenacious nails loose over time. If renailing with ¾-in. to 1-in. long nails does not tighten the roofing down, try driving the nails in new holes or at an angle through the old ones. Fill the old holes with flashing cement. Applying the cement with a caulking gun is more convenient and a lot less messy than troweling.

Resoldering the cracked seams of a standing-seam roof is difficult. Rust and paint must be cleaned down to bare metal along the joint to ensure the solder bonding. Instead, you can use a putty knife to fill any leaking seams with asphalt cement or butyl caulking. Tool the caulked joints with your fingertip or wipe tarred ones smooth with a rag. When dry, they can be painted along with the rest of the roof.

As a rule of thumb, no more than one-third of the total width of a valley flashing should be exposed, with 20 in. being the minimum allowable width of the flashing metal. If, because of careless installation, the metal doesn't extend far enough up under the shingles, the valley will leak, especially during the winter as ice works up under the edges and melts. Applications of flashing cement along and under the edges of the shingles may forestall the inevitable, but the only effective cure is replacement of the flashing.

The roofer's panacea

Fiber-reinforced roof coating (a mixture of coal tar, fibers and solvent, heavier than cold cement but still spreadable by mop or brush) is a sloppy but effective way to prolong the life of a roof on the verge of expiration. Short of reroofing, it's the only way to rejuvenate an old tin porch roof, or built-up or smooth roll roofing. The coating also works wonders for corrugated metal roofs and corroding flashings or valleys, as long as any scale or loose rust is removed first with a wire brush. Brushed over cracked and deteriorated shingles, it is the remedy of last resort to forestall reroofing when appearance is less important than cost.

Apply the coating with a long-handled roofer's mop. If the brush end is submerged in a pail of water after each use, it will stay pliable indefinitely. Keep plenty of kerosene and rags on hand for cleanup—the mix has a way of spattering over windows and walls below.

Reroofing With Asphalt Shingles

You can reroof a house in two ways: by completely removing the shingles down to the decking or by laying new shingles over the old. If the original shingles are not too badly warped and the deck underneath is sound, it will save time and labor to lay new roofing over old. But, if you have old, properly applied wood shingles, they will have been nailed to open purlins—not an adequate base for asphalt shingles. In this case you'll have to strip the roof, then nail new sheathing over the purlins. One other precaution: Most roofs with a pitch greater than 6-in-12 and framed with at least 2x8 rafters at no more than 2 ft. on center can safely support the weight of up to three layers of asphalt shingles (2 psf or 2.5 psf per layer depending on the weight per 100 sq. ft. as specified by the manufacturer); anything less, and you'll have to strip off the old shingles.

Three layers of asphalt is about equal to the dead load of a slate roof, which somewhat belies the argument about the need for extra-heavy roof framing. If there's any doubt about the strength of your roof framing, the recommended load for any given configuration can be calculated from tables in any good carpentry textbook. The real objection to reroofing over existing shingles is more a matter of appearance than structural strength. Unless optimum conditions are present, the new shingles will mirror the irregularities in the roof underneath.

Laying new shingles over old

Careful preparation of the old roofing will minimize undesirable "telegraphing." The goal is to smooth the bumps and wrinkles in the old roof as much as possible. To this end, renail all loose shingles, pull protruding nails, nail warped shingles flat, nail pieces of new shingle into the gaps left by missing shingles and remove the ridge-cap shingles. Some roofers recommend nailing "feathering" strips (beveled lengths of wood similar to thin clapboards) below the butts of each old shingle course, but the extra labor and expense seem harder to justify than simply stripping the roof.

Wood shingles were often used instead of metal drip edge at the eaves. Typically, the shingles cover the open gap between the edges of the roof decking and the angled crown molding that caps the cornice. Since the rotted shingles won't hold nails, break them back to solid wood and nail filler boards cut from 1x6 stock into the gaps to provide solid support for the new roofing. Use narrow lengths of smooth roll roofing or the top halves of strip shingles to bring the surface flush with the old roofing. Then nail metal drip edge to the perimeter of the roof, starting at the eave (the roof overhang at the bottom of the roof) and then running up the rakes (the overhang at the sides of the roof). Drip edge is sold in 10-ft. lengths and in two widths; use the 8-in. along the eaves and the 5-in. up the rakes, allowing 1 in. overlap of all joints. The wider edging is also used to bridge the edges of built-up fascia trim boards (which offer poor nailing, even when new) at both the rakes and eaves. If the edges of the roof deck are solid, remove the old drip edge and break any overhanging shingles back flush to the edge of the deck before putting on the new drip edge.

Corner Detail for Drip-Edge Flashing

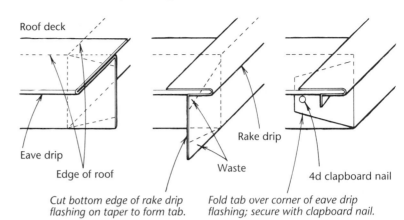

Roof deck

Eave drip

Edge of roof

Rake drip

Waste

4d clapboard nail

Cut bottom edge of rake drip flashing on taper to form tab.

Fold tab over corner of eave drip flashing; secure with clapboard nail.

The difference between applying new shingles over old and installing them over a bare deck is that the starter course at the eave (which is normally a full shingle laid tab-side-up to provide double coverage under the cutouts of the first course) uses only the top half of a shingle to avoid an unsightly hump at the eave. Also, longer nails are needed. Use 1¾-in. nails for reroofing and 1¼-in. for bare decks.

Flashings around vent pipes should be carefully removed and saved for reuse. Clean off debris and old tar by soaking in kerosene. Pry up chimney flashings and fold them up against the brickwork. Now is the best time to evaluate the quality and condition of the metal. Unless they are poorly made, reuse any lead or copper flashings. Consider replacing aluminum or steel; the only exception might be metal that has been tarred or painted and is still uncorroded. Sometimes flashing is buried under the original roofing with the shingles of the second roof cemented over it. When you finally excavate the mess, fill the crater flush to the surrounding surface with scraps of new shingles bedded in tar before re-installing the flashing piece.

Proper installation of end-wall step flashing is one way to prevent leaks. Since these flashings are laid over, not under, the clapboards, this part of the roof will be a chronic problem.

nails within a couple of inches of the cut. New step flashings are slipped up under the siding when the roof is shingled.

The same method is used to flash an addition to a gable wall. When the new roofline or old flashing is parallel to the run of the siding (as where a porch roof meets clapboards), make a vertical cut along the face of the siding at each end of the piece to be removed. Loosen and remove the nails from the overlying clapboard, and slide a knife or hacksaw blade under it to complete each saw cut. Install the flashing to allow at least 2 in. of exposed metal to the first full clapboard. Roofing material should never abut wall siding without an intervening gap of metal. The cut ends of the wood soak up water and soon rot.

Chimney crickets are another potential problem area. These are small pitched roofs built on the upslope side of a chimney that breaches the roof some distance below the ridge. They prevent possible leaks by diverting water and snow away from the backside of the chimney. Unless the chimney is very large, crickets are not usually shingled. Instead, flashing metal or roll roofing is joined to the chimney flashing proper and formed into a valley where it meets the main roof. If you can't extract the metal for installation under the new roofing, cement a piece of mineral-surfaced roll roofing over the cricket and fold it up under cement-coated chimney flashing.

When reroofing, give all flashings and other roof penetrations a fresh coat of flashing cement. Asphalt tends to crack and dry out with time. A hairline crack between a bathroom vent and its boot is enough to cause a leak. Television antennas are especially troublesome. I usually try to remove the lag screws that anchor the antenna mast to the ridge when I am about to slip shingles under it. If the guy wires are still intact, there's enough support to keep the antenna from toppling. Use longer or thicker lag screws and butter the underside of the mast supports as

It is not always possible to work this way with step flashing at an end wall. You'll find that the pieces were laid to fit the original roof, then bent upward and refolded to fit the second. Bending the step flashing to fit yet another layer of roofing will either create a trough almost an inch deep between the shingles and the side wall, or decrease the necessary separation between roofing and wall siding, adding to the likelihood of leakage or rot.

The step flashings can't be raised without removing several courses of wall siding first. If this doesn't convince you to tear off the old roofing first, the next best solution is to make a cut through the siding (but not the sheathing) parallel to and 2 in. or 2½ in. above the roof surface. Use a carbide blade in your circular saw, as you'll run into more than one hidden nail. With a small prybar, carefully lift the bottom of the siding and loosen and pull any

Roof jacks support the staging planks that roofers work from. Because of threatening weather, these roofers are tar-papering each section of exposed deck as soon as they have stripped the shingles.

well as the screws when refastening it. If, for some reason, you can't remove the supports, bury the whole mess in fresh cement. Don't try to cut shingles around the guy-wire screw eyes and antenna-lead stand-off insulators. Unscrew them, one at a time as they get in the way, and relocate them in new holes. If you carefully spread the top of the stand-off screw, the plastic insulator will pop free and you can save the screw for reuse. Seal everything with flashing cement after reinstallation.

Flashing cement has an uncanny knack of smearing itself on everything. Check your elbows, the seat of your pants, your cuffs and your knees before leaning or sitting on anything. Keep a jug of kerosene and a few rags handy to keep tools and hands functional.

Stripping the roof

If the old asphalt shingles are completely deteriorated, or three or more layers of roofing are already present (or the existing roof is wood shingles), you'll have to strip the roof.

Schedule shingle stripping to coincide with an expected run of dry weather. Once the deck is exposed, even a small rainstorm can thoroughly soak attic insulation and ruin plaster, ceilings, furniture and carpets. Around New England the saying is, "If you don't like the weather, wait 10 minutes"; long-range forecasts don't

have much credibility. It makes sense, then, to strip only as much roofing as you think you can replace in a day. Don't strip more than one side at a time.

There are various theories as to the best direction in which to strip shingles—down from the top, up from under the butts, or even sideways. My experience is that all these methods work equally well, and one will work better than the others depending on the layers of roofing and the holding power of their nails. Before Windseal® shingles were invented, roofers used two nails above each cutout to increase wind resistance. If this is the case with your roof, it will certainly have increased stripping resistance.

Exactly how does one get up onto a roof and, more important, work comfortably? The upper limit of a slope that can be worked safely without aid is somewhere between 5-in-12 and 6-in-12. The roof jack, or bracket, provides a safe support for slopes above this limit. Roof jacks are made of steel or wood and are adjustable to various pitches. Fastened to the roof deck, they support the staging planks that create a horizontal work surface. Roof jacks can be rented, although their cost is reasonable enough to allow you to consider owning a dozen.

Getting started is always the slowest part of roofing. There are two options. You can begin from a ladder, stripping away as

Pipe scaffolding creates a safe, spacious work area for roofing. Note the blocking beneath the legs to level across the sections and keep the pipes from sinking into the ground, as well as the 2x4s wired to the uprights to form a safety rail.

many shingles as you can reach, moving along the eaves until the entire bottom section is cleaned off. Never use a lightweight aluminum ladder for this sort of work. These ladders are too light to resist any sideways impetus and will slide easily along a metal-edged roof, especially if you lean out from dead center. They also blow over in a strong breeze. Wood ladders are heavy enough to resist blowing over and they tend to cut into a metal edge, stabilizing themselves to some extent. At all times, exercise caution and common sense when working from a ladder. I can testify from personal experience just how far out you can lean to reach that last little scrap of shingle before a wood ladder will kick out from under you.

A more efficient approach is to rent pipe scaffolding. It comes in panels of several heights, which are easily assembled with crossbraces to create a strong, stable working platform as high as or higher than you'd like to climb. Scaffolding can be rented economically by the week or month. Always lay blocks of dimension

lumber under the legs to prevent the staging from sinking into the ground, which it could otherwise do suddenly enough to topple either itself or you.

The scaffolding panels should be level to prevent binding between sections during assembly and overturning during use. Use blocking under the legs to even out the sections. Scaffolds over 12 ft. high should be roped to the building for safety.

For roofing, the top of the platform should fall somewhere between knee and waist level, relative to the roof edge. Lay 2x10 or 2x12 staging planks across the scaffolding. Sheets of plywood tacked over the planking will make a commodious and comfortable work and materials storage area. The ideal staging would run the entire length of the building, but you can cut down on the number of panels (and the rental cost) by erecting individual towers and spanning the gaps between them with staging planks. Also, since two workers can pick up and carry a 12-ft. high tower where it is needed, the scaffolding can follow the work around the building. Taller towers, which call for more stability, should use a third section of scaffolding.

Pump jacks cost more to rent than scaffolding, but are much more flexible, and are preferable for working on irregular terrain, around shrubbery or for siding application. Two pairs of pump jacks are enough to span the length of an average house. For someone faced with a fair amount of roofing and siding, a couple of pairs would be a good investment. They're easy to sell when you've finished with them. The pump jack works on the same principle as a car bumper jack. When the handle is raised, the jack and the staging planks it carries inch up a 4x4 post braced to the building at its top end. Once the staging is over 10 ft. high, 2x4 diagonal braces are fastened between the jack poles and their bottoms are braced to the wall.

With all these alternatives, home-built staging doesn't make much sense. Lumber costs too much to waste on building a wooden version of pipe scaffolding.

A lot of tedious raking could have been prevented had the roofers spread a polyethylene sheet on the ground before stripping the wood shingles.

Ladder brackets enable the roofer to set up starter staging in places nothing else could easily reach.

Before you set up the staging, cover the ground under the work area with a sheet of polyethylene. Otherwise, rusty roofing nails will be sprouting with the dandelions for years. Shingles eventually rot, but they don't make very attractive mulch for flowerbeds and shrubbery. Set a rented 30-yd. construction dumpster alongside the scaffold to minimize debris handling. You'll be surprised how full it will be by the time you've finished stripping three layers of roofing and old boards. The dumpster should have a door that swings open at one end so you can fill it by the wheelbarrow load once the work zone moves out of dumpster range. Check with local officials about permits and costs before you rent a dumpster.

Working from ladders or the scaffold, strip the shingles as high as you can reach along the entire length of the roof. Look for nails in the sheathing boards that indicate an underlying rafter, and nail a roof jack to the bare deck at a comfortable reach from the staging. Nail another roof jack to support the opposite end of the staging plank you'll lay across them. The third (middle) jack is always added last, after the plank. This way, the plank sits well and any differences in height between brackets that might otherwise make it rest unevenly are resolved. Use three 8d common nails per jack, driven only into solid nailing. For staging, use 14-ft. or 16-ft. planks of planed kiln-dried 2x12 spruce, free from any major knots or defects. Three brackets are enough to support a 16-ft. plank, two workers and three bundles of shingles. If possible, span the entire length of the roof with a course of staging.

As the shingles are stripped, successive courses of roof jacks are added until the peak is reached. Each course is spaced as far apart as you can reach, typically about 6 ft. If you lack enough jacks and planks to stage an entire side of the roof (it takes about a dozen-and-a-half jacks and six long and three short planks for three 36-ft. long courses), run only the bottom course and divide the upper part of the roof in half, cleaning each side separately.

Large polyethylene sheets make the fastest and safest interim waterproofing until the roof is shingled.

A long-handled, flat-bladed shovel is the best tool for stripping shingles. Drive it under the butts and pry upward as you push. Once you get a small area clear, the shingles should begin to rip off in good-sized sections fairly quickly, nails and all. Whatever nails the shovel does not pry out can be removed with a prybar and/or hammer. Keep a flat file handy to touch up the cutting edge of the shovel as it begins to curl over. Next to the shovel, the prybar is one of the most useful items in the reroofer's toolbox. It will pry up ridge shingles, which usually have too many nails to submit to the shovel, and is unequaled for working loose flashings entombed in cement.

Polyethylene film is available in 100-ft. rolls up to 24 ft. wide. Keeping a roll on hand is cheap flood insurance. A sudden shower can sweep over the ridges on even the clearest day. If rain is imminent and the deck is bare, a poly sheet can save the ceilings. Batten the top edge of the sheet to the opposite side of the ridge and unfurl it across the roof, securing it with short vertical battens as you descend the slope and remove the stagings. There's no faster or more watertight way to protect large areas of roof at a moment's notice.

If you've barely gotten beyond the first staging before the weather alert, pull the nails as best as you can from under the first remaining course of shingles and slide the poly up under the shingles far enough so the top edge is covered. For extra protection, shove a strip of tar paper up under the butts of the next course of shingles.

As soon as the shingles are stripped to the ridge, all nails pulled and the bare deck swept cleaned, permanent temporary waterproofing can be installed. You'll need a helper to do this. Consider hiring a young neighbor for the extra hands and feet. Or exchange a day of work with a friend. I know of one fellow who provided the beer afterward for a dozen or so friends and got a new roof on in record time. It wasn't the neatest roof in the world, but it did shed water.

From the rake at the peak of the roof, unroll a dozen or so feet of 15-lb. tar paper along the ridgeline. Staple or nail a roofing "tin"—a thin, flat metal disc 1½ in. to 2 in. in diameter that prevents the paper (or polyethylene) from tearing loose—in the middle edge of the tar paper at the rake. (In my opinion, the Bostich H-2B staple hammer that I use for all my tar-papering and insulation work is the best made. It'll drive a couple of ⅜-in. staples through a tin faster than you can think about it.)

Unroll the tar paper, which is now anchored yet free to pivot, to the opposite end of the ridge, aligning it as you tack it to the roof with tins spaced about 2 ft. apart down the middle of the sheet. Fold the top of the sheet over the ridge and tack it to the shingles still on the other side with another row of tins. Moving downward, align the top edge of a second sheet with the line chalked on the bottom of the tar paper (about 2 in. up). When this sheet is unrolled and tacked along its midline, lift the bottom edge of the upper sheet and slip the lower one under it. Then tack this edge down to the roof.

Repeat the process, working your way down the roof, removing the stagings as you go. Hold the tins at the bottommost course of tar paper up at least 8 in. from the bottom so you can slip the drip edge under it when you're ready to proceed.

As you strip the accumulated layers of roofing and dust from the deck, you may discover that the wood itself is not as solid as it could be, particularly if your shovel pushes clear through the boards. As mentioned on p. 144, open purlins that were fine for wood shingles or slates will not support asphalt shingles. If the purlins were nailed to the rafters in relatively straight courses of even width, you can fill the gaps with boards ripped to fit. But when the original builders used widely spaced "waney" (unsquared) edged boards instead, you'll need to cut tapered and variously sized pieces to close the gaps and make a solid nail base. Snap a chalkline down the edges of the worst boards and rip them to fit the new wood. You'll need a sturdy nail-chewing blade for the job—old roof sheathing holds about as many nails as a porcupine has quills.

Cut any rotted boards back to sound wood over the nearest rafter and replace with new sheathing. Use rough-sawn boards to match the thickness of the old lumber, or add shims along the rafters to raise them up flush. If the top of a rafter is too rotten to hold nails but still basically sound, "scab" a piece of 2x alongside its edge to carry the sheathing.

Sometimes, the shingles will be the only thing keeping the sheathing on the roof. A roof deck too far gone to hold nails or one that is full of gaps can be renewed by "skinning" it with a layer of ⅜-in. or ½-in. CDX plywood. There's a good chance that the edges of the plywood won't break over the oddly spaced old rafters. Screw the sheets to the old decking (enough of the old sheathing should be sound enough

for this) with drywall screws, spaced 2 in. to 3 in. apart. Otherwise, nail the plywood to the rafters with 8d nails, spaced 8 in. apart and 4 in. at the edges. Measure up 4 ft. from the bottom edge of the roof at each rake and snap a chalkline between the points. Trim off any overhanging plywood, or lower the line if more than ½ in. of old sheathing is showing somewhere along a curving bottom edge. The drip edge will hide the ends of the plywood.

Rot traceable to leaks or water blowing under the shingles at the rakes is generally localized. When the whole deck has rotted, the culprit is condensation under the shingles, resulting from poor insulation and insufficient attic ventilation. Water vapor in the warm moist air rising through an uninsulated attic condenses on the cold underside of impermeable shingles. Condensation occurs to some extent in all houses. Frost will crystalize on the nails poking through the underside of a roof deck, even in a well-insulated attic. Most of the time this moisture evaporates harmlessly without turning back to a liquid. But if the attic is poorly ventilated, as is often the case where the attic windows are painted shut or nonexistent and no gable louver has been provided, the vapor condensing under the shingles will soak into sheathing and nurture the spores of dry-rot fungi.

The freshly skinned roof deck can be tar-papered without resorting to staging planks and roof jacks. Horizontal 2x4s, spiked through the plywood into the rafters, are effective stagings, not only for handling and nailing down the plywood, but also for tar-papering. Remove the 2x4s as you work your way back down the roof.

There is one other difference between reroofing over old shingles and reroofing over a new deck: On a new deck, the drip edge is nailed to the deck under the tar paper at the eaves, and over it at the rakes; over old shingles, no tar paper is necessary and the drip edge is nailed on top of the old shingles.

Installing Asphalt Shingles

Like cooking fat, asphalt begins to soften at around body temperature. On a hot day, shingles can become almost liquid. If you stand on them, your footprints will leave a permanent record. The edges of the shingle smear, the protective slate granules are pushed into the base—and the life of the roof is shortened considerably. So consider the temperature when you schedule reroofing. Shingles absorb heat; the darker the color, the more heat they absorb. Although the air temperature may be only 70°F, up on the shadeless roof the shingles can be too hot to touch. The reflective properties of a light-colored shingle are offset by its vulnerability to marring and staining. Footprints that are barely noticeable on a black shingle will scream against a white background.

Try to select a cool, cloudy day for laying shingles. If it promises to be sunny and warm, start early in the morning on the shady (western) side, and try to finish up on the other side by late afternoon. (This plan works only when the roof is small or the crew is large.)

But life seldom flows in the channels we arrange for it. One January day I found myself banging shingles, a man with a pushbroom ahead of me, struggling to keep the deck clear of swirling snow while I fumbled in my nail apron with frozen fingers. A cold, stiff shingle can skin a knuckle as effectively as a block of rough granite. In cold weather, asphalt is as flexible as glass. The ridge shingles, brought up in small batches from the warm cellar where they had been cut and stored since the previous day, were quickly bent over the roof before they could cool and crack.

Then there was the August day I began shingling just before sunrise. By 8:00 A.M. I was working in stocking feet to avoid marking the shingles. At noon, I stumbled down the scaffold, blinded by sweat, my pants hanging wilted and wet from my belt. I spent the rest of the afternoon in an old inner tube in the middle of the pond.

As with every other activity these days, proper footwear is important. Smooth crepe-soled shoes are the best. Sneakers are more comfortable and give greater traction, but they get scuffed apart by the shingles and their soles tend to mark up the roof. Never wear Vibram®-soled boots on an asphalt-shingle roof.

Complete application instructions are generally printed on the shingle wrapper for every type of shingle. What is not explained is how to maneuver an 80-lb. bundle safely up a ladder and onto a roof. There is an art to carrying asphalt shingles; it is a matter of balance more than brute strength. Unless you have access to a mechanical hoist, your shoulder must be the vehicle. You can manage a half-bundle at a time and make twice as many trips. Split bundles actually handle harder than full packaged ones. The loose shingles flop around and bend over your shoulder, throwing you off balance.

To lift a full bundle of shingles, stand it upright, facing you but slightly to your side. Assuming you are right-handed, squat, back straight, and place your right hand under the bottom left corner of the bundle and tilt it so that its center will fall across your right shoulder. Then straighten your legs and hoist the bundle onto your shoulder, still keeping your back straight. The bundle will balance surprisingly well. Your hand stops it from tilting back as you climb the ladder, using the left hand to grip the ladder rails, not the rungs. Always keep one hand in contact with the sides of a ladder at all times. Climb with a steady pace. At the top, roll your shoulder forward, throwing the entire bundle onto the roof. A 16d nail driven into the deck will stop the shingles from sliding down until you can set the first course of staging, if you're working off a ladder.

You'll feel the weight in your calves first, long before your back begins to bother you. After the first "square" (100 sq. ft. of roofed surface, usually three bundles of asphalt shingles) your calves will feel spongy, so carry up no more than a square at a clip. The staging will safely hold that much, and a square will occupy you more than long enough to recover your breath for the next trip down the ladder. Fill up your nail apron each trip. My father told me never to come up a ladder empty-handed. He was used to working piece-work, where every step saved was a penny earned. He was also the fellow who would carry up 12 squares without a pause, collapse for an hour while eating his lunch, and then begin shingling. I guess he liked to work uninterrupted.

Estimating materials

Roofing material is estimated by the square. Measure the roof and multiply length by width to find its area. Divide the total by 100 to get the number of squares. Allow 10% extra for waste and starters, 20% if there are a lot of dormers and valleys to trim. As a rule of thumb, figure an extra square for every 100 ft. of ridge or valley.

Vertical layout

Asphalt shingles are coursed like brick-work. The joints and tabs between courses never break over the ones below. Although three-tab strip shingles can be started from either end or from the middle of the roof, unless the roof terminates at a valley or end wall, it's best to begin the layout from the middle, especially for long roofs. Working outward toward the rakes conserves movement and lowers the chances of the shingles running crooked.

Measure across the rakes at the ridge and the eave and mark the center—roofs are not always square; sometimes the distance across the top is different from the distance across the bottom. Mark another point 6 in. (6½ in.) to one side of center and snap chalklines down the roof from ridge to eave. (Note: All dimensions are for standard nonmetric shingles. Inch equivalents for metric shingles are given in parentheses.) The ends of each successive course alternate between these two guidelines,

Vertical Layout Lines for Asphalt Strip Shingles*

1. Measure across roof at A1 and A2 to get total width. Divide by 2 to locate C—the centerline—in feet and inches.

2. If A1 and A2 are different (crooked roof), use larger number to locate C. Feet = full tabs. Inches = fractional remainder, or filler piece.

3. Filler should be greater than 3 in. Shift C to left or right to correct.

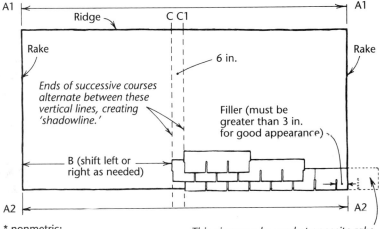

* nonmetric;
1 full tab metric = 13.125 in.

This piece can be used at opposite rake.

giving the required half-tab offset (the shadowline) between courses. Individual tabs are 12 in. wide (13⅛ in.).

To avoid the undesirable situation of needing a ½-in. wide strip of shingle to finish the course at the rakes, the center-line is shifted to one side as necessary. If the roof is 32 ft. 1-in. long, the filler pieces will be either ½ in. or 6½ in. long (2⅛ in. or 8¾ in.). If the roof is an even 32 ft., the shingles should theoretically end exactly on the drip edge, which is highly improbable. Either way, you don't want to start from dead center (the 2⅛-in. wide metric rake filler is at the borderline of acceptability). Shifting the starting lines 3 in. to the left (assuming that the shingles are to be "run out" to the right) gives acceptable rake fillers of 3½-in. and 9½-in. pieces; a 1-in. shift is required for metric shingles to get 3⅛-in. and 9¾-in. filler pieces.

How did I figure this? For standard shingles, it's easy: Divide the total roof length in half. Since each whole shingle tab equals 1 ft., the only significant number is the fractional remainder, in this case ½ in. (32 ft. 1 in. divided by 2 equals 16 ft. ½ in, or 16 whole tabs plus ½ in. left over). This remainder is the width of the rake filler at one side. The filler for the other rake is the same plus the width of half a tab, or 6½ in. Shifting the centerline 3 in. to the left gives a 9½-in. filler on one side and a 3½-in. filler at the other.

The math for metric shingles is more complicated, which is a good reason to stick to standard shingles. Here, unless you have a metric tape, convert half the roof width to inches (16 ft. ½ in. = 192.5 in.), changing fractions to decimals to simplify calculation. Divide that figure by 13.125 (the width of a metric tab) to get the total number of whole tabs and the fractional remainder (14.666). Then multiply 13.125 by the remainder (0.666) to convert the required rake filler to inches (approximately 8.75 in.). This is the width of one rake filler. The other equals that number plus half a tab (8.75 + 6.5 = 15.25). Subtracting the width of a whole tab, the actual required filler is 2.125, or 2⅛ in. A 1-in. shift (and a pocket calculator) is called for.

Figuring all this out may seem like a lot of trouble to go to, but proper centering is critical, especially when the rakes are not parallel, if the shadowlines are to finish neatly at the rakes. Filler pieces less than 2 in. wide are likely to break or blow off the roof.

Since small pieces are equally unwelcome under step flashings at end walls, use the same calculations to determine whether you can start the roof with full shingles at the opposite rake. This is not a consideration when the roof ends in a valley, since every piece will have to be cut to varying and unpredictable widths anyway. To start at the rake end, cut half a tab off every other shingle. These "end starters" are best cut en masse, early in the day while the shingles are still crisp enough to snap when scored across their underside with a utility knife (the blades get dull too fast on the face side). Use a scrap of plywood for a cutting table and an old steel framing square for a straightedge (your aluminum framing square is too expensive and precise to sacrifice to a roof). Most standard shingles feature a factory-made alignment mark on their underside along the top edge that indicates the middle of each tab. Otherwise, save the first piece for a pattern. Use the remaining part of the shingles for starters on the opposite side of the roof or for fillers at the end wall or opposing rake.

Horizontal layout

The starter course at the eaves is doubled to provide full coverage under the cutouts —use a full shingle laid upside-down (it still must be kept gravel-side up) and then offset the overlying course. Snap a chalkline 17 in. (18¾ in.—rounded off to 19 in. is close enough—for metric) up from the drip edge across the roof. If you lay the top edge of the second course to this line, the shingles will run straight, despite any irregularities in the bottom edge of the roof. (Standard 12-in. shingles have a 5-in. exposure, thus 5 + 12 = 17 [5⅝ + 13⅛ = 18¾ for metric]).

Unless it's a very short roof, even experienced roofers snap a series of guidelines across the roof to mark the top of every fourth course. Measure and mark lines 20 in. apart (22 in. for metric) up from the 17-in. starting line. These guidelines keep the shingles from running too far off course. I even use them for the supposedly self-aligning jet shingles, where small differences in shingle widths (some brands are worse than others) can add up to big trouble in a dozen or so courses.

Measure from the last guideline to the ridge at both ends of the roof. If the variance is less than 1 in., lay out the course guidelines as above. If it's greater, the excess must be divided between the last few courses. Otherwise the last course will disappear under the ridge shingles at a singularly unsightly angle. A gradual correction, which doesn't exceed ¼ in. per course over the run of the roof (½ in. is permissible on long roofs where there's more than 3 in. to make up) will be unnoticeable. Divide the excess by ¼ to find the number of courses involved. For example, a 2-in. difference requires 8 courses to straighten out. Mark off 5¼-in. increments at the longest measurement and 5-in. ones at the shortest. Follow these new guidelines to bring the course lines parallel to the ridge.

If there is a noticeable dip in the roof surface, a chalkline snapped across it from end to end will actually describe a curve and wreak havoc with exposure widths. Mark another set of guide points up the middle of the dip (or at intervals of 16 ft. to 20 ft. on a long roof) and run the chalkline out to both ends.

Application techniques

Strip shingles are designed so that the 5-in. exposure falls just above the cutouts. Drive the nails about 1 in. above the cutout, so that they just catch the top edge of the underlying course. Avoid nailing through the weatherseal cement strip (it gums up the hammer head). Roofing staples (I use a Bostich H-6 hammer tacker) must be driven parallel to the shingles, never at an angle. Where a nail finds a crack instead of solid board, renail higher up.

It's easier to run full tabs out over the rakes rather than to cut a filler to fit each time. Hold the nails back at least 4 in. from the edge of the rake. In the morning, before the shingles soften up, snap a line along the rake and trim off the overhanging shingles with a pair of roofing shears (straight metal shears that have been dulled by cutting shingles), working from the top down, and then nail off from the bottom up. If this quick and simple method doesn't fit your schedule and the fillers must be cut as they are installed, use a knife and square. Shears gum up on soft shingles and make a messy cut.

Horizontal Layout Lines for Asphalt Strip Shingles

1. Starter course is doubled for full coverage under cutouts. It follows actual eave drip edge.

2. Snap guideline A 17 in. up from eave (width of one full 12-in. shingle plus 5 in. exposure). Align top of second course to this.

3. Snap guidelines B 20 in. apart to mark every fourth course. Align top of every fourth course to guideline to keep shingles running straight.

4. Measure from last guideline to ridge at each end. If C1 and C2 differ, correct by tilting last few courses (D) as needed, about ¼ in. per course.

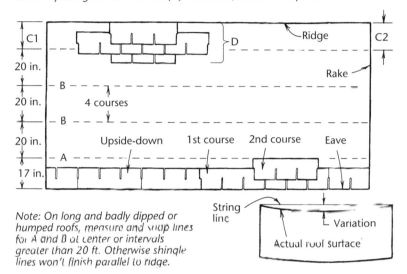

Note: On long and badly dipped or humped roofs, measure and snap lines for A and B at center or intervals greater than 20 ft. Otherwise shingle lines won't finish parallel to ridge.

Shingles are cut to fit where they meet against the lower edge of a chimney or vent. Then the flashing is installed over the shingles, and the top edges are coated with flashing cement. The next course is cut to fit around the flashing or up against the chimney and pressed into the cement. Nail the bottom edge of the flashing to the roof and daub the nailheads with roofing cement.

When cutting and trimming shingles to fit against an end wall, there's an easy way to duplicate the shingles for every other course. Butt the third-course shingle smooth-side up (that is, reversed) against the wall, on top of the first-course end-wall shingle, and mark where it overlaps the edge of the last full shingle (see the

Trimming Shingles to Fit at End Wall

1. Butt third-course shingle smooth-side up (reversed) against end wall.

2. Cut in line with end of first-course shingle.

3. Turn right-side up and install. Shingle will be identical to shingle in first course.

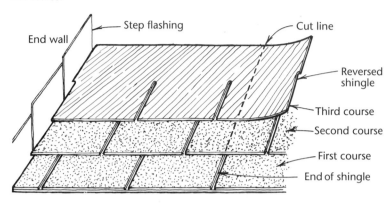

drawing above). Then cut the shingle, flip it and install. (Of course, this assumes that the end wall is square with the shingle courses. If not, each shingle will have to be measured and cut individually.)

Improper placement of roof jacks will cause leaks. Be sure that the nails do not fall under a joint or cutout of the overlying shingle. Likewise, they must be nailed high enough for the nails to be covered by the butt of the tab, but not so high that the tab is lying over the top edge of the jack, where it will be torn by the staging plank. To remove a roof jack, strike the butt of the jack with a hammer to drive it upward, sliding it off the nails. Then hold the tab of the shingle up and drive the nails firmly into the deck to prevent them from working through the shingle.

Ridge-cap shingles

Ridge caps are used to cover the gap at the peak of the roof and whenever two roofs meet to form a hip. Score the underside of a three-tab shingle at an angle back from each cutout. (Order a few bundles of three-tab shingles to cut ridge caps for tabless jet shingles. Ridge shingles are a special order item with architect-style shingles.) This cut keeps an unsightly portion of unsurfaced shingle from showing when the cap is bent over the ridge. Trim the tops of the last two courses of shingles if less than 3 in. or 4 in. are left to fold over the peak.

Center the first ridge cap at one of the rakes so it completely covers any nails in the last full course of shingles and no portion of the shingle above the cutout is showing. Repeat at the opposite end of the ridge, and snap a chalkline between these points to guide ridge-cap installation.

Lay the ridge shingles away from the prevailing winds. Drive a nail into each side of the cap, penetrating the one below it, leaving about 5 in. exposed. Cut the last ridge to width and surface-nail. Seal the exposed nailheads with a dab of flashing cement. To find the number of ridge shingles needed, multiply the length of the ridge by 12 (number of inches in a foot) and divide by 5 (amount of exposure for each ridge shingle). If you divide that number by 3, you'll know how many full shingles to cut. There are 27 shingles to the full bundle for standard strip or jet shingles.

Valley installation

A valley is the intersection of two different roofs. Valley roofing is always installed prior to the shingles. If the original valley is still usable (copper or sound galvanized metal in need only of fresh paint) it can be left in place. If it is between layers of roofing, remove the entire valley and set it aside for reuse. When relaying new shingles over old, it's easier to resurface the valley with fresh roll roofing or metal than to take it up. In regions of heavy snow or rainfall, metal will last longer than mineral-surfaced roll roofing.

To install a new valley over a bare deck, run tar paper vertically down the middle of the valley before running the tar paper across the roof. Then either trim the horizontal sheets to fall within 4 in. of center or allow them to run up onto the adjacent roof in an interlocking weave. Cut a sheet of 24-in. or 36-in. wide flashing metal to length, allowing 2 ft. extra at the ridge and enough at the bottom to overhang the drip edge ¾ in. along its full width at the eave. Use the wider material for pitches under 8-in-12. If possible, use a single sheet of metal; otherwise, allow an 8-in. lap, sealed with several beads of Geocel® copolymer caulk.

Center the sheet in the valley, tacking it at the top with a single nail and then nail off one side only, top to bottom, working downward (if you nail in the middle or bottom first, you're sure to make a wrinkle). With your knee, press and form the metal to curve smoothly into the center, paying particular attention that it lies flat against the roof at the intersecting ridge. Nail off the other side. Cut along a line that runs at a 45° angle from the point of intersection to the edge of the metal, and fold the piece over the ridge. Butter the deck between the edges of the cut with flashing cement, overlapping the metal at least 2 in., and repeat for the valley on the other side, tarring under the overlapping metal and then nailing off the seams. Trim off the projecting sharp points parallel to the main roof.

Always use nails of the same chemical composition as that of the valley metal. Otherwise, because of the electrogalvanic reaction, whereby a more electrically charged metal replaces the less active one, either the nail or the valley metal will corrode. Trim the bottom edge of the valley to overhang the drip edge by about ¾ in. and then fold it over the metal to lock it in place. When, as for example with a dormer, the valley does not end at the eaves, the metal is cut on a line parallel to the run of the main roof from the point of intersection (which should be gently curved).

Metal Valley Installation

1. Install tar-paper underlayment.

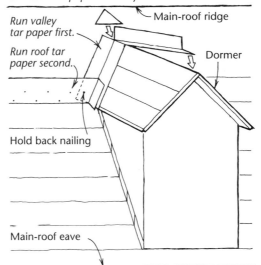

Run valley tar paper first.

Run roof tar paper second.

Main-roof ridge

Dormer

Hold back nailing

Main-roof eave

2. Install metal valley over tar paper. Tack at top with single nail.

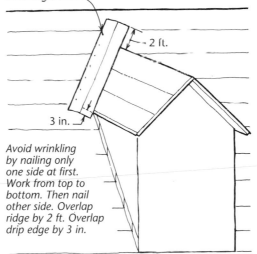

2 ft.

3 in.

Avoid wrinkling by nailing only one side at first. Work from top to bottom. Then nail other side. Overlap ridge by 2 ft. Overlap drip edge by 3 in.

3. Cut and fold ridge.

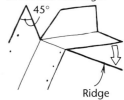

45°

Ridge

4. Cut off points parallel to main roof.

Cement under overlap.

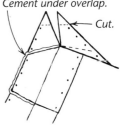

Cut.

5. Cut cover piece and install.

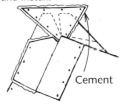

Cement

6. Trim and fold at eave, and repeat steps for opposite side.

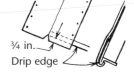

¾ in.

Drip edge

Trim metal to overlap drip edge ¾ in. and crimp to drip edge.

The shingles are rough-trimmed to the center of the valley as they are laid, using roofing shears. When the last course is reached, snap guidelines down each side of the valley and trim the shingles neatly to the line with shears, using the same method as for trimming rakes. Valleys are cut 6 in. wide at the top (3 in. each side of center), and should increase gradually about 1 in. for every 10 ft. of run, to prevent ice from wedging into the bottom as it slides downward. Hold nails back from the exposed metal at least 3 in., and run a bead of butyl caulk under the shingles to seal them to the metal. Run the shingles straight across the intersecting ridge at the top of the valley instead of continuing the cut lines up into a point. Ridge shingles from the opposing roof are likewise run across the peak of the valley.

Installing other kinds of asphalt roofing

Jet shingles are applied in similar fashion to tab shingles, except that end starters (if used) are 18-in. wide pieces made from a full-sized shingle cut in half. The nailing pattern is the same as for a tab shingle: 6 in. up from the bottom every 12 in. across, as judged by eyeball measure. Because of the alignment cutouts on their sides, jet shingles tend to stay on course with less trouble than tab shingles, where it's easier to drop or raise a shingle inadvertently above the cutouts.

Because they lack the cutouts that function like an expansion joint, jet shingles can sometimes buckle, especially when moisture is a problem.

Despite their odd appearance, lock-tab shingles are simple to apply if you observe the same precautions regarding centering and course guidelines as for strip shingles (although the width and height are different). Refer to a good roofing manual (see the Bibliography on pp. 334-338) for the layout of rake and eave starters and ridge caps. The bottom course starter is nailed over standard strip shingles (offset 9 in.) or 18-in. mineral-surface roll roofing.

Roll roofing with a 6-in. lap between courses is used for roof pitches between 4-in-12 and 2-in-12. Between 2-in-12 and 1-in-12 pitches, half-lap roll roofing, also known as "double coverage" or "19-in. selvage" roll, is used. The application principles are the same for both kinds of roofing. The rolls should be cut to length and spread out on a smooth, stone-free surface to soften in the sun. One roll of standard 90-lb. roofing, or two rolls of half-lap roofing, covers one square.

With half-lap, cut the first roll down the middle and cement the smooth-surfaced portion to the edge of the roof. The next full-width roll goes over this starter course. Each roll is nailed along the top edge only, at 4-in. spacing. After all but the last ridge-cap sheet (the other half of the starter roll) is installed, beginning at the top, pick up each piece (it takes at least four hands to prevent tearing) and flip it back over onto the roof. Mop cold cement, called "blind-nailing" cement, over the smooth half of the roll and over the mineral surface to the factory-made chalkline, and pick up the overlying sheet and drop it back into place.

Smooth out any wrinkles with your feet, shuffling from the center outward toward the rakes. Cement the ridge-cap sheet in place last. The exposed edges of the sheets can be left unnailed (hence the term "blind" nailing) or face-nailed for greater resistance to the wind. Vertical laps between sheets should be at least 6 in. and are always face-nailed off. If the edges of the sheets are cemented to the drip edge with flashing cement instead of cold cement, there's less chance of their lifting up.

Reroofing with Wood Shingles

There are several principles to bear in mind when laying wood shingles:

    1. The exposure is determined by the pitch and shingle length. Wood shingles should not be used for slopes less than 5-in-12. A 5-in. exposure is recommended for 6-in-12 and greater pitches.

    2. The shingles should be spaced about ¼ in. apart to allow for expansion when wet. If laid tightly, they will buckle and even split.

    3. Joints on alternate courses should never line up. Observe a minimum offset of at least 1½ in.

    4. Use two 5d galvanized shingle nails per shingle, driven 2 in. above the butt line and 1 in. from the edges (make sure they strike the underlying purlins). Split shingles wider than 10 in. in two to prevent future uncontrolled splitting.

    5. Valleys are 4 in. wide at the top. Use only copper for flashings and valleys. No other metal will dependably outlast the shingles.

    6. Wood shingles should never be laid on a solid deck. Although old, rather widely spaced rough-edged roof boards don't qualify as solid sheathing, longevity of the new shingles is ensured by applying tar paper over the boards, followed by vertical 1x3 strapping nailed over each rafter, and then by 1x3 purlins spaced 5 in. on center to carry the shingles. For long-term security against leaks and possible condensation problems, install sheathing and tar paper over open rafters before the ventilated nailers.

    7. Use clear cedar boards to form the ridge cap. Convert the roof pitch to degrees with a protractor to find the angle of the cut for your saw. The seam at the ridge should be caulked and any butt joints covered with a strip of copper.

Several roofs of wood shingles will wear out before this copper flashing. Always use a long-lasting metal; even with ordinary asphalt shingles, it's too much work to replace corroded flashings.

Cedar Ridge Board for Cedar Shingles

Convert roof pitch to degrees with protractor, and set saw accordingly, e.g., a 6/12 pitch equals a 26½° cut.

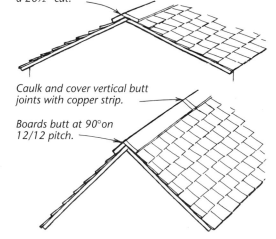

Caulk and cover vertical butt joints with copper strip.

Boards butt at 90° on 12/12 pitch.

Typical Wood-Shingle Installation

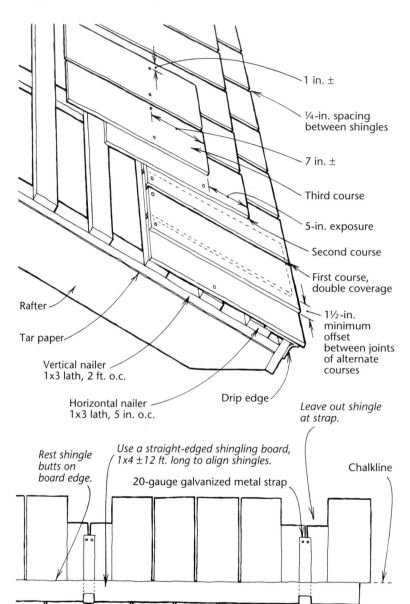

1 in. ±

¼-in. spacing between shingles

7 in. ±

Third course

5-in. exposure

Second course

First course, double coverage

1½-in. minimum offset between joints of alternate courses

Rafter

Tar paper

Vertical nailer 1x3 lath, 2 ft. o.c.

Horizontal nailer 1x3 lath, 5 in. o.c.

Drip edge

Leave out shingle at strap.

Rest shingle butts on board edge.

Use a straight-edged shingling board, 1x4 ±12 ft. long to align shingles.

20-gauge galvanized metal strap

Chalkline

The drawing at left shows the layout and some additional details of typical wood-shingle roofing. The question most novices ask is how to stand on the roof, since, unlike asphalt, wood shingles can't be lifted up to remove a roof jack once they are nailed down. The answer is simply to omit the particular shingle that would otherwise overlap the jack and slide it up under the shingles when the stagings are removed, using the nailing technique shown in the drawing on p. 143.

Courses can follow chalklines snapped across the shingles, but it's a lot faster to align them with a straight-edged board. Fasten three or four galvanized metal straps to the board for attaching it to the roof, like a roof jack (see the drawing at left). The shingle that would overlay the metal is simply not nailed until after the board is removed. Snap a guideline across the shingles to ensure that the board itself is properly spaced and running true. Use blue chalk when working with wood shingles; red chalk doesn't wash off and will stain the wood for a long time. Save it for guidelines on tar paper when working with asphalt roofing.

Reroofing with Steel Sheets

Steel roofing can be applied directly over old asphalt shingles—a convenient solution to the problem of repairing a rotted deck or worn-out shingles with a minimum of effort and expense. But check your local zoning ordinances if you plan to reroof with steel—some towns actually prohibit the use of steel roofing on the grounds that it lowers neighborhood property values.

Roughsawn 1x4 or 1½x4 spruce strapping, laid horizontally 16 in. on center and nailed through the old shingles into the rafters, is used for the nailers (purlins) that support the steel roofing. Roughsawn 1½x4 is 25% cheaper than a milled 2x4, with slightly more strength, and is used over open rafters in lieu of solid sheathing. The 1x4 boards are 17% cheaper than the

Laying Steel Roofing over an Old Roof

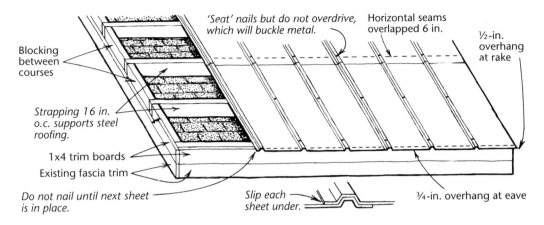

'Seat' nails but do not overdrive, which will buckle metal.

Horizontal seams overlapped 6 in.

½-in. overhang at rake

Blocking between courses

Strapping 16 in. o.c. supports steel roofing.

1x4 trim boards

Existing fascia trim

Do not nail until next sheet is in place.

Slip each sheet under.

¾-in. overhang at eave

heavier nailers, but are too weak to support the roofing unless nailed to a solid deck. The steel masks any differences in thickness, and perfectly consistent width is not an important consideration.

Begin by breaking back any overhanging shingles flush to the edge of the roof. The first nailer should be flush with the edge of the existing fascia trim board. Use a spacer block to keep subsequent courses of nailers on center. Fill in the spaces between nailers at the rakes or, if the deck is solid enough, run a vertical nailer up each rake and butt the horizontals to it. Block around chimneys and vent pipes for solid nailing and triple up the nailers that run down each side of a valley. Use drywall screws to tighten down the ends of any nailers that miss the rafters when nails won't hold. Finish off the edges of the nailers at the fascias with new 1x4 pine trim boards. Allow the roofing to overhang the fascia ½ in. at the rakes and ¾ in. at the eaves.

Steel roofing is installed with its vertical seams opposite the direction of the prevailing winds. Whenever possible, use sheets long enough to cover the roof in one piece. Otherwise, overlap any seams at least 6 in. The overlapping seam must be nailed within 2 in. of its bottom edge. When a standard-length sheet is only an inch or two short of covering the roof, an 8-in. drip edge can serve as an extension. This saves the bother of having to install an unsightly small filler sheet or ordering custom-length steel.

Metal roofing is, to some extent, self-flashing; the sheets can be cut to fold up against a chimney or side wall, as shown in the drawing on p. 162. A 4-in. lap is sufficient. For vent pipes, a hole can be cut through a full sheet and the flashing boot sealed to the metal, but a more watertight job is guaranteed if two overlapping sheets are used instead. The lower sheet, containing the hole, ends about 1 ft. above the vent. The flashing is installed over it and sealed. The second, overlapping sheet is cut to fit around the pipe and over the top of the flashing, just like a shingle. Seal all overlaps liberally with Geocel® caulk, which is much more flexible and durable than flashing cement. Wipe fresh metal with paint thinner to remove any oily film.

Steel roofing is extremely slippery. A 4-in-12 pitch is the upper limit of the slope that can be worked without assistance. Even this will be too steep when wet. Wear rubber-soled high-traction sneakers

Flashing Details for Steel Roofing

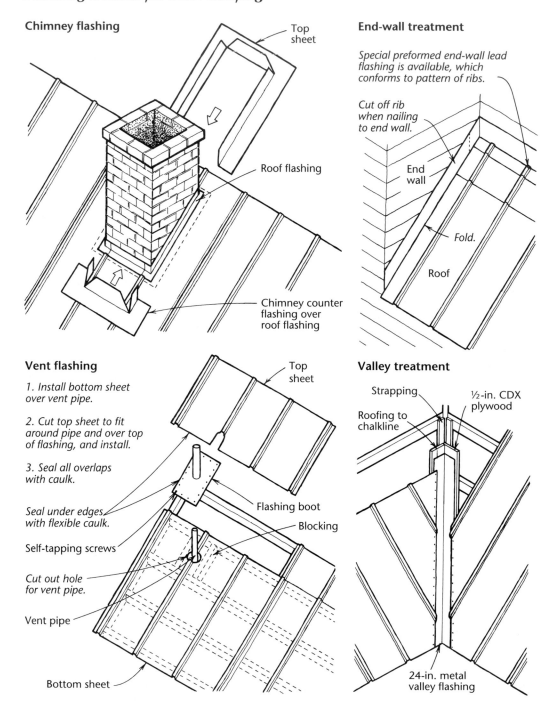

Chimney flashing

Top sheet

Roof flashing

Chimney counter flashing over roof flashing

End-wall treatment

Special preformed end-wall lead flashing is available, which conforms to pattern of ribs.

Cut off rib when nailing to end wall.

End wall

Fold.

Roof

Vent flashing

1. Install bottom sheet over vent pipe.

2. Cut top sheet to fit around pipe and over top of flashing, and install.

3. Seal all overlaps with caulk.

Seal under edges with flexible caulk.

Self-tapping screws

Cut out hole for vent pipe.

Vent pipe

Bottom sheet

Top sheet

Flashing boot

Blocking

Valley treatment

Strapping

Roofing to chalkline

½-in. CDX plywood

24-in. metal valley flashing

when walking on steel. Fortunately, the nailers furnish a built-in staging system from which you reach back over each sheet to nail it. Hook a ladder over the ridge to install the last sheet.

There's very little sideways play in the vertical seams of metal roofing, which means that it's hard to gain more than an inch or so on a skewed rake. Before laying the first sheet, measure across the roof at the ridge and eaves to check for differences. You might be able to compensate by tilting the first sheet over the rake a bit and pushing the following sheets toward the required correction. A tapered cut across raised ribs or corrugations looks pretty poor, but, short of shimming out the cornice fascia trim, there's no choice but to live with it.

Straight or tapered, it's unlikely that the edge of the last sheet will coincide with the rake. Measure the last sheet from the edge of the overlap to the edge of the rake and add ½ in. to the measurement. Tin shears are a slow and painful way to cut steel and an easy way to gash your knuckles. Wear gloves. Better yet, find the burned out blade that you ruined slicing through nails in old roof sheathing and install it backward in your circular saw. This makes a much more durable metal-cutting blade than the carbide composition blades sold for the purpose. Snap a chalkline down the sheet, which should be supported on 2x4s laid under both sides of the cut. Wear safety glasses to protect your eyes from shrapnel and ear muffs to insulate your ears from the banshee scream of metal on metal. Bend the cut edge over the rake with a block of wood and a hammer.

There are two kinds of nails for fastening steel roofing: "lead-heads" and neoprene-gasket nails. The former have a lead washer under the head, which compresses when hammered to form a watertight seal against the roofing. Unfortunately, the washer snaps off rather easily whenever you move a ladder or shovel across the roof or over the years as the nails work

loose. The latter type seals to the roofing with a durable neoprene-rubber gasket. These nails cost twice as much per pound as lead-heads but weigh half as much, so in the long run they're the better buy.

Drive nails through only the top of the ribbing or corrugations—a nail driven into the flat will leak. Strictly speaking, not all steel roofing is corrugated—the term corrugation refers to a continuous ribbed profile, whereas "prime-rib" roofing has a profile of prominent raised ribs followed by alternating flat sections and less prominent ribs. (Prime-rib roofing is more watertight and rigid than corrugated roofing.) Nail prime-rib roofing on each rib and corrugated roofing on every third or fourth corrugation.

Every brand of steel roofing has its own distinctive ribbing pattern, which is seldom interchangeable with other brands. This is of particular importance when selecting factory-made ridge-cap and endwall flashings. Start the roofing from the same end of the roof for both sides to help keep the ribs lined up with the ridge-cap corrugations. Some roofing patterns have a top and bottom orientation as well, which must be observed to prevent leakage along the vertical seams. Check with the dealer for pertinent installation details. If more than one sheet is needed to reach the ridge, finish each course up to the ridge before running the sheets out across the roof. Horizontal seams must interlock so that no top sheet is ever under a bottom sheet.

New galvanized roofing will not accept paint until the coating has weathered for at least a season, unless a special primer is used first. Painting over rusty, but sound, old steel roofing, as described earlier, is best done from a ladder and hook. Tie two lengths of light aluminum ladder together where one is not long enough to cover the roof.

Eave Protection

In regions of heavy snowfall, it is common to find a 2-ft. to 3-ft. wide band of metal along the eaves, especially on slate roofs. Ice dams are a problem in the North, and the metal is intended to prevent water from backing up under the lower courses of shingles and into the house. Even if ice does build up on the metal, there are no overlying seams to work up under.

Ice dams are caused when heat escaping through the attic or sunlight falling on a south-facing roof melts the snowcover. This snowmelt flows down the roof until it reaches the eaves, which, because they project out over the wall, are cold enough to freeze the water. As the layer of ice builds up, it dams further snowmelt, which then backs up higher and higher along the roof slope until it seeps under the shingles and down into the house. This is another reason why ranch houses, with their low-pitched roofs and wide overhanging eaves, are ill-suited to Northern climates. Keeping snow off a roof designed to shield the walls of a house from desert sun requires

energy, either in the form of an electric heating cable or a body behind a snow shovel. After several seasons of ice-breaking with an ax or sledgehammer, the shingles are noticeably tattered.

If the existing metal is in good shape, leave it in place when stripping the roof. Set the first course of roof jacks above it. If your reroofing project includes metal eave protection, proceed as follows:

Measure up from the eave's drip edges to a point equal to the width of the metal, less 1 in., and snap a chalkline across the roof. Add 2 in. to the roof length and cut a roll of 36-in. wide flashing metal to fit. Tack the top corner of the metal to the line, overhanging the rake drip edge 1 in., and unroll the metal, as if tar-papering. Raise or lower the line as necessary to compensate for any unevenness in the eave, but maintain a minimum overhang at the drip edge of at least 1 in. Any excess can be trimmed off afterward. Secure the top edge with nails spaced 6 in. apart, working from the middle toward the rakes to minimize buckling.

Unless you are salvaging existing metal, new copper will easily cost more than all the other roofing materials combined. For anything other than slate shingles, galvanized steel with a baked-on epoxy enamel finish is both cost-effective and attractive. The metal color can match or complement the shingles. Crimp the overhanging metal over the drip edge to lock the bottom and sides to the roof. Vise-Grip makes a sheet-metal tool that will prove invaluable for this and most other flashing jobs.

Because of thermal expansion, a single sheet of metal running the length of the roof will tend to ripple on hot days. This poses less threat of leakage than several smaller sheets joined by vertical seams. Occasional visual imperfection is a worthwhile tradeoff. If it is necessary to join pieces together, add 1½ in. to the length of each overlapping piece, and form a standing-seam type of joint, which can be sealed with Geocel® or high-grade

Installing Metal Eave Protection

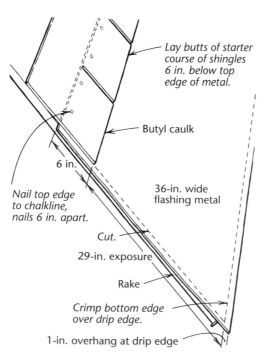

Lay butts of starter course of shingles 6 in. below top edge of metal.

Butyl caulk

6 in.

Nail top edge to chalkline, nails 6 in. apart.

36-in. wide flashing metal

Cut.

29-in. exposure

Rake

Crimp bottom edge over drip edge.

1-in. overhang at drip edge

silicone caulk. When the sheet is nailed down, snap a chalkline 6 in. down from its top edge, and lay the butts of the starter course of shingles to it. Seal the first layer to the metal with butyl caulking (which is compatible with asphalt products and very sticky).

For extra protection under the metal sheet, or for low-pitched porch roofs, wide eaves and especially valleys under metal roofing, omit the tar paper and install a self-sticking butyl waterproofing membrane such as Ice and Water Shield® directly to the bare deck. For protection against ice dams, lay the membrane from the drip edge to one course width past the building line (the transition zone between cold and heated deck).

Eavestroughs and Downspouts

Water falling from the eaves and pooling along the foundation wall can cause a wet cellar. Eavestroughs, or gutters, catch this water at the roof and divert it through a downspout, or leader, away from the building. In regions of heavy seasonal rainfall and mild winters, they are an absolute necessity. But in climates similar to that of northern Vermont, they are not only unnecessary, but potentially problematic.

Gutters can fill up with ice and split apart or encourage especially pernicious ice dams that rot cornices and wall sheathing. Clogged downspouts are easily burst by iceplugs. Unfortunately, there is no practical way to build a house that will be secure from every conceivable weather condition. If a gutter must be under the eaves at all, the only sensible location is a short piece over the front door, which can be taken down in the fall. Although a gable-roofed door stoop is a better solution to the triumph of fashion over common sense that results in an unprotected entry placed directly under the eaves, the gutter will at least prevent a chilling downpour when people enter or leave the house. But it won't do much to protect against a dangerous ice avalanche.

A Yankee Gutter

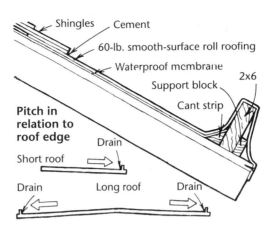

Yankee gutters

In southern New England, it is still fairly common to find gutters built into the roof deck. These Yankee gutters are little more than a sloped trough framed on the deck and covered with roofing material. Besides economy of construction, my memories of them recall another traditional aspect of the Yankee character: cantankerousness. Because Yankee gutters project from the eaves, roofers found them a convenient substitute for the first course of staging planks. Unfortunately, like the fellow who stopped at a fork to ask the old farmer if it mattered which road he took to get to Montpelier and was told, "Not to me, it don't," you can't always know where you stand. You can never quite trust a Yankee gutter not to rip clean off the roof when you put your foot through a hidden rotted place.

I imagine that coastal New England is the natural northern limit of their practicality, since a more ideal environment for a monumental ice dam could not be imagined. However, with an underlayment of waterproofing membrane and a covering of 60-lb. roll roofing (easier to form than metal) and a well-insulated, properly vented attic, a Yankee gutter could be an excel-

Relining Built-In Gutters

1. Whisk-broom surface of gutter and remove first few courses of shingles.

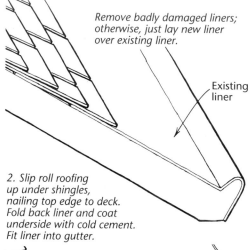

Remove badly damaged liners; otherwise, just lay new liner over existing liner.

Existing liner

2. Slip roll roofing up under shingles, nailing top edge to deck. Fold back liner and coat underside with cold cement. Fit liner into gutter.

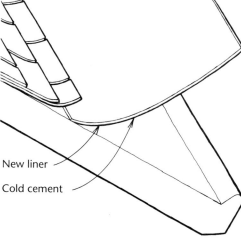

New liner

Cold cement

3. Snap chalkline. Replace and renail shingles, sealing first courses to roof to prevent ice dams.

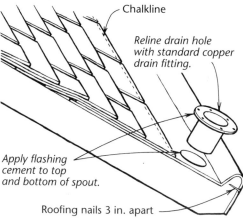

Chalkline

Reline drain hole with standard copper drain fitting.

Apply flashing cement to top and bottom of spout.

Roofing nails 3 in. apart

lent way to capitalize upon the insulating properties of a heavy snowcover. With seasonal cleaning and periodic recoating (use fibered roof coating), it should last as long as the house itself. Unlike conventional fascia-hung gutters, there's no flimsy trough to overflow or split apart.

Most people let their gutters and roofs go unmaintained until a leak becomes too troublesome to ignore. By then, damage has already been done to the roof deck, walls or ceilings. A simple inspection and cleaning each fall and spring would help extend the life of gutter systems and prevent expensive repairs. Any debris from the roof and clotted twigs and leaves should be removed. These frequently plug the entrance to the downspout. Leaves also act like sponges, holding moisture that eventually rots the asphalt composition lining or corrodes metal gutters.

Repairing built-in gutters

The only difference between a Yankee gutter and other sorts of built-in gutters is that the former is constructed on top of the roof deck, independent of the cornice, whereas the others are integral components of it. Repair and relining techniques are basically the same for all built-ins, regardless of style.

Patch small tears or punctures in the gutter lining with flashing cement and fiberglass webbing. Break any bubbles in the asphalt and coat them with flashing cement. Paint the entire length of the gutter with asphalt roof coating, using a wallpaper-paste brush.

Badly split or worn gutters must be relined. First, thoroughly clean the surface with a whisk broom. Allow it to dry out while removing the first few courses of shingles. Take up as many courses as will allow you to slip the new gutter lining up under the shingles with a minimum overlap of 6 in.; a narrow strip of roll roofing makes a good gauge. Smooth-surfaced roll roofing, 18-in. wide, will line a narrow gutter with the removal of only a single course of shingles. If possible, try to save the old shingles for reuse, as it will be difficult to get a good match with new shingles. Nail the top edge of the roll roofing (which has been softened in the sun) to the deck. Lap any seams 6 in.

Lay the liner back over itself onto the roof (as when applying half-lap), and coat its entire underside with cold cement. Form it into the gutter, using your knee to smooth out wrinkles, working from the middle toward the ends. Nail the outside edge of the liner to the fascia board and cover any seams using galvanized roofing nails spaced 3 in. apart. Seal the seams with flashing cement. Snap a line and replace the missing shingles, taking care to seal the first two courses to the roof to protect against ice jams. Reline the drain hole with a standard copper drain fitting, if needed, and apply flashing cement liberally to the top and bottom of the spout.

If a Yankee or other style built-in gutter has deteriorated to the point where the deck or cornice boards have rotted, the gutter should be torn off and the rotted parts rebuilt with new wood. It's probably easier to hang a standard gutter from the fascia than to rebuild the old one. The missing shingle courses are added from the top down, slipping each course up under the one above it. Use a chalkline to mark the bottom of each course. If the distance to the newly installed drip edge will not divide evenly into fives, crowd or spread the courses equally to make up the difference. This way, you avoid ending up with a 2-in. strip of shingle or uncovered cutouts at the last course.

Wood gutters built into the fascia (or even comprising the entire cornice), made of either clear fir, cedar or redwood, were a hallmark of high-quality new construction in the postwar years. If they are still sound, a seasonal coat of asphalt emulsion will keep them that way. Slightly rotted gutters are still salvageable: Reline them with butyl membrane, coated with asphalt cement, or asphalt emulsion reinforced with fiberglass roofer's cloth and topcoated with a final coat after the first has dried.

Filling In Shingles at Eaves

Add missing courses from top down. Snap chalkline to mark bottom of each course.

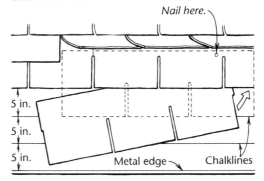

Nail here.

5 in.
5 in.
5 in.

Metal edge — Chalklines

Compensating for odd width

If width doesn't divide evenly by 5, compensate by spreading or crowding courses equally.

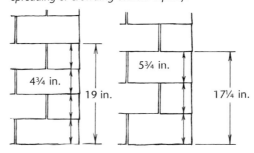

4¾ in.   19 in.

5¾ in.   17¼ in.

Replacing wood gutters

Gutters too far gone to reline must be removed. By this point, expect also to replace most of the trim and even some of the underlying wall sheathing. Remove the bed molding that supports the gutter first. Use a pinchbar to separate the gutter from the cornice. You may have to split it apart with a chisel to ease removal. Try to save the wood end blocks that trim the gutter, or cut new ones if they are too rotted to remove in one piece.

Wood gutters are quite heavy. Pull carefully with the pinchbar until the back edge is barely hanging from its nails. Then tie one end of the gutter to the roof while you slowly work the other end free and lower it to the ground. A helper on a sec-

Built-In Wood Gutters

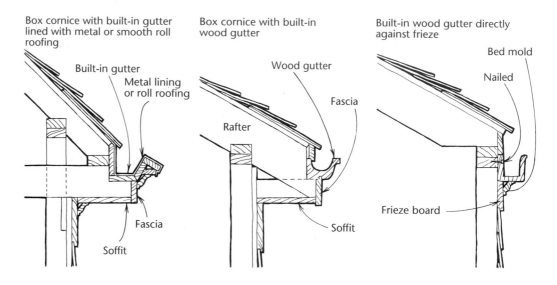

Box cornice with built-in gutter lined with metal or smooth roll roofing

Built-in gutter

Metal lining or roll roofing

Fascia

Soffit

Box cornice with built-in wood gutter

Wood gutter

Fascia

Rafter

Soffit

Built-in wood gutter directly against frieze

Bed mold

Nailed

Frieze board

ond ladder at the other end makes this job a lot easier. Gutters are hard to pull off and tend to go, when they finally do, quite suddenly; enough to throw you off balance and off the ladder as well. The free end of a falling gutter also makes a very good battering ram, and can tear up the side of a house before it smashes through the glass patio doors.

It's unlikely that you'll replace the old wood gutter with a new one, since wood-gutter stock is both scarce and expensive. Cover the missing boards at the wall or cornice with a shim and a trim board sufficient to support a new fascia board.

Metal and plastic gutters

Since the 1960s, aluminum and vinyl have completely supplanted galvanized steel as the material of choice for gutter and leader replacement. With the advent of forming machines capable of turning a roll of "coil stock" into a seamless gutter of any length on site, installation of roof-drainage systems has come into its own as a subcontract specialty.

Prefinished aluminum gutters and leaders have a baked-on enamel finish that makes them virtually immune to corrosion, even in salt-water climates. These systems are available in a wide variety of styles, with corresponding fasteners, hangers and fittings.

Aluminum gutter systems are one of the few justifiably sensible uses of aluminum as a building material. Despite their increasing popularity and heavy advertising, I have reservations about the use of vinyl and other plastic systems. For one thing, they are manufactured from scarce petrochemicals, which might be saved for better uses. For another, all plastics break down eventually after exposure to sunlight, manufacturers' claims notwithstanding. Actually all building materials wear out eventually. The question is, which ones do it most gracefully? Which would you prefer, weathered wood or weathered plastic? Vinyl also becomes brittle at low temperatures, which increases the likelihood of an ice-jammed gutter splitting apart.

Gutters are sized according to the area of the roof surface to be drained—4-in. gutters will drain up to 750 sq. ft.; 5-in. gutters, up to 1,400 feet. If you need a 6-in. gutter, you're probably living in a church. Roofs with over 1,000 sq. ft. of area require 4-in. downspouting; otherwise, use standard 3-in. pipes.

Gutters are designed to mount either directly to the cornice fascia board or to hang from roof-mounted straps. These straps are nailed to the eave starter shingles so that they fall under the middle of the overlapping shingle tabs. When re-shingling the roof at the same time, leave out the first course of shingles and install the gutters after the roofing is finished. Otherwise, lift up existing shingles to slip in the straps. Never lean a ladder directly against a gutter. If the gutters are already in place, use a ladder stand-off bracket to protect them while shingling or doing any maintenance work on the gutters. Carrying a bundle of shingles up a ladder resting against a gutter is like kissing a guardrail with your car.

To drain properly, the gutter must pitch—1 in. for every 16 ft. of run is more than adequate. For spans over 30 ft., make the middle of the eave the high point and pitch the gutter toward downspouts at each end. Shorter spans pitch to a drain at the more convenient end. Snap a chalkline along the fascia to align the top edge of the gutter to the desired pitch and then secure the hangers.

The entire length of the gutter should be pre-assembled on the ground and then installed in one piece. More than one helper and one ladder may be needed to prevent long gutters from buckling when they're raised into place. If the ladders are resting on the wall of the building instead of on a support bracket, protect the siding from scratches by tying rags or socks over the ends of the ladder rails.

Start at the high end and nail the hangers to the roof as you align the back edge of the gutter with the chalkline on the fascia. Roof hangers are most useful when the roof construction won't permit the gutter to rest against the fascia. Other than that, it's a lot less trouble to use spike-and-ferrule hangers. These aluminum spikes, driven through the top edge of the gutter, through a tube (the ferrule) held in place behind it and through the back of the gutter into the fascia, are much stronger than any other kind of support. The ferrule also keeps the gutter from denting. You can lean a ladder over a ferrule without buckling the gutter, or plant your heels in it when you kneel on the edge of a roof to shingle.

Rest the gutter on nails tacked into the fascia until the spikes are driven home. The gutter will have sufficient support if you plant the spikes into the tail end of every other rafter. Fascia strap hangers, while not quite as strong, are the easiest to line up, since they are driven into the fascia board (following the chalkline), after which the gutter is lifted into them. If the existing roof lacks a drip edge, fold a strip of aluminum coil stock to fit up under the first few inches of the shingles and down over the back lip of the gutter.

End pieces, drain outlets and couplers between stock sections of gutter are fastened together by aluminum rivets and sealed with a special aluminum gasket cement supplied by the distributor. Rivet the support straps for the downspouting to the downspout tubing, but leave the sections unriveted for easy disassembly during cleanout.

Although you may have pitched the gutter relative to the fascia, with an old house you can't assume that the roofline is level or that the gutter is actually pitched enough or even in the right direction. Test its effectiveness by dumping a pail of water into the supposed high end and observing the speed and direction of the drainage. It's a good idea not to drive all the supports home until the gutter passes the slope test.

There was a time when copper was used for gutters and downspouts. I suppose today I'd try to resolder split seams

A Cold Roof

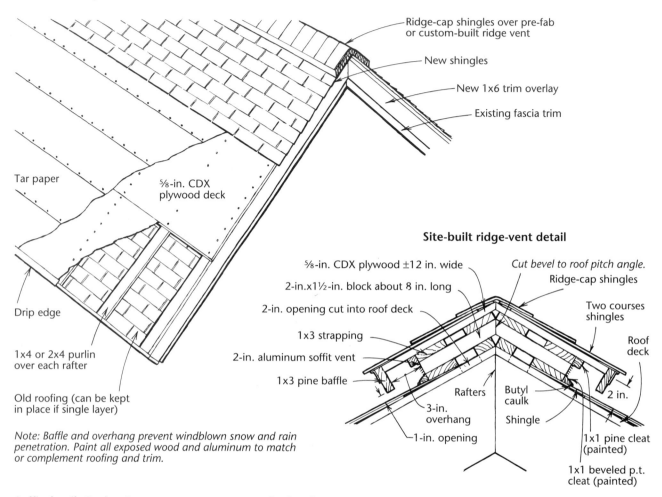

Ridge-cap shingles over pre-fab or custom-built ridge vent

New shingles

New 1x6 trim overlay

Existing fascia trim

Tar paper

⅝-in. CDX plywood deck

Drip edge

1x4 or 2x4 purlin over each rafter

Old roofing (can be kept in place if single layer)

Note: Baffle and overhang prevent windblown snow and rain penetration. Paint all exposed wood and aluminum to match or complement roofing and trim.

Site-built ridge-vent detail

⅝-in. CDX plywood ±12 in. wide

2-in.x1½-in. block about 8 in. long

2-in. opening cut into roof deck

1x3 strapping

2-in. aluminum soffit vent

1x3 pine baffle

Cut bevel to roof pitch angle.

Ridge-cap shingles

Two courses shingles

Roof deck

Rafters

3-in. overhang

1-in. opening

Butyl caulk

Shingle

2 in.

1x1 pine cleat (painted)

1x1 beveled p.t. cleat (painted)

Soffit detail: Option 1

Option 1 works best for uneven eaves since 2x4 purlins can be cut to a straight line.

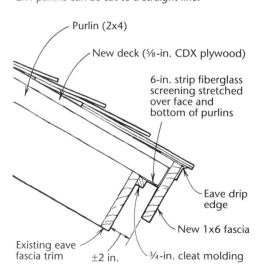

Purlin (2x4)

New deck (⅝-in. CDX plywood)

6-in. strip fiberglass screening stretched over face and bottom of purlins

Eave drip edge

New 1x6 fascia

Existing eave fascia trim   ±2 in.   ¾-in. cleat molding

Option 2

Option 2, which uses 2x4 blocks nailed directly to old fascia to clamp screen and support new fascia, works best for steel roofing (does not require CDX deck). 1x4 purlins give even opening and better nailing for fascia.

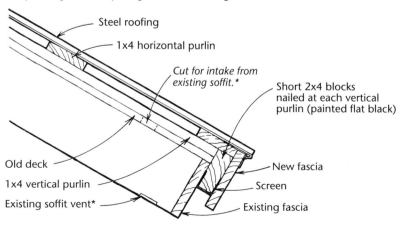

Steel roofing

1x4 horizontal purlin

Cut for intake from existing soffit.*

Short 2x4 blocks nailed at each vertical purlin (painted flat black)

Old deck

1x4 vertical purlin

Existing soffit vent*

New fascia

Screen

Existing fascia

* If there is an existing soffit vent, new vent opening can be eliminated. Simply cut out a 2-in. band of old deck to allow intake venting of cold roof.

rather than tear the old ones down for scrap as we routinely did when I was a kid. Back then, my grandfather would often pay me for helping out by letting me keep the scrap metal. At the end of the summer we'd take a truckload of old flashing, gutters and spouting to the junkyard and leave with a small fortune.

The Cold Roof

Within the last 20 years, the "cold" roof has gained increasing popularity in the North, in both new construction and especially as a reroofing option. A cold roof is a sort of passive air-conditioning and ventilating system that allows cold air to circulate freely under the entire roof deck during the winter, thereby removing the heat that escapes through the attic before it can melt the snow on the roof, pretty much eliminating ice dams (except on the south slopes, where they become much smaller). In the summer, the air flow tends to prevent attic overheating by isolating the hot shingles from the attic sheathing and circulating air beneath them. Unfortunately, these advantages entail a considerable increase in cost for extra decking, trimwork and labor.

If there aren't too many layers of roofing on the deck already, a cold roof can be built right over the old shingles. Otherwise, strip them and tar-paper the roof as for ordinary reroofing, but omit the drip edge. Then nail 1x4s parallel to and directly over each rafter. Let the ends project 1½ in. beyond the fascias (snap a chalkline across the ends to help trim them evenly). Staple a 6-in. wide strip of fiberglass screen to the existing fascia board and leave it hanging downward. Nail blocks of 2x4 (spray-painted black) over the fascia, 2 ft. on center, and fold the screening tightly over the bottom and up onto the face of the blocking. The screen will help keep birds out of your attic.

If you are reroofing with corrugated steel or wood shingles, nail a horizontal course of 1x4 across the vertical strapping, flush to the bottom edge. Finish this with a new fascia board wide enough to overhang the blocking by at least ½ in. Add any other ornamental cornice trim or molding and the drip edge. Continue nailing horizontal strapping across the vertical purlins, 16 in. on center up to the ridge. Fill in the spaces between courses at the eaves with blocking. If you are using any other type of roofing material, simply nail ⅝-in. CDX plywood over the vertical strapping to form a solid deck, and add the new fascia board. Also, only the new deck is tar-papered. The screened opening at the fascia serves as the air intake.

This ventilating air flow is exhausted through a continuous ridge vent. Cut a 2-in. opening through the existing shingles and/or sheathing boards on each side of the ridge (hold the last course of horizontal strapping or plywood sheathing back the same amount). Attic air is vented through this opening much more effectively than through gable louvers.

For years, it seemed as if none of the prefabricated ridge vents on the market were worth installing, at least in the North, where they were soon flattened by snow. The only truly durable and effective vents were contractor-built in place. At an installed price of up to $10 to $15 per lineal foot, they added significantly to the job cost. But recently, several new types of ridge vents have made their appearance (Cor-A-Vent, 16250 Petro Dr., Mishawaka, IN 46544, is one of the better ones). They are not only cost-efficient and effective, but also attractive. Some of these ridge vents are finished off with ordinary ridge shingles; others are self-contained interlocking sections. Custom-built or prefabricated, a ridge vent requires at least five vertical feet of difference (the "thermal head") between the intake and outlet to get the air moving.

Windows, Doors, Siding and Trim

I want a house that has got over all its troubles; I don't want to spend the rest of my life bringing up a young and inexperienced house.

—Jerome K. Jerome

There are several historical inaccuracies and architectural faux pas in this owner-renovation of a classic post-1850s Vermont farmhouse, including the picture window on the second floor, the crossbuck doors and the outside block chimney. (Photo by Joe English.)

A house wears its age on its face. The wrinkles and creases of weathered boards and peeling paint, the arthritic disjointing of cornice and trim, the debilitating diseases of hidden rot—a house shows the weight of life past. But like those beautiful people who fly off to exclusive Swiss clinics for facelifts, old houses, too, can be restored to a semblance of youth. There is nothing exotic to the process, and it need not be expensive. It's fairly necessary for the well-being of the house and can even be fun to do. After the grind of foundation work and roofing, the renovation of an exterior (or interior) wall is a stimulating, pleasurable tonic. Just painting the walls could save a marriage.

In a timber-frame house, the outside walls consist of an exterior finish, which is attached to a supportive inner layer of sheathing boards. The finish is in direct contact with the elements, enduring the constant cycles of hot and cold, wet and dry. Its tightly overlapping structure (clapboards or shingles) is designed to shed water. It is a testimony to the unique durability of wood that it weathers so well. Examine an old barn board. It will be noticeably thicker where the eaves have protected it from direct exposure. Wind and rain will have scoured the grain, leaving a fantastic landscape of ridges and valleys. If kept dry and well aired, wood will erode before it rots.

But as the outer wood wears, the nails draw moisture. When they rust away, small cavities are left to shelter water and rot. The constant shrinking and expanding separates the wood fibers along the grain. As water pries at these fissures, the wood leaches away, cracks open wider and pieces of clapboard curl and break loose. Nails are pulled out as boards warp. The skin becomes loose and flaccid. The house develops a chronic cold; it is continually drafty. Like a deathbed revelation, the old wood glows with a strange beauty in its decay. "Grey" is a mere approximation, an average of the many subtle shifts of color and density as it responds to light and weather. Old boards are a map, a book of verse, the journal of a house's passage through time.

Unfortunately, metaphor alone won't keep you warm and dry. Tourists may think it quaint to live in a weatherbeaten old house, but its inhabitants know it for the mean and constant struggle it is. Driving the backroads in winter, one will often see entire houses swaddled in plastic sheets, buttoned up with tar paper and battens, in the attempt to slam the door on winter's icy fingers.

Infiltration and Heat Loss: Tightening Up the House

It's a common misconception that heavy insulation is the most important requirement for a warm house. Although that may be true for the attic, heavily insulated walls are not as important as tight walls. The infiltration of cold outside air is the major cause of drafts and high heating bills. Wind blowing against one side of the house, warm air escaping up chimneys, exhaust vents and furnace flues, and the temperature difference between heated inside air and cold outside air all create the negative pressure differential or partial vacuum that powers infiltration.

Negative pressure in itself is not a bad thing. The same principle drives passive summer cooling and attic venting. Controlled infiltration is ventilation; uncontrolled infiltration causes physical and financial discomfort. A reasonable amount of air movement is necessary for health. The current wisdom is that a complete exchange of household air about every two hours will exhaust excess moisture, indoor pollutants and other toxic by-products of cooking, breathing and living, without intolerable heat loss. Although some modern superinsulated houses will lose as little as one-tenth of their atmosphere per hour (requiring the addition of mechanical air and heat exchangers to prevent asphyxiation), it's hard to imagine a caulking and weatherstripping program rigorous enough to make an old house too tight.

It's been estimated that the total heat loss through all the cracks and gaps in the envelope of a typical old house is about the same as if the front door were left wide open 24 hours a day. It would take a lot of caulking to fill a hole that big.

Early builders were not unaware of infiltration. To reduce drafts, plank walls were sometimes rabbeted to make tight joints, or plastered over. Cellar walls were sometimes bricked up. The practice of "banking" the house, whereby bales of spoiled hay, spruce boughs or tar-paper strips and battens were placed against the outside foundation walls, was another attempt to block drafts.

Caulking

Modern technology has created a veritable arsenal of anti-infiltration products. No longer does the home owner laboriously have to replace dried-out caulking every couple of years. Today, you can select high-tech polymers that can be applied over a wide temperature range, don't degrade in sunlight, adhere to almost any material and remain flexible for 50 years or more. (This is especially attractive if you need to caulk a high cornice and never want to do it again.) Over the long term, only the best caulk is cheapest.

The best time to caulk a house is when you repaint, just after the surfaces have been scraped, cleaned and primed—even the best caulk won't adhere to loose, flaking or dirty surfaces. Search out and fill any gaps at the joints of door and window frames, especially where clapboards fall short of the trim. Joints between corner trim boards, cornice returns and the wall, or under thresholds are also likely targets. Use a paintable caulk to fill any splits in clapboards. One of the worst infiltration pathways is the gap between the top of

Sources of Air Infiltration

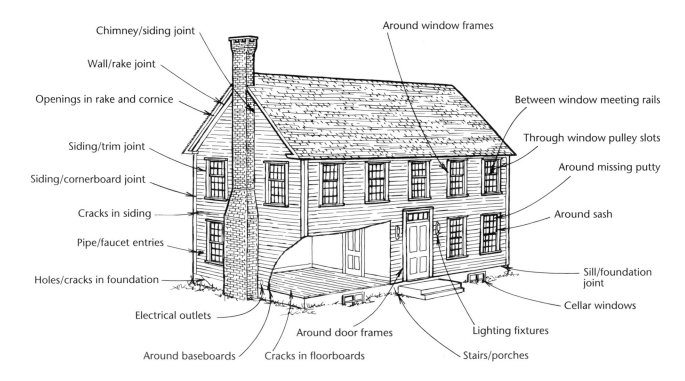

Chimney/siding joint
Wall/rake joint
Openings in rake and cornice
Siding/trim joint
Siding/cornerboard joint
Cracks in siding
Pipe/faucet entries
Holes/cracks in foundation
Electrical outlets
Around baseboards
Cracks in floorboards
Around door frames
Stairs/porches
Lighting fixtures
Cellar windows
Sill/foundation joint
Around sash
Around missing putty
Through window pulley slots
Between window meeting rails
Around window frames

the foundation wall and the sills—plug it with spray-foam insulation. Point any cracks between foundation stones with mortar on the outside. Look for television lead-in wires that enter under window sashes; reroute them through a hole drilled in the wall and sealed with caulk. LP gas lines and outside water faucets also benefit from caulk. If you caulk when the temperature is above 50°F, the caulk will spread and adhere better. Wait until the sun has dried up any morning dew.

The average 11½-oz. cartridge of caulk will fill 50 ft. of ¼-in. deep cracks (or two door or window frames), if it's properly applied. As many home owners can testify, running a neat bead of caulk is not as easy as it looks. The trick is to keep a steady, even pressure on the plunger, and to ease off just before the end of the bead. It helps to use a high-quality caulking gun (which costs five times more than the bargain-basement ones) and to clip the nozzle at a 45° angle. If the gun doesn't force the caulk all the way into the gap or if the caulk rounds up at the edges, tool it into a concave profile with your fingertip. As when using the gun, keep a steady pressure and don't stop until you reach the end of the bead. Wipe your finger clean before smoothing the next bead. Any gaps wider or deeper than ⅜ in. should first be stuffed with some kind of filler. Because of its greasiness, oakum (the traditional crack filler) won't bond well to modern polymer-based caulks—use scraps of plastic foam or roping instead.

Since warm interior air has a higher pressure than outside air, what we call infiltration is actually an exhalation; although the movement is from inside to out, the effect we feel is that of cold air rushing in to replace the escaping warm air. Thus while caulking the outside of the house does help to reduce air infiltration, it can be argued that it is actually more important for preventing water infiltration. Caulking the interior walls at the baseboards and window frames, sealing under electrical outlets, switch covers and attic ceiling fixtures and around plumbing and other wall penetrations, together with a good vapor barrier, is just as effective in plugging heat leaks.

The "smoke test" is an easy way to identify sources of infiltration. Move a lighted cigarette or stick of incense around window trim, closed doors, floors, baseboards and other possible points of infiltration. If the smoke suddenly streams in one direction, you've pinpointed an air leak.

Weatherstripping

Like caulking, modern weatherstripping products are much more sophisticated and specialized than the wool felt and sponge rubber of the pre-energy-crunch era. It requires some study of catalogs and specifications to choose the right product for a particular application. Inspect your doors and windows: Renew or install weatherstripping on every surface that opens, closes or moves against another.

Except for temporary quick fixes, avoid adhesive-backed foam or spring plastic and wool-felt weatherstripping. Foam and plastic soon degrade, crumble or split apart, the adhesive dries out and the weatherstripping falls off; wool felt soaks up moisture and rots. Except for the newer spring vinyl, most inexpensive weatherstripping is not suited for use where it will be subject to friction. Instead, use heavy-duty tubular vinyl or EDPM gasket weatherstripping. These products are durable and easy to install, although their clumsy appearance (the exposed metal mounting flange shows naked nailheads) is a definite disadvantage. One solution is to install them on the outside of windows.

Another alternative is to use a wood-backed vinyl gasket weatherstripping, such as Porta-Seal®. The 1½-in. wide weatherstripping is for sealing doors; the narrower ¾-in. strips are used against window sash. Tubular gaskets mounted in an adjustable metal door shoe or saddle plate are an excellent choice for sealing under doors, and are far less obtrusive than the typical cheap rubber or plastic sweep.

Weatherstripping

Common types

Spring metal

Adhesive-backed
foam strip

Tubular gasket

Wood and foam

Metal-backed felt

Adhesive-backed
spring vinyl

Door-side treatments (top views)

Stop
molding   Jamb
Spring
metal

Foam strip

Tubular gasket

Wood and foam strip

Spring vinyl

Door

Inside

Door-bottom treatments

Do-it-yourself: Inner-tube
rubber slipped into groove
routed in saddle

Inside   Door

Sweep

Saddle

Rubber or
plastic blade

Shoe

Rubber
gasket

Spring
metal

Interestingly enough, spring metal, which is the oldest kind of weatherstripping, also happens to be the tightest and most durable. Although unequaled for buttoning up leaky old double-hung windows, its wide use is limited by the fair degree of skill it takes to install.

It's hard to think of a reason why anyone would ever want to move the upper sash of a double-hung window in the first place. Instead of weatherstripping, why not simply caulk the sash to the jambs and solve the infiltration problem for good? Chances are, it's already glued to the jambs with years of accumulated paint. Along this line, special removable caulking offers a quick fix for the lower sash. Applied in the fall, the transparent gumlike bead is simply peeled off the following spring.

Windows

Windows are always a controversial subject with old houses. The energy savings that can be gained by replacing old, leaky single-glazed windows with modern, tight double-glazed units must be counterpoised against the havoc such radical changes can wreak upon the historical authenticity and architectural integrity of the house. You don't have to be a fanatical preservationist to realize that careless window treatment is a prime example of "remuddling" at its worst. Almost nothing unbalances the harmonious proportions of a classic farmhouse more effectively than a "picture" window punched into its facade.

Storm windows

The same passions are aroused by storm windows. Are traditional wood storm panels, with their attendant maintenance headaches, still a better choice than convenient, but glaringly unauthentic, aluminum triple-track storms? Is there any reasonable compromise?

Proper weatherstripping, repair of loose or missing glazing putty and cracked panes, and caulking of trim will do much to reduce infiltration around old windows. Although insulated glass ("thermopane" or double glazing) will reduce radiation heat loss by 40% compared to ordinary single glazing, double glazing alone offers no significant increase in resistance to infiltration, other than the fact that factory-built windows tend to be much tighter. The addition of a storm panel offers the same radiation heat-loss savings plus a 40% reduction in infiltration. Since the best home weatherstripping cannot come close to equaling the performance of the best factory-made windows, it would seem that if heat loss is more important than strict historical accuracy, double glazing is the answer.

If tradition wins out, then wood storms prevail, at least over aluminum, which loses on the grounds of both appearance and energy savings (more heat is lost by conduction through the frame than is saved by the extra glazing). A possible alternative is the combination storm/screen insert offered by a few manufacturers. Here, a wooden frame permanently mounted to the window sash holds removable aluminum storm and screen panels, which are exchanged seasonally.

All the fuss over storms or other windows may be so much hot air anyway. In the last few years, insulated windows have come on the market that are both energy-efficient and historically accurate. The old windows can either be removed entirely and replaced with new units, or retrofitted with a new replacement sash, fitted to the existing jambs by means of special adapters and hardware without disturbing the casework and trim. Present-day replacement windows are much sturdier and more versatile than those of the early 1980s. But they also cost a lot more.

Rebuilding a double-hung window

There's a lot that can be done to repair and tighten up an old window. When it first appeared in the 18th century, the double-hung window consisted of a fixed upper sash and a movable lower one, which was propped up with a notched stick. As improvements in flat-glass manufacturing brought the cost of glass down and its size up throughout the 19th century, the number of panes ("lights") in a sash decreased from the original "12 over 12" configuration to "6 over 6" in the 1840s, "2 over 2" in the 1860s, ending with the classic single-paned sashes of the Victorian age. The "6 over 6 divided light" (to use the formal nomenclature), which was the signature window of the antebellum New England farmhouse, is currently enjoying a revival of sorts in a double-insulated reincarnation.

Another benefit of the 19th-century march of progress was the replacement of the notched stick with a clever concealed system of counterbalanced weights and

A Double-Hung Window

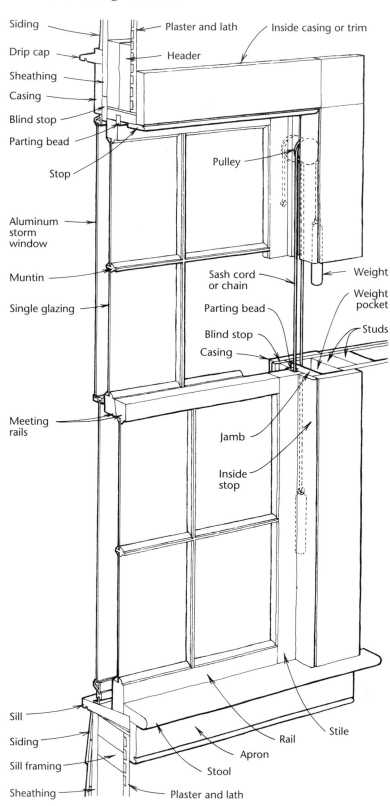

Siding

Drip cap

Sheathing

Casing

Blind stop

Parting bead

Stop

Aluminum storm window

Muntin

Single glazing

Meeting rails

Sill

Siding

Sill framing

Sheathing

Plaster and lath

Header

Inside casing or trim

Pulley

Sash cord or chain

Weight

Weight pocket

Parting bead

Studs

Blind stop

Casing

Jamb

Inside stop

Rail

Apron

Stool

Plaster and lath

Stile

pulleys to raise and lower the sashes. The drawing at left reveals the anatomy of a typical double-hung window.

Assume, for the purpose of discussion, that the sill and other exterior trim components are sound and not in need of replacement. The outside of the sash is most likely to show the ravages of weather and time. Fissures in the wood will show through the flaking paint of the bottom rail. The joint between the rail and the side stiles may be completely rotted. The glazing putty that once anchored the panes to their muntins will have cracked and fallen out.

To remove a double-hung sash, first examine the stop for evidence of painted-over screws. Chip the paint out of the slots and unscrew them. If the screws are long gone, the stop is nailed to the jamb and will probably split when you pry it off unless you are both careful and lucky. Don't worry, stop molding is a stock item. Remove only one stop molding, slide the window up above the stool, and pull it sideways toward you. If nothing budges because the entire sash is painted to the jambs, you'll have to break the old paint with a knife edge or stiff putty knife. The Red Devil Company makes a special tool for this purpose called a Windo-Zipper®, which is available at most hardware stores.

Taking out the parting bead in one piece to get at the upper sash is almost impossible. Chisel it out of the jamb rabbet if you have to and plan to buy or make a replacement. Predrill the new stops for wood screws, and countersink the heads in tapered brass grommets for a traditional touch. This will make future repairs a lot less destructive.

If you find that the sash cords or chains are still attached, lift them out of their grooves and make sure the knot on the end is fat enough to keep the cords from pulling back into the weight pocket behind the jamb before you try to remove the sash.

When a corner of the sash is so badly decayed that no sound wood is left, drill out any remaining wood dowels that secure the stile (which, because of the end grain resting on the sill, tends to rot out first), and remove it. Standard sash stock is carried by most lumberyards. If yours is a unique pattern, a rail, stile or even the entire sash can be duplicated at a local woodshop. Square off the stub of the rail tenon and join it to the new stile with wood dowels and waterproof glue. (Unlike screws, wood dowels won't destroy your saw or plane blade when you need to shave down an edge.) If the joint is wobbly but still basically sound, stiffen it with galvanized drywall screws driven through the tenon. If that doesn't work, use flat angle irons. Excavate the decayed wood and fill the cavity with an epoxy wood filler.

If any glass needs replacing, chisel out the old glazing putty. Avoid placing pressure on the glass, which might crack; work against the wood instead. The pane is anchored to the muntins and sash by small metal wedges called glazier's points. Jamming a chisel into one full-tilt is a good way to crack the glass, so feel for them as you chip out the putty. Pry out the points and remove the pane. Clean the rabbet down to bare wood with a small scraper, and give the wood a light coat of linseed oil. Replace the glass (cut new panes ⅛ in. smaller than the sash opening). With the chisel, force a glazier's point into the wood about 2 in. from each corner, and add one for every foot of length in between.

Prepare glazing putty for use by rolling a ball of it between your palms until it softens. Roll it out into rope-like pieces ⅜ in. to ½ in. thick, and lay it on the glass against the sash. Press it into place with your fingers and then, with a flexible putty knife, press it firmly and evenly into the joint, forming a 45° bevel. Cut and peel off excess putty for reuse. Run your finger lightly over the putty to smooth off any rough edges, clean the panes and reinstall.

A sash that won't raise easily or stay up probably suffers from a cut sash cord or missing counterweight. If the lower sash wasn't attached to a length of chain or cord when you first tried to remove it, the diagnosis will be confirmed. Look for a groove in the top edge of the stiles that looks like it once might have anchored the knot of a cord. A metal pulley set in the top of the inside sash run or a metal plate hidden in the bottom of the run are also signs that the window once worked. Often, broken sash cords were not repaired and the top sash was nailed to its jambs. The bottom sash was held open by friction or the traditional wood stick. Sometimes, the outer sash run was filled in with a stop to keep the top sash in place.

High fuel costs have also led to the abandonment of the counterweight system. In the name of energy efficiency, cords were cut, weights discarded and the hollow weight pockets stuffed with insulation. The sash runs were fitted with metal spring clips or new weatherstripping tracks that allowed the windows to slide and stay open without falling. Traditionalists may find this offensive, but I'm not sure it isn't an improvement.

If authentic operation is more important than heat loss, it's not hard to replace the missing hardware. Sash weights and chain or cord are still available. The new cord is pushed over the top of the pulley and down into the pocket, where it is fished out of the access hole (for earlier windows that lack access holes, the jamb casing will have to be removed) and tied around the weight. The other end of the cord is knotted and pushed into the slot at the top of the window stile. When properly adjusted, the weight should be 3 in. above the sill when the sashes are fully raised. The parting bead and stop must allow enough room for easy movement of the sash. Coating the runs and the edges of the stiles with paraffin wax also ensures smooth operation.

Rebuilding a Rotted Windowsill from Inside

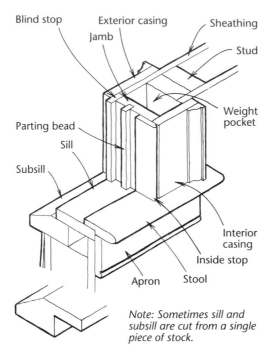

Blind stop — Exterior casing — Sheathing
Jamb — Stud
Weight pocket
Parting bead
Sill
Subsill
Interior casing
Inside stop
Apron — Stool

Note: Sometimes sill and subsill are cut from a single piece of stock.

1. Scribe location of jamb against blind stop or exterior sash. Scribe location of inside stop and parting bead on jamb.

2. Remove inside stop and parting bead. Take out sashes (not shown).

3. Cut paint or wallpaper against trim to prevent tears.

4. Carefully remove interior casings, stool and apron.

5. Split or cut sill/subsill horns as needed to aid removal. Record size first.

6. Pry jambs free of exterior casing with flatbar, pulling window frame into room.

7. Fill weight pocket with solid blocking or insulation.

8. Replace unit. Nail to studs, hiding nails under stops.

To combine authenticity with a high-quality installation, the sashes should be grooved to mate with traditional spring-metal weatherstripping nailed into the sash runs. With a table saw or radial-arm saw, or a router equipped with a veining bit, cut a ½-in. deep, ⅛-in. wide slot into the stiles and the top rail of the upper and bottom rail of the lower sash to line up with the weatherstripping already nailed into the sash runs. The meeting rails must be cut or dadoed to allow the weatherstripping to interlock correctly when closed.

Replacing rotted windowsills

Neglecting routine painting and caulking will eventually rot out the sills and outside casings of any window. If unchecked, the decay will progress inward, attacking the wall, the studs and even the foundation sills.

If the windowsill is too far gone to be saved by an application of epoxy wood filler, that is, if it's nothing but dust held together by dirt, the window can be reconstructed, as shown in the drawing at left. Before removing the sashes, scribe the line of the stiles against the parting bead and inside stop. This way you'll be sure of an exact duplicate for the sash run when you reinstall the sashes. Cut the wallpaper or paint where it adjoins the interior trim to keep the finish from tearing, and carefully remove the inside trim boards, apron and stool. Since there's a good chance that any attempt to remove the sill will destroy it, record the details of its construction and measurements first. If you're really lucky, the jambs will remain intact when you split the sill apart. As there's a much better chance that the bottom ends of the jambs have also decayed, record their layout to facilitate making an exact copy.

Leave the exterior casings in place (if there's a blind stop, it will stay with the outside casings) and pry away the jambs, pulling the window frame into the house. Clip off any protruding nailheads, or pull finish nails through the back of the boards. (Driving them back out the face side will split out some of the wood along with the paint.) To ease removal, cut the sill in half or split off its horns.

Old windowsills were sawn from much thicker stock than is used today, sometimes as much as 3 in. or 4 in. thick; finding a small timber of dry clear pine or fir stock will not be easy or inexpensive. Duplicate the sill (and the jambs if need be), and tack a temporary brace across one corner to keep the new frame square when you reinstall it. Align the jambs with the scribe marks on the old casings, and use cedar-shingle shims to hold the frame tight. Drive finish nails through the jambs into the studs (only where they will be covered by a stop) and renail the outside casings. Renail the inside casings to the new jambs, stuff any cracks or weight pockets with insulation and reinstall the interior trim, the stops and the sashes.

Reinstalling crooked windows

This same technique can be used, without the need to leave the outside casings in place, to reinstall a formerly tilted window to bring it plumb and level. If the sill is sound, the window is pulled outward instead. If the correctly aligned window won't fit the skewed opening, hew the studs with a chisel, a reciprocating saw or an electric chainsaw, depending on the amount of adjustment required. If the jambs and sills are to be rebuilt anyway, the head jamb and sill can be shortened up to ½ in. and the sashes planed down, to minimize hewing.

This is a lot of trouble to go through unless the existing windows are of historical importance, or unless only a few windows are in need of such radical surgery. When most of the windows are beyond rescue, it makes more sense to remove them and replace them with entirely new factory-built units. If you can afford them, high-quality new windows will pay for themselves in years of trouble-free service as well as energy savings.

Adding and subtracting windows

If you need to change any windows, you have a choice between buying replacement windows and replacing the entire window unit. Replacement windows come as kits that use vinyl or metal tracks and various adapters or shims to fit new sash into existing jambs without disturbing the original casings, siding or wall finishes. To replace an entire window unit, you have to remove the window and either shrink or enlarge the opening to accommodate a new factory-built unit. There's little financial incentive to select one method over the other; after all expenses are included, buying replacement windows and replacing the entire unit cost about the same.

Replacement windows are the best choice when there is no need or desire to disturb the interior and exterior wall surfaces. Replacing the entire window unit makes more sense when either the exterior or interior siding is scheduled for replacement, or if it's necessary to change window sizes or placement. A window I wouldn't choose, however, is anything clad in vinyl or aluminum. When the vinyl product begins to disintegrate in 25 or however many years, it can't be saved by a coat of paint or be taken apart and replaced. Since vinyl-clad windows are fastened to the wall by a vinyl flange nailed under the siding, removal and replacement will make a huge mess. The aluminum window cladding may be durable, but if it ever chips and splits, water can work into the wood beneath it and rot out the entire core—undetected and unfixable.

When replacing the entire window unit, if possible, choose a size similar to the window you intend to replace. It's better to be slightly undersize than over. Windows are sized according to the dimensions of the rough opening needed to accommodate the unit. When the new window fits into the old opening, a lot of tedious and messy hacking and framing is avoided.

If the old units are being removed because of energy concerns rather than structural concerns, it's worth taking the time to disassemble them carefully, saving the trim if possible. The windows themselves could be sold or reused for a future outbuilding, and the trim may be irreplaceable. Even rotted old sashes are still a source of usable glass.

Shim the opening with boards or strips of plywood as necessary to fit a smaller-sized window. Since windows look best when their head jambs are all at the same height, any changes should be at the sill, leaving the header height (and framing) intact. Remove the subsill first, sawing through the nails that join it to the studs. Using a reciprocating saw, shorten the cripple studs by cutting through the face of the finished interior wall only. This cut will be hidden under the relocated apron trim. Then renail the subsill, trim the wall siding to the required height, block in under the missing jack stud and install the window as with any new window.

A 1-in. board makes a good half-width jack stud for openings that require only a little enlargement. The board is used in place of the stud that was nailed to the backing stud.

One of the advantages of timber framing is that the wall studs between timbers are not load-bearing—they carry only negligible loads of siding and the interior walls. Thus, enlarging a window opening does not require supporting floor joists or other loads while framing in a new header, as would an opening in a load-bearing stud-frame wall. If the new window opening requires only an extra inch or two, the enlargement can be made by simply hewing the studs with a chainsaw, ax or chisel. To frame a larger opening, cut out existing vertical studs as required and cut off the existing cripple studs to the correct height. Remove the header stud (if any) and subsill and replace with new ones long enough to butt against the next full stud in the wall cavity. Nail these in place, after making sure the insulation batts have been redistributed in the cavities. Nail new jack studs to support the window jamb, and install the window.

The object is to disturb as little interior or exterior siding and sheathing as possible (whichever is to remain intact), so that the wall surfaces will not need patching. Ideally, the scars of the surgery are hidden under the remounted trim boards.

When the enlargement is in a load-bearing stud wall, a properly supported header is required. Short headers (3 ft. or less), can be replaced without any special support. As above, remove enough wall finish to permit a header to be slipped up into the reframed opening. This should always butt against full-length studs. Toenail it in as best you can. Then force a jack

Enlarging a Window Opening in a Stud-Frame Wall

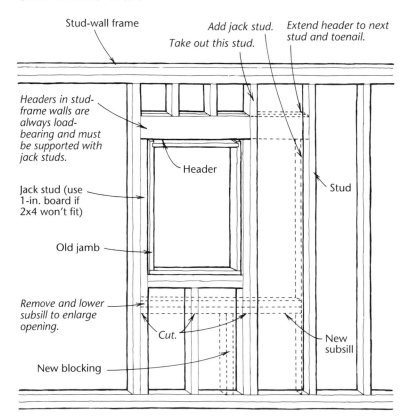

Stud-wall frame

Add jack stud.
Take out this stud.

Extend header to next stud and toenail.

Headers in stud-frame walls are always load-bearing and must be supported with jack studs.

Header

Jack stud (use 1-in. board if 2x4 won't fit)

Stud

Old jamb

Remove and lower subsill to enlarge opening.

Cut.

New subsill

New blocking

stud up under each end of the header. Add cripples to carry the new subsill, insulating the bays before the subsill is nailed home. Then cut and install the window jacks and patch in any missing sheathing. Drive spikes through the finished wall at an angle to join the hidden header to its backing studs. If the nails are countersunk with a punch, a dab of spackle will repair the damage to the wall. Support the ceiling joists with a jacking beam and a couple of 4x4 posts set on planks over the floor joists (jacks are not needed as long as the posts are wedged in tight) when installing larger headers.

Insert the new window, with its exterior casings attached, into the new opening. Tack one corner and adjust it for level. Scribe the siding along the edges of the casing boards and remove the unit. Cut to the inside of the scribe lines. If you use a fine-toothed 3½-in. circular-saw blade, the cut will be virtually unnoticeable. Finish the ends of the cut with a chisel or knife. Reinstall the window and check for fit. If no further adjustments are necessary, remove the window, caulk behind the casing boards and reinsert it. Nail the casing to the wall with 16d galvanized finish nails. Insert a wood drip cap or metal cap flashing above the head casing.

If necessary, rip extension jambs to bring the inside jambs flush to the finish wall surface. These should be glued and nailed (predrill if hardwood) to the jambs, with no reveal. Reinstall the old casings or build duplicates as necessary. The casings should be offset about ³⁄₁₆ in. from the edges of the jambs. A flush edge is difficult to match and paint without being noticeable, whereas this "reveal" actually hides slight imperfections and creates a pleasing detail, especially when rounded over, or eased, with a radius plane or sander.

Unwanted windows, like those on the north side of the house, can also be filled in at this time. Once the unit is removed, 1-in. boards, ripped to the width of the wall studding (ordinary 2x4s are usually too narrow for an old house and must be

When patching around a door or window, new siding should be interwoven with the existing siding for the sake of both watertightness and appearance.

furred out) are nailed around the perimeter of the opening to carry the sheathing. Add additional studs in the opening as needed, either ripped from wider stock or furred to fit, to maintain standard stud spacing. Nail exterior sheathing (if ordinary ½-in. or ¾-in. plywood won't fit flush to the old sheathing boards, add the extra width to the 1-in. boards), insulate the cavity and patch the interior wall.

Patching the opening with clapboards or wood shingles is similar to replacing damaged roof shingles. The new siding should be interwoven with the old for both the sake of appearance and water-tightness. Beginning at the first full clapboard above the opening, remove any nails in its bottom edge and slide out the remains of the underlying clapboard. Work downward, staggering the joints so that no course breaks over or within 6 in. of another. This isn't too difficult in those rare cases where the old clapboards aren't brittle, but it's more likely that you'll find yourself replacing a lot more pieces than you planned on. Sometimes a chisel can loosen the nails enough to insert the blunt edge a prybar. If the clapboard is pried up and then pushed back, most of the nailheads will be left sticking out within pulling range. The cure for those that aren't is to pry the edge up enough to slip the prybar under the point of the balky nail and then push the clapboard down against it.

The replacement clapboards should align with the ends of the old courses, regardless of level or equal spacing. Snap a chalkline or scribe pencil marks across each course to guide installation. Use 4d galvanized nails. Don't forget to staple building paper over any new or exposed old board sheathing first.

Doors

The techniques for repairing windows apply to doors as well. A door has a sill (the threshold) and head and side jambs. The jambs are fitted with stops, weatherstripping and hardware that enables the door to open inward like a large casement window. Like a window sash, a door has rails and stiles that carry thin panels of wood, which float freely in the frame. Because these can expand and contract without affecting the width or height of the door, the stability of the rail-and-stile door is unequaled by any other wood door, and its construction has changed very little since its first appearance around 1700.

An exterior door suffers from the same general debilitations as do windows. But because it is in constant daily use, a door rarely reaches the point of disintegration before someone is forced to fix it.

Replacing a threshold

A worn, wobbly threshold is the first symptom of trouble. The sill under a threshold is especially vulnerable to rot. The worst situation is where stone steps trap snow and water against the band of trim under the lip of the doorsill. Replacing a worn or rotted threshold is similar to repairing a windowsill.

First, remove the door by driving out the hinge pins, and set it aside. Measure the overall dimensions of the threshold from horn to horn. Check the width, as thresholds often taper. Also determine whether its ends are at right angles to its length or at some weird taper to suit a set of skewed jambs. Thresholds are usually cut from red oak, which is durable, heavy and expensive. Unlike softwood, you can't expect to force hardwood into too tight a space—the cut and fit must be exact. Take the time to lay out the cuts properly; you can't afford to make a mistake.

The doorstop molding generally fits flush to the top of the threshold. At least one side must be taken off to pry up and remove the threshold. If the stop is a rabbet cut into the jambs, this step won't be necessary. Use the threshold as a template to guide layout of the replacement piece. New unpleasantries and hidden rot may be exposed when the threshold is removed. Sometimes the finish floor, subfloor, portions of joists and a good section of underlying sill have decayed. A simple hour's job can explode exponentially into a major repair project. But armed with perseverance and bitter resignation, you can rebuild all the rotted structure and finally, several days later, get back to installing the new threshold.

Flash the front face of the new sheathing and the portion of the new subfloor under the threshold and up onto the scarfed wall studs with butyl roofing membrane to reduce the chance of an encore. Check the threshold for fit against the jambs. Then rehang the door and see if it closes properly. Now's the best time to find out if you need to shim it up a bit or lower it into the subfloor. As a general rule, thresholds should be laid flush with the subfloor even if the floor is not level.

It's better to trim the bottom of the door to the threshold than to tilt a threshold to fit the door. Sometimes, though, you'll have to split the difference for the best overall appearance. If everything is satisfactory, run several beads of butyl or silicone caulk over the membrane and especially where the ends of the threshold will butt the jambs, and set it back in place. Drill the wood for finish nails or countersink and plug screws. Seal the threshold with a penetrating oil finish, as any varnish will soon scuff off.

Taking care of doors

Wood doors that stick are one reason why so many insulated steel doors are sold. I suspect that if more attention were paid to proper preparation and maintenance of the door, dimensional stability wouldn't be such an issue. A rail-and-stile wood door is an investment. Protect all faces and edges, especially the bottom and top, with three coats of high-quality exterior spar varnish. Apply the finish when the humidity is low. Renew the finish as soon as it starts to show signs of wear, and recoat any deep scratches immediately. The idea is to prevent the wood from absorbing the moisture that causes seasonal changes in dimension—and sticking. Two coats of an oil-based enamel over a suitable primer are equally effective. The finish should be applied to the door before the hardware is installed and to the jambs as well.

Doors that stick are doors that haven't been taken care of. After decades of erosion by generations of scratching dogs and the sometimes tumultuous comings and goings of daily life, the rails and stiles pull apart. A loose-jointed door can change shape, perhaps becoming wider at the bottom or sagging onto the threshold. When the latch starts missing its strike, the door must be slammed to close. A panel splits, cold air rushes in unhindered. Finally, the exasperated home owner planes down the

Rot starting under this threshold eventually required replacement of the sill, door framing and wall sheathing.

sticking edge. Unpainted, it swells again in the wet fall air and twists so that the door no longer closes against its stop.

Furniture clamps and glue will squeeze open joints back together. Pin the rail tenons with countersunk galvanized wood screws. Check the corners for square before fastening them; years of slack may have allowed the door to fall from rectilinear grace. Panels can be mended with caulk or epoxy filler. The bead molding or even a missing panel can be replaced.

Other than a new door, there's no cure for a warped edge but to remove the stop and renail it to follow the actual rather than ideal edge. Sanding the old door smooth and repainting is more than a facelift; by keeping the door from swelling or joints from drying out and becoming unglued, future problems are prevented. If the door still sticks, the hinge screws might be loose, allowing the door to fall toward the jamb. Replace loose screws with longer or thicker ones. If the screws go through the jamb and into the space behind it without catching a stud, hammer tapered slivers of pine (golf tees work well, if you have them) dipped in glue into the old screw hole until it won't take any more. These restored holes will hold screws as well as any new wood.

If the door still binds, plane down its leading edge. Rub the jambs with chalk and force the door against them. The chalk will transfer to the door, indicating the places to shave down. Give the edge a slight bevel (about 3° or 3⁄32 in.) to ensure a good fit. If you remove the latch bolt and mounting plate first, all but the bottom edge can be planed with the door still hung. Seal the raw edges as soon as the final fit is made.

Before you decide to plane down a door, be sure that the problem isn't caused by something other than the swelling of the door or its jambs. Wood swells in humid weather and shrinks in dry weather. A door that closes fine in the summer but always sticks in winter is not swelling. Examine the gap between the top of the door and the head jamb. If one side is higher than the other, the door frame (and the whole wall) is being lifted by frost heave. Planing down the door to fit in winter will make it too loose in summer. You have a foundation problem, not a door problem.

Although it's true that neglecting a foam-core steel door won't affect its dimensional stability, and that these doors lose much less heat than thin wood panels, there's still at least one good reason not to rip out all your old wood doors and replace them with high-tech surrogates. They just don't look, feel or suffer insults like wood. There's nothing quite as handsome as the soft glow of varnished, well-aged wood, or a feeling as secure as the click of the latch bolt when a heavy solid door closes against its jambs. A sandwich of thin steel sheets and plastic foam rimmed with a skinny wood rind dressed up with nylon muntins and embossed or appliquéd plastic moldings complete with fake wood grain just doesn't seem convincing, even under three coats of enamel. Fixing dings and cuts is more like patching a dented fender than carpentry.

Now that my traditionalist bias is clear, I would like to suggest a compromise: Use steel doors for the rear entry, for cellar hatches, garages, kitchen doors and any other doors that get heavy use, and restore or install a wood door as part of the formal entry. Hardly any other portion of the external house can contribute more to its appearance than the entry—don't cheapen it with a cheap door. And if you do use a steel door, at least choose a pattern consistent with the historical period of your house. Crossbuck frames were never part of the New England tradition.

A shortcut to successful door hanging

Modern prehung door units (with doors factory-installed in the jambs, complete with threshold and trim) have dispensed with much of the finicky (and fairly skilled) carpentry traditionally associated with door hanging. The instructions included with the packaging and the various adjustments typically built into the units allow almost anyone to achieve satisfactory results.

Unfortunately, these labor-saving doors are not always suited for renovation work. It's much more likely that an old door must be remounted in a new frame or adapted to fit an entirely different opening. Also, some might feel that despite the trouble and expense of disinterment, an antique panel door buried under numerous layers of paint makes a better interior door than do the flimsy hollow-core doors that are the hallmark of cheap contemporary construction.

I've found that recycling old doors is cheaper than purchasing new panel doors, even after the cost of professional dip-tank stripping, if you do the touch-up work yourself—the tank process leaves residues of paint in the cracks and along the edges of moldings, which have to be chipped out with hand tools. The raw surface will also require some sanding before it can be either repainted or treated with a varnish or penetrating oil finish. Boiled linseed oil can give good results if the exposed wood has any character to it at all, and is much less costly than tung oil.

The trick to hanging a door is, whenever possible, to fit the frame to the door and not the door to the frame. Check the door for squareness before you begin. If no gap shows against the blades when you lay a framing square along its top corners, the door is square. If the door varies in width or length, it should be trimmed to square. Remove all hardware first, and check for hidden or broken nails or screws before you cut. Because ordinary blades tend to bind up and wander when sawing

through painted wood, use a fine-toothed carbide-tipped blade instead. A straight length of wood tacked to the door will guide your circular saw if a table saw is unavailable. Smooth the cut edge with a plane before hanging. Don't worry about the bottom for now: Unless the threshold is perfectly level, you'll have to scribe this edge and recut it to fit anyway.

The thickness of the jamb stock depends on the weight of the door. Exterior doors are heavier and thicker than interior doors, and require a close fit for weathertightness. Standard thicknesses are 1¾ in. for exterior doors, and 1⅛ in. to 1⅜ in. for interior doors. Jambs for exterior doors are best cut from clear 6/4 (1½ in. thick) or 8/4 (2 in.) pine or fir stock. Common spruce or

Rehanging Old Doors

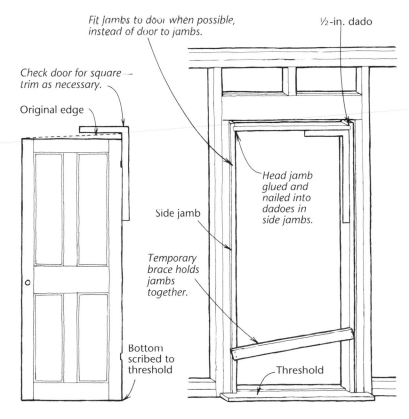

Fit jambs to door when possible, instead of door to jambs.

½-in. dado

Check door for square — trim as necessary.

Original edge

Head jamb glued and nailed into dadoes in side jambs.

Side jamb

Temporary brace holds jambs together.

Bottom scribed to threshold

Threshold

hemlock is too unstable for this purpose. Since the shock of repeated closings will eventually loosen any stop molding nailed to the jamb, it's best to rabbet the stop into the jamb. Compression-type gasket weatherstripping is then applied along the face of the rabbet, or along its edge. With lighter interior doors the stop can be made from stock molding nailed to the jamb. Likewise, because of their more forgiving tolerances, 4/4 (1-in.) or ordinary ¾-in. common pine (knots allowed) stock is more than adequate for interior door jambs.

Lay the door blank on a flat surface and cut the jambs to the length of the door plus ⅜ in. (⅛-in. clearance at top, ¼ in. at bottom) plus the thickness of the head jamb. Allow for the threshold when figuring height. Ideally, if there is room enough in the rough opening, add an extra inch or so to the side-jamb length to permit a dadoed joint with the head jamb. This joint is much stronger and, unlike a simple butt joint, won't open up when the wood shrinks. The head jamb itself is cut to the width of the door plus ¹⁄₁₆ in., plus the width of the dadoes, and then glued and nailed through the side jambs.

Next, attach the butt hinges to the door. Use hinges that are equal to twice the thickness of the door (3x3s for 1½-in. doors, 3½x3½s for 1¾-in. doors, and 4x4s for 2-in. doors). Longer ball-bearing-type hinges (for example, 4x6s) are reserved for extra-heavy doors, such as fire doors, or heavy-duty commercial or institutional applications. Always use loose-pin hinges. Using one of the hinges as a pattern, scribe the mortise into the door edge with a knife (not a pencil).

For a standard 6-ft. 8-in. door, the top hinge is set 7 in. down from the top and the bottom hinge 9 in. up from the bottom. The third hinge (interior doors usually have only two) is centered in the middle. (The top hinge takes the greatest strain and is therefore closer to the edge.) Use a sharp chisel and always push it with the grain. Cutting against the grain will make deep gouges. If you use only two

screws in each hinge to mount the hinges temporarily, any required adjustments will not loosen the hinges, since the remaining screws can be driven into solid wood.

The door is then set into the jamb, resting against the stop rabbet and positioned to allow about ⅛-in. clearance at the head jamb and ¹⁄₃₂ in. to either side (a matchbook cover makes a perfect clearance gauge). Mark the position of the hinges on the jamb, remove the door and, using the other half of the hinges, scribe and cut the mortises into the jambs. Use a screwdriver to remove the hinge pins, separate the two halves and screw the hinges into the mortise, leaving out the top screw only. There is a top and bottom to the hinge as well as a front and back. The face has countersunk holes to seat the screwheads, and the hinge must be aligned so that the pin will not fall out.

Place the door back in its frame and pin the hinges together. Tack a temporary brace across the bottom corners to hold the jambs together, and secure the door by driving a 6d finish nail through the strike jamb into the edge of the door. (This is later removed by pulling it through the jamb with a pair of pliers after prying the door free.) Lift the completed door unit into the rough opening and shim it into place with cedar shingles driven from opposite sides of the frame. Always insert shims behind each hinge and behind the strike. Check for plumb; take care not to force the shims so much that they cause the jamb to bow. The gap between the door edges and the jambs should remain even.

For interior doors, which are hung to clear the finish flooring or carpeting by at least ½ in., the unit is secured to its framing after the door is satisfactorily positioned by nailing through the casing trim. When a saddle is used to cover a break between flooring boards or a change of materials, the piece is cut to fit between the jambs after the door is in place.

For exterior doors, a threshold is required, in which case the bottom edge of the door is scribed to fit and the threshold is installed before the jamb casings, since these must be cut on a bevel to fit against the horns of the threshold. Since the floor under the threshold is seldom level in an old house, the threshold is best installed to fit the existing floor after the frame is mounted. The door bottom must be left long enough so that it can be scribed and cut to fit, leaving no more than ¼-in. clearance, to be taken up by the doorsweep weatherstripping.

The door should close easily without binding. Beveling the leading edge slightly will help. When everything is satisfactory, install the remaining screws in the door and jamb hinges. Use screws long enough to penetrate the jamb and catch into the framing, to keep the hinges from loosening over time and the door from sagging in its frame. Install the lockset and strike plate after the door is hung. A wide variety of hardware is available in kits that contain easy directions and templates to guide installation.

Storm doors

In cold climates, an entrance door should never open to the outside. A tight storm door creates an air lock that helps keep in heat, especially if it is a wood, rather than an aluminum, unit. Even with a foam-core door, conductive heat losses through the metal edges diminish much of the insulation value. Wood storm doors can be painted or stained to match the existing trim colors, and tend to be more durable. A door equipped with interchangeable storm and screen panels will provide summer cooling as well.

When installing a storm door, take care that the latch handle does not hit the doorknob of the entrance door. Another common mistake is to set the latch so close to the edge of the door that you pinch your knuckles against the stop or jambs as you turn the inside handle. Screen doors are usually hung flush to the entry door casing. If the reveal on these casings is increased to ⅜ in. or slightly more, the jamb itself provides a stop.

Exterior Siding and Trim

The earliest Colonial clapboards were fairly thick horizontal boards riven from oak bolts and tapered by a drawknife (the same way as roofing shingles), then nailed directly to the wall studs. Untapered overlapping square-edged boards were a less common alternative. During the first quarter of the 19th century, these sidings were supplanted by the machine-sawn clapboards and wood shingles still in use today. Since these thinner, nonstructural sidings needed a solid nail base, timber frames were sheathed with wide, rough-sawn square-edged boards nailed to studs, most often 4x4s on 24-in. or 32-in. centers, although odd dimensions and irregular spacings are not unusual. When the timber frame gave way to balloon and platform framing, rough-sawn horizontal sheathing was replaced by milled tongue-and-groove boarding applied diagonally for its bracing effect. Although still available today, this sheathing became obsolete with the invention of plywood.

Clapboard siding will last almost indefinitely if kept painted and protected from water damage. Unfortunately, most home owners wait until the siding has begun to weather before renewing the paint. If the paint has been allowed to wear too thin, or if, as with many houses built before 1725, the siding was never painted at all, the exposed wood will begin to curl and split. Water trapped in these crevices fosters decay. Like a threadbare overcoat, the clapboards will start to fall apart, and water and icy winds will penetrate the seams of the house and threaten its structural well-being. Oil-based stains can avert the inevitable if applied after the paint (and before the siding) has worn away. Paint itself will not adhere to weathered wood unless the surface has been prepared by sanding.

When clapboard or shingle siding is too far gone, it must be removed and replaced. Despite the claims of its manufacturers, this is a far more sensible and economical alternative than hiding the old

Clad in new siding, the addition is indistinguishable from the older parts of the house.

siding under aluminum or vinyl cladding. In the first place, synthetic sidings are not really maintenance-free. Like steel-clad doors, both aluminum and vinyl are vulnerable to dents and punctures (vinyl also becomes brittle in extreme cold and will easily split or crack under impact). The only way to fix the damage is to replace the section of siding. But since manufacturers change colors and styles quite frequently, an exact match is unlikely. Also, the enamel finish on aluminum eventually wears or peels off, and solid-color vinyl fades. Neither material will suffer repainting with any great success. Since the 20- to 40-year manufacturer's warranties are prorated, replacement cost near the end of the siding's life span is equal to the initial installation.

By contrast, wood sidings, even when repainting is neglected, will last a comparable time. And they expire much more gracefully than any synthetic material. Government studies have also shown that synthetic sidings offer little real insulation value. Certainly any energy savings gained

are offset by the depletion of nonrenewable resources and environmental damage their manufacture entails.

General considerations aside, there are two specific reasons why synthetic sidings should not be used with old houses. First, these materials can mask, and even cause, serious structural damage. Because of either improper installation, which allows water to enter behind the siding, or a water problem that was covered over undetected and unrepaired prior to installation, or damage to the underlying siding caused by the nails used to fasten the siding battens to the house, rot can progressively destroy the underlying structure. In some cases, the siding itself acts as an exterior vapor barrier, allowing condensation buildup to further the decay. Hidden from view and protected by the seemingly solid siding, termites and other insects can colonize the walls unmolested.

The use of aluminum or vinyl siding also requires the removal or burial of those architectural details and embellishments that give an old house its distinctive character and aesthetic value. Exterior trim and molding are simplified and visually flattened by the application of stock soffit and cladding material. Since original materials and historical authenticity increasingly command a premium, in all but the most utilitarian circumstances, the application of synthetic sidings can actually reduce resale value. Indeed, a potential buyer would do well to suspect that such sidings might actually hide a problem that was never fixed.

Getting under the house's skin

Old clapboards or wood shingles are easily removed with a flat prybar, working from the top downward. To reduce "thermal bridging," remove any protruding siding nails rather than hammering them back into the sheathing. Examine the sheathing boards for soundness and replace any rotted ones. Pay particular attention to the areas above and under windows and doors, where water may have worked behind defective flashings or soaked into open joints. If the drip-cap flashings have rusted out (with luck, the builders used copper instead of galvanized steel), the sheathing beneath them and under apparently solid window casings will most likely suffer from some degree of rot. The wood drip moldings themselves should be sound. Fill any fissures with wood preservative and caulk before repainting. Replace badly split or punky wood. The drawing at right shows construction details. Sheathing behind the horns of windowsills, under door thresholds and at the junction of porch roofs and building walls is also especially vulnerable to water damage.

Clearly, the best time to make wholesale changes in the size, number and arrangement of windows and doors is after the siding has been stripped. This requires advance planning and purchasing, which harks back to the need for a master plan,

Two Wood Drip Caps for Windows

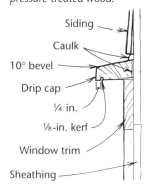

Cut from cedar or redwood or pressure-treated wood.

Siding
Caulk
10° bevel
Drip cap
¼ in.
⅛-in. kerf
Window trim
Sheathing

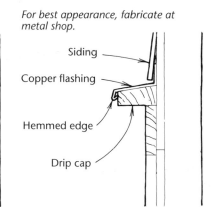

For best appearance, fabricate at metal shop.

Siding
Copper flashing
Hemmed edge
Drip cap

discussed on pp. 46-49. There are two other possible strategies worth considering at this point: strengthening the frame and tightening up the building envelope.

The stability of a timber frame depends entirely on the integrity of its knee braces. Horizontal sheathing boards contribute only marginally to racking resistance. A frame that has suffered a fair amount of racking and then withstood the rigors of realignment is apt to be fairly loose in the joints. Although this might be a desirable state for a practitioner of yoga, it's not one conducive to the long-term stability of a house.

It's not always possible to stiffen the knee braces directly. Quite often, there weren't enough of them to begin with, or critical braces were sacrificed to remodeling. The problem can be solved satisfactorily by adding a layer of ½-in. plywood over the existing sheathing boards, especially when you intend to replace all the old windows. Sealing the joints between panels and at corners with plastic packaging tape eliminates the need to cover the old boards with an anti-infiltration membrane such as Tyvek® housewrap. A bead of caulk under the casings of the new window units likewise reduces infiltration.

Sheathing the old boards with a layer of ½-in. CDX plywood greatly increases the structural strength of the frame. Plywood sheathing also simplifies installing new windows.

If structural strength is not a consideration, but increasing the insulation value of the building shell is, adding a layer of rigid insulating foam makes sense. Adding 1 in. of polyisocyanurate foam will increase the resistance to heat loss of a fiberglass or blown-in cellulose-filled 2x4 wall cavity by almost 40%, without disturbing the finished interior wall or reducing the pleasing reveal of a corner post or plate. If the existing windows are to be left intact, then the outside casing boards are simply removed and extension pieces added to bring the jambs flush to the new surface before reinstalling the trim. As with plywood, the joints between the foam panels should also be taped to reduce infiltration.

If neither of these options is pursued, it is important to wrap the drafty old board sheathing with an infiltration barrier fabric. I can't think of any better use for this product or a compelling reason to use it anywhere else, despite the ubiquitous ads showing new houses swaddled in the stuff. Install the barrier fabric over doors and windows, leaving at least an inch or two extra when you cut out the openings. These flanges are then tucked under the casing boards, which have been pried up to admit them.

Before the invention of these high-tech polyester fabrics, rosin-coated builder's paper was used for the same purpose. Although cheaper (and easier to write on with a pencil or chalk), it can actually contribute to structural decay. Being porous, builder's paper will absorb water from a leaking flashing or exposed joint and hold it against the sheathing. Likewise, never use tar paper (saturated asphalt-felt paper) between the sheathing and any other finish siding. The felt is an effective vapor barrier and can cause condensation (and rot) between itself and the sheathing, particularly with poorly insulated walls or houses lacking a proper interior vapor barrier (see pp. 227-229).

One other problem area is at the junction of the siding with a concrete buttress wall. Proper installation of flashing is absolutely critical in preventing rot and the inevitable replacement of the sills and other framing members. Blistered or peeling paint and moist siding are sure-fire signs of water damage. Replace all rotted sheathing as necessary, preferably with pressure-treated boards (shimmed as necessary to match the thickness of the existing sound sheathing). Correct the pitch of the concrete wall for positive drainage by beveling its edge with a cold chisel, or adding a sloped mortar cap. When the mortar is dry, nail 12-in. wide lead flashing to the sheathing, allowing the bottom to overlap and cover the top of the wall. Seal the metal to the concrete with a bead of highly flexible caulking. Corner joints are folded and lapped similar to the joint between the base and step flashings of a chimney. The finished flashing should extend at least 6 in. up onto the sheathing, with at least a 1-in. reveal between the top of the wall and the bottom of the first course of siding.

Repairing and replacing exterior trim

Ideally, missing or rotted trim boards are repaired or replaced after the old siding has been removed and before the new siding is installed. Cornice returns ("rebates"), with their greater exposure to water and myriad overlapping elements and joints, are especially susceptible to rot. Even sound trim is almost always in need of repainting. Whenever two boards butt together, a potential water trap is formed. Even painted end grain is capable of wicking water into the board, causing the paint to peel and rot to begin. It's important to seal these butt joints with paintable caulk. For additional protection, brush a water-repellent wood preservative into cracks and problem areas prior to caulking or repainting.

The trim on early homes was strictly utilitarian, as the earliest Colonial builders had little time to spare for embellishment. Plain flat boards were used to close the gap between the rafter tails and the side wall at the eaves (the end grain of the rafter tails, if left exposed, would absorb water and soon rot). The rake overhang was clipped back to a single or doubled layer of board nailed flat against the gable wall.

As life became more settled and secure, the desire for ornamentation was indulged. Architectural fashions of Europe were imported along with tea, china and wallpaper. During the 18th century, the Georgian influence resulted in the elaborate cornice entablature typical of country manors and the townhouses of the well-to-do. Freed from the structural restraints of the stonework that was its prototype, wood moldings could be applied in successive layers of pure decorative fancy. Even the most humble farmhouse was often graced with a fluted pilaster or an elaborate capital at the cornice. This decorative impulse reached its apotheosis in the extremes of Victorian gingerbread. Wonderful to look at but hellishly demanding to maintain, it was a true talisman of class distinction.

Before the advent of such elaborate factory millwork, moldings were cut by hand with special planes. Like a modern router or shaper, these planes were fitted with blades designed for a particular shape. Often, several combinations were used to make a single piece of molding. Every carpenter owned his own set of molding planes, and the resulting work was very much a personal signature, which accounts for the wide variation in design.

It used to be possible to buy those old planes quite cheaply in antique shops. But, like so many other formerly functional items elevated by nostalgia to the status of relics, this is no longer so. You could more easily purchase a used industrial shaper than a set of old molding planes today. Lacking either antique planes or modern shaper, it's possible to have the old pattern duplicated by a woodworking shop, working from a small piece provided as a template.

Sometimes the original molding may almost match a modern off-the-shelf pattern. With patience and a contour gauge, it's often possible to reshape it. If the piece being replaced is small, the match need not be perfect, since you won't see the difference from the ground once the patch has been painted in. Unless historical authenticity is very important, using standard stock that recreates the impression of the original if not its exact form is much more economical than custom shopwork. Modern carpentry, by dint of economy, has come full circle to the exigencies of pioneer days. Soffits and cornices on contemporary houses have been stripped to their functional minimum.

Remove and replace any unsound trim boards. If your budget cannot afford clear-grade pine, select the best common pine you can, choosing straight boards with only a few tight face knots. Prime them with a shellac-based sealer to prevent the knots from bleeding through the paint (since knots absorb water more readily than the surrounding wood, they are a prime vector of decay). Small holes are

Before and after: With standard flat boards and cove moldings, the impression, if not an exact copy, of the original cornice trim is recreated. This type of approach is less expensive than the custom milling that is usually needed to match obsolete molding patterns.

best filled with caulk. Plug larger holes and pockets of rot with an epoxy-based wood filler. Keep a can of wasp killer handy when working around cornices; a ladder is no place for fancy dancing. Use the spray to cover your strategic retreat and wait until evening, when all the foraging wasps have returned to the hive, to launch your final assault. Wasps have their ecological niche, but it's better that it be somewhere other than your cornice.

Examine the woodwork for any signs of moisture damage. The source of the leak must be fixed and the wood allowed to dry out before it can be successfully primed and repainted. To prevent spattered walls and to avoid tedious brushwork, repaint the trim before you install the siding, especially when working with different colors.

Retrofitting soffit vents

The underside of the cornice, the soffit, is another area that frequently demands attention, not because of rot but because of potential problems caused by modern insulation methods.

Capping the attic of an old house with insulation gives rise to a problem its builders could not have anticipated. The insulation impedes the otherwise strong convective air movements that ventilate moisture from the house to the outside. Instead, warm, moisture-laden air can condense within the insulating blanket, leading to water damage and eventual rot (more on this mechanism on pp. 227-229). Modern construction practice prevents this condensation problem by providing a ventilation flow from an inlet on the underside of the eaves overhang (the soffit vent) to an exhaust vent at the ridge or gable walls.

Soffit vents are conspicuously lacking in the cornice work of old houses. Retrofitting one can be a troublesome and awkward task. The exact method depends on the construction details of the particular cornice. A widely used but less than satisfactory solution is to drill at least three or four 2-in. holes between each rafter tail in the soffit and install a pop-in aluminum or plastic round louver. Not only is there a good chance of breaking your wrist or fingers should the high-torque ½-in. drill required for the job catch and bind, but the surface area of the louvers is too small for adequate air flow.

If the soffit is comprised of at least two boards, it may be possible to remove one of them (whichever is easier and will do less damage to adjoining trim pieces nailed to it; split the board rather than risk splitting the other cornice members). The edge of the remaining board is then pried down enough to admit the flange of a prefabricated metal soffit vent strip and then nailed back down. A new board ripped to the correct width fills the rest of the opening.

This method is about the only way to open up a pitched soffit. With flat soffits, or where the soffit consists of a single board you'd rather not remove, the vent opening is made by cutting a 2-in. wide slot down the length of the soffit with a circular saw. The edges of the cut are then pried down to admit the vent strip. If this does not prove possible, make the cut wider and then add a filler strip to each side to hold the vent in place. When painted in, it won't be noticeable from the ground.

If your renovation includes a cold roof (see pp. 170-171), you can ventilate the attic by cutting a slot through the roof decking above the soffit and adding an intake vent over the existing fascia. A second option is to cut the vent into the soffit as explained above, which permits the underside of the roofing to be ventilated without the need to disturb the existing fascia board.

Retrofitting Soffit Vents

A. One solution is to drill at least three or four 2-in. dia. holes between rafters and install round louver vents.

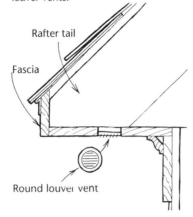

B. A better alternative, when the soffit is composed of at least two boards, is to remove one of them...

Cut nails first.

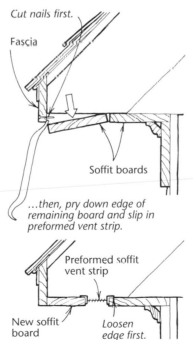

...then, pry down edge of remaining board and slip in preformed vent strip.

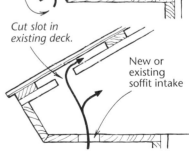

C. When soffit consists of a single board you would rather not remove, cut 2-in. wide vent opening down length of soffit with circular saw. Pry down edges of cut to admit vent strip.

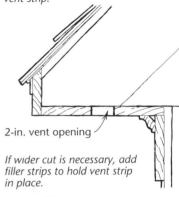

If wider cut is necessary, add filler strips to hold vent strip in place.

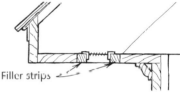

D. Soffit venting for cold roofs

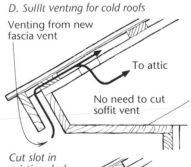

Cutting Timber Plate to Allow Air Circulation

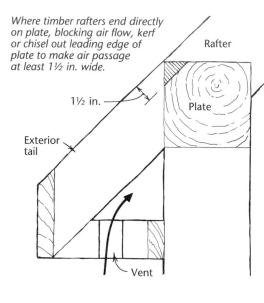

Where timber rafters end directly on plate, blocking air flow, kerf or chisel out leading edge of plate to make air passage at least 1½ in. wide.

Rafter

Plate

1½ in.

Exterior tail

Vent

Opening up the soffit doesn't always provide an air channel into the attic space. Sometimes the spaces between the rafters are filled with a board or solid blocking. Depending on the best access, the impediment can usually be removed with a ripping chisel (a heavy prybar/nailpuller, which is hammered into a board to split it apart), working either from the vent slot or the attic. The drawing above shows a complication found in some timber-frame houses. Here, since the rafters end directly on the plate and the eave overhang is built against the wall, the plate fills the entire space between the rafters. The solution is to cut diagonal kerfs into the top of the plate with a reciprocating saw and chisel back its leading edge to make an air passage at least 1½ in. wide.

If a wood gutter is removed and not reinstalled, it will be necessary to extend the bottom of the roof down and construct proper eaves. Without this overhang, rainwater from the roof will flow directly down onto the siding, shortening its life and increasing the probability of water damage. If the wood gutter is left intact, soffit venting is not possible. Installation of a whole-attic ventilating fan is probably the best solution.

Installing clapboards

Clapboards are manufactured in several grades, species and widths, affecting price and the labor required. The most expensive grade is "extra clear." Because this type is free of knots or face defects, extra clear is well suited for painting. "Cottage" grade clapboards are the cheapest, but not the most economical, since they contain loose knots or defects that must be cut out to prevent leaks. The best compromise is the "second-clear" (also called "clear") grade. Here, any knots or defects are confined to the portion covered by the succeeding course. Clapboards are commonly available in spruce, cedar, redwood and pine. Although unpainted knotty clapboard is ill-matched to the styles of old houses (after 1725, siding was always painted, at least in New England), the knotty-spruce utility grade, which does accept a transparent or semi-solid stain quite nicely, might be an aesthetically and financially suitable alternative to painted clear-grade clapboarding.

Weather exposure for clapboards is equal to half the width plus ¼ in.: for 5-in. clapboards, allow 2¾ in.; for 5½-in., allow 3 in.; and for 6-in., 3¼ in. To estimate the amount of clapboard needed to cover a given area, multiply the square footage by the width of the clapboard and divide the result by the width of the exposure. The answer is the number of lineal feet of clapboard to order.

On bare surfaces, begin installing clapboards by leveling a line around the building ½ in. below the bottom edge of the wall sheathing. This is, of course, an imaginary line, since there is nothing below the bottom edge of the sheathing on which to mark it. In actuality, mark the line on the wall at a point ½ in. lower than the nominal width of the clapboard up from the bottom. The first course is set with a spacing block held to the line.

Several problems may come to mind. Ideally, the bottom edge of the sheathing should be level. In reality, at least for an old house, it's very likely that it will vary by several inches. By means of a water level or builder's transit level, mark the level point at all corners of the house and at several points in between.

If the variation is not too great, begin the first course at the lowest corner and run it as level as possible, letting it overhang the wall as it will. For best appearances, try not to let its bottom edge fall below the ends of the corner trim boards. Instead, tilt the last clapboard upward to meet the trim board. If this won't work, it's probably best to adopt the technique used to run roof shingles against a wavy drip edge: Let the first course more or less follow the sheathing and run the second course straight and level. It may take several courses to bring the clapboard line gradually up to level.

In extreme cases, as, for example, when a windowsill is not level, visual effect may be more important than true level. If the line of the siding is parallel to the line of the windowsills, head trim and cornice, the eye tends to read the siding as level. The effect is a lot less jarring than a tapered clapboard disappearing into a trim board. If the courses are slanted gradually, the deviation from true level will not be apparent. For example, measure the distance from the last level course of clapboards at least eight courses below both ends of a crooked sill. Divide the difference between these two measurements by the number of courses. Continuing the example, assume a difference of 1½ in. between measurements. This translates into ³⁄₁₆ in., which is the extra height each of the eight courses must be lifted on one side to bring the last one parallel to the underside of the tilted sill.

Compensating for Crooked Walls when Installing Clapboards

Slant courses of siding gradually, so deviation from level will be inconspicuous.

Divide deviation by courses (here, 1½ in. ÷ 8) for slant of each course (here, ³⁄₁₆ in.).

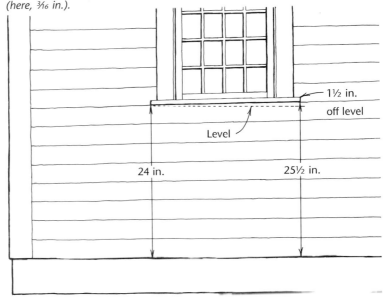

The same technique works well for running clapboards up under a frieze board if you wish to avoid finishing up with a narrow strip. In this case, the total distance is divided by the exposure width to find the number of courses needed to reach the last one, and then the desired adjustment is calculated. For example, with a 3-in. exposure and a distance of 37 in. to the soffit, 12 full courses will end with a 1-in. strip. Increasing the exposure by about ³⁄₃₂ in. allows the last course to end with a full-width exposure.

When installing clapboards, the object is ultimately to end up where you started from: That is, a line extended around the house from the starting point ends up on the starting point or close enough to it so that the difference is not noticeable. The line of each course continues around each corner. Even if you are very careful about checking the run of the courses, it is still

Four Ways to Install Clapboards

Method 1: From top down

Nail first course only in upper portion so next course can slip under it. Tack bottom of course only when course beneath it is aligned.

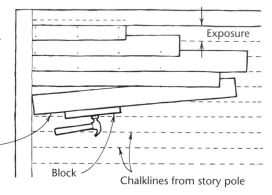

Exposure

Tap up clapboard with wood block.

Block

Chalklines from story pole

Method 2: From bottom up (using 2-course spacer jig)

A. Nail first course to bottom of wall.

B. Align top edge of spacer to line of next course plus one. Bottom of spacer will align with bottom edge of second course.

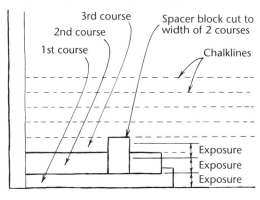

3rd course

2nd course

1st course

Spacer block cut to width of 2 courses

Chalklines

Exposure
Exposure
Exposure

Method 3: With guide jig

Lay clapboards to top edge. Hook bottom edge over lower clapboard.

16 in. long

1x stock

Width of exposure

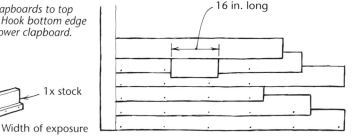

Method 4: Filling in short sections of wall

To work from bottom up, mark pencil guidelines across clapboards with a straightedge. Working from top down, snap lines between ends of each course and fill in where necessary.

From top down

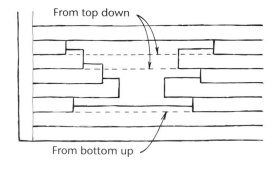

From bottom up

fairly easy for them to run quite a bit off level by the time you've rounded a house, especially when covering long walls unbroken by windows or doors. This can be avoided by using a story pole to mark the layout lines for the course spacings.

Carefully divide a straight length of 1x2 into segments equal to the width of your clapboard exposure. Lay the story pole against the wall next to a corner trim board with its bottom set to the bottom of the first clapboard. Transfer the markings onto the wall. Repeat this at each corner and next to each window and door, and then snap chalklines on the wall between each set of marks. As for roofing, on long spans or walls with bows or dips that interfere with the string, establish intermediate sets of marks.

There are several ways to lay clapboards. Each has its advantages.

Method 1: Starting at the top of the wall, nail the first full clapboard in place with its bottom edge even to the chalked line. Take care to nail this first course only in the upper portion, so that the following course can slip up under the butt of the preceding one. Continue down the wall, slipping each course up under the one above it. Tack the nails in place rather than driving them home, using only a few nails per clapboard and always leaving the bottommost edge unnailed until the next clapboard has been slipped under it. Driving the nails home makes it harder to slide the clapboards up under the edge, and you could easily split one trying. Use a block of wood to tap the clapboards into place in any case. Once a section is finished (all you can reach from your ladder or staging), nail it off. The nailing pattern looks best if it follows a more-or-less straight line down the wall.

It might seem more sensible to work from the bottom up, lining up the top edges of clapboards with the chalklines. So it would be, were it not that clapboards are so thin that their top edges are usually broken, split and generally uneven.

Method 2 solves this problem with a 1x4 spacer block cut to the width of two courses. The first course is nailed to the bottom of the wall (always tack a cant strip cut from the top half of a clapboard under the first course to give it the proper pitch first). Hold the top edge of the spacer block flush with the line corresponding to the next course plus one. The bottom of the spacer block will now line up with the bottom edge of the second course. Since every course is constantly referenced to a chalkline, errors and misalignment are kept to a minimum.

Method 3 avoids the time-consuming business of layout lines altogether. Because it sacrifices accuracy to speed, this method is better suited for replacing small sections of wall that have no reference to other walls. After the first course is nailed level, subsequent courses are kept aligned by means of a guide jig cut from a 16-in. length of 1x stock to which a cleat is fastened at a point corresponding to exposure width. When hooked over the bottom of the clapboard, the following course rests on its top edge. Check the run of the courses from time to time with a 4-ft. level.

Method 4: When only a small section of clapboard must be filled in to match existing clapboards, as, for example, when patching over a window or door opening, leveling the courses is not important. Snap a line between the ends of each course and fill in each course, working from the top down as in Method 1. You can also fill in from the bottom up, drawing lines across each clapboard as you go.

Clapboards are secured with 4d galvanized nails spaced about 12 in. on center driven within ½ in. of the butt. Don't drive them too deeply into the surface of the wood, as it can easily split. Blunt the points when nailing off the ends of a piece. Joints should never break above each other. Stagger the joints between overlapping courses at least 3 in. If you use a fairly consistent pattern when breaking joints, the nailing lines will remain fairly straight. Since clapboards are available in bundles of different lengths and almost any piece can be used, there's little excuse for waste when laying out the nailing pattern. Trim the ends on a chopsaw before installation, since you cannot assume that they have been cut square at the mill. A portable table saw is the best tool for ripping long cuts to fit over and under windows. Hand-held saws vibrate dangerously in such thin stock.

Clapboards should butt snugly against window and door casings and other trim. For the neatest appearance and to avoid tedious cutting in, paint the edges of the adjoining trim before applying the clapboards. Caulk these joints before painting the clapboards. For inside corners, butt the clapboards against a 1x1 trim board.

Wood-shingle siding

Along the New England coast up into the Maritimes and throughout the Pacific Northwest, cedar shingles have always been a traditional siding. This naturally decay-resistant wood weathers to a soft silvery grey, requiring no other finish or paint. The shingles are durable, watertight and cost less than clapboards. The only real difference between roof and wall application is the maximum permitted exposure. Since wall shingles are not so directly exposed to rain, the exposure can be greater (the rule is: half the length of the shingle less ½ in.; for example, for a 16-in. shingle, 7½ in.), and they don't require extra spacing for expansion. When fitted tightly together at their butts to reduce rain and wind infiltration, the natural taper of the shingle from bottom to top provides all the spacing needed.

As with clapboards, level a starting line and use your story pole to mark off the courses. But don't snap chalklines on the sheathing. Instead, after the first (doubled) course is nailed with its bottom edge projecting about ½ in. below the sheathing, snap your line across the shingles themselves. To avoid staining the shingles, use the washable blue (not the permanent red) chalk. The butts of the next course follow

Board-and-Batten Siding

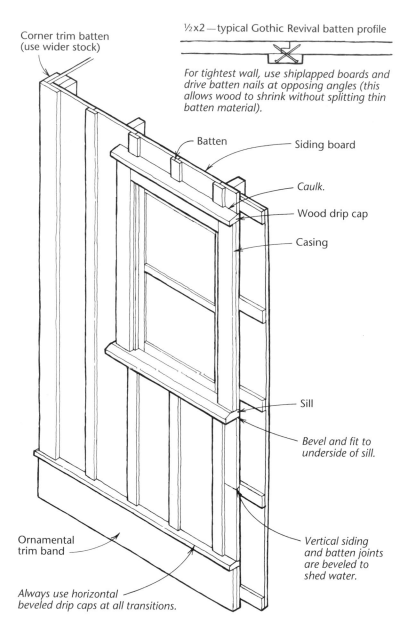

Corner trim batten
(use wider stock)

½x2 —typical Gothic Revival batten profile

For tightest wall, use shiplapped boards and drive batten nails at opposing angles (this allows wood to shrink without splitting thin batten material).

Batten — Siding board

— *Caulk.*

— Wood drip cap

— Casing

— Sill

— *Bevel and fit to underside of sill.*

Ornamental
trim band —

Always use horizontal beveled drip caps at all transitions.

Vertical siding and batten joints are beveled to shed water.

this line, and so on, up the wall. Although these chalklines are enough to guide installation, using a length of shiplapped board as a straightedge is more convenient and ensures accurate courses. The lip of the board holds the shingles against the wall, and strips of galvanized metal clinched to it make attachment or removal easy. The missing shingles are filled in after the straightedge is removed.

Wood shingles are typically butted to trim boards and window casings, although cornerboard trim is sometimes omitted and the shingles are mitered or butted together. Because shingles taper, they must be cut to fit square against trim boards. A utility knife, a framing square and a small block or finger plane are the most efficient tools for cutting and trimming wood shingles. A portable table saw kept close at hand on the scaffolding is also helpful, especially for repetitive angles and crosscuts.

During the Victorian and Queen Anne periods of the late 19th century, several styles of siding were often combined for a highly ornamental effect. Scalloped and hexagonal wood shingles were combined with wavy and diagonal clapboards and regular square-edged sidings. When only a few novelty shingles need replacement, the pieces can be cut from standard shingles on a bandsaw. Fortunately, thanks to the current interest in preservation and nostalgic variations on old themes, these siding patterns, along with Victorian gingerbread, are now becoming more commonly available.

Some other siding choices

Board-and-batten siding, which often characterizes contemporary "rustic" styles, sheds, barns and other rough structures, was actually a distinguishing feature of the mid-19th-century Gothic Revival style. Planed vertical boards were nailed to horizontal blocking let into the studs or directly to the sheathing boards. The joints between them were covered with thin strips of wood ("battens"), either plain or decoratively beaded, to create an attractive and economical siding. Fitting and cutting are simplified since the corner boards, window casing and other trim boards are nailed over the boarding. The battens simply butt against the trim. When a board must be spliced, the joint is beveled to shed water.

A variety of ornamental banding effects can be created with a minimum of labor and expense. The drawing on the facing page shows some of the details. For a tighter wall, use modern tongue-and-groove or shiplapped boarding instead of square-edged boards, but don't eliminate the battens and ornamental trim. Unadorned vertical board siding is much too contemporary to suit an old house.

Board-and-batten siding can be retrofitted to plywood or foam sheathings with the addition of 1x3 nailers, called strapping or furring. Fasten the siding with ring-shank stainless-steel siding nails to prevent rust stains and minimize movement. To reduce the chances of excessive swelling and shrinkage, which will loosen the siding and cause splits, boards should not be wider than 8 in. Also, if the nails are driven at opposing angles (only two per board) to each other, the board will tend to slide down the nail as it shrinks, preventing splits and keeping it tight.

Another 19th-century siding that enjoyed limited use and is still employed today is the "novelty" pattern. Its dished-out upper edge enables it to shed water when applied horizontally, resulting in a siding that is self-aligning, and extremely fast and economical to install. As with board-and-batten siding, the fit to trim boards does not have to be exact, since the boards and casings are applied over the siding. Nails are driven through the boards directly into the studding, using 8d stainless-steel siding nails.

The drawing at right shows another siding option, which is especially suited for application over foam sheathing. Narrow 1x4 or 1x5 shiplapped boarding, when overlapped clapboard-style, is almost indistinguishable from the real item and much less costly and labor intensive; 10d

Two Clapboard-Like Sidings

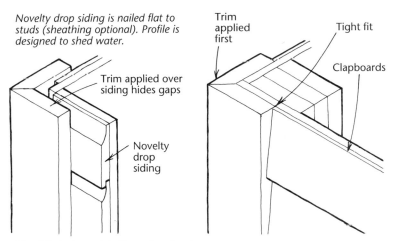

Novelty drop siding is nailed flat to studs (sheathing optional). Profile is designed to shed water.

Trim applied first

Tight fit

Trim applied over siding hides gaps

Clapboards

Novelty drop siding

Simplified trimwork is the main advantage of novelty siding: Unlike clapboards, trim is nailed on top of siding cut to rough opening. No precise fitting required.

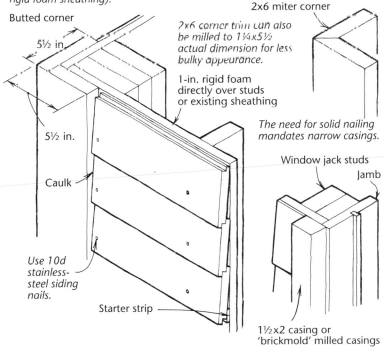

Shiplapped board laid clapboard-style is nailed directly to studs (often over rigid foam sheathing).

2x6 miter corner

Butted corner

5½ in.

2x6 corner trim can also be milled to 1¼x5½ actual dimension for less bulky appearance.

1-in. rigid foam directly over studs or existing sheathing

The need for solid nailing mandates narrow casings.

5½ in.

Window jack studs

Jamb

Caulk

Use 10d stainless-steel siding nails.

Starter strip

1½x2 casing or 'brickmold' milled casings

This style of asphalt-impregnated fiber siding is intended to mimic stonework. When damaged, the fiber base typically soaks up water like a sponge, causing the walls underneath to rot.

stainless-steel nails will penetrate the foam and secure the siding to the studs. Because of the extra thickness, corner and casing trim and frieze boards must be at least 1¼ in. thick. If custom milling is unavailable, substitute standard 2x stock instead.

This mock-clapboard siding works best with the narrow "brickmold" supplied with modern factory-built windows, since the end-nailed siding must catch into the studs beside the window jambs. Old-fashioned flat casings are usually too wide to allow this, unless extra jack studding can be added to the interior wall cavity.

Painting Protocol

The main purpose of paint is protective rather than decorative. Paint protects the wood beneath from attack by wood-destroying fungi and harsh weather. But no paint lasts forever. Because a paint film is relatively impervious to moisture, water vapor migrating from the interior of the house through the porous wood siding will push against the underside of the paint film. When the bond between paint and wood eventually breaks, the surface peels and cracks. Even the best-quality paints will inevitably fail under this relentless pressure. Since each additional layer of

paint adds to the barrier effect, constant repainting will only hasten the inevitable. At some point the old paint must be stripped down to the bare wood and the process begun anew.

When is repainting necessary? Only when it can no longer be put off—a regular schedule of repainting in the misguided attempt to avoid total stripping only shortens the lifespan of each successive coat of paint. This is a case where procrastination is a virtue. Repaint only when the vast majority of the paint has begun to peel. Otherwise, touch up isolated areas of paint failure or any spots where bare wood is showing. Don't repaint a wall just because the color has faded. A thorough washing may allow you to put off the job for a few more years.

Paint problems

There are several symptoms of paint failure. To cure them successfully, it's important to diagnose their underlying cause. Unless you've used the discount-store clearance-sale brand, most paint problems are not caused by cheap paint but by improper application. The other culprit is moisture penetration, either internally (as discussed previously) or from the outside.

Stains and discoloration that won't wash off are most likely caused by mildew, a fungus that is actually living off the paint. Shrubs and trees growing too close to the house will prevent the sunlight and air movement that discourage mildew's growth. Water splashing back up onto the walls or from leaking or clogged gutters and downspouts will also foster fungal bloom. Once these factors have been corrected, kill the fungus with a solution of 3 qt. hot water, 1 qt. bleach, 1 cup detergent (Spic and Span® is a favorite) and ½ cup trisodium phosphate (available in hardware stores) applied with a rented power washer. If this treatment fails to remove the stain, cover it with an exterior-grade shellac primer (such as BIN®).

Chalking (when the paint turns powdery and washes away) is a common symptom of cheap paint. Some exterior paints are actually formulated to chalk, so that the color will always appear fresh. But there's a difference between such "self-cleaning" paints and one that is literally running down the walls. If good paint was applied over badly weathered or bare, unprimed wood without proper preparation, the binder (the resin that holds the pigment together) is too quickly absorbed into the fibers, leaving the pigment scattered on the surface, where it soon washes away. Weathered wood needs to be treated with a water-repellent preservative (such as Thompson's Water Seal®) or a solution of two parts boiled linseed oil and one part turpentine before priming.

All bare new wood must likewise be primed before finish coating. If there is no evidence of raw wood under the chalky areas, the culprit is probably cheap paint with inferior binding agents. The cure is a thorough washing followed by repriming with a high-quality oil-base primer.

If blisters are a problem, cut one open to reveal its cause. If another layer of paint shows under the blister, it's likely that the paint was applied in the hot sun, causing the outer film to dry and trap a pocket of solvent beneath it. When bare wood is visible, interior moisture has ruptured the surface bond. Solvent blisters are easily repaired by spot-sanding and repainting. Moisture problems must be corrected and the wood allowed to dry before repriming and painting.

Wrinkles are also caused by improper technique. Once again, the outermost film dries before the underside. This happens when the paint is applied too thickly without being brushed out, or in direct sunlight (especially with dark colors) or over a cold surface. Avoid applying oil-based paints below 40°F or latex below 50°F. Scrape or spot-sand to remove the wrinkles and recoat.

The partnership of color and siding variations reached its apotheosis with the Victorian style and its variant, the Queen Anne shingle style. The many layers of exposed decorative trim require constant attention to caulking, flashing and painting to maintain their good health.

Cracking or crazing occurs when old or cheap paint becomes hardened and can't move with the wood as it contracts and expands. The condition is progressive, since the tiny cracks allow moisture to penetrate beneath the paint, causing further swelling and larger cracks. Once the damage extends beyond a few isolated spots that can be scraped and patched, the only cure is complete stripping and repainting. Cracking eventually leads to "alligatoring," which is a terminal failure of the paint bond, usually brought about by the accumulation of too many layers of paint.

Intercoat peeling is usually caused by poor surface preparation, which prevents new paint from bonding to the old. Failing to wash the walls prior to repainting will leave a greasy film. Applying paint under adverse conditions or when the surface is damp will also prevent a good bond, as will painting over a hard and glossy undercoat (or too many previous coats).

When paint peels off bare wood and not just between coats, moisture problems exist. Small patches are traceable to water absorbed into the exposed end grain of improperly sealed or caulked joints, splashback from roof runoff, or leaks somewhere into the wall itself. These must be fixed before repainting.

Wholesale peeling due to interior moisture will be a chronic problem unless the sources of moisture buildup are reduced, if not eliminated. When the peeling is on a bathroom or kitchen wall, you can be sure an interior vapor barrier is lacking. Installing an exhaust vent or a whole-house fan can help reduce moisture movement. Add a continuous vapor barrier over the insulation when replacing interior walls, or use a specially formulated vapor-barrier paint or wallcovering over existing walls to prolong the life of your exterior paint.

Another major source of moisture is from earth-floored crawl spaces or cellars, which should be retrofitted with an appropriate polyethylene barrier (see p. 98). As mentioned earlier, eventually paint buildup alone will lead to peeling. Stripping and repainting are ultimately unavoidable. The goal is to prolong the life of the latest paint job.

Stripping exterior paint

Stripping exterior paint is messy, tiresome and potentially dangerous. Despite the wide array of tools and methods recommended for paint removal, hand-scraping —the most tedious and strenuous—is the least harmful. Never use a blowtorch to remove paint. Even greater than the risk of fire is the health hazard associated with inhalation of toxic lead fumes made volatile by the high-temperature flame. Almost all old paint contains lead pigment.

Electric heat guns are safer, since they typically operate at temperatures too low to boil off lead. They work like an oversize hair dryer, blowing a stream of hot air over the surface, which makes them useful for reaching into awkward areas and for removing paint from curved balustrades and other ornaments difficult to strip mechanically. Other than this limited application, heat guns are too slow for large areas.

Heat plates, which are held directly over the surface until the paint blisters, are useful on flat surfaces. They work fairly quickly, but there is danger of flaming if the coil is held too long in one area or allowed to touch the paint.

Unless they are handled delicately, rotary sanders can shred the surface just as fast as they can remove paint. Since sanders create a fine airborne toxic dust, their use for paint removal is actually illegal in some communities. Wire-brush attachments for drills also tear up wood and are too slow for large-scale work. The various flapping and wire-mesh strippers are also effective only on small areas.

Sandblasting is an efficient way to turn siding into barnboard. The abrasive action will gouge out the grain of the wood along with the paint, and forever alter its character. In addition to the same dangers of surface destruction, high-pressure water sprays (over 2,000 psi) can break windows and force water up under the siding and into the walls. Although low-pressure (400 psi) sprayers will remove some flaking paint, these tools are best used for washing the walls prior to repainting.

Chemical paint strippers are not only toxic, they're too expensive for use on large surfaces. Save them for difficult interior projects.

Since all loose, peeling, cracked or alligatored paint must be removed for a successful paint job, there's really no alternative to hard labor and a stiff putty knife or scraper blade. Always wear a dust mask when scraping.

Latex vs. oil

Whether to use latex instead of oil-based paints is one of those perennial questions that incites strong partisan arguments not necessarily based on fact. Oil paints tend to shrink and harden as they age, whereas latex paints are more stable and flexible. Because of these different rates of movement, a latex paint applied over an oil paint will peel more readily than an oil paint over an oil paint.

On bare wood, either paint will perform just as well. The only reason to use oil paint is that most old paint is oil-based. For best results, use an alkyd primer (synthetic oil-base) over oil paint before applying a latex top coat. On new work, one coat of high-quality latex paint applied over an alkyd primer will probably last longer than two top coats, since latex is actually somewhat more permeable to moisture. On areas subject to abrasion or standing water (such as windowsills), the standard double finish coat is still recommended. The question of oil vs. latex may soon be moot: In some states, oil-based finishes are prohibited.

Stain

Paint is the traditional finish for old houses. Although stains are suited to early Colonial-style saltboxes and Capes, you might consider dispensing with historical accuracy and employ a stain instead of paint on old houses of later styles. Stains differ from paints in that they lack a film-building binder. Because the pigment is merely suspended in a solvent that soaks into the surface grain, the color gradually washes away. There is no resinous film to impede moisture movement, so it won't crack or peel. Recoating does not cause a buildup. Modern stains also contain fungicides, wood-preserving oils and water repellents that accomplish the same protective functions of paint. They're also cheaper, self-priming and easier to apply.

The darker solid-color stains, at least for a few years, are indistinguishable from paint. Since lighter stains can't hide knots, mask grain and joints or cover old paint, their application is limited to new siding. Unless they eventually replace the siding, the owners of a painted house are consecrated to the eternal ritual of repainting.

Cleaning brickwork

Houses built of brick are another story. Any attempt to keep a brick wall painted is doomed to failure. Bricks are so porous that moisture migrates through them easily and soon pushes the paint film off the surface. The quick fix, especially favored by commercial developers, is sandblasting. But, as with stripping siding, sandblasting is the worst possible way to clean or restore a brick wall. The harsh abrasion of a high-pressure stream of sand can strip away as much as ¼ in. of the bricks' surface along with the grime and paint. Corners and other details are blunted and obscured. Soft mortar is blasted out of the joints. Even worse, once the hard face of the brick is gone, the soft inner core weathers much faster, seriously compromising the building life.

Steam cleaning, which uses 140 psi to 150 psi of pressure, is a much gentler and effective way to remove accumulated grime. Working on 3-ft. square sections at a time and rinsing them clean with a garden hose, it's possible for the home owner to clean brickwork with a rented steam generator. Stubborn deposits are removed with a wire brush or a dull paint scraper and a solution of near scalding hot water and TSP (trisodium phosphate) and washing soda (sodium carbonate), 2 lb. of each per gallon.

To remove iron stains from brickwork, try a mix of 7 parts glycerine, 1 part sodium citrate and 6 parts water, with enough whiting (powdered chalk) to make a paste; apply, let dry, then scrape off. A paste of one part TSP and one part whiting mixed with water, when left to dry for 24 hours, will often remove oil stains. Remove whitewash from brick with a 1 to 5 solution of muriatic (hydrochloric) acid and water. Wear rubber gloves, eye protection and use a long-handled synthetic-fiber scrub brush.

Attachments, Additions and Alterations

The majority of old houses did not have any sort of protection for the front door. Porches were the exception, not the rule. It is obvious from a study of the physical depreciation of dwellings that have not been kept in first-rate repair that the porch (where one existed) was the first part of the building to become decrepit. This may explain why so large a majority of dwellings never had one; it was considered a luxury, something unnecessary.

—Herbert Wheaton Congdon, *Early American Homes for Today* (Dublin, N.H.: William L. Bauhan, 1985)

Porches and verandas provide protection from summer sun and act as buffers against the winter wind, creating a socially useful space—inviting, but not too intimate, a perfect place to watch the world go by.

*T*he porch is as much a part of the iconography of the American house as the fireplace. The word and the form are derived from the Latin *porticus,* an architectural element designed to draw attention to the formal entries of the aristocratic townhouse or country manor. Although it did provide some protection from roof runoff and winter winds, the portico, with its fluted open columns and classically detailed triangular pediment, was never intended as an outdoor living space. It was too small.

The influence of Andrew Jackson Downing's naturalistic theories, as expounded in his book, *Landscape Architecture* (1844), transformed the portico from an ornament into a "necessary and delightful appendage, a place for warm weather living and cold weather protection." As the passion for porches swept across the country, old farmhouses and stately manors alike were "modernized" by the indiscriminate addition of porches, verandas and piazzas. No new house was considered complete without one.

Porches and Verandas

Properly speaking, a porch is a roofed gallery supported by columns that does not cover an entire wall. A veranda covers one or more walls. The term "piazza" is synonymous with both.

In northern climates, the porch can screen the house from the direct force of the wind and, when glassed in, help to reduce heating bills through solar gain. It is a place to hang clothes to dry on a rainy day or to start trays of seedlings in early spring. It makes an ideal winter workshop, where heavy power tools can be set up and boards cut while the main areas of the house are both rebuilt and lived in, safe from sawdust. If the door between the house and porch is left ajar, the porch will reach a comfortable working temperature —any heat loss is offset by stoking the stove with construction scrap. In hot, sticky Southern climates, a veranda catches and encourages the slightest breezes.

Open or enclosed with glass or screen, a porch or veranda is a place to gather or sleep, a cool and shady refuge. Though the usefulness of a porch is counteracted to some extent by the diminished light level of the rooms behind it, this is not altogether undesirable: The rooms will seem cooler in summer and cozier in winter.

Common problems and repairs

Although porches are psychologically part of a house's living space, they are physically outside the domain of the house. Thus their routine maintenance is often neglected until repair or demolition is unavoidable. This is unfortunate, because with proper construction and upkeep, a porch should last as long as the house.

Water destroys porches; the greater exposure of a porch to rain and snow demands special protective features. The drawing on the next page shows some typical trouble spots that can lead to structural damage.

The well-built porch begins with a tight roof that is properly flashed to the side wall. Because of the relatively shallow pitch, which encourages snow and ice buildup, porch roofs are more susceptible to leakage and the effects of wind-driven rain. Early porches were often roofed with tin sheets, soldered at the seams; unless the metal was kept painted, it eventually rusted. Asphalt coatings not only have the unfortunate effect of hastening corrosion, they also dry out and crack fairly quickly. Leaks in porch roofs soon cause structural decay. Sagging, warped or water-stained ceiling boards are a telltale sign of a chronic leak. It may take extra blocking between the ceiling joists to screw distorted boards back down after the leak and any structural damage have been repaired.

Today, half-lap mineral-surfaced roll roofing applied over an adhesive butyl membrane is cheaper and easier to use than metal. Fiberglass-asphalt shingles could also be used over the same membrane (which is superior to a cemented felt underlayment), even on roofs with slopes

Porch Trouble Spots

Wherever water can enter and collect will eventually become a site for decay.

- Side wall
- Leaking or damaged flashing
- Worn-out roll roofing/rusted tin/ bubbled or dried-out tar
- Rafter
- Leaking gutter
- Fascia
- Ceiling joist
- Rotted ceiling boards
- Dried-out caulking

Rain gets into columns through fascia, roof and gutter leaks. Moisture condenses beneath paint film and is trapped at base of column. Drill 1-in. vent holes to prevent condensation, and pop in plastic midget louvers.

- Column
- Knots, splits
- Open joints
- Torus
- Plinth (pillow block)
- Runoff from deck
- Joist
- Exposed end grain
- Rim joists or girder
- Heaving foundation post, steel or masonry pier
- Rotted lattice (in direct contact with ground)

lower than 4-in-12. Organic felt shingles, however, should not be used, because they would rot as they soaked up the moisture inevitably trapped between their undersides and the waterproof membrane.

The porch roof should be joined to the side wall of the house with copper or galvanized enamel-coated steel flashing. This flashing must extend up under the siding and down over the last course of roofing, with the bottom edge of the flashing embedded in flashing cement. More than on any other part of the house, gutters are a mandatory feature of porch roofs, since rainwater should not be allowed to splash against the porch skirts, foundation posts and steps.

The floorboards, which are so open to weather, are likely to be at least partially rotted. This decay can often infect the underlying framing. The bottoms of the posts or columns and rails and balusters are also likely victims of weather and neglect. Wherever a joint has opened up or end grain is left exposed, there is an opportunity for water to seep in and for fungi to begin their insidious work. Preventing joint failure and rot is as much a matter of attention to proper construction as it is to timely maintenance.

The advent of pressure-treated lumber in a wide variety of stock widths and styles, including ornamental turnings specifically designed for outdoor structures, has dramatically increased porch longevity and simplified repair work and upkeep. To take advantage of its benefits, the old and damaged material must be removed.

Unless a multi-story porch is involved, the load carried on porch columns is quite light. No special jacking or support is needed to carry the roof while the columns, floor and joists are removed. Use 4x4 jack posts, lifting from the porch deck to relieve the roof load. Then lower the roof back down onto 4x4 posts jammed between the ground and the underside of the porch headers. (These posts should be set at an angle to facilitate framing removal.) Don't worry if the roof sags some during repairs; it's a simple matter to jack it back to level from the rebuilt porch deck. Use 2x12 pads above and below the posts to distribute the force. Often, as the roof is lifted, the porch columns or posts and their attached railings come up with it. It's safer to remove these elements than to leave them dangling.

Replace rotted framing with pressure-treated lumber. Don't forget to pitch the joists so that the porch floor can drain. Since the flooring joints must follow the direction of the water flow, the floor joists must run perpendicular to the width of the porch. A slope of ⅛ in. per foot is sufficient. Use strings to establish level and straight lines for the sills and joists. These will also show the amount of correction needed to straighten sags and bows in existing framing caused by settled or lifted foundation posts or structural failure. An automobile screw jack will provide all the lift you'll need.

Cut any sections of decayed flooring back to sound wood over the middle of the nearest joist and replace with similar stock. The traditional material for porch decks is 1-in. thick by 4-in. wide clear-grain Douglas fir or yellow pine tongue-and-groove flooring. Soak each board in a trough filled with wood preservative for at least three minutes, and let it dry for two days before you paint it.

Use two coats of oil-based porch-and-deck enamel on both sides and all edges of the board. When installing the flooring, seal each tongue-and-groove joint with caulk as the pieces are installed. This tedious step will greatly reduce water penetration and paint failure. The exposed ends of the flooring boards must be protected from water exposure by nailing a bullnose molding cut from an extra length of flooring over them. Apply a third coat of enamel to the finished deck.

Square-edged pressure-treated board is an alternative to the expense and labor of traditional decking. If a tighter floor is desired, you'll have to cut a tongue-and-groove joint into the edges of the boards

It takes very little to support a single-story porch roof.

Protecting Exposed End Grain of Porch Decking

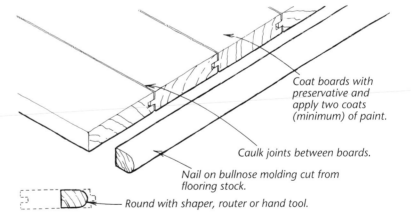

Coat boards with preservative and apply two coats (minimum) of paint.

Caulk joints between boards.

Nail on bullnose molding cut from flooring stock.

Round with shaper, router or hand tool.

with a table saw or router, since treated decking milled to a tongue-and-groove pattern is unavailable. Always wear a dust mask and observe recommended safety precautions when working with pressure-treated wood.

If the existing floor framing is still relatively sound, treated joists can be sistered alongside partially decayed old wood. To extend the usefulness of the existing joists, coat their top edges with preservative and a layer of flashing cement. Joists can also rot along their bottom edges if they are too close to the ground—8 in. is the minimum recommended clearance.

Fortunately for the porch restorer, the typical ornamental turned-wood porch post has a squared section at top and bottom. Replacing these rotted areas with a prosthetic section requires a lot less skill than duplicating the carved portions. Mate the new section to sound old wood with a dowel or rebar pin. Should complete replacement be necessary, lumberyards stock turned hemlock and pressure-treated posts. Salvage yards specializing in architectural antiques are another source if the standard patterns are not a good enough match. If all else fails, an exact replacement can be custom-turned at a woodworking shop.

Once the paint peels, hollow round columns start to split. These splits admit water, as does the exposed end grain at the column base and any open joints between elements of the capital. Water can then collect in the interior of the column and cause rot. These surfaces should be stripped, sanded, sealed with preservative and then primed, caulked and given two top coats of latex paint (latex films are slightly more permeable than oil and will thus permit some vapor migration from the interior of the column).

Hollow columns will last a lot longer if vented. Drill several 1-in. holes in an inconspicuous part of the column just below the capital, away from the prevailing wind. Cover the openings with pop-in plastic midget louvers. Drill a hole up through the floorboards and column base from underneath the porch to allow trapped water to drain. Or drill ¼-in. weep holes around the base of the column, just above its plinth block (the square base upon which the column sits).

Because water is easily trapped under them and sucked into the cracks between their joints, the plinth block and the torus (an ornamental wood disc between plinth and column proper) will almost always rot first. A common mistake is to fashion replacements from a solid block of wood, which leaves too much end grain exposed. Using pressure-treated stock makes this less of a problem, although even here, a section of mitered molding on each side of the plinth block will prolong the life of the paint.

If the rot has progressed an inch or so up into the column base, shorten the column and increase the depth of the plinth or add another torus. This is one place where epoxy consolidation (the process whereby rotted wood fibers are filled with a stiffening resin) is easier and probably more economical than the highly skilled shopwork demanded by the repair of severely deteriorated columns. For one thing, the work can be done on site.

Because of their many joints, balusters and railings are especially prone to decay. A lot of future repair can be prevented by ensuring that the railings are properly supported by blocking inserted between the bottom rail and the deck every 3 ft. or 4 ft. This prevents the rails from sagging under stress and the joints from opening. Constant caulking and repainting will preserve ordinary wood for a long time. If the railing needs replacement, use pressure-treated lumber and turnings for new work. It's not unusual for porch railings to terminate at a turned post sawn in half and set directly against the wall over a trim board. If this board has rotted, or worse, was omitted, the new one should be made of treated wood.

Because of their intimate contact with the ground and shrubbery, the lattice panels that skirt the porch bottom are usually the first part of the porch to rot. Prefabricated pressure-treated lattice has simplified repairs; the panels are easily sandwiched between treated boards. In regions where the ground freezes, always leave

Bracing Porch Steps

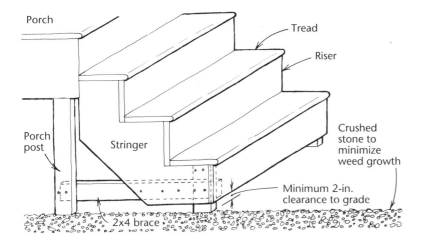

Porch

Tread

Riser

Porch post

Stringer

Crushed stone to minimize weed growth

Minimum 2-in. clearance to grade

2x4 brace

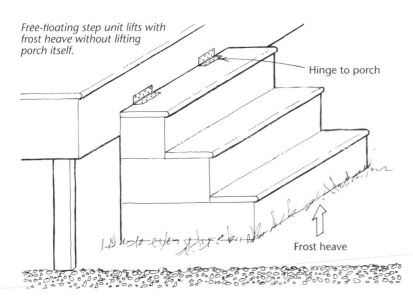

Free-floating step unit lifts with frost heave without lifting porch itself.

Hinge to porch

Frost heave

about 2 in. of clearance under the bottom edge of the panel. Otherwise, frost heave could destroy the panel or even lift the porch. Don't replace the lattice with solid panels, as this would impede ventilation.

Steps are another problem area whose longevity has been greatly improved by pressure-treated wood. At the very least, the undercarriage and riser boards should be cut from treated stock even if the treads are made with ordinary fir or yellow pine. Even so, never simply set the risers on a board or stone resting directly on the earth. If the stairs are too large to be supported by bracing against the porch framing, additional footings that extend below the frost line must be provided. For less formal porches, if the steps are built as a separate unit that simply rests against the porch, they are free to rise and fall with-

This porch has a host of problems: poor roof flashing, no gutters, sinking foundation posts, rotted flooring and concrete steps that have rotted out the wood behind them.

A remuddling disaster almost beyond repair: One possible solution might be to remove the clumsy siding detail above the door and soften the impact of the steel door with an appropriately scaled stoop roof.

out damage. If this independent stair is hinged to the porch frame, it is still free to move, but not too much.

Very often the problem with a porch is not so much rotted framing as it is unstable foundation supports. Porch sills and posts often rest on rocks or concrete blocks set directly on the ground. Sometimes they are carried by steel pipes driven into the earth. The seasonal lift and settlement of such foundations can sometimes rack a porch so badly that it starts to tear loose from the house.

The solution is a footing that extends below the frost line. Although poured concrete piers (using Sonotubes® or another brand of paperboard form) still enjoy wide use, pressure-treated posts set directly into the ground are becoming a popular alternative because of their labor-saving features. They're certainly a lot easier to cut to length or shim to height than concrete.

Since the undersides of porches are seldom protected by snow cover, frost penetration will be deeper than normal. The post holes should be dug 1 ft. deeper than the standard frost depth. An 80-lb. sack of concrete mix (Sakrete®) yields about 1 cu. ft. of concrete, which is enough to make footing pads for two posts when poured into the hole (dig it at least twice as wide as the post). Let the concrete harden a day or two before setting any posts.

Another solution, which is particularly effective in wet soil, is to excavate a trench along the entire porch perimeter and set precast footing blocks on a layer of crushed stone. Lay perforated drainpipe and provide an outlet at grade as for a standard perimeter drain system (see pp. 68-70). Backfill with more crushed stone around the bases of the porch support posts and then with gravel to grade. Ideally, the porch drainage should be teed into the rest of the foundation drainage system, especially if it is part of a general foundation overhaul.

Stoops

Despite a preponderance of porches, the formal portico never became extinct. The "stoop," a platform or small set of steps at the front entry sheltered by a small triangular roof, is its vestigial descendant.

The success of these additions is questionable. Sometimes, utility triumphs over good taste and a perfect facade is marred by a clumsy, ill-matched stoop. But then, a trellised stoop and its climbing vines or roses are certainly part of the charm of a country cottage. Since country people rarely use their front doors anyway, it's better to tear off a decayed or ugly stoop rather than rebuild it, or move it around back to the kitchen door where it will do some good. In the country it's not unusual to find the front door walled over with a polyethylene sheet, sometimes even year-round. In the city, the back door is the service (delivery and servants') entrance; the front door retains its formal character and remoteness even today. City people new to the country can be identified by which door they walk up to first.

Proper flashing of a stoop roof to the side wall of the main house is the key to preventing rot. One detail that is often overlooked is the need for some sort of backing board between the roof brace (or bracket) and the siding. Scribe and cut away the siding so that this piece (use pressure-treated stock) can lie flat against the sheathing. Backers should always be used under anything that would otherwise be mounted directly against the siding, such as light fixtures and rail or baluster supports. An exception might be covered electrical outlets or outside water spigots, if they fit into a single clapboard. Otherwise water and debris can collect behind the fixture, or seep into splits opened by its fasteners and rot the siding. Bevel the top edge of such trim boards to shed water. Backers also provide a much firmer attachment for porch railings.

Support Bracket and Backing Board for Stoop Roof

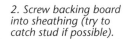

1. Scribe backing-board profile on siding and cut out clapboards using fine-toothed saw and utility knife.

2. Screw backing board into sheathing (try to catch stud if possible).

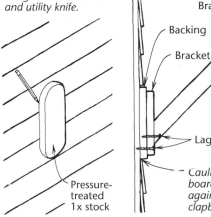

Brace

Backing

Bracket

Lag screws

Caulk under board and against clapboards.

Pressure-treated 1x stock

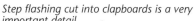

Step flashing cut into clapboards is a very important detail.

Extending an Attached Shed

1. Because improper grading allowed snow to pile up against the rear of this attached shed, the back wall and floor framing were so badly deteriorated that replacement was the only sensible cure.

2. The light roof load is easily supported on the old wall posts while a new foundation is poured. The new foundation is 'bumped out' to increase the floor area of the original shed.

3. The original roof was removed and a new, shallower-pitched roof added to preserve full ceiling height in the extended shed. (Photos this page by Joe English.)

Sheds and Garages

Like the seed at the heart of a fruit, the core of an old house is often buried under an accretion of later additions. Unlike the New England joint houses built in the latter half of the 19th century (see the photo on p. 6), the additions were not always conceived as a harmonious whole. In fact, thoughtlessly attached wings, sheds, garages and walled-in porches are some of the best examples of "remuddling" one can find.

The question of whether to renovate or remove an addition depends on architectural and structural considerations. Additions were not always built with the same care and skill as the original house. Attached sheds, in particular, usually lack real foundations and often have settled, racked and rotted beyond reasonable hope of repair. It may prove more economical to tear the thing down than to tinker with it. Or you can always live with it until nature takes its course, as long as its continued decline does not threaten the health of the main house.

Conversely, because its framing is accessible and relatively light, a small barn or shed on the threshold of collapse is more easily rescued than a house in similar condition. Concrete foundations are not necessary. Any rotted sills are simply replaced with pressure-treated timbers carried on treated posts set below frost. If the structure provides useful space and the bulk of its framing is still sound, it's probably worth shoring up.

A sound but ill-fitted structure, such as a 20th-century garage attached to a 19th-century house, can be retrofitted to the main house by replacing discordant architectural details, sidings and window styles with historically appropriate materials and siding. If an exact match is not affordable, a stripped-down version won't strike an inharmonious note as long as it captures the essence of its more ornate prototype. In hope of sidestepping the ideological crossfire of preservationists, restorationists and renovators, I suggest this as a guiding philosophy for undoing the "improvements" wrought upon a house by insensitive remodeling.

Finally, a note on vocabulary. An "ell" is not the same as a "wing." Properly speaking, wings are added onto the short (gable) end of a house, usually offset slightly from the main house—the rooflines are thus parallel. Ells, as the name suggests, are added perpendicular to the long walls of the house. Sometimes these additions are so large or numerous that the original house is literally swallowed up within them.

Radical Changes: Attic and Roof Retrofits

The attics of many old houses have a rough and pleasing beauty, and they can be treasures worth living in. But if you choose to leave beams, rafters and roof boards exposed, insulation must be installed on the outside surface of the roof deck and a new roof system devised to cover it. An easier alternative, depending on the depth of the rafters and the desired reveal, is to install rigid foam insulation between the rafters and to finish the ceiling with drywall or plaster. Nail 1x2 cleats along the rafters against the underside of the roof deck to provide a ventilation channel behind the insulation. This can outlet into a ridge vent or gable-vented space.

If you choose to apply rigid foam to the outside surface of a stripped roof deck, the problem, at least in northern areas, is to get enough insulation onto the roof with the least disruption of the existing roofline and a minimum of expense. Urethane foam roofing panels bonded to a waferboard nail base are available in thicknesses of up to 6 in., but they're not cheap. Also, there are some doubts about the long-term stability of waferboard and its nail-holding ability.

Some builders suggest nailing 2x8 joists (or even 2x12s) parallel to each rafter and filling the bays with ordinary inexpensive fiberglass insulation. But not only do you run the risk of soaking the insulation (which takes forever to dry), unless the existing rakes and eaves are cut back flush to the wall and refitted with siding and trim (a lot of trouble and expense), but the new roof will also present a thick and ungainly profile. Wide fascias may suit a contemporary design, but I don't think an old roof can stand more than 4 in. of added sheathing, that is, two 2-in. layers of foam insulation.

Nail a 2x4 (a ½-in. shim added later brings the 2x4 flush with the top of insulation) on edge along the edges of the roof to support the foam panels and the new fascia board (Option A in the drawing on p. 216). The foam is glued to the roof with an appropriate construction adhesive in overlapping layers. On steep roofs, build the sandwich as you work up the roof, gluing ⅝-in. CDX plywood on top of the insulation and securing it to the underlying rafters with 6-in. long ring-shank nails (pole-barn nails). The plywood will hold 2x4 cleats or roofing brackets (attached with drywall screws instead of nails) and prevent damage to the insulation.

Roof Insulation on Retrofit Sections

Option A: Section through rake

Here, all insulation is on top of the roof deck. The disadvantages are a wide fascia profile and the need for 6-in. long nails.

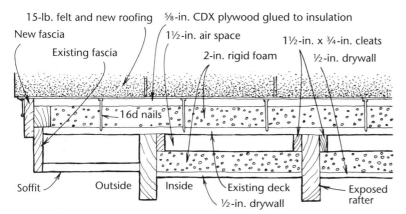

15-lb. felt and new roofing

⅝-in. CDX plywood glued to insulation

6-in. ring-shank nail through roofing tin to rafters or solid deck

Drip edge

½-in. shim

Remove existing drip edge.

New fascia

Existing fascia

2-in. rigid foam

Existing deck

2x4s

Note: If rake offers solid nailing for 2x4 on edge, flat backing 2x4 can be eliminated.

Existing deck

Existing fascia

Option B: Section through eave

Installing half of the insulation layer on each side of the deck results in a narrower fascia profile and the need for shorter (less expensive) nails, but less interior exposure of rafters.

15-lb. felt and new roofing

New fascia

Existing fascia

⅝-in. CDX plywood glued to insulation

1½-in. air space

2-in. rigid foam

1½-in. x ¾-in. cleats

½-in. drywall

16d nails

Soffit   Outside   Inside   Existing deck   Exposed rafter
½-in. drywall

Note: Can be adapted for cold roof by addition of 1x4 vertical nailers over each rafter on top of existing deck.

This is a lot of trouble to go to and not altogether satisfactory. Installing a single 2-in. layer of foam to the roof (this reduces the extra fascia trim to an unobtrusive narrow band) and a second layer on the underside between the rafters is an attractive compromise (Option B in the drawing at left). In most cases, the undersides of the old roof boards are peppered with nails and marred by so many splits and unsightly stains that it makes more sense to cover than expose them. The attic will seem more spacious and brighter and the rafters will appear more dramatic against a light (and easy to clean) background. If vertical strapping is nailed to the outside insulation on 16-in. centers, the underside of the roof deck can be vented to the ridge and the benefits of a cold roof enjoyed.

Removing the roof

When a low-ceilinged attic is converted into full-sized living space, as discussed on pp. 52-55, a deteriorated roof becomes an ideal candidate for removal. If you are living in the house when you decide to remove the roof, gather all the possessions, rugs and furniture that can be removed and store them in a safe, dry place. The house is about to become a camp, a minimalist life-support system that provides water, washing and toilet facilities, and, depending on the weather, perhaps sleeping and cooking quarters. If you can't sleep out in a camper or van for the duration and cook on an outdoor barbecue or camp stove, get the job done as quickly as possible. Invite a few handy friends over one fine day, arm them with wrecking bars and hope for a run of good weather.

A day or two before the help arrives, strip the roof deck of its shingles and cover it with plastic sheeting. For safety's sake and an uncluttered work area, remove all debris to a pile out back or truck it to the landfill. When your friends arrive, begin

Removing Heavy-Timber Rafters

With ridge beam

Drill or drive out pegs or cut with chainsaw.

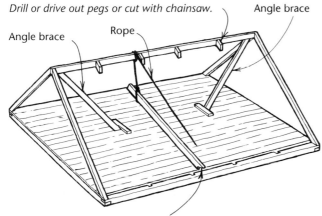

Have an assistant pry rafter tail off plate with pinchbar while beginning to lower rafter.

Without ridge beam

Remove temporary ties as each rafter pair is disassembled and lowered.

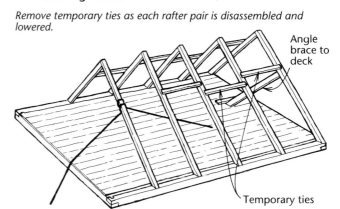

Another alternative is to free rafters from plate and lower as a pair (no bracing required). Start at an end wall.

removing the roof decking. Start at the peak and work down, standing on the boards (nail 2x4 cleats to steep decks). Using the rafters as a fulcrum, lever off the boards with a pinchbar. Stubborn boards are "persuaded" by pounding them upward from their undersides with a sledgehammer. The ground crew (a great job for older kids) pulls the nails from salvageable boards and stacks them out of the way. To keep the work area clean, consign all scrap to the rubbish pile.

Remove the trim boards and cornice framing as you move down the rakes. Try to save any sound trim for reuse. Once the decking is stripped, the rafters can be removed. Ordinary common rafters are easily taken down by sawing through the nails at the bird's-mouth (where the rafter seats against the plate) with a reciprocating saw, and then twisting them free of the ridge board. If splitting is not objectionable, a prybar will also free the seat joint. Because the gable-wall framing and sheathing is still intact, there's little danger of the other rafters collapsing.

Lowering pole or timber rafters is not quite as easy, especially if they are mortised and pegged into a ridge beam. The descent must be carefully controlled, else their weight could injure you as well as the attic floor deck. If there is a ridge beam, nail a temporary angle brace from the peak of the gable wall down to the floor deck. Beginning in the middle of the ridge span, tie a rope around the top of the rafter and cinch it once around the ridge beam itself. Drill or drive out any pegs (if this proves difficult or impossible, saw through the rafter tenon). While an assistant pries the rafter tail free from the plate with a pinchbar (excessively stubborn joints may also need cutting), loosen the rope and begin to lower the rafter. The levering action will help lift the bottom of the rafter off the plate. Working off a pipe scaffold on wheels is safer and more convenient than from a ladder leaning against the ridge.

Work toward the gable ends, leaving the end-wall rafters supporting the ridge. If the ridge is not continuous, leave a rafter pair on either side of the splice and take down each half of the roof frame separately. Tie ropes to both ends of the ridge beam. Remove the last freestanding rafter pair, and separate the ridge splice, leaving the end of the beam tied to the remaining ridge section. From the scaffold against the gable wall, and with a helper at the peak of the remaining rafters, cut the ridge beam free and lower it to the deck. Now slide the scaffold under the last rafter pair, support the ridge (by hand if it's not too heavy, with a sawhorse or temporary bracing off the staging planks if it is), lower the last rafter pair and then drop the ridge to the scaffold. Cut the gable end free and lower the ridge beam down the ladder and then off the scaffold. A continuous ridge is simply roped at both ends, cut free and slowly lowered, one end at a time, using the rung of a ladder set alongside it as a pulley block.

Early Colonial houses typically lacked a ridge beam. Instead, squared timber rafters were pegged together with a tenoned joint at the peak. To lower them, brace the gable end to the floor deck and tie the rafter pairs to each other with short lengths of roofing boards. These are successively removed as each rafter pair is unpegged and rested against the sides of the scaffold. After each rafter is freed from the plate, it is lowered to the deck. Another approach is to remove the end wall first and then, using a control and a lowering rope, free the rafters from the plate and lower them as a pair.

Lighter 4x4 rafters can be lowered by hand, without ropes. They can even be pushed over and allowed to fall to the deck like a run of dominoes. But using ropes guarantees that nothing will be broken and valuable timbers will be salvaged.

Once everything else is removed, tear the sheathing off the end walls. Starting at the peak, drive the boards and siding off the framing from inside with a sledgehammer. Then turn the hammer loose on the studding. Remove the diagonal brace and let the rafters drop to the deck, braking the fall with a control rope as above.

Sweep the exposed deck clean and remove all the timbers and other obstructions. Using the widest possible sheet of polyethylene you can find (24 ft. is not always available), cover the deck and batten the edges to the side walls. If seams are elevated above the floor deck by lengths of strapping and folded over each other like standing-seam roofing before being stapled to the board, leakage will be minimized. Likewise, use duct tape to seal the plastic to the sides of protrusions such as chimneys and vent pipes. Leave any electrical wires and attached outlet boxes beneath the plastic. This may not keep your house completely dry, but it will prevent it from turning into a gigantic shower stall during the next downpour. Where the plastic sheet is unsupported, as, for example, over a staircase opening, raise the sheet upward with a T-shaped brace to prevent puddling. Pray for dry weather to hold long enough to get the new roof on, and don't take the plastic up until it's finished. You will frame new walls and plates right over it. Leave one section of sole plate out between the studs so that the deck can drain off.

If you can organize another work party or have hired a crew of carpenters, aim to frame the entire roof in a single day. At least two pairs of hands are needed to frame a roof in any case. Precut the rafters and organize the materials before the help arrives. Use the extra bodies to their maximum potential by having them raise the rafters and nail off decking instead of carrying boards and erecting staging. If the new roof includes a dormer, raise all the common rafters first, leaving out those under the dormer; these can be framed by a single worker while the main roof is sheathed by the crew.

The object is to get the bulk of the work done while you have the weather and the help. Gable-end walls and other details can be filled in later. In a pinch, gable walls and dormers can be closed in with polyethylene and battens. Another sheet stapled to the interior will make a warm and secure, albeit somewhat noisy, temporary wall. The night winds will play that plastic like a sail in a storm. Plastic and tar paper can keep you warm and dry longer than you might suspect—or intend.

Finally, make sure the work area is kept clear and nails are always bent over or removed from waste boards. The larger the crew, the greater the chances for injury. Cover open stairwells and any exposed framing with plywood. (A friend almost lost his mother when she stepped off the floor deck and fell across the open joists covered by plastic, breaking three ribs on the way.)

When wholesale removal of the roof is not an option, adding a dormer is a satisfactory and traditional way to increase attic living area (see pp. 52-54). The same basic module can shelter one window, be repeated at intervals or be expanded to cover most of a wall (a saltbox is nothing more than a Cape with a shed dormer across its front wall). Laying out and cutting openings for dormers is easiest if the dormer width coincides with a multiple of the rafter spacing. Disruption of the existing ceiling is minimized and framing greatly simplified.

Remove shingles in the general area of the dormer opening, leaving at least half a tab's width between the edge of the remaining shingles and the dormer opening. Cut the sheathing alongside the rafter. Ideally, this will become the outside face of a tripled-up "trimmer" rafter (the rafters on either side of a dormer must be beefed up to carry the extra weight without sagging). Depending on the exact layout, it may end up as the inside or middle piece.

The large volume of useful space gained by adding a shed dormer is obvious in this interior view. The jack post supports the ridge beam, preventing it from sagging while the roof decking and shingles are applied. It will be left in place until the interior partitions and ceiling joists are installed. (Photo by Joe English.)

Ultimately, the outside member of the trio will carry the existing roof sheathing and the other two will support the new dormer framing, which is typically nailed flush to the framing and not over the sheathing.

Support the ends of the jack rafters inside the dormer area with a header nailed between the trimmers at ceiling level. One of the advantages of adding a dormer to an existing roof is that the jack rafters for a gable dormer are cut to fit onto the sheathing, which avoids the need for a valley rafter. The same is true for shed-dormer rafters. Save the rafter tails of any removed rafters. These are cut to fit against the front-wall studding of the gable. Remove shingles along the general line of the valley as needed to simplify laying the new valley after the dormer roof is sheathed. Step flashing and valley installation are a lot easier if the new dormer is added as the first phase of a reroofing project.

Walls, Ceilings
and Floors

*It has been said that "dirt is matter out of place,"
but if it has come to be in the right places through the long years,
we call it "patina" and admire it.*

—Herbert Wheaton Congdon, *Early American Homes for Today* (Dublin, N.H.: William L. Bauhan, 1985)

It's a rare old house that doesn't need at least some plaster repair—but with luck, not as much as this one.

As with the sagging features of the formerly young and beautiful, a facelift is futile if it renews only exterior appearance without a corresponding improvement on the inside. For tired faces, we deal with self-esteem; for old houses, with plaster.

From the earliest Colonial days until just after World War II, plaster was an almost universal interior wall finish. It was cheap, the raw materials were readily available, and it made for a tight wall with fairly good vapor resistance, a fact of no small importance in the era before modern insulation and caulkings. It could be argued that plastered walls contributed to the longevity of old houses by helping to reduce excessive condensation in wall cavities. But the plasterer's craft was a demanding one, both because of the skill it required and the amount of time it took to finish a house. With the introduction of prefabricated plasterboard panels (drywall), the plastered house became nearly extinct within a few years after World War II.

What to do about Plaster

Whatever its merits, plaster seems to have the annoying ability to remain sound for years and then, quite suddenly, to give up the ghost, literally falling off the ceilings and turning to dust behind the wallpaper. The first major question the old-house renovator must answer is: What to do about the plaster? How bad is it and how feasible are the repairs? Are there any historic features that should be conserved at all costs? Should the walls be gutted or does it make more sense to leave them intact? Are there any reasonable alternatives between traditional plastering and drywall? Are professional subcontractors required?

Conservationists will argue that the original plaster finish should be repaired, or restored with new material mixed and applied according to traditional recipes and finishes. Preservationists are not averse to using modern materials to repair the original plaster or, should repair prove impractical, hiring a professional plasterer to "duplicate" the original texture. Likewise, they suffer no qualms over using modern latex ceiling paints in place of the traditional calcimine or whitewash finishes. Utilitarian remodelers, depending on their sensitivity (or lack of it), will not hesitate to gut the entire house at the first sign of a bulge in the ceiling and wrap every available surface in drywall and texture paint. Except for those few houses where a plaster ceiling is distinguished by ornamental medallions and cornice castings of historical value, which are worthy of professional restoration, I confess that once again my sympathies lie somewhere between the liberal preservationists and the conservative remodelers.

Plaster repairs

Identifying the cause of plaster problems is the first step toward assigning these repairs a place in the hierarchy of repair feasibilities. Hairline cracks, which are the most innocuous form of plaster failure, usually result from the normal settling of a house over time. Assuming that the settling has stabilized (and there are no foundation problems), such cracks are easy to repair.

Insert the blade of a stiff putty knife or a utility knife into the crack and cut back its edges to form a keyway (see the drawing on p. 222) to help lock the patch into place. With a 5-in. wide taping knife, trowel joint compound into the crack and embed a strip of fiberglass-mesh joint tape in the compound. If you don't use the tape, the crack will usually reappear a few months later. Knock off any ridges or bumps in this coat after it dries and apply a second coat, smoothing it outward with a 12-in. wide taping paddle. Sand this coat to blend in with the rest of the surface. A third coat feathered out at least 12 in. on either side and sanded smooth will make the repair all but invisible.

Because joint compound shrinks and cracks when used to fill deep holes, it's best to use plaster of Paris to fill such holes and any patches of fallen plaster caused by

Patching Hairline Plaster Cracks

1. Undercut edge of crack with putty knife to form keyway.

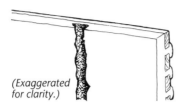

(Exaggerated for clarity.)

2. Using 5-in. wide taping knife, cover crack with joint compound and bed joint tape into it.

Joint compound

Joint tape

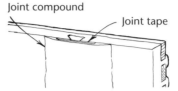

3. Apply second coat with 12-in. taping paddle. After drying, apply third coat, feathering out edges.

mechanical injury. The size of the patch is limited by plaster of Paris's very short drying time. Trowel the patch level and sand it smooth. Fill large patches with plaster or drywall.

The situation is potentially more serious when the plaster has begun to fall from the wall or ceiling. Sometimes a ceiling will sag because the nails anchoring the plaster lath to the joists have rusted away. A chronic water leak or corrosion caused by countless generations of mouse droppings is the usual cause. Drywall screws will secure the fallen lath back in place and reduce the problem to simple crack repair.

A ceiling will also sag when sections of plaster are no longer attached to the underlying lath. This happens when, for a variety of reasons, the keys that bind the plaster to the lath have broken off. Sagging ceilings are repaired by pulling the plaster back up onto the lath with plaster washers, which are perforated metal discs with a countersunk screw hole. Unfortunately, bits of broken plaster key and a truly remarkable quantity of rodent droppings and seed husks usually make it impossible to flatten out the sag without some delicate surgery first.

With a sharp utility knife, carefully cut through the center of the bulge and delicately pry the edges of the incision away from the lath with a spatula. Hold the crevice nozzle of a vacuum cleaner directly under the cut. Gently move the spatula around, to help the vacuum cleaner suck up the rubble. The worst that could happen is that a section of plaster will fall down and you'll need to do some unanticipated patching. After the bulge is cleaned out, drill pilot holes through the plaster and screw the washers into the lath with drywall screws to draw up the sagging plaster tight to the lath. The crack and the washers are covered with patching plaster or drywall compound.

Because early plasters were mixed by hand, inconsistencies in the proportions and impurities in the materials would eventually cause it to crumble and fall off the wall. Brown stains on the ceiling or walls are evidence of water leaks, which, over time, would also weaken the plaster.

Wallpapered ceilings are an ominous sign in an old house: Suspect a quick fix for powdery plaster. When the paper is stripped, what's left of the ceiling could come with it. To assess the state of the damage, the wallpaper must be stripped. Fortunately, the bond between wallpaper and old plaster is unlikely to be strong. Assisted by occasional sponging with warm water, the paper should lift off easily with a scraper. Stubborn paper can be dislodged with a rented wallpaper steamer. If most of the plaster is still on the ceiling or wall after the paper has been removed, crumbled areas can be patched and sags and cracks repaired.

Cut any hanging or loose plaster back to a solid area. Undercut the margins of the patched area to help key in the patch. Secure the edges of the plaster adjoining the damaged area to the lath with drywall screws, spaced 6 in. apart and set just slightly below the surface. (If the screws are turned too far, the plaster will break apart under the screwheads. Ideally, the paint film should pull in slightly.) Unless the lath is directly over a joist, don't use nails. The lath will bounce and you could suddenly have a much larger repair job on your hands.

Tighten down any loose lath and replace any broken sections as necessary. Wet down the lath with a spray bottle to prevent it from sucking the water out of the plaster. Mix a wetting agent (from a photographic-supply store) with the water to help it penetrate the dusty old lath. Then, using a flat plastering trowel, force the plaster into the keys. If possible, the first coat should be about ⅛ in. below the surface of the surrounding area, but no thicker than ⅜ in. Depending on the thickness of the original plaster, a second ⅜-in. thick coat may be needed before the finish coat can be applied.

A traditional three-coat plaster wall is about ¾ in. thick. The first coat is called the "scratch" coat, because its surface is grooved with a serrated trowel or wire brush before it hardens to improve the bonding surface for the second "brown" coat (which is softer and not bright white like the finish coat). The scratch coat is dampened with a spray bottle and the brown coat troweled level with the surface and lightly scratched. To prevent excessively rapid drying, which causes hairline cracks, the brown coat is "damp-cured" (sprayed with fine mist) for two days. The final coat gets its hard, smooth finish by the addition of extra lime to the premixed plaster. Follow the instructions on the bag. Since plaster has a fairly short shelf life

(less than a year), it may be difficult to find a building-products distributor who stocks it. Masonry suppliers are the best bet. Premixed perlited gypsum plaster (as opposed to the kind you mix yourself from sand and hydrated, or slaked, lime) is sold under the brand names Gypsolite® or Structolite®.

The scratch and brown coats are applied with a heavy steel trowel, working from a "hawk" (a square metal or wood plate equipped with a handle). The brown coat is brought true to the surface with a "darby," which is a 4-ft. long strip of wood equipped with handles that is slid up and down diagonally and horizontally over the surface. The finish coat is floated smooth using a wood trowel in a rotary motion. An entire ceiling or wall is not the place to learn plastering skills. If more than a few square feet are to be replaced, I would recommend hiring a professional, or repairing the area with drywall.

Two-coat plastering, which gives about a ½-in. thick wall, is a much more common technique than three-coat plastering. Patching large areas of damaged plaster with drywall of equal thickness is thus an alternative to replastering for those to whom authenticity is less important than convenience. As before, the fallen plaster is cut back to sound material, and the patch is made as square as possible to simplify fitting the drywall. A paper template can be used for complicated pieces. The drywall patch is simply screwed to the lath, and the joints taped and filled with joint compound as for patching cracks.

Throughout the late 18th and much of the 19th centuries, ceilings were whitened with calcimine, a mixture of powdered chalk, glue and water. Although a single coat will easily wash off with water, over many years and repeated applications the glue becomes hard as rock, making its removal quite difficult. As the layers of calcimine thicken, the ceiling becomes irregular and can start to flake off. Although a strict conservationist might insist on complete removal in order to restore the original finish, this tedious task is one compelling reason to rip down the plaster, or at least switch over to modern latex ceiling paint.

Neither paint nor wallpaper will adhere to a calcimined ceiling unless it has first been thoroughly scrubbed with a solution of warm water and ammonia. Fill in gouges, nail holes and hairline cracks with spackle before applying a latex primer and a good-quality ceiling paint. Although this may not have the texture of a genuine calcimine ceiling, it will save endless hours of tedious scraping and cleanup, and is certainly better than replacing the plaster with drywall.

Gutting the plaster

If the plaster is truly unsalvageable, it's easier to strip the interior walls and ceilings down to the lath and replaster or apply some other finish material. In fact, some might argue for the complete removal of all plaster regardless of its condition, on the grounds that it's the only affordable way to revamp the wiring, plumbing and insulation and make other major interior changes. Except for museum-quality historic houses, where the owners are obligated to make every effort to retain or restore the original finishes, the average old-house owner must decide whether to save the plaster strictly on the basis of personal taste and budget.

Despite the objections of purists, old-house aficionados will strip plaster to expose old hand-hewn ceiling beams (see also pp. 253-255). The original builders covered them over as soon as the householder could afford to hire a plasterer. Exposed beams were a sign of poverty; a successful man celebrated his wealth with successive layers of plaster and paint, demonstrating, perhaps, the pioneer's mastery of nature with artifice and ornamentation. Our present fascination with exposed ceiling beams may belie a longing for reconnection with the natural world. The undeniable feeling of security that emanates from the rude strength of these old timbers is a revelation of structure in harmony with nature.

Of course, if the plaster ceiling is removed to reveal closely spaced pedestrian sawn joists rather than hewn beams, it would have been best left undisturbed. Unless the visible framing in the attic and cellar is timbered, don't expect to find buried treasures under the plaster. If the floor joists are sawn lumber, the ceiling joists will be, too.

Should you decide to gut the plaster, the job is best done all at once. Piecemeal removal only means extended mess and continued inhabitability. Walls that may have appeared sound upon initial examination will begin to crumble the first time a molding is removed, a window casing pried or a door slammed. Start with the attic and work toward the cellar. Plaster by itself is dusty and gritty. Mixed with mouse droppings and decades of house dust it is hazardous to your health. Wear a dust mask or respirator.

If the wall cavities or ceilings have been blown full of fiberglass or mineral wool at some point during the past, the material most likely has settled enough to make it worthless. The itch and choking dust of insulation removal will add a new dimension to the torture of plaster removal. The stuff seems to expand as it pours from the walls, until the entire house is full of it. Days later, you'll feel it in your clothes and between the sheets and taste it in your food. The insidious itch becomes more psychological than physical—you can never be quite sure if you are imagining it or not. If the house gutting coincides with foundation repair, the stuff can be thrown out the windows and into the trench (and it will make the house lighter if you have to lift it). Otherwise the plaster must be hauled off to the landfill or buried somewhere on the property before it gets rained on and reduced to pudding.

At this stage, renovating a house calls for a tool seldom mentioned in the how-to books—the pickup truck. There is little you can do in the rebuilding business without one. Not everything you need can be delivered, and a lot of it won't fit into the trunk of a car.

Ideally, the plaster is funneled from the upper story into the truck by a chute built from old boards. What can't be thrown out the windows and into the truck is carried over plank ramps with a wheelbarrow. Separate the lath from the plaster to reduce the bulk and simplify disposal. Although lath makes great kindling, your enthusiasm for it will wane after you snag yourself a few times on the needle-sharp stubs of rusty lathing nails. If local ordinances permit open burning, you could pile it out back for a bonfire to celebrate the project's completion.

Smashing through the walls with the hooked end of a crowbar and ripping down great chunks of plaster and lath is a great outlet for fantasies of destruction or revenge. It can be a job for the whole family, at least as cathartic as television and probably healthier. Use snow shovels to scoop up the fallen plaster. The destruction is best done in summer, when an afternoon's dip in the pond will wash away the memories and grime of a miserable day's work. Once the rubble is removed and the floors mopped clean, the rewiring and other structural repairs can begin and the walls can be reinsulated with fiberglass batts in preparation for the new wall finish.

Plaster walls and insulation
Even without major changes, gutting the plaster is one sure way to deal with the problem of retrofitting new insulation to an old house. Insulation can be blown into the stud cavities from outside the building, but that's not necessarily the best way to do it. Blown-in insulation is prone to settling. Even at densities that will not settle (which cost considerably more than the usual estimate), the problem of providing an adequate vapor barrier still remains. Insulation contractors will assure you that the material (usually cellulose fibers) has been treated to be water-resistant, vermin-proof and fire-retardant. What this actually means is that if water condenses in the wall, the insulation will soak it up like a sponge so that the wood can start to rot. With blind blown-in, it's virtually impossible to fill every stud cavity completely. Cold spots, as evidenced by frost on the inside walls, are not unusual.

Although special paints designed to form an effective vapor barrier over intact old plaster are now available, these won't solve the cold-spot problem or prevent moisture movement through areas that can't be painted (for example, behind the wood baseboards, wainscot and casings, to name just a few places). Applying a vapor-barrier paint is still better than ripping out sound old plaster, but it's no cure-all.

If the lath is left intact when stripping off the plaster, the stud cavities can be filled (or topped off) from the inside, allowing the insulator to see how well the spaces are filled. The lath holds the insulation in place. A polyethylene vapor barrier is then stapled over the lath before the new wall finish is installed. Although electrical outlets and cables can be worked behind the lath, horizontal strapping nailed to the studs simplifies wiring changes. These spaces can be filled with rigid-foam panels to increase the heat-loss resistance of the walls. Also, a formerly uneven wall surface can be straightened out by inserting wood shims behind the strapping. An alternative is to replaster the lath and use vapor-barrier paint.

There is an alternative to complete removal of interior plaster worth considering. Staple a polyethylene vapor barrier directly over the existing plaster. For best results, remove existing baseboards, ceiling moldings and window and door casings. Next, screw drywall directly over the old walls and into the underlying studs. If the original plaster butted up to the baseboard and not behind it, nail shims to the

How to Install Drywall without Removing Casings

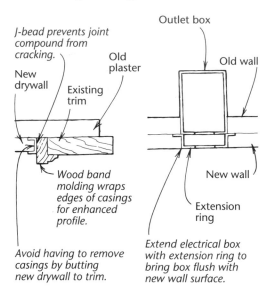

J-bead prevents joint compound from cracking.

New drywall

Existing trim

Old plaster

Outlet box

Old wall

New wall

Extension ring

Wood band molding wraps edges of casings for enhanced profile.

Avoid having to remove casings by butting new drywall to trim.

Extend electrical box with extension ring to bring box flush with new wall surface.

studs before installing the drywall. Add extension jambs to bring the window and door jambs flush with the new surface. Prime and paint the drywall before replacing the casings and other surface trim.

Removing and replacing the trim is a lot of trouble. Instead, you can simply butt the drywall to the existing trim. Some may object that this treatment flattens out the trim profile, but a solution is to wrap the edges of the casings with a narrow band of molding of slightly greater depth. Edges of the drywall panels that butt against the trim are inserted into metal J-beads to prevent cracking of joint compound. Electrical boxes will need extension collars to bring them flush to the new wall.

Since these methods preclude replastering and are also a lot slower than wholesale plaster removal, they are best suited for use in individual rooms or on single walls, and especially for walls that are to be papered rather than painted. Adding drywall over the plaster also offers the advantage of extra sound-deadening, a bit more thermal mass and a lot less debris.

Alternatives to plaster

Drywall finishing requires the application of three coats of joint compound and a lot of sanding (see pp. 248-249). It's messy, time-consuming and a lot harder than it looks. After all this, the wall surface still has to be primed and painted. If you add up all the costs and labor, it's not such a great bargain.

Personally, I lean toward replacing plaster with drywall finished with wallpaper. This seems more suited to an old house than the usual featureless white expanses typical of the modern style. Machine-made wallpaper has been used in the United States since 1837 (hand-painted wallpapers had been imported by wealthy home owners since the mid-1700s), so it's hard to argue against it on traditional grounds. And since the joints will be covered over, they don't need as careful a taping job as when the walls will be painted.

Conventional drywall is not the only alternative to traditional multicoat replastering. A single coat of perlited gypsum plaster (Structolite®) troweled over Rocklath®, a gypsum-board-based plaster lath, requires minimal skill, is inexpensive and gives a pleasingly rough and traditional-looking finish. The lath boards are 16-in. by 48-in. ⅜-in. thick panels. These are nailed or screwed to the studs every 4 in. on center, leaving a ⅛-in. to ¼-in. gap between the panels for a plaster key. The vertical joints should break over a stud. To prevent future cracks, don't join sheets over doors and window head jambs. Because the sheets are small, they are easily handled and generate little waste. Wet the lath panel with a hand sprayer before applying an ⅛-in. coat of plaster. The plaster can either be left natural or painted to facilitate washing.

Herbert Wheaton Congdon, writing about plaster ceilings in his classic treatise, *Early American Homes for Today* (see the Bibliography on pp. 334-338), recommends the application of a coat of thinned-down "cheap varnish" followed by a second coat, to recreate the mellow and pleasing patina of age. Of course, this rough finish, which will show trowel marks and vary in texture, is architecturally more appropriate to early Colonial (or fairly rustic) farmhouses and cottages than to Victorian mansions. It wouldn't be out of place in a southwestern-style ranch house either. Old-time plasterers strove to achieve a polished, smooth finish, a finish that looks like drywall mellowed by four or five layers of paint.

Inside the Walls: Insulation Theory and Practice

So far we have discussed insulation and vapor barriers with only the most cursory explanation of terms. It is important to have a thorough understanding of the art and science of insulation, as much damage can be done by incorrect application.

The passage of heat through solid materials is called conduction. An insulator is anything that retards this movement. Trapped (dead) air is an excellent insulator. A hollow wall itself is not a dead-air space because the volume of air is large enough to allow the transfer of heat by convection. Currents of air, which arise whenever a temperature difference exists across an enclosed space, transfer heat between moving molecules — an air space wider than ¾ in. will permit the formation of convection currents.

Fiberglass insulation works because it is comprised of a tangled web of surfaces that trap air and prevent its circulation, whereas foams work because they contain closed cells filled with inert gases that are poor conductors of heat. Materials used in common residential insulations include spun glass and mineral fibers, organic fibers made from recycled paper and synthetic plastic foams. The old-timers understood the principle of dead air when they filled the walls of their houses with corn cobs, sawdust, straw and mud and even bricks. Although old-timers knew nothing of insulation theory, the plaster wall finishes they favored were an efficient vapor barrier. Otherwise, condensation occurring

within these primitive loose-fill insulators would have quickly rotted them and the surrounding wood framing.

A wall is a relatively porous membrane. Because in cold weather the inside air is much warmer than the outside air, heat moves through the wall by conduction and convection in an attempt to establish equilibrium. The infiltration of cold outside air through cracks around windows and doors, and between siding boards, increases this transfer. Infiltration is a pressure-driven process. The warm air inside the house is at a higher pressure than the cold air outside and so forces itself out through any opening. Meanwhile, a negative pressure is created on the side of the house opposite the prevailing winds, which acts to drive cold air in. The partial vacuum within the house created by warm air rushing up the chimney (the stack effect) also sucks in cold air through the cracks.

Because people and plants live in the house, the inside air is heavy with water vapor (although the terms are often used interchangeably, vapor is water in a gaseous state, whereas moisture is actually microscopic droplets of liquid water diffused in the air, that is, fog). Warm air holds more water vapor than does cold air; vapor in rapidly moving air is less likely to condense than in still air. Air is said to be saturated when it is holding all the vapor it can at a given temperature. Its vapor content, together with the air temperature, determines the dew point, which is the temperature at which saturated air gives up its water by condensation. Relative humidity is a measure of the amount of vapor the air is holding compared to the amount it could hold at a given temperature, expressed as a percentage.

In an uninsulated wall cavity, the convection currents usually prevent condensation within the air space itself. Warm, vapor-laden air diffuses through the wall until it strikes the cold interior surface of the outside wall, whereupon it suddenly freezes. Although much of this frozen water will sublimate (return to gas without going

Insulation, the Vapor Barrier and Condensation

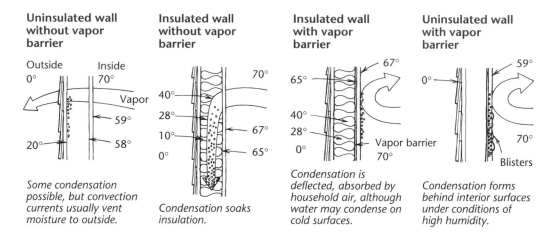

Uninsulated wall without vapor barrier

Some condensation possible, but convection currents usually vent moisture to outside.

Insulated wall without vapor barrier

Condensation soaks insulation.

Insulated wall with vapor barrier

Condensation is deflected, absorbed by household air, although water may condense on cold surfaces.

Uninsulated wall with vapor barrier

Condensation forms behind interior surfaces under conditions of high humidity.

through a liquid phase) as soon as the temperature rises above the dew point, under the right (or wrong) conditions, some of it will condense into the liquid phase and be absorbed into the wood or flow down the studs to collect on the sills.

At temperatures above freezing but still low enough for the dew point to occur within the wall cavity, the relatively large convection currents help lower the chances of a miniature cloudburst while rapidly ventilating any moisture to the outside. The vapor-retardant effect of the interior plaster also helps. In addition, since houses were much colder in the days before insulation and efficient central heating, the inside air would not hold as much water vapor as a modern house. The fact that most old houses did not rot away in a few short years shows that condensation within uninsulated wall spaces was not a common occurrence.

All this changes when the wall cavity is filled with insulation. Convection currents are almost nonexistent. Condensation can occur anywhere within the insulation where the temperature is below the dew point. Since the insulation will also warm up slowly, sublimation is not possible, and the liquid water soaks into the

insulation, coincidentally reducing its insulative value and increasing the likelihood of further condensation.

But when an impermeable film is installed on the warm side of the wall under the finish surface, water vapor cannot pass through to the cold side. Heat can still move through the wall by conduction and also through infiltration, which brings in cold outside air to replace escaping warm inside air.

With a good continuous barrier, the water vapor stays inside, where it is taken up as new air is warmed by the heating system. If there's too much vapor present, that is, if the relative humidity is high, the water will condense on any convenient cold surface, especially windows and cold pipes. Water can hold a lot of heat. When it condenses, it loses this "latent heat," which means that the room becomes a little bit colder every time a drop of water runs down the window pane to collect on the sill. A vapor barrier installed against an uninsulated wall will cause condensation on interior surfaces where high humidity is present, such as bathrooms or kitchens. Since high-gloss oil paints applied over plaster make a fairly good vapor barrier, paint always peels off the bathroom ceiling first.

Although it might seem sensible to lower household relative humidity as much as possible to prevent condensation (some energy experts recommend eliminating showers, green plants, cooking and just about anything else living creatures do within the house, including breathing), this is not desirable. Studies and common sense have shown that people feel most comfortable and are healthiest at a temperature of about 70°F, with a relative humidity ranging from 35% to 70%. When interior humidity is low it takes more heat for us to feel warm, because moisture evaporates faster from the skin in dry air, lowering body temperature. Maintaining proper humidity will enable the home owner to turn down the thermostat, feel warm and keep the family's mucous membranes from drying out.

There is a trade-off: Keeping the humidity high enough to ensure comfort will inevitably cause some condensation. This is one of the best arguments for adding an external infiltration barrier (such as Tyvek® housewrap) when replacing siding, and for a general program of caulking and tightening up. Replacing single glazing with insulated glass or storm windows also contributes to comfort by increasing the surface temperature of the room-side glass. The tighter the house, the easier it is to strike a balance between comfortable humidity and minimal condensation.

R-values

The effectiveness of insulation is rated by its ability to slow heat transfer, as measured by its R-factor. Because the R-factor varies according to the density and other properties of a material, it is also related to thickness—an important consideration when determining the cost-effectiveness of a given insulator for a particular application. Generally, the price of insulation is directly proportional to its R-value per inch. The synthetic foams are the best insulators, but also the most expensive. Loose-fill material is cheap, but the required professional application is not.

The chart on pp. 230-231 lists the R-values of some commonly used residential insulation materials and their applications. The materials used in a wall's construction also have an R-value. So does the very thin layer of air that sticks to each side of the wall. The R-value profile of a typical uninsulated wall in an old house might look something like this:

Outside air film	0.2
½-in. clapboards	1.0
1-in. sheathing boards	2.0
Air space, wall cavity	1.0
½ in. plaster	0.5
Inside air film	0.2
R-value total	4.9

Does this mean that adding 3½ in. of fiberglass will boost the wall's R-value to R-16? Not really, since the cavity is necessarily filled with solid wood (the wall stud) every 16 in. or so, which reduces the overall gain. Because of these "thermal bridges" and other built-in heat-loss factors (such as outside wind speed), heating engineers usually average out the wall's R-value to equal that of the insulation. The bottom line is: As heating costs rise, added insulation becomes more cost-effective. The economic "dew point" of diminishing returns shifts upward. Two inches of fiberglass installed in a bare wall may decrease heat loss by 80%. Four inches will save 90%. But 8 in. will save only 95%.

Is the extra cost of the insulation and/or the added framing lumber justified by the fuel savings over a short enough pay-back period? Today, the answer is yes. In the 1960s, when architects and engineers recommended values of R-11 for walls and R-19 for ceilings, it wouldn't have been. At the height of the energy crises of the 1970s, the minimum jumped to R-19 and R-38, respectively, and super-insulated homes with values up to R-40 and R-60 were built throughout the Snowbelt. Today, these heavily insulated houses

Residential Insulation Characteristics

Material	Description	Application	R-value per inch	Comments
Fiberglass	Continuous rolls and precut batts sized to fit between framing on 16-in. or 24-in. centers. Unfaced, or with reflective foil or kraft-paper vapor barrier. Also loose fill for blowing and pouring; rigid panels for sheathing.	Stapled between studs and ceiling joists through paper flanges. Unfaced batts are friction-fitted. Requires polyethylene vapor barrier.	3.2 (batts) 2.2 (loose fill)	Least expensive and most versatile. Short-term skin and lung irritant; wear respirator, goggles, gloves and loose-fitting clothes. Preferred nesting material of rodents (absorbs feces and smell). Noncombustible, nontoxic, will not rot. Holds water like a sponge. Blown-in settles in wall cavities.
Mineral wool	Precut paper-faced batts. Blown-in wool.	Stapled through flanges, poured into attic bays, blown into walls.	3.5	Inexpensive. Finer, sharper particles, more irritating than fiberglass. Batts tend to flatten, blown-in wool will settle. Noncombustible, won't rot, holds water. Same precautions as for fiberglass.
Cellulose fibers	Shredded newspaper (with various additives). Loose fill for blowing or pouring into cavities and attics.	Poured from bag into attic bays, blown-in with rented machine or by subcontractor from outside walls. Mainly used for retrofitting old houses (better than nothing) and for capping attics.	3.5	Inexpensive, though professional installation is not. Can settle in walls if not enough blown in. Flammable. Some condensation problems reported in retrofits without proper vapor barrier. Soaks up water. Does not itch. Wear dust mask and eye protection; additives are hazardous if breathed in.
Adhesive cellulose fiber (K-13®)	A mixture of cellulose, glue and whitening agents.	Machine-sprayed directly over walls, into stud cavities, over masonry and onto steel sidings and beams. It can be left exposed or covered over as desired. Will adhere to almost any dry surface.	5.5	Excellent for insulating metal buildings and problem surfaces such as the cellar side of brick or stone foundation walls. Needs masking to protect adjacent areas. Can be used as combination insulation and finish ceiling. Will flake off when rubbed. Noncombustible, water-resistant. Not cheap.
Extruded polystyrene foam: blueboard (Styrofoam®), pinkboard (Foamular®)	2x8 tongue-and-groove sheets, 1 in., 1½ in. and 2 in. thick (other thicknesses also available). Cells filled with air.	Glued to surfaces or friction fit. Used extensively for insulating outside of foundations, under concrete slabs, exposed crawl spaces. Also used on interior basement walls, between attic joists and over roof decks.	5.0	Water-resistant, rigid. Releases toxic gases when burned, must be covered with fire-rated drywall for interior use. Nontoxic, nonirritating. No installation precautions. Degrades in sunlight. Manufacture involves ozone-depleting chemicals.

Material	Description	Application	R-value per inch	Comments
Expanded polystyrene foam "bead-board" (Durovon®)	2x8 and 4x8 sheets, 1 in. to 6 in. thick.	Used on interior of basement, crawl space, between studs and joists with appropriate fire-rated drywall.	4.0	Not for burial or outdoor use, will absorb water, easily broken or crushed. Burning emits toxic gases. Less expensive than extruded foams. Very popular mouse-nesting material.
Polyurethane foam	4x8 sheets, unfaced or kraft-paper covered. Cells filled with Freon® gas instead of air.	Same as for expanded polystyrene foam.	6.2	Expensive, releases toxic gases when burning. Possible long-term thermal degradation (loss of R-value).
Polyisocya-nurate foam (Thermax®, Hi-R®, R-Max® et al.)	4x8 sheets, ½ in., ¾ in., 1 in., 1½ in., 2 in. and 4 in. thick. Aluminum-foil faced both sides, fiberglass-fiber reinforced, closed cell, gas-filled. Sandwiched with waferboard drywall panels to make stress-skin panels, used for prefabs and energy-efficient timber framing.	Installed by nailing, gluing, friction-fit. Widely used as exterior wall sheathing, over-roof deck insulation, and for maximum R-value where space is at a premium. Often used under drywall for a vapor barrier over fiberglass batts.	7.4 to 8.0	Most expensive. Greater fire resistance, lower toxicity when burning. Irritating fiberglass fibers and dust released when material is cut and handled. Not for exposure to weather or sunlight. Will absorb water. Thermally stable. New product, test results need long-term verification in field.
Impregnated fiberboard (Celotex®)	4x8 sheets, ½ in. thick. Made from ground corn husks, other organic and vegetable waste fibers, sometimes impregnated with asphalt as a moisture repellent.	Widely used for nonstructural sheathing, occasionally found under drywall or plastic wall tiles in remodeled old houses.	2.0	Nonasphalt types will absorb water easily and hold it against the framing until the whole mess rots. Fiber "IB" panels will smolder if ignited. Sawdust is an irritant.
Perlite, vermiculite	Perlite is a natural mineral foam of volcanic origin. Vermiculite is a kind of mineral "popcorn" made from mica-rich rock.	Both are loose fill, poured into cavities. Widely used to insulate cores of concrete block walls.	2.5	Both are nonflammable, rot-proof. Perlite dust is hazardous. Vermiculite will absorb water. Contains asbestos, can cause lung and liver cancer. Should not be used as attic insulation (a very common use). Wear respirator when handling.
Sawdust	Widely used as early form of insulation.	Loose fill.	1.0	Soaks up water, causing wall framing to rot. Also settles and is flammable. Solid wood has the same R-value as sawdust.

Where to Insulate

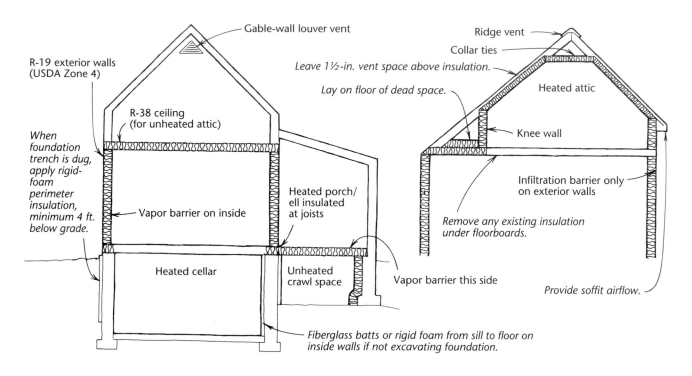

Gable-wall louver vent

R-19 exterior walls
(USDA Zone 4)

Leave 1½-in. vent space above insulation.

Lay on floor of dead space.

Ridge vent

Collar ties

Heated attic

R-38 ceiling
(for unheated attic)

*When
foundation
trench is dug,
apply rigid-
foam
perimeter
insulation,
minimum 4 ft.
below grade.*

Knee wall

Vapor barrier on inside

Heated porch/
ell insulated
at joists

Infiltration barrier only
on exterior walls

*Remove any existing insulation
under floorboards.*

Heated cellar

Unheated
crawl space

Vapor barrier this side

Provide soffit airflow.

*Fiberglass batts or rigid foam from sill to floor on
inside walls if not excavating foundation.*

seem a bit extreme, but who knows when the next fuel shortage will make that last 3% of heat-loss resistance more affordable?

Adequate insulation is only one element of the old-house energy-conservation program. The existing structure of an old house limits the amount of insulation you can stuff into the walls and the options you have for doing it. But after the windows, most of a house's heat loss is through the roof, not the walls. Retrofitting dollars are best invested in the attic, where it's usually easy to add extra depth.

Installing insulation

Fiberglass insulation is widely used because it is cheap, easily installed and versatile. It is suited for almost every application in both old and new houses. Together with rigid polyisocyanurate foam panels, it's possible to add more than enough heat-loss resistance without spending a

fortune or seriously compromising the old house's original features (granted, if gutting the walls is considered only a minor compromise). The drawing above shows the general areas where insulation should be installed in an old house.

Although it might seem that foil-faced insulation would increase the total R-value (the reflective surface bounces radiated heat back toward the room from which it escaped), the advantage is mostly theoretical. To be effective, the foil must be separated from the backside of the wall surface by at least ¾ in. Ideally, stapling the flanges of the batts to the inside edges of the studs accomplishes this; in reality, the batts sag forward. The only way to maintain a dead-air space is to nail spacers to the studs over the insulation, which is a great deal of trouble and expense for a questionable benefit, since once the shiny surface tarnishes it loses its reflectivity.

Some builders insist that kraft-paper-faced insulation be stapled over the studs to prevent "fishmouths," puckers in the batt flange that would act as holes in the vapor barrier. Others maintain that the only way to staple the batts is to the sides of the studs, to prevent the paper from lumping up behind the drywall. The supposed vapor barrier provided by the kraft-paper facing is about as effective as the reflective-foil facing. Even if it were possible to staple the paper perfectly flat, without rips and tears, asphalt-backed kraft paper is not much more of a vapor barrier than ordinary plywood. The only reason to use paper-faced insulation is to decrease the amount of fibers floating around the room and into your clothing and lungs. Stapling the paper flange is also the only way to attach batts to the ceiling joists.

Unfaced insulation is actually much easier to cut to size and faster to install than faced batts or rolls. Hardly any more fibers are released than from faced insulation. The batts are simply pressed into the stud cavities, and cut and folded around obstructions—never mash fiberglass batts to fit under or around a pipe or other obstacle. Compressed fiberglass loses its R-value (the dead-air spaces shrink).

An exception to this rule are the cracks between window and door jambs and the wall studs. Here, preventing infiltration takes precedence over insulation. Stuff the gaps with fiberglass or, better yet, fill them with urethane spray foam insulation. (A wood shingle makes an unparalleled stuffing spatula.) Although foam sprays are expensive and messy to use, they offer both superior R-value and infiltration protection. Cut out the batts to fit tight against and beneath electrical boxes. Back-cut and fold insulation around cables. Don't leave any gaps at the top or bottom of the bays or where the batts butt together. If you insulate above ceiling-mounted light fixtures, make sure they are designed for that purpose; otherwise the buildup of trapped heat could start a fire (don't use fixtures that won't permit insulation).

If you can find a supplier who stocks them, "full-thick" unfaced batts are even better than standard unfaced insulation. The fiberglass is stiffer, which makes for a tighter fit and produces less airborne fibers. It also has an R-value of R-13 instead of R-11.

The rule for insulation is cover the warm side, vent the cold side. The plastic vapor barrier is always installed on the warm side of a wall. Vapor barriers are effective only when they are tight. Since vapor migration, like infiltration, is pressure-driven, a small puncture in the membrane is the same as small puncture in a balloon. Use plastic tape to patch any rips or holes. Overlap seams between sheets at least the width of a bay (the space between studs). Seal the edges with tape. Cut an X over electrical outlets and tape the plastic to their sides. It's not possible to install a perfectly continuous barrier in an old house since there's no way to retrofit the membrane around floor joists and over partitions. Nevertheless, it's still important to be as thorough as possible.

Adding insulation between the floor joists of an unheated cellar or crawl space presents several difficulties. Short of taking up the flooring boards, there's no way to install an effective vapor barrier over the insulation. The common wisdom calls for stuffing fiberglass batts, paper-side up, against the flooring and stapling chicken wire to the bottoms of the joists to keep the stuff from falling down. Sliding the batts up between rows of strapping is another suggestion. Metal hangers (E-Z Hanger®), up to 4 ft. long, hammered between the joists to support the insulation are also a possibility. Having eaten more fiberglass than I'd like to think about, I long ago decided that this is the kind of situation for which rigid foam was made. Because of the vapor-barrier effect of the aluminum facing, use a layer of ½-in. rigid polyisocyanurate foam board, followed by two 2-in. layers of less expensive extruded polystyrene bluebuard or expanded polystyrene beadboard. An alternative vapor barrier could be fashioned from strips of polyethylene cut to fit between the joists and taped along their edges.

If one were condemned to use fiberglass, I'd apply the polyethylene, staple the insulation paper-side out, and then, to ensure vapor movement, cut a series of diagonal slashes through the facing. Nail Celotex® to the undersides of the joists to prevent a constant rain of glass fibers into the household air. When the crawl space is exposed to the outside (as with a heated porch or house on piers), protect the insulation against infestation by rodents or insects with asphalt-impregnated fiberboard or pressure-treated plywood.

In some old houses, the wall studs might be spaced as much as 32 in. on center, much too far apart to support wall finishes. It's quite common to find pole or timber rafters spaced as much as 4 ft. on center. An alternative to adding an extra stud or rafter between each bay is to nail 1x4 strapping over the framing, spaced horizontally on 16-in. centers. Although the vapor barrier will keep the insulation from falling out of the bays, the strapping prevents the whole thing from bulging into the room like an unbelted beer belly until the wall finish can be applied.

If your schedule and budget won't permit immediate finishing and you must live with kraft-paper decor for a time, it is imperative to cover the insulation with plastic film. Foil-faced decor has a way of growing more pleasing day by day, as the urgency to do more slips away: The house is warm, why bother? The facing on one brand of insulation is even printed with a woven-mat pattern, almost as if the manufacturer had expected the product to double as a decorative wall finish. I remember spending the night in such a house, sleeping on a guest bed next to the wall and waking up feeling as though I'd spent the night in a nettle patch. A fine rain of fiberglass slivers had fallen into the blankets and from them, onto me.

Interior Partitions: Moving Walls

The desire to convert an old house to modern sensibilities, to change the sense or use of space or quality of light are frequently compelling reasons to remove or relocate interior walls.

Some people find the many small rooms and labyrinthine turnings of an old house constricting rather than charming. In the Victorian manor, for example, the kitchen was closeted away from the dining room, and often a separate maid's or butler's pantry was appended to the kitchen proper. This suited an age when the housework of the well-to-do was performed by domestic servants, but a modern family that often gathers around the ritual of food preparation might prefer to join these compartments into an open space. A preservationist might regard such proposals with alarm, but as long as they are carried out sensitively, they won't automatically tear apart the architectural or spiritual fabric of the house.

Whatever the reasons that justify removing a wall, there are two kinds of partitions: those that carry weight and those that do not. Removing a load-bearing partition is not likely to be a problem encountered in a timber-frame house. Here, the floor joists are carried by girts or a massive center beam (the summer beam, so called after the old English "sumpter," a pack mule bred for carrying heavy loads). Unless a beam has been cut or otherwise weakened by later alterations, interior partitions are almost never load-bearing.

In stud-framed houses, floor joists are usually supported by bearing walls. You can be almost certain that any interior wall running parallel to the length of the building, that is, perpendicular to the run of the floor joists, is a bearing wall. Any partition running parallel to the joists is always nonbearing.

Partitions that run perpendicular to the run of the joists are almost always load-bearing.

Removing nonbearing walls

What's behind a wall is almost as important as what's above it. Rerouting concealed wiring and plumbing isn't necessarily a major operation, but it can eat up a lot of time and expense (the plumbing more so than the wiring). Try to discover that cast-iron vent stack in the middle of the new kitchen island before you rip off the plaster. Go down into the cellar or up into the attic and look for wires or pipes running into the partition.

Remove light fixtures from their mountings or remove outlet covers and note which direction the wires take off from the outlet box. Cables that loop down to a switch from the attic or rise up out of the floor will be easier to reroute than ones that enter the partition from an adjacent wall. With some forethought, pipes that are too much trouble to move can often be concealed in some element of the new design.

Unless the walls are already gutted, begin by removing baseboard and ceiling moldings. If a molding must be cut, use a jigsaw or fine-toothed handsaw to start the cut, and finish what the saw won't reach with a sharp chisel. To remove a section of plaster or drywall from a wall without damaging the adjoining finish, score the division with a sharp utility knife. It's better to dull a few knife blades and cut the plaster down to the lath than to hack through it with a reciprocating saw. The wallpaper or paint won't tear off where it shouldn't and the plaster next to the cut will stay on the wall. Plan your opening so that its edge coincides with a full stud if possible; there's less chance of rattling the lath if you saw over solidly backed wood. Hang a curtain or polyethylene sheet to protect the rest of the house from the dust, and then rip off the plaster and lath to reveal the framing.

The partition is nailed directly to the joists through the sole and top plates. If kindling is more useful than salvaged lumber, a sledgehammer aimed at the joint between the stud and the sole plate will quickly relocate the studding. With the bottom free, the studs are easily twisted off the nails at the top and removed. Cutting through the nails that join the stud to the plates with a reciprocating saw is also a fairly quick method, and does less damage to the wood. Pull out or bend over any protruding nails. Even if you don't intend to recycle the wood, it doesn't take long to get the point of this exercise if you step on a rusty nail. Loading and dumping the scrap is also easier.

Instead of disconnecting the power and rerouting wires in order to remove the studs they run through, saw through the studs just above the holes where the cable runs through them and pop out the remaining wood with a chisel or screwdriver, thereby releasing the cable. The attached outlet boxes and switches will then remain functional until the circuit is shut off and everything rerouted at a convenient time.

Finding the Hot Feed Wire in a Junction Box

Separate black leads: The only black wire that lights the test probe is the hot feed. Use this test to be sure you've turned off the circuit, too.

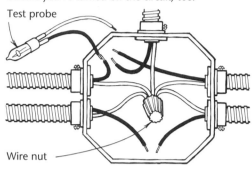

Test probe

Wire nut

Isolate the wire that feeds power to the circuit in question. Somewhere in that tangle of cables is one wire that will stay "hot" when the switch is off. Think of a switch as a drawbridge: When it's up, the traffic can't get across; when it's down, don't be standing in the middle of the road. Use a test light to find which side of the bridge you're on. (If working with live circuits makes you nervous, call in an electrician to make the necessary changes.) Press one probe on the tester against the outlet box and touch the other to the switch terminal. When the test light stays on, regardless of whether the switch is open or closed, you've found the hot side. Now you can go down into the basement, find which fuse or breaker controls the circuit and shut it off. This is a job for two people: One person unscrews fuses or flips breaker switches while the other watches for a light plugged into that circuit to go off when the correct fuse is pulled.

With the circuit deactivated, disconnect the switch, pull the wire out of the box and back through the floor and screw an insulating wire nut on its exposed conductors. Wrap the nuts with electrical tape just to be sure they don't get knocked off. Now the rest of the wiring can safely be re-moved at leisure, even if the circuit is reactivated. This is sometimes necessary when other branches of the circuit feed vital appliances or zones of the house that cannot be left without power for long periods.

For reasons that will be explained in the chapter on the electrical system (see p. 276), don't confuse a feed with a switch leg. If the switch has only one cable coming into the box instead of two, it is not a feed. The hot wire supplying the circuit is somewhere else, usually in the box directly under the fixture controlled by the switch. Disconnect the fixture and unscrew all the pairs of wire nuts in the box to unjoin the spliced cables (novices should do this only with the circuit off). Only one of the incoming cables is hot, the others just draw power from it. With the circuit back on, touch the probe to each black wire (black is always hot) until the tester lights up. That's the feed. Cap the hot lead with a wire nut as before and proceed with the demolition. Always use electrician's pliers to cut cables; the insulated handles will prevent a nasty shock if you happen to cut a live wire by mistake.

Rerouting dangling wires is a bit tricky when they run through a ceiling between floors instead of an attic or basement (see the drawing on the facing page). Since the ceiling over the missing partition will need patching anyway, push the cable up behind the lath boards and chisel a groove into the wall stud so the cable can round the corner and slip into a hole drilled through the stud and into the wall cavity. Then it can be fished down into the basement, up into the attic or out a hole in the adjacent wall cut for a new outlet box, as necessary.

Cover the exposed cable in the groove with a steel plate (use side pieces of discarded outlet boxes) to protect it from nails or drywall screws. If the cut cable isn't long enough to reach, install a steel junction box in the ceiling above the old wall and splice a new length of cable to it. Refer to pp. 268-276 for a more complete discussion of old-house rewiring.

Another option is to reroute the wires through the floorboards, which are usually easier to take up than the ceiling is to take down. Square-edged floorboards will lift without damage. Baseboards and ceiling moldings are also another route of concealment. The studs and wall plaster behind them are grooved and notched for horizontal cable runs. Cut a fist-sized access hole through the lath so the wire can turn up into the wall or down into the floor.

Removing load-bearing walls

Since a load-bearing partition carries the joists above it and any upper-story bearing walls, a temporary support beam must be jacked up under the joists as close as possible to the partition before removing it. The bearing wall is then replaced by a carrying beam, supported on posts at both ends and, for spans over 16 ft., at midspan as well. If such a post (or posts) are undesirable, a steel girder will be required.

Follow the same general procedure as when removing a nonbearing wall. Once the studs are exposed and the work area cleaned up, bring in the jacking equipment. A 4x8 or three 2x8s spiked together is usually adequate for the jacking timber; 4x4s or doubled 2x6s will serve for jack posts. A few short lengths of 2x12 plank act as jacking pads for distributing the load across the underlying framing. Three screw jacks are ideal, but with patience, one will do.

Support one end of the jacking beam close to the ceiling with a ladder, then lift the other end against the ceiling and hold it there while a helper slips the jack post under it. Raise the jack post high enough so that the ceiling joists are lifted off the partition, and insert a support post cut to length. Do the same at the other end, and in the middle of the timber. Since a 16-ft. timber is about the longest length three or four pairs of hands can comfortably handle, longer walls must be removed a section at a time.

Rerouting Cables when a Partition is Removed

Circuit A feeds from the cellar to the attic via the ceiling.

To reroute via the floor:

A1 Cut cable close to base of wall. Remove cable staples.

A2 Pull cable up into attic and bore through into end wall.

A3 With fish wire, pull cable down into cellar, where it can be rerouted to 4A.

A4 Splice cable together.

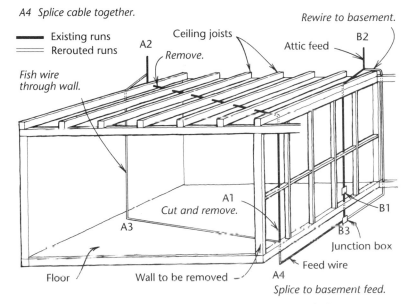

Circuit B feeds from the attic to the outlet and then down into the basement.

To reroute into the side wall:

B1 Remove cables from outlet box —draw feed up into attic at B2, draw down into cellar at B3.

B2 Bore top and bottom of side-wall partition and fish cable down into cellar.

B3 Install junction box and reconnect feed cable to run cable, ensuring continuity of circuit.

Once the timber is in place, the partition can be removed. Floor joists are typically butted together or overlapped on top of a bearing wall. Most of the time, the ceiling joists and attached flooring are stiff enough so that a single jacking timber will hold up the ceiling, despite the offset. If only one side of the ceiling lifts, or if the wall is part of a multi-story bearing system, a second jacking timber on the opposite side of the partition is needed. Place these timbers and jacks at least 2 ft. off the centerline to allow enough elbow room.

The ceiling joists themselves are most likely toenailed into the top plate of the partition. Attempting to pry the plate free could damage the adjoining ceiling finish, even if you insert a protective block under the prybar. Instead, split the plate apart with a chisel, or pull out the nails with a cat's-paw, if the reciprocating saw can't get at them. Nip off any protruding nails or at least bend them back against the wood. If the new carrying beam is to be concealed under plaster or trim, the plate is simply left in place.

The carrying beam should match or at least suit the style of the existing finish. If the ceiling has exposed hand-hewn beams, use a hewn timber, stained to match. A smoothly planed beam, stained or with a natural finish, might suit a more contemporary home. But exposed beams of any sort would be an egregious mistake for a formal Colonial or 19th-century home with flat-finished ceilings and painted trim. Here, the carrying beam, typically tripled 2x10s or 2x12s, is cased with decorative trim or plastered over. If the style allows, the corners can be curved to form an arch.

Depending on the choice of beam, it should be supported on exposed posts of similar material, by built-up studs concealed within the wall framing or a fin wall, or incorporated into existing or new masonry. The carrying beam itself is also jacked into place to compensate for the inevitable sagging of the ceiling joists. The requisite correction is determined by strings stretched across blocks on the ceiling, or a good "eyeball" level, before the carrying timber is raised into place. Even with the weight distributed across the floor by the jacking pads, the floor may also sag a bit.

Because the load that was previously spread across a wide area is now concentrated onto two or three posts, they must have solid support beneath them. General-

ly, a bearing wall rests on a corresponding partition or girder directly below it. Fill in the space between floor joists under the new posts with solid blocking and make sure there are posts below them footed onto solid concrete or rock pads. Knee braces will stiffen girders and compensate somewhat for offset posts. If this underpinning work is done before the ceiling is jacked up, the floor system won't sag under the new posts.

If sections of plaster have fallen from the ceiling or been cut away for wiring changes, patch the holes with drywall (or patching plaster) once the carrying beam is installed. Spackle any nail holes and patch any damage behind the posts where new work meets the old plaster.

The finish floor will probably stop at the edges of the former sole plate. Even if a patch is cut from the same species as the original wood, the color of new wood won't match the patina of the old. Obtain small tubes of yellow ocher, burnt sienna and lampblack oil tinting colors from a paint store and mix them by trial and error with a palette knife. Add the color a dab at a time to a cupful of kerosene, and brush the mix onto a scrap of the patching wood. Rub the color in with a towel and set it aside to dry overnight. Make a number of samples and observe which one most closely duplicates the original. If the color is applied lightly to the patch so that additional coats can darken the tone as needed, it should be possible to create a synthetic patina indistinguishable from the original.

Small holes left by the removal of wires or pipes in the finish floor itself are best filled with circular plugs cut from similar material. Larger holes, resulting from the removal of heating registers, a chimney or drainpipe, are better filled with a rectangular patch. Square the hole and, if possible, screw cleats to the sides of the floor joists to support the patch. If the area is too small, cut the finish flooring back so that an inch or two of subfloor is exposed, apply a bead of construction adhesive and insert the patch, securing it with finish nails or countersunk screws. Hardwood strip or tile flooring requires the additional support of a subfloor, even over small spans. The flooring must be taken up to the nearest joist; otherwise, headers nailed between joists can support the subfloor.

Another method for repairing small floor patches is to a cut a piece of plywood several inches larger than the missing area and angle it into the hole, below the subfloor. Screw a drawer pull to its face. Apply a bead of construction adhesive to the plywood and use the handle to hold it tight against the underside of the subfloor. Pull the patch up tight against the subfloor with drywall screws, driven through the subfloor into the patch, and then remove the handle. Fill in the subfloor with more material and add the finish-floor patch.

Adding straight walls to crooked houses

The sole plate of a new wall is set to a line chalked across the floor. Remember: Neither the floor, ceiling or walls are likely to be level or plumb. If the partition is built as a tilt-up unit, frame it to slightly less than the height and width of the shortest dimensions, so you can tip it up and shim it into place. This method works only if the overall variance is less than 1 in.

A simpler method, especially when the walls are badly skewed, is to build the new wall in place. Begin by nailing the sole plate to the chalkline. Plumb the wall to find the location for the plate at the ceiling. Measure and cut each wall stud to length. Check the walls behind the end studs of the partition for plumb and add or subtract the amount the first stud is out of plumb to the spacing modules to lay out the remaining studs. (To accommodate finishes like drywall, the wall studs must follow 16-in. on-center spacing. Compensating for the variance from plumb enables finish surfaces to fit studs without waste.)

When the new wall is perpendicular to the run of the joists, simply nail the top plate into the ceiling joists. If the ceiling is already in place and the wall runs paral-

---

Two Ways to Install New Partitions in Crooked Rooms

Prebuilt partition shimmed and nailed in place

Frame partition to slightly less than height and width of shortest dimensions and shim in place.

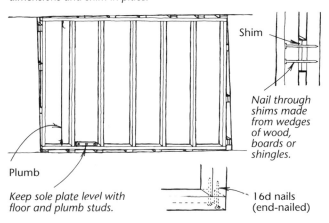

Shim

Nail through shims made from wedges of wood, boards or shingles.

Plumb

Keep sole plate level with floor and plumb studs.

16d nails (end-nailed)

Partition built in place to fit walls

1. Snap chalkline on floor at desired location and install sole plate, nailing into floor.

2. Plumb wall to locate plate on ceiling.

3. Nail end stud to wall first. Determine proper spacing to center of studs to compensate for wall's deviation from plumb. For drywall, studs must be 16 in. o.c. to minimize waste.

4. Plumb each stud, cut to length and toenail to plates.

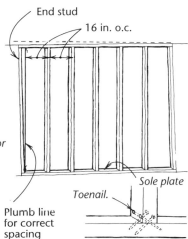

End stud

16 in. o.c.

Sole plate

Toenail.

Plumb line for correct spacing

lel to the joists, blocking cannot be added. Instead, secure the top plate to the ceiling with construction adhesive. Drywall screws driven into the lath will hold it up until the studs themselves wedge it tight. Molly-bolt drywall anchors will hold where screws can't, as, for example, when the existing ceiling is drywall, not plaster. These fasteners are particularly useful for securing end studs to an existing wall, as it's unlikely that solid blocking is behind the wall finish.

Depending on the type of material, there are several ways to attach wood framing to a masonry wall. With brick, drill a hole through the stud and allow the point of the bit to nick the brickwork. This marks the center of the hole you'll drill with a masonry bit, into which a lag shield or similar expansion anchor is inserted, bolting the wood to the wall. Expansion fittings also are useful in stone. Because rock is usually a lot harder than brick, use a hammer drill to make the hole.

Powder-actuated fasteners are the tool of choice for joining wood to concrete. Either rent a powder-actuated nailer (because of liability problems, these aren't rentable in many states), borrow one or purchase an inexpensive tool. Hardened masonry nails can also be hand-driven with a 2-lb. sledge. The nails should penetrate no less than ½ in. or more than ¾ in. into the concrete; less won't grip and more will chip out. Hardened nails and lag shields tend to crack concrete blocks. Use screw anchors designed for the purpose or toggle bolts. Whatever fastener you use, for extra strength, run a bead of construction adhesive behind the stud.

A word of advice concerning the removal and repair of masonry walls (other than foundation walls): Don't. If a portion of your brick bearing wall or an arch has bulged or cracked open, hire a mason experienced in repairing structural damage before attempting it yourself. One exception is the simple case where a brick wall that supports a floor deck has cracked or bowed. If the load is relieved as described above, the wall can be taken apart brick by brick and rebuilt, or else be demolished and replaced by a carrying beam or wood partition. When rebuilding a masonry wall, the underlying cause of the failure must be correctly diagnosed and repaired if the rebuilt wall is to succeed.

Although it may sound formidable, installing a steel beam in place of a bearing wall is not really any harder than adding a wood beam. In fact, some of the steel beams I've installed weighed a lot less than some of the wood ones. Any good carpentry book outlines the procedure for calculating the load on a wood girder and sizing the girder to carry it. Some of these books also include tables for determining the sizes of steel beams needed for a given span. Local building codes may require these calculations to be performed by a licensed structural engineer. You may also feel more comfortable consulting with one, in any case. There are also tables in architectural and millwright's manuals that give the weight per foot for standard steel beams.

An average steel beam, suitable for residential spans, weighs about 22 lb. to 24 lb. per ft. Although it is commonly assumed that steel beams are "I" beams, the "WF" (wide flange) beam is better suited for connection to wood framing. Its wider cross section gives more strength with less depth and weight. The profile is also flatter, which makes it easier to attach wood nailers than with the more sloped and curved cross section of an I-beam. A 10-in. deep WF beam 18 ft. long weighs only about 450 lb., which is at least 100 lb. lighter than the same length 8x12 beam cut from green hemlock. Sawhorses and cleats spiked to the wall framing, together with four strong shoulders, can easily lift one end of the beam a step at a time until it is alongside the post that will support it.

The key is to lift no higher than is comfortable, alternating between opposite ends of the beam, adding blocking or scaffolding until the whole beam is at the right height. Jack the ceiling at least an extra ½ in. to allow room enough to slide the beam sideways onto its posts. Steel beams should not rest on wood posts—the different rates of expansion between wood and steel will create an instability that will crack ceiling finishes. Instead, support the beam on steel Lally columns to which flat plates have been welded. These plates are either welded to the bottom of the beam or drilled and bolted. Two-by-four trim and framing nailers are fastened to the metal with powder-actuated fasteners. The appropriate power charge can easily pierce steel, which is a lot faster than drilling holes for self-tapping screws. Use construction adhesive with either method.

Building and Repairing Stairs

In his book, *Early American Homes for Today* (see the Bibliography on pp. 334-338), Herbert Wheaton Congdon writes: "...the staircase is the largest single element of decorative construction inside a house, as well as the most important functional one. It is much more than just a means of getting to the next floor." He also says "...It must be acknowledged that the comfort of those using them seems to have been of little concern to the long-legged pioneers, but they did make an effort to make stairways decorative...."

Since safety seems to have been a concern that the old-time housewrights disregarded, Congdon tells us that "the stairs in old houses are excellent in appearance and sturdily built, but their steps are seldom comfortable and sometimes really dangerous." Thus, the desire to make a staircase more usable (if not safer), the need to repair damage caused by abuse or neglect, and general changes in layout occasioned by remodeling may call for the removal of existing stairs or the construction of a new set.

Rise and run

Although stairbuilding can be one of the most demanding forms of the woodworker's art, the theory of stair design is actually quite simple. A stair is, basically, a de-

vice for travel between two levels of a building in comfort and safety. The rest is simply ornamentation. As such, a successful stair depends on the proper ratio of rise (vertical height of each step) to run (horizontal width of each tread).

Rules of thumb distilled from custom, practice and not a few treatises state that for the average person, the most comfortable and useful stair will embody a ratio of rise to run such that the sum of two risers and one tread will equal 25 in. Thus a 7½-in. riser requires a 10-in. tread.

There are several variations on this rule, but they all give similar results. The idea is that steeper stairs take too much effort to climb and the treads are so dangerously narrow that one must set the foot down diagonally to negotiate each one. Lower stairs may be safer, but their extra tread width converts valuable living area into stairwell opening. Although less fatiguing, low risers encourage one to take two at a time, which is even less safe than steep steps. The acceptable range for the rise of frequently used stairs is between 7 in. and 8 in. Seldom-used attic stairs can have a 9-in. rise. But cellar stairs are too well used to permit such a dangerously steep angle. For safety, all treads and risers in a flight of stairs must be the same size; otherwise people tend to trip where the stair changes size.

To apply the rule to a given stairwell opening, begin by dividing the total rise in inches by 7. Round off the result to a whole number, which represents the number of risers. Divide that number into the total rise to get the actual height of each riser. Use the rule to find the width for each tread.

For example, assume a total rise of 8 ft. 1 in., or 97 in.: 97 ÷ 7 = 13.85, or, rounded off to a whole number, 14. This is the number of risers necessary. Calculate tread width as follows: 97 ÷ 14 = 6.92 in. To fit the rule, we'll round off to 7; so 7 + 7 = 14, and 25 − 14 = 11. Hence the treads should be 11 in. wide. The total number of treads is always one less than

Basic Stair Anatomy

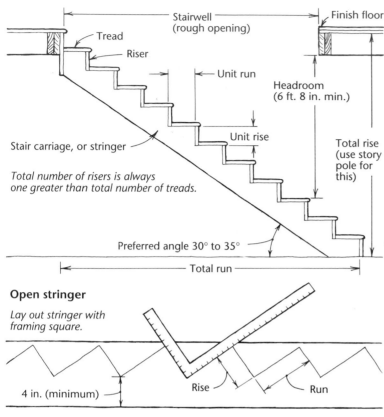

Stairwell (rough opening)

Finish floor

Tread

Riser

Unit run

Headroom (6 ft. 8 in. min.)

Stair carriage, or stringer

Unit rise

Total rise (use story pole for this)

Total number of risers is always one greater than total number of treads.

Preferred angle 30° to 35°

Total run

Open stringer

Lay out stringer with framing square.

4 in. (minimum)

Rise

Run

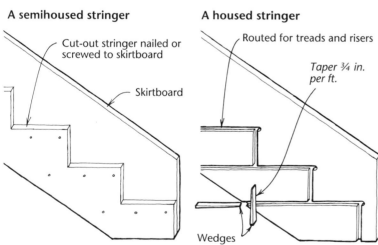

A semihoused stringer

Cut-out stringer nailed or screwed to skirtboard

Skirtboard

A housed stringer

Routed for treads and risers

Taper ¾ in. per ft.

Wedges

the number of risers (the last tread is actually the upper floor), in this case, 13. Now 13 x 11 = 143 in., or 11 ft. 11 in., which is the total length of the opening required for the stairwell.

If the hallway is long enough to accommodate such an opening without losing room space, this would give a very comfortable stair. In most cases, a little comfort is sacrificed to living space. The stairwell could be considerably reduced with only a slight increase in riser height. If, following the example above, we use 13 risers instead of 14, we have 97 ÷ 13 = 7.46 in. A 7½-in. rise is considered by many stairbuilders as the ideal compromise between utility and economy: 7.5 + 7.5 = 15 and 25 – 15 = 10, which is a standard tread width. The dividend comes when the stairwell opening is calculated: 12 x 10 = 120 in., or 10 ft., a savings of almost 2 ft. Calculations of this sort are important when space is limited, as, for example, when a stair must ascend under a steep roof.

Another factor that determines the angle of the stairs is the requirement for adequate headroom. The distance between the tread and the ceiling should never at any point along the stairs be less than 6 ft. 8 in. Otherwise, a person's forehead could smack into the stairwell ceiling, especially at the header where it joins the ceiling at the bottom of the stair. To gain extra headroom in tight spots, the joist header is sometimes set back and the wall at the foot of the stairwell actually projects into it.

Framing the stairwell

Framing for stairwell openings is exactly the same as for window openings or skylights. The joists parallel to the run of the stairs are doubled up, or "trimmed." Doubled-up headers also distribute the extra load to the trimmer joists. Where the opening contains room for a turn, the unsupported corner is posted to the floor below or carried on a wall. Stairwells are either closed, semiclosed or open, depending on whether the stairs are hung from a wall on both, one or no sides. The treads and risers are attached to the stair carriage, which consists of two or three steplike notched timbers, or "stringers." Stringer layout is the most important element of stair rough-in. All the rest is just fancy trimwork. Since a number of books have been written about stairbuilding, our discussion is necessarily confined to the simplest outline and some peculiarities of old houses that affect stair layout.

Laying out the stairs

To apply the numbers derived from the formulas to stringer layout, first cut a story pole to the height of the rise, as measured between finish floors. If the finish floors are not yet installed, tack blocks equal to their thicknesses to each subfloor. With a 4-ft. level and straightedge, check the floor for a difference between the head and foot of the stairwell opening. Measure across the opening at the foot for a pitch in that direction also. With old houses, it's not unusual for the floor to be several inches off level. The difference is added to or subtracted from the length of the story pole. If there's a difference across the stringers as well as along them, their average is used as the total riser height, and the first riser shimmed or shortened as needed to keep the treads level.

Set a pair of dividers to the calculated riser height. Since even $1/32$ in. will add up to almost a $1/2$-in. error over 13 risers, it's important to be exact in setting the dividers and stepping off each riser on the story pole. If the calculations are correct, the last step will coincide with the end of the story pole, plus or minus any observed variation in floor level noted previously across the foot of the stairwell. Keep trying until you get it right. More than $1/8$ in. difference in the actual stringer is unacceptable and quite noticeable.

Installing the stairs

Once the layout coincides with the calculations, the stringer can be set up. Use straight, knot-free 2x12 stock. Stair gauges are slotted brass nuts that lock onto the blade of a framing square to hold it at the proper angle as it steps off the layout on the stringer stock. The short blade is set for the rise while the long blade marks the run. Mark the cut line with a scratch awl rather than a pencil. Cut the first stringer and try it in the opening. It should rest against a mark leveled across the header one riser length below the finish floor height. The treads should read level and the risers plumb. If it fits, use the first stringer as a pattern for the others.

Before the stringer is installed, it's shortened at its bottom edge by the thickness of the tread stock, so that the last riser is the same as the others. The finished treads should project 1 in. beyond the face of the riser trim board. This nosing makes for a safer stair and prevents stair climbers from striking their toes against the riser.

The stringers are placed against the finish wall and nailed through to the studs. The riser boards are nailed to the stringer first, and then the stair treads follow. In closed-stair construction, the treads and risers either butt against a skirtboard fastened behind the stringer (a "semi-housed stringer") or slide into notches cut in the skirtboard (a "housed stringer"). The notches of a housed stringer are routed level and plumb across the face sides of the treads and risers, and angled slightly on the backside. Wedges are glued and driven tight to prevent the treads from squeaking and the risers from shifting. In this case, the treads are installed and wedged tight before installing the risers, working from the top down.

Stair repair

The treads and risers of housed stringers cannot be removed unless you gain access to the underside of the stair carriage. If this has been plastered over, it must be stripped. Fortunately, for the novice stair

Stair Rails, Balusters and Newel Posts

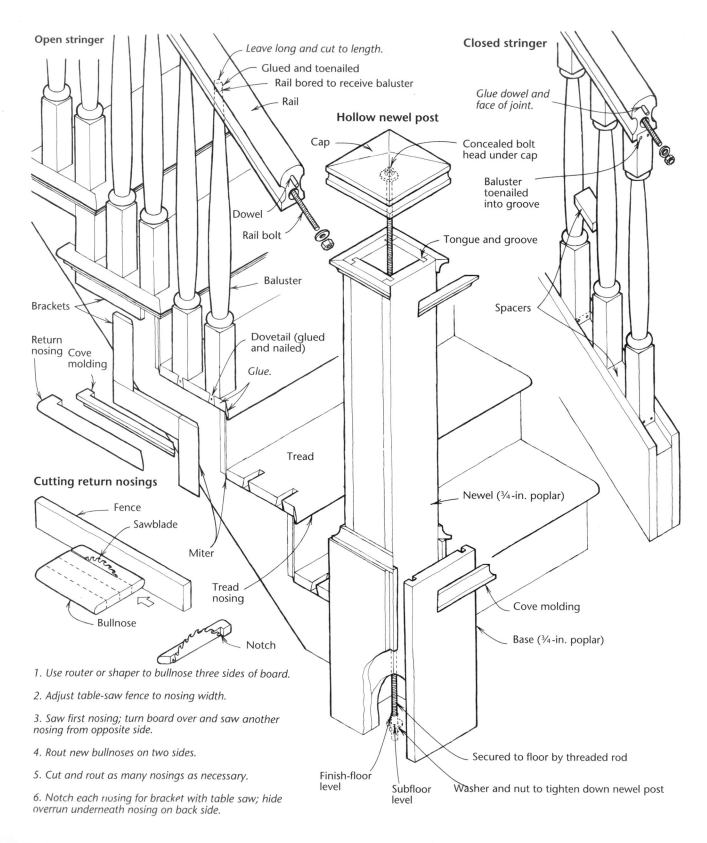

Open stringer

Leave long and cut to length.

Glued and toenailed

Rail bored to receive baluster

Rail

Dowel

Rail bolt

Baluster

Brackets

Return nosing

Cove molding

Dovetail (glued and nailed)

Glue.

Hollow newel post

Cap

Concealed bolt head under cap

Tongue and groove

Tread

Newel (¾-in. poplar)

Closed stringer

Glue dowel and face of joint.

Baluster toenailed into groove

Spacers

Cove molding

Base (¾-in. poplar)

Secured to floor by threaded rod

Finish-floor level

Subfloor level

Washer and nut to tighten down newel post

Cutting return nosings

Fence

Sawblade

Miter

Bullnose

Tread nosing

Notch

1. Use router or shaper to bullnose three sides of board.

2. Adjust table-saw fence to nosing width.

3. Saw first nosing; turn board over and saw another nosing from opposite side.

4. Rout new bullnoses on two sides.

5. Cut and rout as many nosings as necessary.

6. Notch each nosing for bracket with table saw; hide overrun underneath nosing on back side.

rebuilder, at least, housed stringers were used only for first-class jobs. The treads and risers of most stairs were simply face-nailed into the stringer and set flush to the skirtboards. In such cases, damaged treads and risers are simply pried up and replaced as needed.

Some renovators look at a set of treads worn by the scuffing of generations of feet, and buried under iron-hard layers of porch and deck enamel, and conclude that the only alternative to tedious stripping and peeling is complete removal and replacement with new material. This is a tragic mistake. New material can never match the unique and satisfying sculpture that a worn tread has become, the visible evidence of the house's connection to the past. If the treads and risers are carefully disassembled, they can be much more easily stripped of the old, caked-on finish. The skirtboards are also much more accessible to the scraper or sander. I remember discovering exquisite cherry hidden under brown paint so ugly the owner was about to have me tear the old stairs out. Quite by accident, a helper had found a stock of triangular cherry boards that looked a lot like the pieces left over from a skirtboard, hidden in the attic. This got us to wondering what was under the paint.

There are only a few repairs to the newel posts, the rail and balustrade that anyone but a skilled carpenter should attempt. Broken or loose balusters are one of them. These often decorative, but quite necessary pieces are typically dovetailed into the tread in an open stringer. The joint is hidden behind a strip of bullnosed "return nosing" nailed to the end grain of the tread. When this is removed, the joint is exposed. The drawing on the facing page shows an easy way to make bull-noses, should any be damaged or missing.

Sometimes the damaged baluster is identical to a stock pattern, or you may find a replacement at a salvage warehouse. If a baluster has sheared off at the dovetail instead of at the top where it plugs into the rail, a new dovetail can be fashioned

and doweled into the bottom of the baluster. You might even be able to remove the old dovetail in one piece and dowel it back to its baluster. Loose balusters are tightened by driving glue-coated wood shims into the dovetail joint. Remove any loose balusters and clean off the old dried-out glue before regluing.

When balusters are inserted into a closed stringer, they are locked into place with flat pieces of wood that fit into the baluster groove at the top of the stringer. Pry up these pieces or replace any missing ones. The balusters are secured with toe-nails driven into the stringer. Predrill nail holes in hardwood, to prevent splitting the wood or bending nails.

Newel posts are either solid or boxed (hollow). Turned newels are usually solid. A solid newel is tightened by drilling through its face and screwing it to the underlying stringer. The bore hole is plugged with a dowel. Boxed newels are normally secured to the floor by a threaded rod. Access is gained by removing the newel cap. The nut on top of the rod is turned down to stiffen the newel post. If such a rod is missing, it can be retrofitted by bolting it through a metal bracket screwed into the floor. Rail repair usually involves finding and removing the wood plugs that give access to the various star nuts and concealed rail bolts that tie the railings together. These bolts are either tightened or replaced.

Interior Wall Finishes

The modern home owner is faced with a bewildering choice of materials for interior wall finish, almost all of them inappropriate. To me, materials such as imitation bricks, plastic beams and prefab wall panelings have no soul; they negate whatever spirit the house may be struggling to articulate. If people could feel the emptiness of these products, they would never consider living with them.

With some reservations, I would maintain that these objections don't hold for drywall, an undeniably versatile material.

It is not so much the nature of the product itself that sometimes may be offensive, but rather the way it is thoughtlessly used. Drywall is, above all, a neutral material. If used with wood or a contrasting surface, the tension between texture and space is highlighted. Dramatic planes are defined, dark rooms lightened. Drywall can be a noncompetitive background for furniture and artwork, or offer relief in what might otherwise become a tyranny of busy wood. But remember that the labor and costs of finishing and painting diminish drywall's economy. Drywall is unmatched, however, as a base for papered walls.

Although drywall lacks the quality of a good plaster finish, the difference is not so noticeable that one couldn't learn to live with it. In fact, the rounded quality of plastered edges can be duplicated by nailing quarter-round molding to outside corners instead of the conventional square-edged metal corner bead.

Installing drywall

A popular misconception about drywall is that finishing is a job easily done by the amateur. The picture of a smiling woman, trowel in hand, tailored jeans and neat bandana—if she can do it, anyone can—is an outright lie. Patience, a steady hand and lots of practice are the recipe for successful taping. Nothing looks worse than a poor taping job, which is all that most neophytes succeed in accomplishing. This is a strong argument for hiring a professional drywall contractor, or else figuring out a clever way to avoid the issue altogether.

The long edges of a drywall panel are beveled. When two sheets are butted together, the resulting depression makes it easier to embed the joint tape and compound. It takes a lot of skill to make an invisible tape joint over unbeveled edges.

The fewer seams to tape, the easier, faster and better the job. Drywall is cheap: Use a full sheet instead of piecing several smaller pieces together. For example, cut out window openings in a full sheet instead of leaving a joint over the top cor-

ner of the window header. Any such joint directly over a door or window jamb will be the first to crack, as this particular area moves more than the rest of the wall. Break joints over and under the middle of a wall opening instead.

Unless a vertical piece can cover the entire wall, the sheets are always laid horizontally. On long walls, offset the vertical joints at least 4 ft. A "crossroad" (where vertical joints cross horizontal joints) is just about impossible to tape neatly. Save the cut pieces for the insides of closets, which usually require lots of small pieces and where the joints aren't exposed to close scrutiny. A larger piece that won't fit through the closet door opening can be bent around the obstructing corner if it is scored on its backing side first. Don't actually fold the sheet; otherwise the finish side will show a crease. Make the scoring cut so that it falls over a stud.

Drywall is available in 8-ft., 10-ft., 12-ft. and sometimes 14-ft. long panels, in thicknesses of ⅜ in., ½ in. and ⅝ in. Order sheets sized to minimize butt joints. For example, the increased expense of using 12-ft. long sheets on a 10-ft. 9-in. wide ceiling is more than offset by the elimination of a joint.

Drywall application begins with the ceilings. With old houses in particular, the run of the joists should be checked for square (that is, perpendicularity) with the run of the walls. Since the ends of each sheet must fall on the middle of a joist (unlike plywood, drywall cannot be toenailed along an edge; the fasteners won't hold if they break through the paper facing), the edges of the first sheets that butt the walls may have to be trimmed. Line up the edge of the first panel with the joist and measure the width of the gap (if any) that opens up between the sides of the panel and the wall. Assuming that the wall is not curved, convert the measurement to a ratio. For example, a 1-in. gap over 8 ft. means that the wall is running out of square ⅛ in. per foot. Thus, a 13-ft. wide room will require an adjustment of 1⅝ in.

Mark a point on the ceiling at 48 in. from the ending corner, make another at 46⅜ in. from the beginning corner, and snap a chalkline between them. Trim the edge of the panels that abut the wall so that they fit to the chalkline. Once again, trimming a full sheet is always easier than patching in a tapered piece. Depending on how skewed the walls are, the long, the short or even both ends may require adjustment to keep the sheets falling over the joists.

Since tape and joint compound are forgiving of many sins, the fit between panels need not be glove-tight. Never cut a panel so closely that it must be forced to fit—this risks breaking the edge behind the paper, making for a very difficult repair. As long as the sheets line up along the factory edges, gaps of up to ¼ in. are not a problem on cut edges. If, as sometimes happens with ceilings, the sheet is screwed halfway home before you notice that it has slipped, and an edge now requires some gentle "persuasion" to fit, hammer on a length of 2x4 held over the stubborn spot. If this won't do the trick, cut away the overlap with your knife.

The pros use a panel lift to hold the drywall against the ceiling. These can be rented. Or you can use a "deadman," which is a braced 2x4 tee that wedges a sheet tight to the ceiling. Even with a deadman, it takes two people to put up ceilings, especially with panels over 8 ft. long.

Fasten the panels with blued, rust-resistant ring-shank nails driven straight into the joists. The head of an angled nail will cut the paper surface, canceling its holding power. The head of the nail should rest in the dimple formed by the hammer blow—deep enough to lie below the surface, but shallow enough not to break through the paper. Space the nails 2 in. apart every 12 in. along the joists. Missed joists (and hard-to-cover nail holes)

will be prevented if the joist or wall-stud centerlines are marked on the panels before installation. Hardly anyone uses drywall nails anymore. Screws have much greater holding power and, if you have a screw gun (they can be rented), are faster and less tiring to install.

When the ceiling joists are spaced on 2-ft. centers and the space above is used for living, the ceiling should be strapped. Screw 1x3 furring on 16-in. centers across the joists. The strapping need not be perfectly perpendicular, since the sheets will line up to it and not the joists. Strapping is also the method used to flatten out an uneven ceiling. Strings set on blocks indicate where shingle shims must be wedged between the joists and the strapping to bring the ceiling into the same plane.

Drywall is trimmed by making a scoring cut through its face side using a utility knife and a straightedge. A 4-ft. long T-square is indispensable for work with drywall and any other panel-type materials. The scored sheet is stood on edge and bent backward to snap the core, and the backing paper cut through. It's time to change the knife blade when it begins to tear rather than slice the paper. Use a Surform® block plane to smooth any rough edges. Make larger adjustments with the shank of a steel hammer held scraper-like or with a knife.

Holes and other irregular cuts are made with a coarse-toothed drywall keyhole saw; its pointed tip is plunged into the sheet to start the cut. Holes for electrical outlets will line up better if only their centers are marked and the openings cut after the panel is installed. Don't do this if the boxes are already energized. A drill-mounted hole saw makes neat, fast cutouts for pipes and other circular penetrations.

Wall panels are hung horizontally from the top down. This way, any cut edge is usually hidden by the baseboard molding, eliminating yet another unbeveled joint. The first sheets may also require trimming where they butt against the ceiling, to square up with the studs.

Sweep and vacuum the floor area after all the drywall is hung and the scraps are disposed of. The dust has a way of appearing all over the house. The stuff is so fine that it clogs up vacuum cleaner filters in just a few minutes. Even worse than this, small crumbs of drywall seem to have a special affinity for joint compound. They're forever showing up as streaks and gouges under the taping knife.

Taping drywall

Joint compound is sold in 1-gal. and 5-gal. pails. Unless you are taping only a small patch, buy the larger size. Even a 5-gal. pail won't go very far. "Mud" is cheap; it's better to throw some away than to find yourself a quart short on a Sunday afternoon. Allow the pails to warm up to room temperature (70°F is optimum) before use. The house itself should also be maintained above 60°F for several days prior to and after taping to ensure good drying.

Upon opening the pail, stir the compound to mix any separated liquids. Scoop it onto an aluminum hawk and keep it mounded up, cleaning the edges to prevent dried compound from contaminating the fresh compound.

Fill the trough between the beveled edges of the horizontal joints first. Use a 5-in. taping knife to run an ample bead down the center of the joint. Embed paper joint tape in the compound, over the joint. Smooth the tape and run the knife over it to squeeze out excess compound. Repeat on each side to level off the extra compound, running the edge of the knife along the center of the tape. Apply a light skim coat over the tape when done. (If, instead of paper tape, self-sticking fiberglass mesh tape is run over the joint before the mud is applied, one step is saved.)

Inside corners can be a bit tricky. Fill half the knife with joint compound and run it down each side of the corner. Fold the tape and embed it, then smooth it out with the full width of the knife. Nail (don't screw) a metal corner bead to any outside corners. To avoid hard-to-cover buckles,

use only enough nails to hold the metal firmly against the drywall. Rest one edge of the knife on the beaded edge and the other on the drywall, and apply enough compound to fill the gap under the blade, exerting a steady pressure. Use a metal "L" bead for a clean edge where the drywall butts against wood trim and a "J" bead to finish and protect exposed edges.

After the first coat is dry (usually overnight), run over the surface with the taping knife to knock off any bumps and ridges. Feather the second coat over the first, applying the full width of the taping knife on each side of center. Use an 11-in. or 14-in. wide taping paddle to smooth out this coat, at least 2 in. beyond the first coat. The compound should blend smoothly into the drywall at the edges of the patch. At inside corners, use the full width of the knife to run the second coat and level it out with the paddle. Some people prefer to use a special corner trowel which can level both sides at once, theoretically eliminating ridges at the inside. It doesn't seem to make much difference. Outside corners, especially at fin walls or wall openings, are easily leveled using the corner beads as a screed guide.

The second coat is the most difficult to apply, and the most critical. Craters (pockets in the compound formed by air bubbles) will refuse to disappear, a Himalaya of ridges will show where layers cross, humps and valleys will betray the intersection of seams, and gouges will show the scars of meteorites that somehow fell into the bucket. Wherever the knife lingers, a telltale ripple is left behind. Exert a steady, but not overly firm, pressure when running the compound down the joint, moving the paddle in a graceful sweep without pausing. Lift off and return the paddle to the compound gradually, like an airplane taking off or coming in for a landing. Frequently wipe the edge of the paddle and the hawk clean to prevent dried particles from contaminating the compound. Don't reuse any material that has fallen to the floor. Keep the bucket covered and its sides scraped clean. Half-full pails of compound that have been kept too long should be thrown out.

A good part of the taper's art is to know when to stop. It's better to leave a small ridge or gouge in an otherwise smooth joint rather than to risk messing it all up with yet another pass of the paddle. When the second coat is dry, sand it smooth with 120-grit paper and a sanding block, or with an abrasive sponge. If used carefully, a small orbital finish sander is less tiring and a lot faster. Smooth out any ridges and feather the edges of the compound into the paper. Always wear proper eye and lung protection when sanding.

Take care not to sand away so much compound that the tape shows beneath, which is the worst part of finishing untapered butt joints. It's difficult to apply enough compound to cover the tape without making a noticeable bump in the wall. The trick is to use the widest paddle and feather out the compound so broadly that the hump is indiscernible. This is especially important at the intersection of vertical and horizontal joints or at a patch between old plaster and new drywall.

If the first two coats were done well, the third coat can be a touchup. Using the widest paddle, feather butt joints even more, and fill any ripples, craters or gouges that were not removed by sanding. Not much thicker than a film of paint, the third coat will often dry within an hour or two and can be touched up once again if needed. A light sanding is all that is needed to clean up any minor imperfections. Nailheads or screwheads always require at least three coats. Scratches and places where the paper has been torn off are hard to hide, and often require a surprising amount of feathering even though no tape is needed.

On paper at least, that's how taping is done. In real life it's apt to be a lot more frustrating. Good luck.

Wood paneling

The interior partitions of many of the earliest American houses consisted of vertical planks finished with whitewash. This explains why a renovator will sometimes find a painted wall under the plaster lath. Around the last quarter of the 18th century, plank walls gave way to vertical boards nailed to studs. These "ceiled" boards were often given a decorative bead along their edges. Walls that were not plastered were often paneled.

Early American wood paneling bears no resemblance to its modern namesake. Instead, it was more like a continuous door, a series of grooved rails and stiles in which floated thin beveled panels of remarkable width. Indeed, any door set in such a wall was designed so that its rails matched the rails of the wall paneling. The term "wainscot" was also applied to this floor-to-ceiling paneling. Later on it came to refer almost exclusively to panels run halfway up the wall and capped with a "chair rail." It wasn't until the mid-19th century that rail-and-stile paneling was supplanted by the narrow-beaded matchboard that we have come to regard as traditional wainscoting.

The lucky renovator may sometimes uncover antique paneling or ceiled boards under incrustations of wallpaper or plas-

New work in a traditional style: Paint or dark varnish is the usual finish for 19th-century matchboard wainscoting. The flat oak baseboard and chair-rail trim are simple yet elegant.

Installing Tongue-and-Groove Board Paneling

Provide solid nailing for vertical boards, either by nailing 2x4 blocking flatwise between studs 2 ft. o.c., or nail 1x3 strapping over studs 2 ft. o.c.

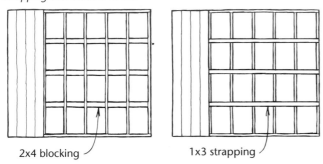

2x4 blocking

1x3 strapping

Detail A: Blind-nailing
Secure boards by blind-nailing through tongue.

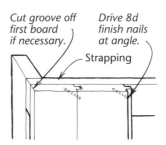

Cut groove off first board if necessary.

Drive 8d finish nails at angle.

Strapping

Detail B: Fitting last board
Shave off back of groove on last board with knife, so board can be forced into place at an angle.

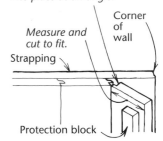

Corner of wall

Measure and cut to fit.

Strapping

Protection block

Using a level and a ratio to find taper cut for crooked corners *(Deviations exaggerated for clarity.)*

$$T = \frac{d \times h}{l}$$

T = width of taper (in.) d = deviation from plumb (in.)
h = height of wall (ft.) l = length of level (ft.)

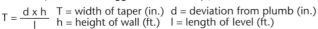

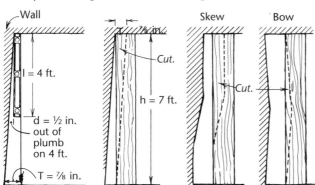

Wall

l = 4 ft.

d = ½ in. out of plumb on 4 ft.

T = ⅞ in.

⅞ in.

Cut.

h = 7 ft.

Skew

Bow

Cut.

Two ways to scribe a bowed board to fit a rough edge

Set divider to widest gap, trace contours onto board.

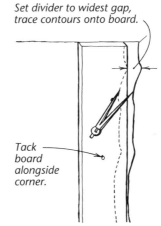

Tack board alongside corner.

Width of board (use wider board if needed to avoid small gaps)

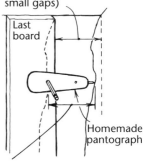

Last board

Homemade pantograph

Offset board by width of distance from pencil to point of pantograph.

ter. The paneling requires little more than a good scrubbing and a coat of boiled linseed oil to restore its beauty.

Although hardly traditional, matched wood paneling boards are nonetheless preferred by many as an alternative to drywall, wallpaper or plaster. Despite the added costs, this species of paneling offers some undeniable advantages. Individual boards are easily installed without the back-wrenching labor of lifting and aligning heavy sheets. There are no joints to tape or sand, no dust to inhale, no footprints tracked throughout the house and

no expensive wallpaper, primer or paint to apply. Wood paneling can be left natural or finished with a coat of boiled linseed oil or varnish.

Unless the boards are installed horizontally, blocking must be nailed between the wall studs or timbers. Install 2x4s flatwise to prevent thermal bridging, and cut the existing insulation to fit behind it instead of compressing it. If this seems to compromise the R-value too much, nail strapping over the studs instead. Strapping can even be nailed over an existing plaster wall. Of course, this approach calls for the removal of existing casing and the installation of extension jambs. Whether you choose blocking or strapping, the nailers should be installed on 2-ft. centers, as measured from the floor. Snap level chalklines across the studs.

Paneling boards are usually shiplapped or tongue-and-grooved. If square-edged boards are used instead, first staple tar paper over the studs where boards meet so that the insulation won't be visible between the gaps when the boards shrink. Tongue-and-groove (also called planed-and-matched) boards are blind-nailed, a method that leaves no nails showing on the surface. Drive 8d finish nails at about a 45° angle through the tongue into the blocking. Set the nailhead below the surface with a nailset.

If the joint won't fit together, don't force it with a hammer. Instead use a short piece of matching paneling to drive the boards tight. Sometimes, the boards will arch upward, and no amount of pounding will draw them together, whereas the pressure of your palm is often enough to flat

ten the hump, mating the boards almost as if by magic. Paneling boards are fairly flexible. If a finish nail doesn't draw a bent board in far enough, carefully drive an 8d box nail through the tongue and sink it. If you still need more pulling power, and there's still enough of the tongue left to hold a nail, drive a 10d nail alongside the first one.

When a board bows so much that the nails can't pull it in, drive a wedge between it and a tapered block tacked across the nailers as shown in the drawing below. Any board that won't draw tight by this method will split first. It's better to select paneling boards with an eye to straightness than to go to such extremes. Cut badly warped or bowed boards through the worst part and save them for places that need short pieces.

As the boards approach the corner, blind-nailing becomes increasingly awkward, and, finally, impossible. Shave off the bottom half of the groove on the very last board with a knife (or cut it on the table saw) so that it can be forced at an

Working with Misshapen Boards

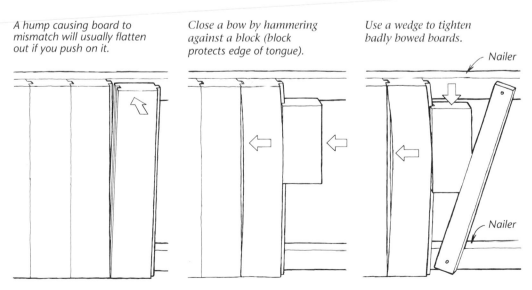

A hump causing board to mismatch will usually flatten out if you push on it.

Close a bow by hammering against a block (block protects edge of tongue).

Use a wedge to tighten badly bowed boards.

Nailer

Nailer

angle into place. Use a block of wood and hammer the edge flat into the corner. The joint need not be perfect, since it will be covered by the first board of the adjacent wall. The first and last pieces of paneling are face-nailed on the outside edge.

As with drywall panels, the first board on each wall is installed plumb. Check the corner with a 4-ft. level. Use the level to determine the amount of taper and the ratio in inches per foot that the board must be trimmed to fit the wall (see the drawing on p. 250). This assumes that the wall is skewed in only one direction. If, as sometimes happens, the wall bows, the board must be scribed to fit. Tack the board alongside the corner in a plumb position and with a pair of dividers set to the widest part of the gap, trace the actual contour onto the board.

Dividers don't work as well when a board must be fitted against a very rough and irregular surface, such as a brick wall or fieldstone fireplace. It's hard to keep the dividers perpendicular to the plane of the wall. Tilting them throws off the scribed line. Instead, use a makeshift pantograph (see the drawing on p. 250).

Drill a pencil-sized hole through a tapered length of wood shingle at the point equal to the greatest distance between the last full board and the contour to be traced. Plumb the next board and tack it to the wall. For a perfect fit, this board should overlay the last full board by the width of a full board less the distance between the pencil point and the tip of the marking tool. If this amount is greater than a full board, either use a wider board or scribe small filler piece. Use a jigsaw or bandsaw to make the cut. Any gaps can be masked with translucent Phenoseal® caulk, which will cure to a clear amber that picks up the color of the wood better than any other sealer.

The same general rules apply when fitting a horizontal board to an uneven floor. First, measure up the width of a full board from the floor at the lowest point where the floor meets the wall. Next, level a line across the wall from this mark. Then tack the board in place and scribe it with dividers as above. If the fit need not be perfect but the overall difference is quite large, take measurements between the floor and the level line at 1-ft. intervals and transfer them to the board. Connect the dots and cut along the line. If the overall difference is small and baseboard trim will cover any gap, simply level the board from the highest point of the floor.

Shiplapped boards are face-nailed to the wall. Some carpenters use finish nails, set below the surface and filled with stained putty. Others feel that instead of concealing the fasteners, they should be accentuated. Square-headed cut nails or spiral flooring nails (which have a small head) are good choices for this. Be wary of replicas of old-fashioned nails with huge "decorative hand-forged" heads. Although such nails were used for framing and flooring, a Colonial craftsman had more pride in his work than to leave them exposed in finish paneling.

Wood and plaster are a traditional combination. Although wainscoting is technically rail-and-stile paneling run up a wall, in modern popular usage the term refers to almost any wood boarding applied either horizontally or vertically partway up a wall. The height is somewhere between 30 in. and 42 in. The treatment of the chair rail, the decorative trim which capped the top of the wainscot, varied from a simple rounded molding to elaborate pseudo-cornices.

Ceiling Treatments

The natural logic of interior finishing is to work from the top down. Begin with the ceilings, proceed to the walls, trim and cabinet work, and conclude with the floors. Whatever drops from the ceiling does not stain a finished wall, and spatters from the wall strike only a rough floor.

At the beginning of this chapter we discussed some of the problems and cures for plaster ceilings and the possibility of stripping the ceiling to reveal hand-hewn beams. Exposing the ceiling beams creates the problem of how to finish the spaces between them. Some folks are quite enamored of the rough-sawn subfloor boards now revealed. They simply brush them clean, cut off any protruding nails with a pair of nipping pliers, and leave it at that. But eventually the ceiling begins to grow a beard, as the household dust is snagged from the air by the rough boards, and as it rains down from cracks in the floor above. The dark wood becomes dingy and the room seems dense and almost gloomy. This cave-like atmosphere may suit a den or private retreat, but it almost defeats the reason the beams were exposed in the first place; the timbers are lost in the gloom.

Ceilings with exposed beams

The intensity of the sunlight entering the house, the height of the ceiling, and the finish of the floors and walls contribute to the effect of the ceiling. Bright walls and light floorboards may benefit from the counterpoint of a dark ceiling. Another possibility is suggested by the Colonial practice of whitewashing the unsheathed interior walls: Simply paint the subfloor boards with a white latex ceiling paint or semitransparent white stain. This preserves their texture and brightens the room at the same time.

If this approach is a little too rough, or if the subfloor boards are too shabby to leave uncovered, there are several ways to construct a new ceiling between the exposed beams. Choices of material include wood paneling, drywall and plaster.

One rather tedious but necessary task that must precede the installation of a new ceiling is the cleaning of the beams. A stiff bristle brush removes clinging dust and cobwebs. Scrub the beams with detergent and hot water. If, after the beams dry, the results are pleasing, no further treatment is necessary. But a lot more can be done. They can be stained to a uniform tone; darker colors look good against light ceilings, especially if the beams are rough-

Although some may object to the practice of exposing ceiling beams, many home owners find exposed beams pleasing. (Photo by Joe English.)

sawn rather than hand-hewn. Experiment with turpentine and tinting colors to find a suitable tone.

Old beams darken with age, often so much so that the wood appears featureless. A drill-mounted wire brush will remove this accumulated obscurity. It also wipes out the bulk of the stains left by plaster lath. Short of sanding, there's no practical way to remove all of the plaster stain. Sanding would take forever and leave the surface unnaturally smooth to boot. A wire brush does a really good job. It removes the grime and scale and, because of its rapid rotation, leaves only minute scratches. The dark grain of the wood is left to contrast with its lighter background in a swirling dance of delight. A coat of boiled linseed oil or other penetrating sealer will accentuate this play of structure and light.

Once the beams are clean, nail 1x1 cleats directly to the sides of the beams up against the subfloor; 1x3 spruce strapping ripped in half makes a good cleat. So do strips ripped from leftover trim boards and pine paneling. Spruce holds nails better than pine, but splits easier.

Use 6d or 8d box nails (not screws) and blunt the tip so the nail will crush the wood fibers rather than wedge them apart. Box nails are thinner than common nails and less likely to split thin wood. They also bend more easily. Run any cables through

Three Types of Ceiling Finish between Exposed Beams

Wood paneling over cleats

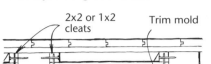

2x2 or 1x2 cleats

Trim mold

Drywall (or gypsum lath for plaster)

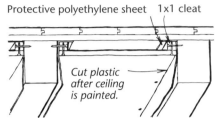

Protective polyethylene sheet   1x1 cleat

Cut plastic after ceiling is painted.

Metal lath and plaster

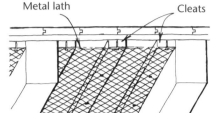

Metal lath

Cleats

the ceiling as needed. Use a "nail-biter" electrician's bit when boring through the top edge of a beam, which is likely to contain more than a few flooring nails. Half-inch deep shallow ceiling boxes screwed to wood support blocks between the beams allow the installation of ceiling light fixtures.

Tongue-and-groove boards can make a handsome ceiling between exposed beams, particularly if the boards have a V-groove profile. The smooth new wood is light in color, and when rubbed with linseed oil or a tung-oil varnish, it takes on a soft, warm glow, much more pleasing than the hard gloss of polyurethane varnish. Hold the boards up against the cleats and drive two finish nails through their ends angled up toward the beam. It would be quite a chore to scribe and fit each board to the uneven contours of a hand-hewn beam. Unless the timber is sawn, don't try for a perfect fit; the results won't be encouraging and the joints will open up anyway due to seasonal shrinkage. Instead, nail a ¾-in. quarter-round molding or a flat ½-in. by 1-in. band molding against the beam to conceal the ends of the ceiling boards. The ceiling boards can also be toned down with thinned-down oil stains, which won't deny or mask the nature of the wood. A light grey or sandy wash could be very soothing.

There can be such a thing as too much wood. Wood floors and wood walls may be fine, but a wood ceiling can overdo it. Painted drywall or the rougher texture of perlited plaster may be more appropriate between the ceiling beams.

Although it is possible to screw drywall directly to the subfloor, it isn't a good idea. Not only will you lose the opportunity to run wiring across the ceiling, but the boards will flex and bounce as the floor is walked upon, and the fairly wide boards will expand or shrink seasonally, causing taped joints to crack and nails to pop. Unlike wood paneling, drywall cannot be toenailed. Although it's possible to screw drywall along a cut edge without all the nails breaking through the paper, given the fact that the beams are likely to be spaced at least 32 in. on center, the long-term prospects for such a wide sheet of otherwise unsupported drywall remaining on the ceiling are questionable. Even if this weren't a problem, the screws are likely to split a ¾-in. wide cleat.

Rip a 2x4 into 2x2 cleats or, if the extra depth is troublesome, glue a 1x2 cleat flat against the subfloor and nail it to the beam with 12d box nails driven through pilot holes. Add additional cleats wherever one sheet butts another to support the joint. Before nailing any cleats to the beam, staple a strip of plastic film against the top edge of the beams, wide enough to hang down past the bottom. This will protect the beam during painting and save painstaking cleanup when the edges of the drywall are filled with joint compound. Force the point of a utility knife at a slight angle up into the joint to cut the poly-ethylene when the job is finished.

When the space between the beams is greater than half the width of a full sheet (over 2 ft.) don't try to piece together the leftovers in a mistaken effort to avoid waste. This may seem extravagant, but a poor taping job shows up more clearly on a ceiling than on any other surface. Rock-lath® might be more economical, but the thin, narrow panels will require a continu-ous center cleat for proper support. This will tend to transmit the bounce from the floor above directly to the plaster, and probably cause a fair amount of joint crack-ing. Then again, the floor may not be very bouncy, and because plaster is thicker than drywall, it may never crack.

Rocklath® is used for a plaster base because the plaster can key into the joints between sheets. Theoretically, plaster applied over drywall won't hold as well, since there are no keyways, especially on a ceiling. But in actuality, surface adhesion is the primary force binding the plaster to gypsum lath. I don't think this would be the case with a multicoat job, but the plas-ter seems to grip drywall equally well— I've had satisfactory results troweling it directly over drywall between beams.

Variations in the width of the bay and inwardly tilted beam faces will conspire against a snug fit for the drywall. Mea-sure between the beams at several places along the run of the drywall, to determine whether the sheet must be tapered and by how much. A ¼-in. tolerance at each side will ease its fitting. Fill the gaps and screw-heads with joint compound. It may take several coats, since there is no effective way to install L-bead or joint tape.

Drywall ceilings are usually finished with a flat (or matte) latex ceiling paint. These are formulated for extra brightness and more covering power than regular wall paint. To diffuse light and soften glare, and most important, to hide blem-ishes in the taping job, sanded texture paint is often used as a ceiling finish. In my opinion, if texture is desired, use the real thing and trowel on rough plaster. No taping is required at all and the finish is, if not architecturally quite correct, at least well suited to exposed beams.

Covered ceilings

Baring of the house's bones is not a pan-acea. Some ceilings are better left covered. Although isolated examples persisted in-to the early 20th century, timber framing was pretty much obsolete by 1860. That leaves a lot of ceilings to deal with that are over 100 years old. Falling plaster was a problem for turn-of-the-century reno-vators, too. Stamped metal ceiling panels were widely promoted as an inexpensive, safe and decorative way to conceal dam-aged plaster. At the height of their popu-larity, from the 1890s until World War I, over 400 patterns were available, includ-ing cornice moldings, floor-to-ceiling wall panels and a cornucopia of decorative me-dallions and borders.

Surprisingly, tin ceilings are not obso-lete. Although the selection of patterns and accessories is far less varied, tin ceil-ings are still available and still an inex-pensive, easy-to-install cure for damaged plaster ceilings.

The 2x8 tin sheets are nailed to strap-ping laid right on top of the old plaster and screwed into the ceiling joists. A help-ful hint: Staple 4-mil polyethylene to the old ceiling first to keep dust and grit from falling on your head while you install the ceiling. Ceiling preparation begins by screwing strapping around the perimeter of the room. Next, snap chalklines diago-nally between the corners to locate the center of the room. The layout is similar to that used for floor tiles: The sheets are aligned to perpendicular axes radiating from this point. This ensures that the last sheets will be the same width on both sides of the ceiling.

Tin-Ceiling Installation

1. Screw strapping to perimeter. Snap chalk layout lines to find ceiling center.

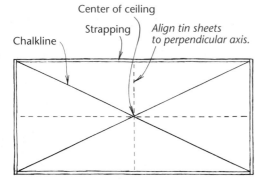

Center of ceiling

Strapping

Align tin sheets to perpendicular axis.

Chalkline

2. Install first course of strapping to follow centerline. Continue with parallel courses on 12-in. centers.

Pieces of strapping fastened perpendicular to vertical strapping on 8-ft. centers secure ends of sheets.

First course

12 in.

3. After ceiling sheets are installed, nail strapping to wall to support cornice trim.

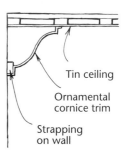

Tin ceiling

Ornamental cornice trim

Strapping on wall

The first course of strapping runs along the centerline of the ceiling, followed by parallel courses on 12-in. centers. Short pieces of strapping are fastened perpendicular to these on 8-ft. centers to secure the ends of the sheets. If necessary, the strapping should be shimmed to level out the ceiling. Attach the tin with 1-in. long common nails driven into the preformed nailing beads. Experienced installers can put up a ceiling working unaided. They literally use their heads (and a piece of strapping) to hold up the loose end of the sheet being nailed. A novice would probably find it more comfortable to work with a helper. A word of warning—wear thin leather gloves when handling tin; the edges can be razor-sharp.

Once the ceiling sheets are installed, strapping is nailed to the wall to support the cornice trim. Flatten any open seams by gently tapping them with a hammer and a blunt chisel or nailhead. Stubborn seams can be filled with paintable caulk. Wipe the tin with paint thinner to remove any oil and apply oil-based metal primer. The final finish can be either oil or latex. Metal ceilings can also be left unprimed and finished with a clear lacquer or multi-purpose sealer like Masury Oil®.

If wallboard, new plaster or tin seem like too much trouble for your ceiling, there's always wood. I'd suggest using beaded matchboard (⅜-in. to ¾-in. thick panels about 5½ in. wide with a beading pattern that makes them look 3 in. wide), which was a common treatment for turn-of-the-century commercial buildings.

A less expensive substitute, which has much the same feeling as matchboard, is 1x3 V-groove board. Board finishes are easily installed over 1x3 strapping nailed over the ceiling joists. (Once again, it's not necessary to remove the original ceiling.) The boards can either be varnished or painted. For a unique effect, cut curved plywood brackets and fasten them to the wall studs at the ceiling to serve as nailers for the boarding, as shown in the drawing on the facing page. Curving the ceiling into the wall was a standard decorative touch for matchboarded ceilings.

High vs. low ceilings

During the energy crisis of the 1970s, experts counseled home owners to lower their high Victorian ceilings to help conserve energy. It never occurred to them that these high ceilings, by allowing heated air to collect above the living zone, might actually keep the house cooler in summer. Adding a ceiling fan is both cost-efficient and energy-efficient, and does no violence to the special character of high-ceilinged rooms. I can think of more reasons to raise a ceiling than lower it, especially where some misbegotten remuddler turned a house into a church basement by "improving" the old ceilings with acoustical tile. No matter what lies under them, it couldn't be as bad as this depressing and tacky quick fix. Tear the stuff down and fix the old ceilings as soon as possible.

The only good reason I can think of for lowering a ceiling is to accommodate plumbing changes. An exception might be the kitchen. Here, a high ceiling requires impractical extra-tall cabinets or some sort of soffit construction from which ordinary cabinets are hung. Some modern kitchen designers find this unbearable. Although there's something to the argument against high ceilings and small rooms on proportional grounds, dropping a ceiling could do irreparable damage to the "rightness" of a house by cutting off an important element of its connection with the past. Uprooting the whole tree is a poor way to prune an overabundance of foliage. Besides, kitchen soffits are a good place to hide those troublesome plumbing changes and heating ducts.

Although it's not cheap, traditional matchboarding is versatile. It can be used to finish both porch and interior ceilings as well as for wainscoting.

Wood-Ceiling Detail

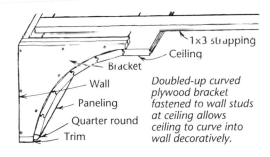

1x3 strapping
Ceiling
Bracket
Wall
Paneling
Quarter round
Trim

Doubled-up curved plywood bracket fastened to wall studs at ceiling allows ceiling to curve into wall decoratively.

A Note on Trim

Many old-house owners, in the belief that "natural" must always be better, are convinced that all interior woodwork and trim should be liberated of its paint, so that the bare wood can express its true nature fortified by an oil or varnish finish. But unless the underlying wood is a species worth rescuing, such as cherry, walnut, mahogany, oak or other semiprecious hardwood, it's usually not worth the effort. Most woodwork was painted because it lacked any particularly interesting grain. With many softwoods and even some hardwoods, the paint is absorbed into the surface so that it cannot be entirely removed without sanding away a great deal of wood.

Trim that has accumulated so much paint that its detail is lost or that has been the victim of previous careless stripping can benefit from stripping before repainting. A little detective work will determine whether the underlying work is worth rescuing. Select an inconspicuous piece of trim and, with a single-edged razor blade, carefully excavate the paint strata, one layer at a time. If it's paint all the way to the bottom, the wood is probably only worth painting. If you uncover a layer of varnish or shellac, the wood was probably interesting enough to someone to leave it unpainted.

Stripping trimwork *in situ* is one of the least stimulating tasks imaginable. It's easier to remove the trim, number and record its location and take it to a commercial strip shop. Although the hot-dipping process does leave a fuzzy grain that will have to be sanded smooth, this isn't a major problem (except for precious antiques, which must always be cold-stripped to avoid raising the grain). Seal hot-dipped wood with shellac before sanding to stiffen the fibers.

The key to removing moldings and other painted trimwork without splitting them is to break the paint bead first with a putty knife inserted along the margin of the molding. A trick experts use to loosen the piece is to insert a chisel, heavy screwdriver or small prybar between two putty knives and lift up. This opens a crack into which a larger prybar can be inserted, without damaging the edges of the trim piece.

A flatbar (such as a Wonderbar®) is the tool of choice for the actual removal. Place a flat block of wood between the bar and the wall or ceiling to prevent damage, and gently pry along its length, gradually widening the gap. Don't hurry and try to pull off the piece too quickly.

A good deal of the nails will pull through the back of the wood. Cut those that won't budge with a hacksaw blade. Drive any protruding nails into the wall rather than risk damaging the finish by trying to remove them. Pull out any nails left in the trim piece from the back side with nipping pliers to avoid splintering the face side. The curved edge of a vise-grip plier will lever out the most stubborn nail. Last, scratch or stamp a identifying mark into the back of the piece, since pencil or markers will not withstand the stripping process. Neither will glass. If you strip old window sashes, remove the glass first, or else apply cold stripper yourself.

Finished at Last:
The Floors

The floors of an old house are an archaeological adventure. The various dynasties of a house's past are chronicled in the flooring strata. Rare is the old house without at least one layer over the original floorboards. Tired of scrubbing at the scars left by years of heedless boot heels, progressive housewives of the post-Civil War era soon had the old "hard pine" floors of the much-trafficked ground-floor rooms covered over with new and readily available hardwood strip flooring. Upstairs floors, much less abused, were only painted — with countless coats of steel-grey, iron-hard paint.

Excavate the floor before the ceilings and walls are finished. The old baseboards, trapped behind several layers of later additions, can then be removed from the wall without danger of splitting and saved for refinishing.

Most often, the topmost layer of flooring is a battered sheet of linoleum. Since this wildly popular flooring material remained in use for over a century (invented in 1863, production ceased only in 1974), there's a good chance you'll need to dig through more than one layer of the stuff. Usually, the cement has become so dry that the old linoleum can easily be taken up with a wide, stiff putty knife, although either a square-edged shovel or ice scraper, when sharpened with a file, will be faster and easier on the back. The same method of attack will work for asphalt floor tile and glued-down carpet. A bit of close work with a paint scraper should remove any stubborn patches of old adhesive, to reveal the same hardwood strip floor that someone couldn't stand to wax or wash one more time.

Personally, I despise strip flooring. Perhaps because of childhood associations with school corridors, the stuff somehow just seems too hard for comfortable living. Curiously, wider plank floors don't have that impersonal feel. Why the width of floorboards should make such a difference defies analysis. Why is it that wide-board floors are prized above all others? Perhaps it is the difference between the signature of the machine and a filet of a living tree; there's more life to the wood.

Nevertheless, unless the flooring is warped and damaged beyond repair, there is no structural reason to take up a hardwood floor—especially since it might be covering a really bad floor. Repairs are generally not hard to make.

Repairing floors

Squeaks are usually caused by slightly warped or shrunken boards that rock up and down in response to weight. The cure is to drive finish nails at an angle into both sides of the tongue-and-groove joint. Drive a flooring nail into the underlying joist to tighten down loose floorboards. If a joist is not convenient, drive two nails at opposing angles into the subfloor. Drill pilot holes first. Screws will usually work where nails fail. Make the pilot hole through the floorboard slightly wider than the screw, so that it pulls the board into the subfloor rather than tending to push it up. Countersink the head and fill with a dowel plug. If the floor can be accessed from underneath, the screws won't show.

The only practical way to replace a cracked or rotted strip of flooring is to split it out. Use a carbide blade in a circular saw set to the depth of the flooring and saw down the middle of the board to be removed. Finish the cut at the ends with a chisel. Pry up the split pieces. Oak, birch and maple strip flooring are readily available. Other species or nonstandard widths can be custom-milled from square-edged stock. To fit the replacement piece, saw off the bottom edge of the groove. Spread a bead of construction adhesive on the subfloor and face-nail the patch with finish nails—cleats attached to the faces of the joists support the replacement flooring. Set the nails and fill with colored putty.

If you share my feelings about hardwood strip floors and investigations in other parts of the house have revealed softwood floors beneath, salvage the old hardwood—for reuse on a countertop, a workbench or for someone else's floors—and dig further to uncover the underlying original flooring. Some old-growth pine, spruce and hemlock was denser and had a higher resin content than second-grown timber; the characteristic patina of old softwood flooring cannot be reproduced with new wood, even after years of mellowing. To my mind, the value of this treasure is so great that it should not remain hidden under a plebeian hardwood strip floor.

Strip flooring is removed with the least damage if it is pulled up from the tongue side. Since flooring is always laid tongue out, the last board laid (which is usually narrower than the first board) is where you start. Remove the baseboard and insert the curved end of a flatbar into the gap between the edge of the board and the wall (if there's room). If the gap is too tight, split the flooring apart at the next joint. If you're lucky, the old nails will be more rust than metal, and most of the strips will lift up without splitting. As long as the face side is intact, the pieces are reusable. When you have room enough to work, stand facing the flooring and drive the blunt end of a pinchbar under the boards. Lift up and push them away from the nails; pulling with the curved end of the bar tends to cause more damage. Pull out any protruding nails and sweep the area clean.

Refinishing floors

The original wide boards, sawn from trees larger than any growing today, won't look like much. It takes an act of faith to see the clear grain masked by the grime of years, pocked with nail holes and separated by wide rubble-filled gaps. It takes more than faith to exhume the wood hidden under that cladding of paint.

Prepare the floor for refinishing before renting a drum sander. Nail down any loose boards. Set all nailheads at least 1/8 in. below the surface. Clean out old caulk or

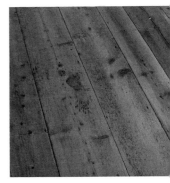

Flooring cut from old-growth hard pine is denser than today's lumber, with small, tight knots, similar to spruce. When stripped of paint, sanded and refinished, even these relatively narrow boards make a beautiful floor.

other debris from the cracks between boards with a screwdriver. Patch-in missing boards. If there are more than a few badly split or rotted boards, or if the gaps between them are excessive, it might be possible to take up the entire floor and relay it without too much trouble. Check the attic or barn: These are often partly floored with boards of the same age and species as the main floor. Otherwise, new wood must be colored to blend in with the old. Applying a chemical paint stripper to loosen the first few layers of old paint will save a lot of sandpaper and sweat.

Although rented drum sanders are not as powerful or easy to use as those employed by professionals, the careful amateur can still do a reasonably good job. If you are unusually lucky, the rental agent may actually know more about running the machine than just how to tighten the belts. In any case, take home more belts than you think you'll need; until you get the feel for the machine, you'll tear several to pieces the moment the drum hits the floor. Besides, unused belts are returnable and you don't want to run short.

Here are some tips on running a drum sander. Always work with the grain, never across it. Cross-grain sanding not only leaves hard-to-remove scratches, the sander also follows the dips and humps in the floor instead of leveling them. The speed at which the machine pulls itself across the floor will determine the depth of the cut. Never let it linger in one place or it will scoop out the wood. Ease the sanding drum into and out of action by leaning it on its backstop. It should be running at full speed when it contacts the floor and shut off only after contact is broken.

At the end of a pass, pull the sander backward over the cut to pick up sawdust and smooth it out. Overlap each pass 3 in. to 4 in. If the dust bag is emptied before it fills up, a lot less dust will escape into the rest of the house. Even so, you'll need to wear a dust mask, especially when sanding painted wood. Since this sawdust could be toxic, don't use it for mulching the shrubbery. To avoid sanding through the cord, sling it over your shoulder.

On painted floors, start with 32/0 coarse open-coat paper, which won't clog as fast as other grits. The same grade is also used for badly worn and pitted, cupped and irregular floors where a great deal of material must be removed. This is the grade you'll need the most of.

Once the wood is clean and level, the rest of the job is dedicated to smoothing out the scratches left by this initial sanding. Start the restoration with 60-grit or 80-grit paper. On unpainted and more-or-less level floors (especially hardwood), the coarser of these can often be used for the cutting coat. If the 80-grit clogs too quickly, use 60-grit. When the scratches have been reduced to faint swirls and the grain is beginning to stand out from the background, the floor is ready for fine sanding —100-grit will generally do for softwood floors; hardwood may require an additional pass with 150-grit paper. Wear crepe-soled shoes or socks while finish-sanding, or you risk marring the wood. The finished floor will be smooth to the touch. Look at the floor obliquely under strong light to check for dished-out areas

Sanding floors requires patience and skill. Here, the gouges left by careless use of the edger are highlighted by the stain. The surface has also been dished out by unskilled work with the drum sander.

left by the sanding drum or any renegade scratches. The job is done when you can see clear, unscratched grain in the knots.

An edge sander is used in corners, along walls and in areas too small or awkward for the drum sander to reach. The edger follows each pass of the drum sander using the same grits. Remove the baseboards first. Use a sharp chisel or scraper to pare down the arc at the inside of each corner where the edger can't reach, and smooth it with a finish sander or a piece of sandpaper wrapped around a block of wood. Sometimes, especially when the grain runs in the wrong direction, the edge sander is the only machine that can reach into closets and hallways. If you're lucky, there won't be too many places like this, since no better torture for the lower back could be imagined than the stooped-over position demanded by the edger.

Clean the finish-sanded floors with an industrial-strength vacuum cleaner, paying particular attention to the cracks between the boards. Go over the floors once more with a tack cloth; you'll be surprised how much dust the vacuum cleaner left behind.

The selection of a floor finish defies easy resolution. Every type of finish has its partisans, who recommend it above all others and condemn any alternatives. Basically, there are only two kinds of floor finishes: penetrating oils or surface resins. A penetrating finish (such as linseed or tung oil, or "Danish" oils such as Watco®) is generally easy to renew by simply cleaning and adding another coat. Surface coatings, such as varnish, polyurethane and other synthetic resin finishes, have more resistance to scratches, but look the worse for it and can be renewed only by stripping and sanding. The choice comes down to soaking your floors in oil or covering them with plastic.

A penetrating oil finish will help maintain the patina of a fine, old softwood floor. Spar (marine) varnish makes an excellent finish for hardwood strip floors. A splintery softwood floor can be rescued

with a polyurethane glaze. The real problem with polyurethane is its unpredictable bonding to previously finished wood (even after sanding) or response to temperature and moisture conditions, which can cause a cloudy finish. New water-based polyurethanes are easier to apply. They dry so fast that you can recoat in a day, but they are expensive.

Three or four coats of gloss urethane is the most wear-resistant finish you could apply over hardwood, especially for floors that aren't subjected to heavy traffic. Bedroom floors will remain like new forever, whereas kitchen floors will need refinishing every four or five years unless people get into the habit of taking off their shoes at the door. Never wax polyurethane, as it makes refinishing impossible.

Whatever finish you choose, follow the directions on the label religiously. And give some thought as to where you'll live while the finish cures. Not only must the rooms be kept heated and ventilated (which is hard to do in the winter), but a house full of evaporating hydrocarbons is neither pleasant nor healthy to live in. This is another argument for using water-based polyurethane.

In spite of your efforts with the vacuum cleaner, the cracks between wide boards will still contain sanding grit and flakes of debris that are easily picked up by the brush bristles. To imprison the dust and reduce further frustration, first flood the cracks with floor finish as you start to coat the floorboards proper. Wider cracks can be filled after the first sealing coat is dry with lampblack-tinted glazing compound. Force the material into the cracks with a putty knife and then wipe the surface clean with mineral solvents before applying the second and third finish coats.

The beauty of old floorboards is worth the effort of uncovering, sanding and refinishing. New wood, even when stained, cannot duplicate their tone. More than a color, it is a palpable warmth distilled from the heart of the wood.

The Electrical System

Electricity becomes uncontrolled when the wrong kinds of materials are used or when the right kinds of materials are wrongly installed.

—H. P. Richter, *Practical Electrical Wiring* (New York: McGraw-Hill Book Co., 1972)

The entrance panel is the heart of the household electrical system.

*L*ying in bed on some cold nights, poised on the edge of sleep, I hear a noise that seems to come from within the walls of the house. It is the 60-cycle hum of electric current, the sound you hear when there is no other sound. Sometimes the sound fills the entire house, pounding like an idling diesel engine outside the windows. The very walls vibrate. I wake my wife and ask her if she can hear it too. She can. We both lie awake, stomachs tight, listening to the walls pulse. Adult as we are, it is still frightening, and the point is that electricity itself can be frightening. There are those who cannot fix a plug, who react to a spark with the same terror as they react to a lightning bolt. Others find it a mystical and irrational force. But if electricity is thought of as invisible water, it becomes friendlier—electrical problems are remarkably similar to plumbing problems.

Basic Electrical Theory

Water flowing through a pipe exerts pressure, which is expressed in pounds per square inch. When electricity flows through a wire, the pressure is expressed as volts. The rate of flow for water is measured in gallons per minute; the rate of flow for electricity is measured in amps. The friction of water against the walls of the pipe is measured in poises; with electricity, this friction is called resistance and is measured in ohms. The longer the wire, the greater the resistance. To reduce friction and the need for stronger pumps, larger pipes are needed to carry increased volumes of water. The same is true of wires: They must increase in diameter to carry larger currents over longer distances. The electrical analog to the loss of pressure that occurs in water pipes over long distances is a "voltage drop." Heat is the byproduct of electrical resistance, which is why an undersized extension cord can melt down.

The relationship between these aspects of electrical flow is contained in Ohm's Law: volts x amps = watts. Watts are a measure of the work done by electricity, convertible both to horsepower (kinetic energy) and Btus (thermal energy). Water is sold by the cubic foot, electricity by the kilowatt hour (kwh), with 1,000 watts being used for one hour.

Just as water flows through the empty space contained within waterproof pipes, electricity flows through the spaces between atoms in conductors, bound by an electrically impermeable insulator. In a water circuit, such as an outdoor fountain, water is pumped from a reservoir and then collected and returned. In an electric circuit, a current flows because of a difference in potential between source and ground—the charge. This charge is positive with respect to the ground, which is negative (think of high and low). A lightning bolt is nothing more than a very big spark that marks the completion of a circuit between positively charged clouds and negatively charged earth. Like water flowing downhill or heat moving from warm to cold, electricity is pumped from a source—the generator at a power station—to your house and then returned by the ground. Think of the ground as an omnipresent wire connecting everything with the generator.

An electric current flows whenever there is a continuous path between its source and a ground. Along the way, it will perform tricks like turning motors, heating coils and emitting light, according to whatever device is inserted in the circuit. When a pipe springs a leak, the water will flow until the reservoir is emptied. An electrical reservoir is, for all practical purposes, infinite. If a leak (a short circuit) occurs in an electrical insulator, all the power, all the way back to the generator, will flow through it to ground, unless some protective device intervenes first. A short circuit allows more current to flow through a wire than it can hold, increasing resistance and heat until the insulation melts and the wires and the house surrounding them burn up. A fuse is simply a thinner wire that vaporizes first, breaking the circuit and preventing the flow of current. A circuit breaker is a heat-sensitive switch that opens when a preset current limit is exceeded. Proper circuit protection and grounding are critical—consult one of the electrical wiring manuals listed in the Bibliography (pp. 334-338) for details.

Real (as opposed to schematic) electricity runs through standard color-coded wires. For the sake of safety, the National Electrical Code (and common sense) insists that this code be strictly followed. The basic house-wiring circuit consists of a black "hot" wire and a white "neutral" wire. Chassis grounds or grounds between an appliance case and the wall outlet, via the power cord, are always green.

The code also specifies that all metal fixture boxes and wiring devices be connected to an independent continuous ground. This is the bare copper wire observed alongside the other conductors in plastic-jacketed cable or armored (steel-jacketed or BX) cable. The ground protects against shock should there be a short circuit between the device and its box. When more than one hot wire is needed, the extra conductor is usually red. Switches and plugs are likewise coded for polarity. Brass-colored terminals are always connected to the black or red (hot) wire; the white (neutral) wire connects to the silver-colored terminals, and the bare or green (ground) wire to the green screw.

Alternating current

Because alternating current (AC), unlike direct current (DC), can be transmitted over large distances without excessive voltage drop, it is the most commonly used form of power. In this country, the current changes polarity 60 times (or cycles) per second. Power comes into the home through two hot wires and a neutral wire. At a given moment, the charge on one of these wires with respect to the ground is 110 volts positive while the other is 110 volts negative. But if these current pulses are properly timed (in phase), the voltages will add together instead of canceling out, which means that the power coming into the house is 220 volts, measured across both hot wires.

A 220-volt service makes it possible to deliver two different voltages into the house: 110 volts for devices that consume relatively little power, and 220 volts for those with a greater appetite. Electricity travels from the power station at high voltage to a stepdown transformer mounted on the pole outside your house, where it is reduced to 220 volts. Power through the "service drop," the connection between pole and house proper, is measured by the electric company's meter before it feeds into the entrance panel. This box contains a safety device, the main breaker, which will shut off all the power to the house, and a number of circuit breakers to protect and distribute power to individual circuits at the appropriate voltages and capacities. Older installations rely on plug- and cartridge-type fuses for circuit protection. The house's electrical system radiates out from the entrance panel like nerves from the brain stem.

Evaluating Your Electrical System

Thomas Edison designed and supervised the first electric power system in New York City in the 1880s. Until 1897, when pressure from insurance companies and fire marshals led to the adoption of the first National Electrical Code (NEC), the installation of house wiring was haphazard and frequently unsafe. But by the close of the 1920s, the electrical appliances that we take for granted today had become standard features of the American household, and electrical systems had advanced to the point where they would not be unrecognizable to a modern electrician.

There is no law that requires you to improve or replace the wiring in an old house, but the NEC does require that any new work conform to current standards. Likewise, the code doesn't state that you can't do your own electrical work. But municipal regulations vary. Some (mostly rural) impose no restrictions, others provide only that any work must pass an inspection for conformance to the code, while others (usually cities) allow only licensed professionals to fool with wiring. Sometimes a lending institution requires that the work be inspected or performed only by professionals, local ordinances notwithstanding.

Even if there are no restrictions, doing your own wiring is a job that should be undertaken with extreme caution. An improperly wired house is a fire hazard. Carelessly handled, electricity can and does kill. Complicated jobs are often best left to professionals. An experienced electrician can make sense of the rat's nest of wires and feeds, three-way switches and other enigmas that may greet you upon ripping into a wall, and have it neatly rewired before you could even find the hot wire.

If there's only one circuit to move, by all means consider doing the work yourself. Since the language of the code is incomprehensible to the ordinary mortal, you should definitely purchase one of the many easily understood wiring guidebooks that interpret it for you.

Types of wiring systems

The earliest electrical installations used "knob and tube" wiring. In this system, rubber-coated conductors were run between wall studs or floor joists, protected by porcelain insulators (the tubes) where they passed through a framing member, or wrapped around other insulators (the knobs) where they passed over framing or changed direction. Since each conductor was separated from the other by several inches, these installations were actually quite safe, unless, as was frequently done, the wires were routed through old gas piping or buried under plaster. The lime in plaster would eat away the insulation. So would rats. Even worse, the rubber coat-

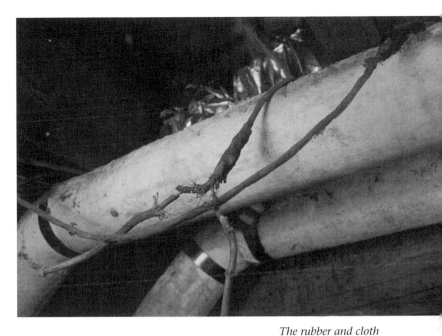

The rubber and cloth insulation used on old wiring becomes brittle with age and cracks. The exposed bare conductors, if left live, are hazardous and one of the leading causes of house fires.

ings became brittle with age and cracked, causing short circuits and fires. Still, it's not unusual to find modern wiring spliced into part of an old knob-and-tube network in a remote part of the cellar or attic. The most dangerous situation is when such hybrids are hidden behind a wall.

Cloth-covered rubber-insulated cable was a later improvement, but it also tended to break down over time. If your wiring system uses a black braided-fabric outer shell covering a pair of rubber-coated conductors, I'd consider replacing it. Also suspect is the later silver braided-cloth cable. Here, the rubber-covered conductors were often wrapped in jute and paper as well, which would absorb moisture and eventually rot the insulation.

Under normal circumstances, the plastic jacket of modern nonmetallic cable (type NM or Romex®) is almost indestructible and much safer than any of its predecessors. Steel-armored cable (BX) is also safe, unless it is in a moist location where it could rust. As long as the rest of the installation is properly done, two-conductor cable that lacks a separate ground conductor is not inherently unsafe. Although the risk of a shock is negligible, never plug appliances or motors into two-conductor outlets without the protection of a proper grounding adapter. It's safer than trusting that the wiring was done correctly.

As successive owners struggled to adapt their house wiring to the demands of increased electrical usage, the wiring often became tangled up in a web of over-extended circuits and mismatched cables. Sometimes, a previous attempt to "modernize" the wiring could result in a situation more dangerous than the one it replaced, especially when the alterations were performed by unknowing home owners. There is one especially hazardous condition, which professional electricians inadvertently helped create. Throughout the 1960s, aluminum was promoted as a low-cost alternative to expensive copper cable. The wiring devices for connection to this cable, although listed as safe, turned out not to be. The connections would corrode and short out. It wasn't until 1971 that the UL (Underwriter's Laboratories) called for stricter listings. In the meantime, many houses and lives were lost to fires that could have been avoided.

If your house was rewired with aluminum cable, it's a good reason to rip out and redo the electrical system. If the walls are already gutted, you have an excellent opportunity to ensure your safety and peace of mind by renovating the wiring, whatever type of cable it may contain. Renewing the electrical system without removing the walls can be done, but I'd hate to hire an electrician to do it. It's slow work, and unless you are funded by a historic preservation grant, too costly for the average budget.

Inadequate wiring usually begins at the service drop. Houses wired before the advent of electric ranges and clothes dryers might have 60-amp service. I've even seen isolated farmhouses wired for 30-amp service. Today, the minimum rating for electrical service is 100 amps; 200-amp service is required for electric heating or for 100-amp service more than 300 ft. from the power pole. The electric company will run its wire from the transformer to a wall or mast-mounted weatherhead, and also provide the meter. The rest of the service installation is up to you. Since code requirements are fairly numerous, this is one place where hiring an electrician might make sense, unless you really do know what you're doing.

The utility company has the sole legal right to tinker with the meter they install in your meter box. They own it. There is a plastic seal affixed to the lock, and if it is broken, they can hold you liable and impose all sorts of penalties, especially if they think you were trying to tamper with the meter to cheat them out of their rightful profits. I know of several people who had need upon occasion to disconnect a meter for perfectly legitimate reasons, such as turning off the power while moving or replacing a service entrance panel. Reversing the meter to make it run backwards was not their intent. These people simply broke the seal and removed the meter, thereby shutting off the power. But I certainly wouldn't recommend that course to you, even in a rural area. Instead, let the utility company handle it.

From the meter box, the entrance cable proceeds to the entrance panel by the "most direct path." Considering the cost of the cable, there's an incentive to comply with this code directive. Depending on code specifications, the meter box and/or the service panel are grounded to a buried steel water main or an 8-ft. long copper-clad steel rod driven fully into the earth. The diameter of the entrance cables will indicate the rating of the service feed in the unlikely event that the fuses or main breaker are not marked. Stranded conductors rated for 100-amp service are about ¼ in. in diameter, without their insulation; 60-amp conductors are about ³⁄₁₆ in. in diameter.

As electrical needs increased, cables radiated outward like tentacles from the undersized service panel to satellite sub-feed panels or distribution boxes, stuffed with the fuses, breakers, switches and splices dedicated to the burgeoning circuitry. For the sake of simplicity alone, if not safety, these jungles should be clear-cut and a new entrance panel with adequate capacity installed. Even relatively recently upgraded installations can sometimes cause trouble.

Entrance cable is almost always aluminum. Although the terminals inside the panel are not supposed to react with this metal, the connections sometimes corrode or loosen, especially if an antioxidant coating (No-Al-Ox) was not applied first. Corrosion increases resistance, which leads to a potentially dangerous heat buildup or arcing to ground, which can cause the neutral wire to become sporadically energized. Circuit breakers can also become corroded, especially in damp cellars. This has the effect of increasing the amount of current needed to trip the breaker. When a circuit designed for 20 amps is overloaded to 25 amps before the breaker opens, the fire hazard is more than theoretical. Routinely tripping the breakers once a month will help prevent corrosion buildup.

The service cable feeds into the entrance panel. Each conductor is connected to lugs on the main breaker, which also functions as a disconnect switch. In older systems, the disconnect switch was typically separate from the service panel. Sub-feed boxes usually don't have disconnects either. The strands of the aluminum jacket are twisted together to form a wire, which is fastened to the main grounding lug. Flat metal bars (the "bus bars") deliver the current to the individual circuit breakers. The hot (black) wires from each circuit are connected to the breaker terminals. The grounding bus is fitted with screw terminals for the neutral (white) leads and bare conductor ground wires. Special ganged breakers enable both black and white leads, or black and red leads, to tap 220-volt instead of 110-volt power.

Designing a Circuit

A few basic principles distilled from the welter of code requirements govern residential circuit design. The most important is that the total current draw on a circuit not exceed 80% of its capacity. Recalling Ohm's Law, it's obvious that this requirement determines wire sizes, lengths of circuit runs, the number and wattage of fixtures, circuit-breaker ratings, and whether or not you can perc the coffee at the same time you toast your muffins. The code also insists that lighting circuits for bedrooms, living rooms and hallways contain no more than 12 outlets and/or fixtures, protected by a 15-amp breaker. Circuits for kitchen plugs or outlets must be separate from the lighting circuit.

The code calls for at least two 20-amp appliance circuits to handle the current demands of a modern kitchen. Anything with a motor or a large heating element, such as a refrigerator, freezer, water pump, water heater, electric range, dishwasher, clothes dryer or air conditioner, is required to have its own individual circuit, with wire size and capacity determined by the wattage or horsepower of the appliance. Finally, because of the probability that someone with wet feet or hands could encounter an electrical device, the bathroom and any outdoor outlets must be protected by a Ground-Fault Interrupter (GFI), a device that automatically breaks the circuit within microseconds at the slightest flow of current from hot to ground, which means that you won't fry if you are standing in bare feet on the wet floor and touch an appliance that is electrically live.

Since normal household circuits (not including heater, range or dryer type) use either 15-amp or 20-amp breakers with 14-gauge or 12-gauge wire (the smaller the number, the larger the wire), circuit design is basically a matter of adding up the wattages of each proposed fixture or appliance and seeing if the total is within the 80% of maximum capacity specified by the code (actually the total is adjusted by a demand factor, since it's unlikely all the fixtures will be in use at the same time). The current-carrying ability of a wire depends not only on its gauge, but on the length of the circuit. Your electrical handbook should include tables for sizing wires to loads.

So to answer the important question posed above, given a 20-amp breaker, can you run a coffee maker and a toaster oven at the same time? The plate on the bottom of the toaster oven says 1,050 watts, the one on the percolator, 700 watts. The maximum capacity of a 20-amp circuit is 20a x 110v = 2,200w; the allowable load (80%) is 1,760 watts. You can toast and brew without blowing a fuse and have the satisfaction that you are also complying with the code. Adequate capacity is the rationale for two or more separate kitchen outlet circuits.

One more example. What size breaker is required for an electric clothes dryer? The dryer contains two elements that draw 5,000 watts at full tilt. But the dryer also is wired for 220 volts. Thus 5,000 ÷ 220 = 23 amps, which is the current it will draw. Twenty-four is 80% of 30, which means that the dryer should have a 30-amp breaker, and use 10-gauge wire for the connection (this from standard tables). If the dryer had been wired at only 110 volts, it would have drawn over 45 amps, twice the current, which is why it's more economical to use higher voltages to meet large demands.

Rewiring an Old House

Rewiring old houses without tearing out the walls or pulling down ceilings is more a problem of carpentry than electricity. It's a game of hide-and-seek, where you look for hidden wires and reroute them through or around unseen obstacles. If, as they say, one picture equals one kw (kiloword, not kilowatt), then the rulebook for this sometimes frustrating game is found in the drawings in the rest of this chapter.

Tools for rewiring

Before discussing the moves of the game, a few notes on the playing pieces. The fishwire, used to pull cables through walls and around corners, is indispensable. Although you can manage with one, there are cases where two are useful. You'll also need a ½-in. right-angle-drive heavy-duty drill. Ordinary home-handyman ⅜-in. drills don't have enough torque and power to drive the 16-in. or longer electrician's augers you'll need to bore through multiple layers of framing or between floors. The angle-drive feature makes it possible to bore between stud cavities, which you couldn't do with a regular straight-drive drill. Since a contractor-grade drill can cost upward of $200, you may want to rent one if your rewiring is not extensive.

For close work, you'll need a short (7¾-in.) "nail-eater" bit. The hardened steel chews through the inevitable hidden framing nails with ease. Fitted with one or more extension bits, your drill will fearlessly bore through just about anything. A neon-bulb circuit tester will show you if a wire is live, but a pocket-sized multi-tester is a lot handier, since it gives voltage and resistance readings as well. Plug-in circuit analyzers are also useful. When plugged into an outlet, the combination of glowing lights indicates whether the circuit is correctly wired or, if not, what is wrong with it. This will prove invaluable when troubleshooting the handiwork of the previous home electrician, who may have been color blind when it came to observing the wiring color code. Finally, you'll need a wire stripper/crimping tool, insulated electrician's pliers, an insulated screwdriver, needle-nosed pliers and the usual basic carpenter's tools.

Surface-mounted wiring systems

If you're less than excited at the prospect of trying to hide wires behind fragile moldings and crumbling plaster, or crawling through dusty insulation and attic cobwebs to fish the lost end of a cable up a blind hole, there is an alternative. You can add a fixture, switch or outlet with one of the numerous readily available surface-mounted wiring systems. In these systems, single-conductor wire (type THHN) or regular plastic-jacketed cable is routed through metal or plastic raceways between boxes that hold the individual wiring devices. All the components are screwed to walls, ceilings and baseboard moldings by mounting tabs, and are usually painted to match the wall finish. Where exposed cable is not objectionable (garages, cellars, attics and outbuildings), the familiar dark brown Bakelite surface-mounted device is an inexpensive alternative.

Personally, I think of surface-mounted raceways as a means of last resort, just the thing a preservationist might approve of if forced to electrify a historic house, or the simplest way to power the light fixture the electrician forgot to wire without tearing down the finished ceilings. Otherwise, I feel that wiring is best hidden behind the walls, both for safety's and appearance's sakes. The drawings on pp. 273-275 show how to accomplish this with a minimum of destruction and frustration.

Wiring within the walls

Special outlet boxes with beveled rear corners and internal cable clamps simplify the procedure of adding new plastic-jacketed cable in a finished wall. The square corners of the boxes used for "new work" (installing wiring in the easily accessible bays of exposed framing, as opposed to the "old work" of retrofitting it to finished walls) bind the cable against the sides of the opening in the wall when you try to push the box into it, especially if cables enter at both the top and bottom of the box. By contrast, the sloped shoulders of old-work boxes permit the cables to slip

Even when you can trace a cable exposed between wall studs, labeling the feeds and other connections saves time, confusion and blown circuits.

Beveled-Corner Outlet Box for Old Work

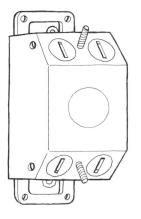

An outlet box with beveled corners and internal cable clamps simplifies retrofitting wiring to finished walls.

270

Installing an Outlet Box in a Plaster Wall

1. Locate studs. Drill test hole to find lath center and position template.

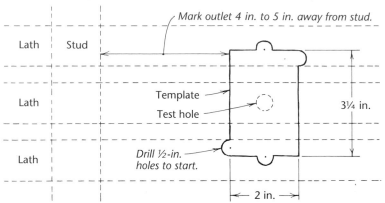

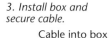

2. Cut box outline with keyhole saw. Cut away one lath and part of each of two others, never through two complete laths. Hold plaster to prevent it from breaking. Fish cable from opening into box.

3. Install box and secure cable.

Cable into box
Screw box to lath.

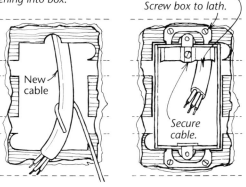

Secure cable.

you get carried away, drill a test hole through the underlying plaster lath. Since the box is best supported when only one complete lath piece is cut away, you may need to relocate the opening slightly. You also will need to notch the two laths above and below the one you have removed.

Once you've determined the exact location of the outlet, drill ½-in. holes at the points indicated on the template. Insert the tip of your keyhole saw and support the plaster with your hand while gently sawing through the lath. If you are using armored BX cable, you'll have to slip a connector clamp over the cable before you pull it into the box. Unfortunately, sloped boxes with internal clamps aren't available for BX cable, so there's no way to pull the box into the opening without pinching against the cables. Leave about 1 ft. of wire sticking out of the cable and into the box, and use this to pull the clamp up into the knockout after the box is installed, as shown in the top drawing on the facing page. Then secure the clamp by slipping a locknut over the wires and onto the clamp.

Unlike new-work boxes, which are designed to fasten directly to the studs with spikes, there are at least four ways to mount square-cornered or bevel-cornered old-work boxes in the wall, depending on whether the attachment is to wood, lath, plaster or drywall. The bottom drawing on the facing page shows how the mounting ears can be reversed to suit plaster or wood, how special compressible spring clamps anchor boxes to walls too flimsy to hold screws, and how special metal hanger strips pull the box against the back of drywall panels as the plug or switch is screwed into the box.

To avoid damaging irreplaceable wallpaper when cutting the outlet opening, first cut a flap in the paper with a sharp utility knife. Dampen the paper until the glue loosens enough so that you can carefully lift up the paper flap and tack it out of the way. Then cut the box opening,

back into the wall opening without pinching. But check your local code requirements before installing these boxes. Their smaller volume limits the number of connections and wires they can contain.

You can use an electronic stud-finder to locate the framing, though I've found that for electrical work, at least, all you need is to listen for the change from a hollow to a sharper tone while rapping along the wall with your knuckles. Use a template to mark the location of the new outlet box about 4 in. or 5 in. away from a stud (see the top drawing above). Before

Installing BX Cable in a Box

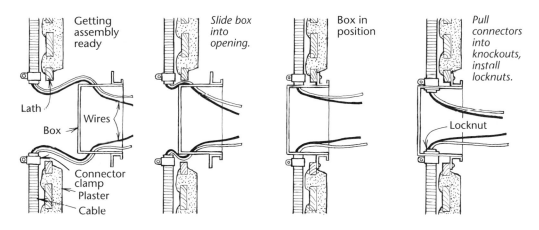

Getting assembly ready

Slide box into opening.

Box in position

Pull connectors into knockouts, install locknuts.

Lath

Box

Wires

Connector clamp

Plaster

Cable

Locknut

Fastening Old-Work Boxes to Existing Walls

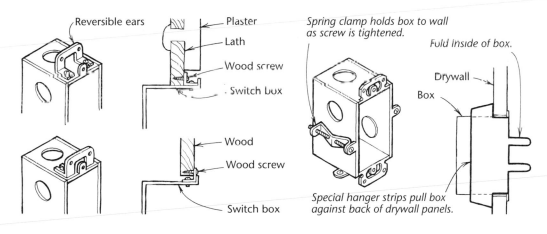

Reversible ears

Plaster

Lath

Wood screw

Switch box

Wood

Wood screw

Switch box

Spring clamp holds box to wall as screw is tightened.

Fold inside of box.

Drywall

Box

Special hanger strips pull box against back of drywall panels.

fold the paper back down, trim around the box and reglue. If the cut was neat and kept clean, the patch will be invisible.

It's often desirable for more than one wiring device to be included in an outlet box. Make sure that the boxes you use can be "ganged" together; there are some that won't permit this option. Ganging two or more boxes together (six is the most that cover plates are made for) is simply a mat-ter of loosening a screw to remove one side plate on each box and then hooking them together and tightening down the screws.

Another type of ganging occurs when a new outlet is added back-to-back to an existing one. Unless the existing box has an internal cable clamp, the only way to protect the wires running between the two boxes is to join them with a length of threaded ½-in. galvanized pipe nipple.

Shallow Boxes for Old Work

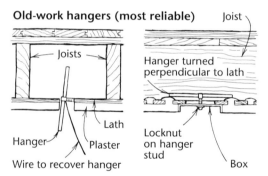

For direct attachment

For use with old-work hanger

For heavy ceiling fixtures

Joist
Plaster
Lath
Box
Wood screw

Install on substantial timber where possible.

For lighter ceiling fixtures

Wood screws
Box
Plaster
Lath

Mount box to two laths, not just one, to distribute weight of fixture.

Old-work hangers (most reliable)

Joist
Joists
Hanger
Lath
Plaster
Wire to recover hanger

Hanger turned perpendicular to lath
Locknut on hanger stud
Box

The code requirement for a 1½-in. minimum outlet box depth is waived for old work, where, for example, disturbing lath could loosen delicate ceiling plaster. Here, ½-in. deep boxes are allowed (see the drawing above). The boxes are screwed through plaster lath into a ceiling joist when supporting a heavy fixture, such as a chandelier. For less substantial fixtures, the box can be screwed directly to the lath. If an old-work hanger is used, the weight of the fixture will be distributed over numerous laths. The hanger is simply inserted up into an access hole, rotated perpendicular to the lath, and tightened down by a locknut when the shallow box is slipped over the hanger stud. Attach a piece of wire to the hanger when slipping it into the hole; then there's no danger of losing it between the ceiling joists or wall studs. Since there's no need to cut the lath with shallow boxes, these are ideally suited for working with the fragile plaster of old houses. But even when you work carefully, the vibration of a sawblade as it pulls through springy lath can break adjoining plaster keys.

Adding a switch

One of the most annoying things about old houses is their lack of outlets and switches. Not only is a thicket of extension cords sprouting from a single baseboard outlet unsightly, it's also a fire hazard. And anyone who has groped in the dark for the pullchain on a ceiling lamp would certainly appreciate the convenience of a wall switch to control room lights.

Adding a switch to control a wall-mounted light fixture already wired and controlled by a switch on the fixture itself is fairly simple. Begin by cutting the opening for the new switch. Then remove the baseboard and cut two more holes in the wall behind it, directly below the existing fixture and the new switch. With the power off, remove the fixture. Then slide a fishwire through a knockout in the outlet box and down the wall until it comes out at the hole at the baseboard. Attach the cable to the fishwire and pull them up into the fixture box. Next, run the fishwire from the new outlet box hole down to the other baseboard hole and snake the other end of the cable up into the opening.

Install the new switch box, and then connect the cable so it controls the light fixture. Before replacing the baseboard, cut a groove in the plaster and/or lath deep enough to accommodate the cable.

Be very careful not to drive any nails into the new cable when renailing. This same method is used to add additional wall outlets (for extra convenience, some of these could be switch-controlled) by tapping off existing ones.

Wiring between floors

Wiring changes are a lot less trouble if the new cables are run across the attic floor or between ceiling joists. Then, the only wall openings are for the new wiring devices. The fishwire is dropped into a hole bored through the wall plate. Attic floorboards (if any) are pried up and the underlying joists drilled to run the cable. There is no danger of splitting baseboards or cracking plaster where it could show. Just make sure you have correctly located the underlying partition before drilling. You don't want to find the point of an auger sticking out of the ceiling or the face of the wall. Because partitions are usually built to the joists before the ceilings are put up, the top of the wall should be plainly visible from the attic, once any insulation has been pushed aside.

Since cellars are even more accessible than attics, it might seem even easier to make first-floor wiring changes by simply boring up into the partitions from below. As long as you can accurately locate interior partitions from below boards (look for nails protruding through the subfloor or take measurements from known points), this is certainly the case. But when the wire must run through an outside wall, the foundation and sills will obstruct any simple boring. Instead, bore up into the wall cavity at an angle from the cellar or, if the space between the floor joists is inaccessible, down from above, after removing the baseboard.

Things get more complicated when a cable must run between floors and into partitions. Since it's likely that the top of the partition will be blocked by a plate, you'll need to make a temporary opening at the top of the wall, as shown in the drawing at right. If there is a ceiling crown

Running Cable from a Ceiling Fixture to a Wall Outlet

1. To get cable from A to B, make temporary hole at C.

2. Feed first fishwire through C and out A.

3. Feed second fishwire through C and out B.

4. Hook fishwires together at C. Push into hole.

5. Attach cable to fishwire and pull from A out B.

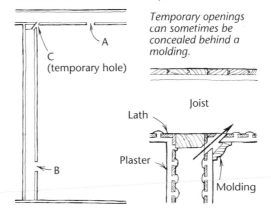

molding, it can be removed and the hole concealed behind it. Otherwise, you'll have to spackle the hole over later.

To run a cable from the ceiling fixture to the wall outlet (or down into the cellar), feed one fishwire into the temporary hole and wiggle it along the joists until it can be pulled out the ceiling opening. Feed a second fishwire into the temporary hole and out through the wall opening. To do this right, you'll have to use a fishwire with hooks at both ends, not the single-ended kind that rolls up into a dispenser. Hook the fishwires together at the temporary opening and pop them back into the wall. Pull one of the wires until you have a continuous loop from ceiling to wall outlet. Then attach the cable and, feeding it into the ceiling hole, pull it out the wall with a fishwire.

Running Cable between Floors with Partitions above Each Other

1. Remove upper-floor baseboard. Bore down through top plate of lower wall.

2. Bore second hole through sole plate of upper wall.

3. Insert fishwire and work down through plates.

4. Pull out fishwire at B to run cable from A to B.

or

5. Bore up into partition from cellar at C, insert second fishwire to hook first wire.

6. Attach cable to fishwire and pull from A to C.

You can also loop cable so that the circuit runs from A to B to C.

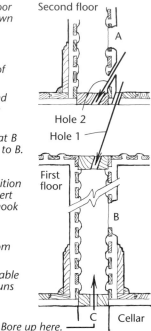

Second floor

A

Hole 2

Hole 1

First floor

B

Bore up here. ——— C   Cellar

To run cable between floors when the partitions are directly over each other, first remove the baseboard of the upper partition and bore a hole downward through the top plate of the lower partition. Then bore a second hole through the sole plate of the upper partition. Push the fishwire through this hole and work it down into the lower partition. You'll probably need to snag it with a second fishwire worked up from the outlet opening in the wall below. If the upper outlet is to be mounted in the baseboard, use the fishwire to pull the cable from that point down and out the opening in the lower partition. Otherwise, push the end of the first fishwire back into the upper partition and snag it with yet another fishwire (a bent coat hanger can also do the job) fed into the wall from the new outlet opening.

When the partitions on the two floors are offset from each other, bore a temporary access hole at the top of the lower partition and another behind the baseboard of the upper wall, as shown in the top drawing on the facing page. Then, as with the installation of the ceiling fixture, use two fishwires to run the cable. The operational principle is always to end up with a single loop of fishwire between the two points for pulling cable.

In these examples, we have assumed that the cables were run parallel with the ceiling joists. Since you obviously can't push a fishwire or cable through solid framing, a length of the overlying flooring must be removed to run cable perpendicular to the joists. It's easier to take up flooring than to refinish a plaster or drywall ceiling. Square-edged softwood boards are not hard to pry up with an ordinary chisel. Attic floorboards are often not even nailed down. But lifting tongue-and-groove hardwood strip flooring isn't so easy (see p. 259). Once the joists are exposed, they can be notched or drilled for the cable. Any holes bored through the flooring are filled with plugs of matching hardwood.

Not all electrical obstructions are between floors. Sometimes a cable has to turn a corner. If you can't run the cable in a groove behind the baseboard, use the temporary-hole technique described previously to bore through the corner post. Use two fishwires to pull the cable through the corner.

When the wall is interrupted by a door, the cable can either be looped down into a cellar or into the ceiling joist cavity. Otherwise, remove the door casings, cut a channel into the jack studs and across the header and run the cable around the door. To be safe, I'd use armored cable here, to protect it from unwitting puncture.

In new work, studs are bored for cables near their middle to reduce the likelihood that a trim or paneling nail will pierce the wire. Even then, carpenters typically note the location of the wires and avoid nailing near them. When running wires between lath across the faces of studs or through notches cut into the edge of a joist, use the steel plates left over from ganged boxes to protect these shallow wires. If a cable has been concealed in a notch cut across the top of an exposed ceiling beam, it should be run through a length of galvanized steel pipe. Thin-walled electrical conduit will not deflect a nail. If you need to fit more than a single cable in this pipe, use individual type THHN wires instead. You can fit up to five conductors in the same space occupied by a single Romex® wire.

Other wiring solutions

Another alternative to removing base-boards and to the unsightliness of surface-mounted wiring is to box out the base-board around the perimeter of the room. With some planning, this can become an integral part of shelving, window seating or other built-in cabinetry. The bottom drawing at right shows how a baseboard raceway can facilitate extensive wiring changes without disturbing a finished wall. With such a system, one could even insulate and finish the interior walls without having to wait for the electrician to show up first. An added bonus is that the interior vapor barrier isn't punctured by outlet boxes and cables. Variations on this theme can also be used to hide plumbing pipes and heating ducts that run between floors and along exposed ceiling beams.

The profile of a baseboard raceway can be greatly reduced by incorporating it into newly applied wainscoting (see the drawing on p. 276). A 1½-in. deep outlet box will just fit flush to the surface of the base-board if applied over ¾-in. thick paneling. Check with your local electrical inspector first, since code restrictions may not allow the use of these boxes. If the wainscot paneling is applied over horizontal furring, standard-depth boxes can be used instead.

Running Cable between Floors with Offset Partitions

1. Attach cable to fishwire and feed from A into joist cavity.

2. Feed fishwire from B to snag first wire.

3. Push into wall at B.

4. Snag fishwire from B with another fishwire from C.

5. Pull cable from A to C.

Using Baseboard Raceways to Hide Wires

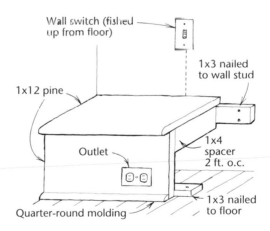

Wall switch (fished up from floor)

1x3 nailed to wall stud

1x12 pine

1x4 spacer 2 ft. o.c.

Outlet

1x3 nailed to floor

Quarter-round molding

Wainscoting Wiring Ducts

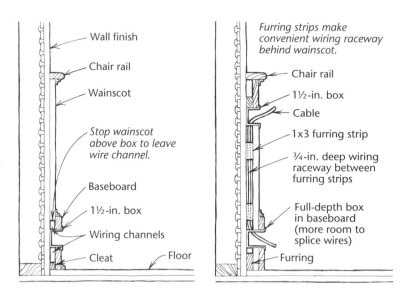

Wall finish

Chair rail

Wainscot

Stop wainscot above box to leave wire channel.

Baseboard

1½-in. box

Wiring channels

Cleat

Floor

Furring strips make convenient wiring raceway behind wainscot.

Chair rail

1½-in. box

Cable

1x3 furring strip

¾-in. deep wiring raceway between furring strips

Full-depth box in baseboard (more room to splice wires)

Furring

Making the Right Connection

Now that you understand at least some general principles governing the design of circuits, and have some idea how to run wires from one part of the house to another, the only question remaining is how exactly to connect the wires at each device and fixture so that the lights and not the kitchen blender go on when you flick the switch, the television set doesn't melt down when you plug it in and the fuses don't blow out of the service panel as soon as you turn the power back on.

It helps to remember that house wiring is color-coded—black is always the "hot" wire and white the "neutral" in ordinary 120-volt house wiring. (In 220-volt circuits used for electric heating and some heavy-duty appliances, both wires are hot. Look in the entrance panel for circuit breakers that occupy the slots of two normal breakers; these are for 220-volt circuits. If you have any doubts about the voltage at a fixture, check it with your multi-tester.) In the three-wire circuits used to control fixtures from two or more points, the red wire is also hot.

The color coding also extends to the terminals themselves. The white neutral wire must always be connected to the silver terminal. The black hot wire is always connected to the brass terminal except with three-way switches, where the red wire connects to the brass and the black (which is here called the "common" wire) is connected to a special black or copper-colored terminal. The green chassis ground wire and/or the bare continuous ground wires are always connected to the green terminal. If you observe these protocols, your wiring will be safe and work properly.

Another useful rule to remember is that all the white wires are always connected. It's only the black (and red) wires that are interrupted by switches and other control devices. Finally, all circuits consist of a "feed" that brings current into a device or joins with other wires inside a steel junction box, and a "run" that carries the current from the box or fixture to the next. Feeds bring power in; runs carry power out. It's important to know the difference if you are working with live wires or trying to figure out where everything goes when you can't see anything more of a circuit than the tangle of connections inside a switch box. A "leg" is an extension of the feed to a switch placed to control a fixture from a convenient location.

This is the kind of information you can find in most wiring books. But even so, the full range of possible connections isn't always presented in one place or in clear detail. When I first started wiring, I used to carry around a handbook so I could look up the connections for whatever I needed at the time. This was not only time-consuming, but it also ruined the book. Finally, I made up a schematic chart that outlined all the typical connections and the resultant combinations that one might ever need to wire a house. If you photocopy the chart on pp. 277-279, you'll be able to keep this reference handy while you work, without smudging and tattering the pages of this expensive book.

Thirty Ways to Wire an Electrical Device

Key

—— Black (hot wire)

—— White (neutral)

----- Red (hot wire)

.... Blue (hot wire)

Feed = Power in

Run = Power out

═══ 2-wire run

▨▨▨ 3-wire run

▨▨▨ 4-wire run

▱ Wire nut (for splicing)

⬡ Octagon junction box

▢ Outlet box

W→B White conductor
marked as black
at terminal

* Break common bond
between hot terminals.

Assume:

Black to brass terminal

White to silver terminal

Red to brass terminal

Like-colored terminals
in duplex outlets have
common bond.

Black 3-way circuits to copper
or black terminal

Note: Continuous bare copper
ground wire not shown for
clarity. These conductors are
always spliced together and
joined both to the device and
to the box with grounding
clips or grounding screws.

**1. Fixture at end of run
(integral switch
controlled)**

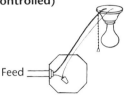

**2. Fixture at middle of run
(integral switch
controlled)**

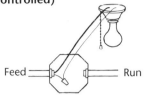

**3. Outlet at end of run
(always hot)**

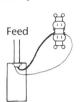

**4. Outlet in middle of run
(always hot)**

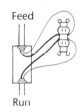

**5. Fixture at end of run
(switch controlled)**

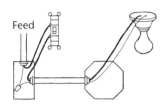

**6. Fixture at end of run,
controlled by switch leg**

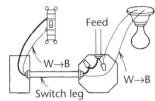

**7. Fixture in middle of run
controlled by switch leg**

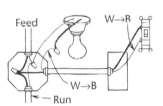

**8. Outlet in run, unswitched fixture and switched fixture
at end of run (typical for closet light in bedroom circuit)**

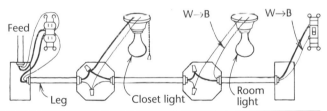

**9. Two or more runs from
one feed**

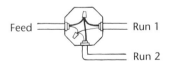

Feed —— Run 1

—— Run 2

*Note: Use square box for more
connections. Follow code specs.*

**10. Switch-controlled fixture in middle of run with
unswitched fixture at end of run**

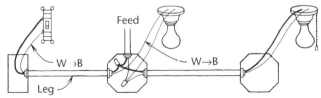

11. Two fixtures controlled by switches at end of run

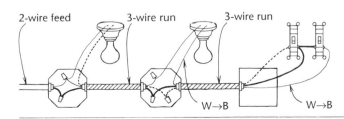

**12. Fixture at beginning of run controlled by switch in
middle of run with live outlet at end of run**

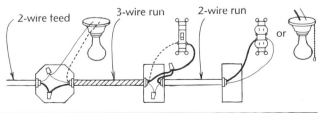

Thirty Ways to Wire an Electrical Device

13. Switch at beginning of run controlling fixture in middle with live fixture (or outlet) at end of run

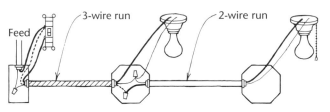

Feed · 3-wire run · 2-wire run

14. Fixture at end of run controlled by switches at two points

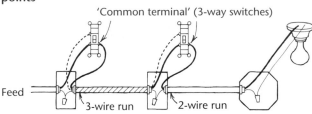

'Common terminal' (3-way switches)

Feed · 3-wire run · 2-wire run

15. Fixture at beginning of run controlled by switches at end of run

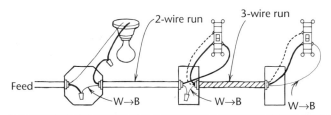

Feed · 2-wire run · 3-wire run · W→B · W→B · W→B

16. Fixture in middle of run controlled by switches at beginning and end of run

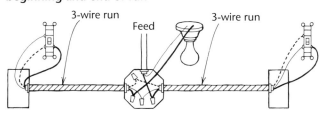

3-wire run · Feed · 3-wire run

17. Switch controlling fixture in run with combination outlet at switch leg

Feed · 3-wire run

18. Switch/outlet controlling fixture at end of run

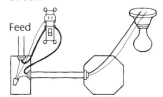

Feed

19. Multiple outlets controlled by switches at two points

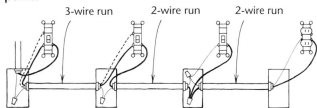

3-wire run · 2-wire run · 2-wire run

20. Switch-controlled outlet at beginning of run

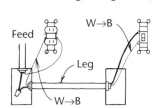

Feed · W→B · Leg · W→B

21. Switch-controlled 'hot' outlet at end of run

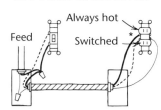

Feed · Always hot · Switched

22. Switch-controlled and hot outlets

* Break common bond between hot terminals.

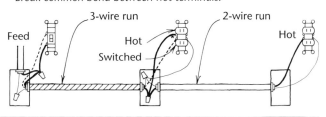

Feed · 3-wire run · 2-wire run · Hot · Switched · Hot

23. Fixture at beginning of run controlled by two switches at end of run with live outlet

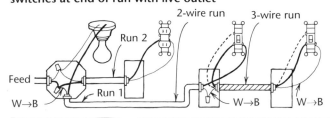

Feed · Run 2 · 2-wire run · 3-wire run · Run 1 · W→B · W→B · W→B

24. Two switches at beginning of run controlling light with live outlet at end of run

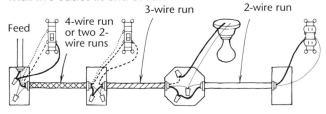

Feed · 4-wire run or two 2-wire runs · 3-wire run · 2-wire run

25. Four-way switch to control fixture at end of run from three points

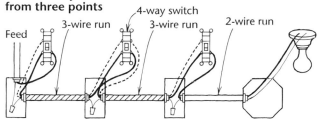

Feed · 3-wire run · 4-way switch · 3-wire run · 2-wire run

26. Same as at left, but different internal wiring

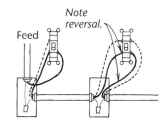

Note reversal.

Feed

Note: Four-way switches can be internally wired two ways — connections change accordingly.

Type A   Type B

27. Fixture at beginning of run controlled from three points

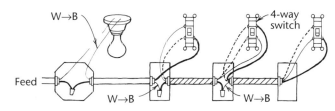

W→B

Feed

W→B   4-way switch   W→B

28. Fixture at end of run controlled from more than three points (4-way switches for all intermediate points)

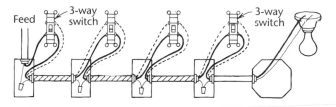

Feed   3-way switch   3-way switch

29. 'Zoned outlets': Each half of a duplex outlet on its own circuit with last outlet on only one circuit

Note: Red to one circuit breaker, black to another.

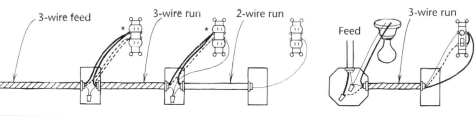

3-wire feed   3-wire run   2-wire run

30. Switch with pilot light

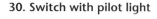

Feed   3-wire run

Household Plumbing

Plumbing is a vast body of knowledge composed of little bits and pieces. This is what makes plumbing seem so complicated—all the different kinds of pipes, valves, faucets, fittings and fixtures, each requiring simple, yet somewhat different treatment to assemble, join and repair. When you realize that a plumbing system is put together much like an Erector set, you will have no hesitancy in tackling the problems that arise.

—Max Alth, *Do-It-Yourself Plumbing* (New York: Sterling Publishing Co., 1987)

Antique plumbing fixtures are often worth preserving for their beauty alone.

The word "plumber" is derived from the Latin word for lead, *plumbum*. The basic principles of the trade have changed very little since the ancient Romans circulated their household water and wastes through lead pipes. Plumbers, like masons, have jealously guarded their secrets. And until recently, there was perhaps some justification for the aura of mystery in which plumbers cloaked themselves. They worked with ancient and heavy elements, with lead, cast iron, copper, bronze and tin. They were heirs to the alchemists, they plied their trade in dark and moldy cellars. You can't expect a wizard to come at your beck and call.

Plumbers have a sizable investment in specialized tools: pipe threaders, reamers and cutters, wrenches, torches, augers and drills. They must carry a warehouse of fittings and connectors, pipes, solders and fluxes. No wonder then that plumbers place themselves at the apex of the blue-collar elite and adjust their wages accordingly. But the introduction of plastic pipe has shaken the foundations of the plumber's hoary hegemony. The plumbers' unions and trade associations, which help enforce and write plumbing codes, fought bitterly against the adoption of the new materials. What latex paint did to the professional painter, plastic pipe has done to the plumber. Except for special cases where codes still require cast-iron or galvanized-steel pipe for drainage lines, professionals and home owners alike will rarely have occasion to deal with these intractable materials.

Nevertheless, all the reasons that justify the employment of an electrician apply equally to plumbers. They have the tools, the right parts and the experience. As with wiring, local building codes or mortgage regulations may require the work to be performed by a licensed plumber or inspected for compliance with the Uniform National Plumbing Code. The subject of codes, permits and inspections as they pertain to home plumbers and electricians is

a complex tangle, for local codes can limit or take precedence over the requirements of the national codes.

Many municipalities have laws that prohibit anyone from engaging in the *business* of plumbing or wiring without a license. The question of whether or not someone who is working on his or her own premises is engaged in the business of plumbing or wiring is a legal morass. Although you may have to go to court to prove it, precedent has established that people can plumb or wire their own homes. But before proceeding, a permit from city, county or state officials is usually required. Obtaining this permit automatically engages the inspection process. Until the local inspector is satisfied that your work complies with code requirements, an occupancy permit won't be issued. If it is possible to do your own work, there are any number of guide books that will acquaint you with the requirements for safe installation.

Plumbing Materials and Theory

A domestic plumbing system is actually two subsystems. The supply system is a distribution network that moves water from a source to the fixtures where it is used. The waste system collects the used water and takes it somewhere else, along with any pollutants it has acquired along the way.

For the plumbing system to work safely and efficiently, certain methods must be followed. As with electricity, which demands absolute separation of white and black wires, supply and waste must never meet—if clean water becomes contaminated with waste water, anyone who uses it could get very sick. Much of the plumbing code derives from the Victorian obsession with germs and sanitation. Some of this may seem like overkill, but just as the excesses of unregulated and unscrupulous tradesmen led to the adoption of minimum building standards, the possibility of infection and even explosion caused by shoddy plumbing led to stringent codes.

Pipe systems

There are four basic nonmetallic pipe systems: polyethylene, CPVC or PVC, ABS and polybutylene.

Polyethylene, the familiar flexible black plastic pipe, has all but replaced the galvanized-iron piping that once was used to deliver water from the well to the house. Iron pipe can develop hardening of the arteries, especially with hard water. As the diameter of the pipe decreases, friction increases; the pump has to work harder to draw less water and it can burn out. Minerals won't adhere easily to the slippery and chemically inert surface of polyethylene pipe. It can be buried directly in the ground, is impervious to corrosion, will expand when frozen without breaking, and since it is available in coils of up to 1,000 ft. long, it's possible to eliminate potentially troublesome splices.

However, plumbing codes prohibit the use of polyethylene pipe in residential systems for good reason: It softens at about 120°F. Since the temperature of domestic hot water runs from about 120°F to 150°F, it wouldn't take a fire to turn the stuff into limp spaghetti. It isn't used for cold-water lines because it is prone to failure at the joints. The nylon fittings used for connections are secured with stainless-steel clamps; over time, in pressurized systems, the momentum of water slamming into a joint when the flow is stopped can force it apart or break the nylon fitting.

In rural areas, polyethylene is widely used to bring water from a well into the house in a single length, uninterrupted by splices. It is also used for exposed water systems in barns and other outbuildings and for the cold-water lines of a low-pressure gravity-feed system. Even though the pipe itself will not burst if frozen, the fittings are not as flexible. Since they do break, such systems should be drained if installed in an unheated space.

CPVC (chlorinated polyvinyl chloride) or PVC (polyvinyl chloride) plastic is rigid enough to withstand pressurized water systems. The most significant difference between the two is that CPVC is stronger and approved for water up to about 180°F. PVC should not be subjected to pressurized water hotter than 100°F. Most of this pipe is used for drainage systems.

Despite its intense promotion as a low-cost and easy alternative to conventional sweat-soldered copper tubing, CPVC plumbing is an idea whose time has come and gone. Although the evidence is not conclusive, there is a real possibility that over time, aided by the solvent power of hot water, CPVC can break down into its parent monomer, vinyl chloride, a proven potent carcinogen. To make things worse, CPVC gives off toxic fumes when ignited.

If these aren't big enough drawbacks, CPVC pipe will shatter when frozen even more readily than copper splits. True, it is easily cut, and the fittings are quickly installed, but as the price of copper has fallen and the price of oil gone up, it is no longer as economical as before. Also, if a joint springs a leak or was misaligned, unlike copper, it cannot be taken apart and reassembled. Instead, the piece must be cut out and replaced with a coupler and new fittings. But there is nothing wrong with using PVC pipe for drainage lines. Be sure, however, to use Schedule 40 grade pipe. Most of the PVC pipe sold at do-it-yourself outlets is a lighter, inferior grade.

ABS (acrylonitrile-butadiene-styrene) pipe is structurally stronger than PVC and CPVC pipes. It is also reputed to be less toxic if burned. But because it cannot withstand high temperatures or pressures, ABS pipe is used mostly for electrical conduit and drainage lines. This is where plastic pipe has had the greatest impact upon plumbing. Large-diameter copper pipe is too expensive for drainage systems and the traditional cast iron is not only costly, but heavy.

In the last few years polybutylene pipe (PB) systems have won grudging acceptance. In some regions, most notably the Southwest, the material is widely used in new construction. In other areas, like New England, you'll be lucky if the distributor has even heard of it. This is unfortunate, since it is well suited to the demands of remodeling. Unlike PVC plastics, the material is approved as safe for drinking water and food processing. It is freeze-proof down to –50°F, and heat stable in pressurized systems up to 180°F.

PB pipe is available in 5-ft. rigid lengths or flexible coils of up to 400 ft. Indeed, flexibility is one of its most attractive features (½-in. diameter pipe can be bent to an 8-in. radius without kinking). The pipe can be snaked through walls like electrical cable, run through holes drilled in the studs and bent around corners with a minimal number of fittings. Since the fittings themselves are quite expensive, this is a good thing. A variety of adapters allow PB to interface with other kinds of pipe. Compression-type fittings are the most common. These are virtually leakproof, strong, stable and easy to make, requiring only wrenches or pliers. The pipe itself can be cut with a sharp knife.

A PB plumbing system is easier for an inexperienced plumber to install than copper tubing and much more forgiving of mistakes than either copper or CPVC. Since plastic is an insulator, cold-water pipes won't sweat so easily and hot water will stay warmer. The sound of running water is also muffled.

Traditional copper tubing is still the favorite type of pipe, with good reason. It is strong, noncorroding, unaffected by heat, and safe. Sweat-soldered joints seldom pull apart and are not difficult to make once the art is mastered. Copper plumbing also contributes to a higher resale value. Because its use is so widespread, almost any fitting is available.

The design of a domestic plumbing system or a discussion of the many fittings available and techniques for their use is beyond the scope of this book. In any case, the system in your house is already a *fait accompli*. The outline that follows is intended only as a guide to the basic principles and repairs.

Springs and Wells

A spring is a naturally occurring water source, a point where the water table coincides with the surface, or a vein of underground seepage that can be tapped by digging a hole down to it. In many parts of the country, houses cannot be occupied without a certificate indicating a potable water source. State health labs offer water-testing services that check for the presence of coliform bacteria, which indicates a potential health hazard.

If a spring is to be a safe source of drinking water, and capable of passing the water test, it must be carefully constructed. Most old springs, especially those walled in with stone or wood, are easily contaminated by surface runoff and will probably have to be replaced. With a drilled well, a steel pipe (the casing) penetrates loose soils and unconsolidated rock until it reaches bedrock. The pressure of the drilling bit polishes the hard rock into a smooth-sided and impervious bore hole. Completely isolated from the surface, a drilled well is almost impossible to contaminate, unless of course the water table itself has been affected by subterranean pollution.

A good spring is lined with concrete spring tiles, sealed together with a thin mortar grout. The immediate area of the actual water source is excavated and filled with clean washed chestnut stone, at least 1 ft. below the level of the first tile and for several feet around it. The stone creates a reservoir. Punch a hole through the first tile and insert the water line so that the intake is about 6 in. off the bottom. Fit it with a foot valve and/or strainer.

The rest of the excavation is backfilled to within 2 ft. of finish grade with washed gravel, which will help filter out impurities in the ground water. The gravel is topped with a filter fabric and impervious clay soil, sloped away from the last spring tile on all sides. Contrary to popular opinion, rainwater is no longer pure but is filled with all manner of industrial contaminants. Even if it were pure, surface water can wash ground-borne pollutants from animal wastes, herbicides and fertilizers into the spring. A heavy concrete cover tops the last tile. If the static level is high enough, add an overflow pipe to carry out the excess water.

A pencil-thin trickle of water, if constant, will fill a pond in a few months and will more than supply a household's needs as long as the water is not drawn down faster than the reservoir can be replenished. Unlike municipal water supplies, most springs and wells won't run forever. You will soon come to know your spring's capabilities and learn when to use it gently. Drawing your own water involves you as intimately in your life-support system as heating with wood or the sun.

Problems at the source

With changing use patterns and increased development, springs frequently run dry. The solution is to locate a better source for a new one or to drill a well. Although expensive, a drilled well almost always yields enough water. A flow of 3 or more gal. per minute (gpm) will suffice for a single family. If the well is over 200 ft. deep, its bore hole will furnish an adequate reservoir even with flows as low as ⅓ gpm. Although finding water can never be guaranteed, drilling a well is considerably less risky than developing a spring. I once spent hundreds of dollars retrofitting my old spring so it could pass the water test, only to have it run dry the very next summer. Unless you have positively located an excellent source, go for the well.

It may be that your present troublesome spring is only tapping a capillary rather than an artery of the aquifer. Modern technology has not been able to locate water with any more certainty than it can predict the weather in the mountains of New England. Whatever science and the skeptics may say to the contrary, empirical evidence shows that dowsing works far too often to be merely coincidental. Theoretically, anyone can dowse for water, but some are more attuned than others. When we had our dowsing done, I wondered if there was an element of collusion in the fact that the well-driller's uncle happened to be a dowser, but after three weeks without water we were willing to try anything:

The old man stood wizened like last fall's fruit, clinging to the Y-shaped branch of apple wood he held tensioned between his outstretched arms. The branch seemed alive, quivering as he slowly moved across the lawn. He seemed to be following an invisible trail, pausing as if to sniff out the scent of underground water. The branch dipped sharply. He moved off at an angle to his left, the branch now vibrating like the wings of a honeybee as he followed a new scent. It dipped again, harder. "Just as I thought," he said, "t'was a vein. Here's the real source. There's goin' t' be a lot of water down 'bout one-twenty, one-twenty-five feet." The drill struck water at 123 ft., hitting a vein that gushed 23 gpm.

A water-supply line should be laid from the source to the pump without splices if at all possible. A slug of water 300 ft. long traveling through a pipe at about 10 mph develops considerable momentum. When a valve in the plumbing system is closed or the pump cycles, this column comes to a sudden stop, with an effect similar to an auto slamming into a concrete abutment. A car is ultimately compressible, water is not. The shock waves of this collision travel through the pipe, and the joints absorb a good deal of this energy. Fittings should be tightened with double clamps (two on each side of a coupling). Use the more durable brass fittings instead of nylon for underground burial. Soften the pipe slightly with a quick pass of a propane torch before inserting the fittings, and tap them home with a block of softwood. Don't scrimp on clamps or fittings; digging up a leaking pipe for lack of a 69-cent clamp or a $3 coupler is not cost-effective. When filling the excavation, protect the pipe from damage by covering it with at least 6 in. of sand or stone-free soil.

I remember one summer when the well seemed to be running an awful lot. Several days later, I noticed that an area of lawn was very wet. I also remembered that the line from the well to the garden hydrant was somewhere in the vicinity of this wet spot. Before the backhoe even found it, the broken water line announced itself by a geyser streaming up through the underground mud hole it had formed. When the muck was cleared away, the pipe revealed itself to have been split open by the sharp edge of a stone.

Water Pumps

The owner of a country home, untethered to the municipal water supply, may discover that the spring that never ran dry in the living memory of man suddenly has, causing the faithful pump, in a fit of burning wires, to give up the ghost. Such are the trials and tribulations of rural life.

Pumping systems

There are four basic pumping systems for on-site water supply. The simplest (and in some ways, most efficient) is gravity feed. When a source, such as a spring, is located sufficiently high enough above the house, the water will flow downward through a pipe into the house. The higher the source, the greater the pressure. It's like filling a milk carton with water and punching a series of holes in it: The hardest stream comes from the lowest hole.

This difference in pressure points out the disadvantage of a gravity system as well. Since the pressure decreases as the water rises within the house, a second-floor fixture may not get sufficient flow to operate. Since the pressure in a gravity system equals ½ lb. per sq. in. (psi) for each foot of drop, a source 40 ft. above the house will supply 20 lb. of pressure in the basement. Twenty feet higher than that,

up in the second-floor bathroom, 10 lb. of pressure won't operate a clothes washer and will give a rather unsatisfactory shower.

In the days before rural electrification, gravity-feed water systems were common. The pipes for these old installations were galvanized (and even made of lead), and since the trenches had to be dug by hand, seldom buried below frost line. Usually the snow cover kept the ground from freezing. A tap was also left open since moving water wouldn't freeze as easily.

Other than digging up the old pipe and replacing it with polyethylene in a new trench below the frost line, there is no reason not to continue using a gravity-feed supply. Adding a simple electric piston pump in the cellar will solve the pressure problem. Install a check valve (a one-way valve) in the incoming line before the pump to prevent pressurized water from flowing back up the line to the spring. To reduce friction, gravity systems require oversized pipes. Use 1½-in. for runs over 100 ft. instead of standard 1-in. pipe. Where the pipe cannot be buried below the frost line because of an underground ledge, cover it with 2 in. of rigid foam and a layer of straw mulch topped with burlap and at least 1 ft. of soil. If this fails to prevent freezing, wrap the pipe in electric heat tape.

The rich uncle of the gravity-feed system is the artesian well. Here, a drilled well or spring strikes a vein of water confined between sloping impervious soil strata. The water supply is self-pressurized. Depending on the location of the house relative to the slope, the pressure can be just enough to bring the water to the surface, or so great that a pressure-reducer must be installed before it can be used in the house.

The shallow-well pump is far more common than either of these naturally powered systems. The hand-powered pitcher pump and the windmill-driven piston pump, veritable icons of country life, have been replaced by an electrically powered piston pump, but otherwise the principles of operation have stayed the same for almost a century and a half. Because a shallow-well pump pulls water by suction (which is less efficient than pushing) its effective vertical lift is limited to about 25 ft. Horizontal pull, however, is limited only by friction, especially if the run is slightly downhill.

A more powerful version of the shallow-well pump, which also requires less maintenance, is the centrifugal pump. The pump operates by drawing water through an impeller (a set of spinning blades in a sealed chamber). It is less noisy and a lot more efficient than a piston pump. Never let a centrifugal pump run dry; the heat generated by the friction between the closely fitted nylon blades and the walls of an empty pump chamber will quickly melt them.

A jet pump will bring water up from wells as deep as 125 ft. The pump requires two pipes to operate, one for the water coming up from the well and another that returns some of that water to the bottom of the well, where it is jetted through a special orifice at high pressure to force water up into the intake pipe. Thus the jet pump pushes water up by boosting its pressure, instead of pulling on it by suction. A jet pump uses more power than a piston or centrifugal pump but it is the only kind that will work for sources below 25 ft. Since it is located in the cellar and not the well, it is as easy to service as the other pumps.

When a well is more than 100 ft. deep, a submersible pump, which can force water up from depths of 500 ft. or more, is the only practical choice. A submersible pump (as its name implies) is lowered to the bottom of the well, connected by polyethylene pipe and its power cable. Although installation and replacement are not beyond the ability of a home owner, the peace of mind provided by a warranty that includes repairs in case of pump failure is probably worth the extra cost of a professional installation.

Because the buried 220-volt power cable that connects the motor to the house is about as good a ground as could be imagined, deep-well pumps are susceptible to damage from lightning strikes. Motors encased in an insulating oil bath are less easily damaged. Since lightning can travel underground to the power cable and into the house from quite a distance, you should protect the pump and the household electrical system by installing a lightning arrester across the line from the service panel to the pump control relay. This is a kind of one-shot fuse that literally goes off with a bang when a nearby lightning strike sends a power surge into the system. It's also a good idea to turn off the pump during severe thunderstorms. Polyethylene pipe rated for 140 psi can be safely used to depths of about 250 ft. Beyond this, stronger pipe or even galvanized iron is needed to withstand the pressure exerted by a very long column of water.

Pump problems

Deep-well pumps are virtually trouble-free. Shallow-well pumps fall prey to several common ailments. The intake opening at the bottom of the well is fitted with a foot valve, a species of check valve attached to a strainer that prevents debris from being sucked into the line and the pump. The foot valve prevents the water in the line from flowing back down into the well whenever the pump shuts off. Sometimes, especially if the well is pumped almost dry, an accumulation of gravel, twigs or mud can prevent the valve from closing, causing the pump to lose its "prime."

Pumps are designed to suck water, not air. But they'll keep trying until the pump or the motor itself overheats and seizes. When a pump runs continuously and no water flows out of the tap, the pump has either lost its prime or its piston or impeller has failed. An empty water line will feel warm and light and lack a pulse (you can feel water moving through the intake pipe). The pump chamber will also feel warm to the touch. Working pumps sweat with condensation on their ground-water-cooled surfaces. If the pump is cold and running, the problem is not lost prime, but lost suction. A pump that takes forever to reach shut-off pressure is probably suffering from this kind of problem.

Like a bicycle pump or the familiar camp stove, a piston pump pushes air out of a chamber with a rod (the piston) creating a vacuum that sucks water up the line on its backstroke. The piston is sealed to the sides of the air chamber by flexible leather washers, which will eventually dry or wear out. Replacement kits, available from the manufacturer or distributor, will give new life to a pump that runs a lot but doesn't seem to draw much water.

Dried-out leather washers can sometimes be rejuvenated by soaking their edges with light machine oil. Centrifugal pumps lose their suction when overheating wears down their nylon or brass impellers. Abrasion from dirt sucked into the pump chamber when the well ran too low or was flooded with surface debris will also damage the impellers. Since this is not a far-fetched occurrence, these parts are designed to be easily replaced.

If the pump has lost its prime and you can see water in the bottom of the well or spring, examine the foot valve. If the intake strainer is not choked with dead leaves or mud, unscrew the strainer and see if any dirt has lodged between the spring-loaded flapper valve and its gasket. Check the spring itself for proper opera-

tion. Clean or replace the valve as necessary. A 1-in. line 300 ft. long takes 30 gal. to fill completely; to reprime a pump, all the air between the foot valve and the pump must be replaced with water.

The first step is to shut the valve between the pump output and the pressure tank (if there is one) or the main system shut-off (you don't want to fill all the pipes in the house too). Unscrew the priming plug located on top of the pump head (usually a ½-in. square plug, top dead center of the impeller housing or pump chamber). Insert a funnel and slowly pour water into the line, allowing the air to bubble out. This will take a long time. If you can't get any water in at all, look for a check valve at the inlet side of the pump and remove it. When the line will accept no more water, screw the plug back in loosely and turn on the pump. You should hear a whooshing sound and the intake pipe will jump as slugs of water lurch up the line. Air should bubble out the sides of the plug along with water.

When only water squirts out of the plug, you've recaptured the prime. Most often, it will take several (sometimes dozens) of tries before the line is emptied of enough air so the pump can grab water. If there are high spots along the line (for example, where it rises to cross a ledge) no amount of priming can clear the resulting air lock. Suspect this condition if the pump won't prime and yet refuses to take any more water through its priming plug.

A force pump, a kind of oversized bicycle pump that can be rented from your local plumbing store, will take up water from a pail and push it into the line with enough force to dislodge the offending air bubble. Ideally, it should be connected to the end of the intake line, with the foot valve removed and its intake hose let down into the well. It will also work, with a bit less efficiency, at the pump end, connected to the priming hole. When relaying a water-supply line, anticipate priming problems and install a tee connected to an above-ground priming valve at any high spot. Maintaining a constant pitch (upward or downward or level) will also prevent problems.

Water pumps are set to switch on automatically when water pressure falls below a preset limit and to turn off when it reaches the desired pressure. A pressure-sensing diaphragm (it looks like a flying saucer tethered to a thin copper tubing) is connected to a relay that switches the pump motor on and off. There are adjusting screws on the relay to change the high and low limits. These should be set so that the pump cycles on at 20 psi to 25 psi and off at 40 psi. Although shut-off pressure can be increased slightly to supply a third-story bathroom, exceeding the normal working range of the plumbing system will cause joints and fittings to spring leaks.

If the pump cycles constantly whenever the smallest amount of water is drawn off, the problem is in the pressure tank, not the pump itself. Piston pumps are usually mounted directly on top of the pressure tank. Centrifugal and jet pumps (and of course, submersibles) are usually separate. To reduce excessive pump cycling, water in the tank is pressurized by a diaphragm and a cushion of compressed air at the top of the tank. All tanks gradually replace the air cushion with water as seals loosen and air dissolves in the water. When the air cushion no longer exerts enough pressure, the pump comes on whenever water is drawn off and the tank is said to be "waterlogged." Shut off the pump, close the main valves to prevent backflow into the tank, and allow it to drain. If the problem persists after the tank refills, check the air valve (which is exactly the same as a tire valve) at the top of the tank to be sure it is not loose or leaking air. A defective diaphragm, although less likely, will render the tank useless.

An Old-House Plumbing System

The drawing on the facing page shows a generic plumbing system likely to be found in any old house. It takes no account of any connections with a heating system, which is considered completely separate from the plumbing, both in theory and in practice.

The supply system

Cold water entering the house from a well or municipal supply is separated into a hot-water supply and a cold-water supply, pipes for which are run to all fixtures. When more than one fixture is on a given line, the supply feeder should be ¾-in. pipe and the fixture feeders ½ in. If all lines are only ½ in., a pressure drop occurs when, for example, you run the shower and flush the toilet at the same time. The increased diameter allows more water to be delivered, preventing one fixture from pre-empting another, and you from being scalded as cold water is suddenly drawn off to refill the toilet.

Individual shut-off valves should be installed between the hot and cold feeds for all fixtures and the main supply pipes. In the event of repairs, the defective fixture can be isolated without shutting down the entire system and inconveniencing the household. All supply lines should slope slightly so that the entire system can be drained if necessary. Long lines can pitch toward a drain valve in the center of the line. In-line stop and waste valves are fitted with a screw-type drain cock. Use boiler drain valves at the lowest points of the system and on water storage tanks and heaters. These can be coupled to a garden hose to empty the entire system into a basement floor drain.

To prevent frozen pipes, never route water lines inside exterior walls. A drainable system can be emptied out when the house must be left vacant and unheated for a while. Pour a pint of methanol-based antifreeze (the glycol antifreeze will harm septic-tank bacteria) into the toilet bowl

Anatomy of an Old-House Plumbing System

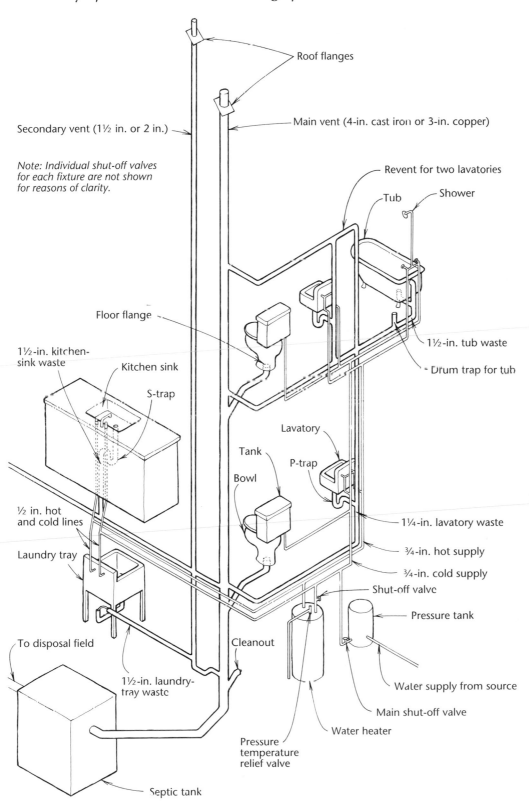

Roof flanges

Secondary vent (1½ in. or 2 in.)

Main vent (4-in. cast iron or 3-in. copper)

Note: Individual shut-off valves for each fixture are not shown for reasons of clarity.

Revent for two lavatories

Tub   Shower

Floor flange

1½-in. tub waste

Drum trap for tub

1½-in. kitchen-sink waste

Kitchen sink

S-trap

Lavatory

Tank   P-trap

Bowl

1¼-in. lavatory waste

½ in. hot and cold lines

¾-in. hot supply

¾-in. cold supply

Shut-off valve

Laundry tray

Pressure tank

To disposal field

Cleanout

1½-in. laundry-tray waste

Water supply from source

Main shut-off valve

Pressure temperature relief valve

Water heater

Septic tank

after the supply is shut off and the tank flushed to keep the water in the trap from freezing and cracking the bowl. Pour some more antifreeze down each sink trap.

The drainage system

A drainage system has three parts: drainpipes to carry waste water away, a vent to aid drainage and exhaust toxic sewer gases, and fixture traps to prevent them from leaking into the household air. Like a tree that increases in size from the upper branches down to its trunk, a drain system must always increase in diameter as it flows downstream. Branch lines are always smaller than the main stack, and always enter it at an angle to prevent clogging and aid cleanout.

The decomposition of human and household wastes produces hydrogen sulfide gas, which is poisonous and smells like rotten eggs; methane, which is explosive and smells even worse; and carbon monoxide and other noxious gases. Water-filled traps keep sewer gas from seeping into the house, while the vent exhausts

it to the outside. Fresh air in the system also prevents corrosion and limits the growth of bacterial slime. Vents also prevent siphoning, which could empty the traps if there were a sudden heavy flow of water through the drain system. If a drainpipe were ever to fill completely with water, the momentum of its movement could suck the water out of the trap. The longer the pipe, the greater the chance of siphoning. The importance of keeping traps full and preventing soiled water from backwashing into fixtures is the reason behind the complicated code prescriptions for proper venting.

Drain systems clog when pipes are not properly pitched or are too narrow, or when too much greasy kitchen waste is dumped into them. Plastic has such a strong affinity for grease molecules that it's not unusual to find a branch drain plugged solid with a butter-like sludge after only a few years. Of course, some drains clog because someone has thrown insoluble objects like hair, toys, bobby pins or construction debris into them. Plaster is not soluble, and will often collect at the bottom of a trap if tools are washed out in the sink.

On-Site Sewage Disposal

Indoor plumbing has been widely used in this country for little more than a century. Until its adoption, the pit privy and the open gutter were the only waste-disposal systems. The greatest contribution of the Victorian age to the advance of civilization may well have been the development of sanitary engineering, and the discovery of the scientific basis for the folk wisdom that prescribed defecating downstream of your drinking water.

Victorian bathrooms were, above all, sanitary. Unfortunately, late 19th-century sewage treatment consisted of little more than an "out of sight, out of mind" attitude. Waste water was "treated" by dumping it into the nearest river. Even now, despite the advances made in sanitary engineering, raw sewage is still being discharged into lakes and rivers. Without commenting on the ultimate wisdom of using 5 gal. of water to remove ½ pt. of urine, it can be said that there is no such thing as a waste-disposal problem. There is only a recycling problem.

The costs of supplying public services in an era of diminished public income have led to a reversal of the policies that formerly encouraged, and in some municipalities even forced, home owners to hook into town sewer lines. Septic tanks are now being promoted as the ecologically sound, dependable and economical means of treating waste water that they always were.

Plumbing codes and health officers distinguish between two kinds of waste water: "grey" water and "black" water. Grey water is the effluent from kitchen sinks, tubs and washing machines. Black water carries human wastes. Despite their very different nature, both kinds of water are usually carried into the same sewer. Some have argued that grey water, with its low level of pathogens and high level of plant nutrients, should be separated and recycled as fertilizer for greenhouse crops or kept in a dry well, where it can leach slowly into the soil. Systems for processing grey water have been designed and employed. One benefit is an extended life for the septic system.

On-site sewage-disposal systems have two parts. The waste water enters a septic tank via the household sewer. The septic tank is a 1,000-gal. box arranged so that its inlet is typically about 4 in. higher than its outlet. The wastes are digested anaerobically (without oxygen) by bacteria living in the tank. Undigested solids fall to the bottom. The liquid digested waste moves out of the tank as new water enters, flowing through solid pipes to a distribution box that directs the effluent to perforated pipes set in crushed-stone-filled trenches. These absorption beds comprise the second part of the system, the leach field. Here aerobic bacteria digest the effluent and pure water re-enters the ground-water cycle.

The suitability of a septic system depends on the soil type, the level of the seasonal water table, the depth to bedrock and several other factors. A "perc" test determines how fast the soil can absorb water. Heavy clay soils absorb water too slowly, and sand releases it too quickly for a leach bed to work properly.

Since, in some regions, the soils are unsuited for septic systems, alternatives have been sought that would allow on-site sewage disposal. Composting toilets have met with mixed success. These systems are more of an ethical statement than an economic alternative. Where they have been approved, a separate system is required to process grey water, anyway. Proper use of composting toilets also requires a greater degree of awareness and a certain change of lifestyle that most people aren't willing to make. Health officials take the position that since no one can guarantee that the next occupants of the house won't misuse the system or even hook up a flush toilet to a leach field designed only for grey water, a conventional system must be installed anyway.

Mound systems and other expensive variations on conventional absorption trenches are about the only approved alternative for marginal soils. If you are considering the purchase of an old house that must have an on-site system installed, the best alternative is to ask for a copy of a successful perc test or an approved system design before signing the contract.

Septic-tank problems

Septic-tank ills are often chronic and vary with the seasons. The first symptom of a clogged tank is a toilet that will not flush properly or drains that empty slowly, even though a drain auger has failed to locate any obstruction in the drain or sewer lines. Be especially wary in the spring, when the water table is highest and the carrying capacity of the soil is therefore at its lowest. Another symptom is an outflow of malodorous water in the area of the leach field.

Septic tanks fail for a number of user-related reasons. If too much water is discharged into the tank, the bacteria won't have enough time to digest the effluent; it passes directly into the leach field, where it plugs the pores in the soil and fills up the pipes. The aerobic bacteria aren't equipped to deal with this overload. Large families and houses equipped with clothes washers require a large tank and a greater absorption area, especially in marginal soils. Dumping kitchen grease, which is almost indigestible to the tank bacteria, down the drain will also plug the leach field. It creates a crust on top of the tank, which interferes with the effluent release. Some codes call for a grease trap to be installed between the sink and the sewer line. Kitchen grease can be saved, fed to pets or dumped into the compost pile or a discreet spot in the yard where it will be absorbed into the soil.

The worst offender for septic-tank overloading is an in-sink garbage disposal. These appliances should not be allowed with on-site systems, because they send huge amounts of coarsely chopped organic material directly into the leach beds, where they overload the system and plug the pipes. Careless dumping of spent paint thinner, photographic chemicals and caustic or acid drain cleaners into the sewer destroys the tank bacteria, bringing digestion to a halt. The only cure is to dump a packet of bacterial starter down the drain and wait for the colony to recuperate.

The undigested solids will eventually accumulate at the bottom of the tank until they take up so much room that the water begins to flow through too fast. Pumping out the tank is thus a normal part of septic-system maintenance. A healthy and properly used tank should go about two years between pumpings. Before you can pump the tank, you've first got to find it. Mark the line of the sewer where it leaves the cellar. The tank is almost always 10 ft. from the house (the length of one section of cast-iron soil pipe). Locate the tank by hammering a length of rebar into the ground until it strikes something hard about the size of a kitchen table 1 ft. to 2 ft. below the surface. In the winter, the tank will be under the area where the snow melts first. Hire a professional to pump out the tank. Whatever you do, don't stick your head into the inspection hole of a freshly opened tank. It's full of poisonous methane gas. Don't smoke near it either, since methane is explosive, too.

If the system still doesn't work after the tank has been pumped, the leach field is probably plugged up, either because of abuse or old age. The only cure is to dig it up, clean out the pipes and replace the crushed stone with clean material.

Plumbing Problems

In new construction, a plumbing system can be laid out rationally, with consideration given to the proper sizes and installation of pipes and fixtures. In an old house, plumbing is limited to repair and upgrading of existing facilities, unless all the plumbing had burst when the house was abandoned, or its galvanized-iron pipe had rusted out so that the entire system needs replacing.

One usually learns to live with whatever insanities of design come with the house. The existing plumbing will be a weedlike tangle, having been patched together during the tenure of the house's previous owners. It can take half a day just to discover that there is no shut-off valve for the toilet supply. The rule is: If it doesn't leak, don't fix it. There is little point in renovating a plumbing system just to make it more sensible.

Supply-line repair

If the plumbing has not been renovated in the last half-century or so, the galvanized-iron distribution lines will probably be plugged with rust and begging for replacement. If water barely trickles out of the faucets, you can count on it. There's no good reason to replace old iron pipe with new. Change over to copper or polybutylene pipe instead.

Where dissimilar metals are joined, electrogalvanic action will cause corrosion. This brass faucet is rusting the iron nipple. Over time, the joint could spring a pinhole leak. Wrapping the threads with Teflon® tape will prevent corrosion.

Water stains on ceilings, floors or walls are a sign of plumbing trouble, a leaky roof or condensation problems. If the stain is dormant, the problem has probably been fixed. But if actual water shows up, you've got trouble. Obviously, if the leak is active only during a rainstorm, especially when the wind is blowing from a certain direction, the roof or exterior siding is leaking. When the moisture buildup occurs seasonally, during the coldest winter months, condensation or an ice dam on the eaves is the culprit. If the water stain manifests suddenly and continues to grow, you've got a plumbing problem. And a carpentry problem, since you'll have to tear out a section of wall or ceiling to find the source of the leak. Fortunately, since much of the plumbing is concentrated in the cellar, most of the leaks will be, too. Finding the leak is the first step toward fixing it.

Sometimes basically sound galvanized pipe suffers from spot corrosion, which causes a pinhole leak. Factory-made repair patches are a simple and effective cure. The patch consists of a rubber sheet gasket, which is tightened between two curved metal clamps. Of course, it's unlikely that you'll just happen to have a clamp of this sort lying around waiting for a leak to hap-

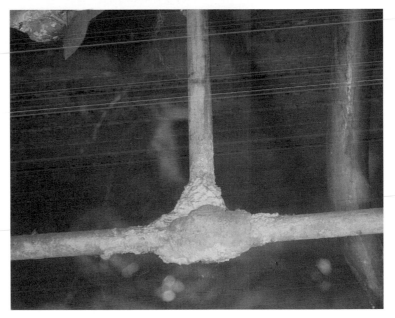

Sloppy but effective: Rather than disassemble the pipes to fix this leaky tee, someone kept smearing lead putty over it until the leak stopped. It took a lot of putty to do the job.

pen. When you're awakened in the middle of the night by the hiss of high-pressure water streaming out of a pipe between the cellar floor joists, you can't dash off to the hardware store either. But you might just happen to have a curved piece of metal

Repairs for Leaking Galvanized Pipe

1A. Seal leak in thick-walled pressurized pipe with gasket and clamp assembly. Shut off water before repairing.

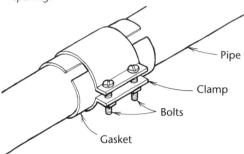

Pipe
Clamp
Bolts
Gasket

1B. Or use an automotive-type clamp, a curved piece of metal and some rubber or gasket sheeting.

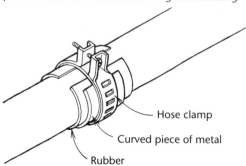

Hose clamp
Curved piece of metal
Rubber

1C. This temporary patch will hold until you can get to the hardware store to buy the clamp and gasket. Drive wedge farther under the wire after fastening the coils, then drive a small nail into wedge at X to secure it.

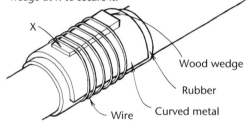

X
Wood wedge
Rubber
Curved metal
Wire

2. To repair a hairline crack in thick-walled pipe, drill holes at crack ends and a few along its length. After roughening the surface with a file, apply pipe-sealing cement, which will enter holes and fill the crack.

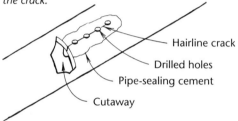

Hairline crack
Drilled holes
Pipe-sealing cement
Cutaway

3A. To fix a small leak at a threaded joint, try tightening the pipe into the joint. If you're lucky, you'll be able to back out the thread at the other end of the pipe without causing another leak.

Leak

3B. An alternative is to dry and roughen the outside of the joint, then seal with liquid steel or plumber's epoxy patching compound.

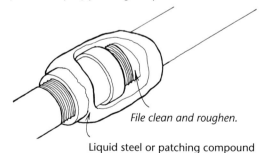

File clean and roughen.
Liquid steel or patching compound

3C. A sure-fire method is to cut the leaking pipe at an angle, swing the cut ends out of line and unscrew them. Make a new section from a union and two pieces of pipe, screwing them firmly into their joints.

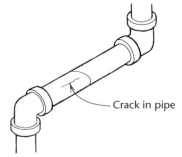

Crack in pipe

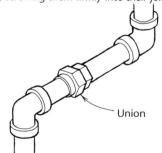

Union

(bend one if you don't) and a piece of rubber cut from an inner tube or a deflated basketball. The drawing on the facing page shows how these can be combined with wire and a wooden wedge to make a temporary patch that will hold until you can get to the hardware store. A stainless-steel hose clamp or automotive radiator clamp will also permanently tighten a rubber and metal gasket over the leak. Whatever you use, turn off the water before patching.

When the pipe leaks through a hairline crack instead of a pinhole, a rubber gasket may not work as well as pipe-sealing cement. The pipe must be dry first. Before applying the sealer, drill a small hole at each end of the crack and several more along its length. The end holes stop the crack from opening farther and the others help the cement grip the pipe.

Galvanized pipes usually leak at threaded joints because the joints are not tight enough. Unfortunately, unless the pipe is fitted with a union somewhere along its length, you can't loosen one connection without tightening the other end. If you're lucky, the good joint might be so well made that it can be backed off just enough to tighten up the leak without leaking itself. Failing this, you can disassemble the joint, which typically involves taking apart an entire series of joints all the way back to something you can unscrew without tightening something else.

Threaded joints loosen for a number of reasons. If pipe-joint compound ("pipe dope") wasn't applied to the threads when the joint was originally assembled, they could expand from the heat generated by turning unlubricated metal surfaces against each other. When the joint cools off, the threads are loose. Sometimes loose joints will hold for years until a change in water pressure causes them to leak.

A joint that was overtightened and then taken apart for some reason and reassembled will often leak, since the metal deforms so much that it can never be tightened properly again. Rethreading is a sure cure for deformed pipe threads. The fittings should be replaced with new ones. But if having to use a pipe-threading machine is too much trouble, try cleaning the threads and coating them with automotive gasket cement. If this doesn't stop the leak, roughen the outside of the pipe with a file, let it dry and then coat it generously with liquid steel or plumber's epoxy patching compound.

There is an alternative to taking apart a lot of joints (which might create more leaks to fix) that is also foolproof. Cut the leaking pipe at an angle so that the ends of each section can be swung out of line and unscrewed. Make a new section up from two pieces of threaded pipe and a union joint. If stock "nipples" (short lengths of threaded pipe) won't bridge the distance, have a piece cut to length and custom-threaded at the hardware store. When it is the union itself that is leaking, check the ground faces of the joint for corrosion buildup or scouring. If cleaning and reassembly doesn't work, try inserting a rubber or lead gasket between the faces.

Copper-pipe repair

In some ways, copper pipe is a lot easier to repair than thick-wall galvanized pipe, but in one way it isn't. Before a leak can be soldered shut, the pipe must be emptied of water. Otherwise the metal won't heat properly and the solder won't stick. Steam will also blow out through the molten metal. In theory, it should be easy to drain the pipe. In practice it always seems that the shut-off valves never quite work, allowing just enough water to trickle through to prevent the solder from taking. Sometimes there aren't any shut-offs on the troubled line. Sometimes, the pipe is run so that it cannot be drained.

Pinhole leaks in copper pipe caused by a careless carpenter or drywall installer can usually be repaired with a simple solder patch. Drain the pipe and open a valve somewhere along the line to vent steam. Clean the area around the leak with steel

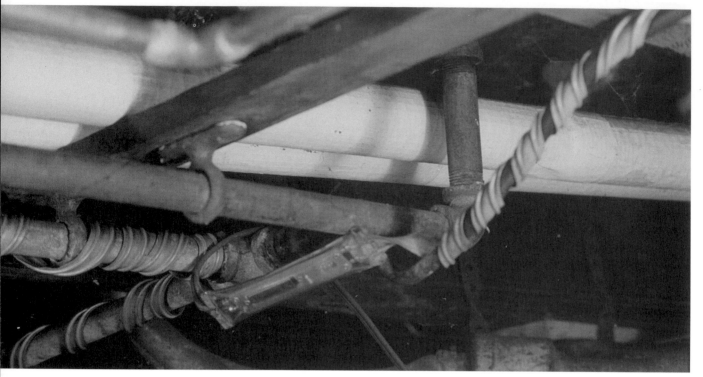

wool and apply paste flux and a dab of solder. A well-bonded solder patch will hold under pressure.

If the hole is bigger than 1/16 in., solder will fall into the hole instead of plugging it. In such cases, clean around the pipe and solder a curved piece of copper or small section of copper pipe over the hole.

Pipes that have split because of frost damage can sometimes be repaired with patching compound. The only sure cure is to cut out and replace the damaged section. Fortunately frozen copper pipes usually break apart at the solder joint before they split. When a pinhole leak appears at a fitting, it is sometimes possible to repair the joint without taking it apart. As earlier, drain the pipe and open a valve. Heat the fitting and sweat acid-core solder (which cleans out any contaminants) into it. If the leak persists or gets worse, you'll have no choice but to take the joint apart, clean it thoroughly to dislodge the offending speck of dirt or oxide, and resolder it with ordinary solder and non-acid flux.

If the fitting is part of a valve or close to it, take the faucet apart and remove the core to protect its rubber washer from the heat. If the pipe cannot be drained, cut it apart (you may need a special mini-cutter designed for tight spaces) and rejoin the pieces with a coupler after the leaking fitting is successfully soldered.

If, despite everything, one side of the pipe still dribbles water, you can solder the coupling to the dry side first, prepare the dripping side, and then pack the pipe full of bread, and quickly solder the coupling together. By the time the bread has absorbed enough water to soften, the joint should be completed.

A leaking flare joint in a copper or chrome-brass pipe (which is usually used to connect kitchen faucets and toilet supplies and also extensively with LP gas tubing) is ideally fixed by cutting out the old flare and reforming a new one. The local hardware store should carry the flaring tool that you'll need for making new joints. If there isn't enough tubing left to allow this, the alternative is to apply a bead of trusty automotive gasket cement to the flared end and retighten it. Faucet packing thread wrapped around the pipe under the flange nut might also do the trick. Short of complete replacement, the final solution is to solder the flare to its fitting, file off the excess and screw the flange nut back down.

Compression-ring fittings are the most common joint for toilet and lavatory supply risers. Most leaks respond to tightening. Some leaks will stop when packing thread is wrapped above the compression ring. Short of stripping the threads off the fitting, you can't damage a compression ring by overtightening. But because the metal is soft, use a wrench on both sides of the fitting to prevent twisting it apart. If the leak doesn't stop, you can't take the joint apart and try to retighten it. The metal will be too deformed. Install a new riser pipe and ring instead.

Drain-line repair

Leaks in drain lines are easier to repair by patching than are leaks in supply lines. For one thing, a drain line (if properly sloped) has water in it only when a fixture is actually in use. Since drain water is not pressurized, patches are not likely to loosen or spring a leak several hours later.

The joints and fittings of old-fashioned "hub-and-spigot" cast-iron drainpipes (or soil pipes) were sealed (or caulked) with a packing of oakum and molten lead (see the drawing at right). As the house settled over the years, some of these rigid joints might have shifted and cracked open.

Although making a poured lead joint is not difficult, it can be dangerous. If you let it sit too long before pouring the lead, the oakum packing could absorb moisture, which then instantly turns to steam, splattering hot lead out of the joint. Leather gauntlets (gloves with sleeves) are a must for working with hot lead. When pouring, hold the ladle at arm's length and to one side. Fortunately, unless you're adding and

Making a Vertical Caulked Lead Joint

1. Center spigot of one cast-iron pipe inside hub of another.

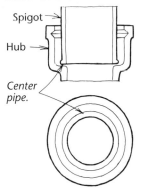

Spigot

Hub

Center pipe.

2. With a yarning iron, which has a blunt edge, pack oakum as shown.

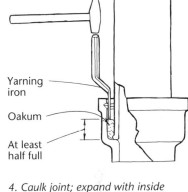

Yarning iron

Oakum

At least half full

3. Pour molten lead into joint.

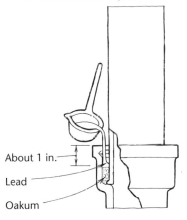

About 1 in.

Lead

Oakum

4. Caulk joint; expand with inside caulking iron, which has a beveled edge.

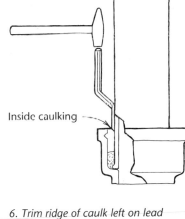

Inside caulking

5. Caulk outside circumference with outside caulking iron. Note difference in bevel angle.

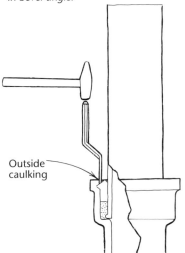

Outside caulking

6. Trim ridge of caulk left on lead surface, if desired.

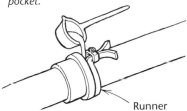

Flatten or leave.

For horizontal joint, use an asbestos joint runner clamped around pipe and pushed up against hub, as shown. This forms a small opening through which you pour hot lead into the pocket.

Runner

An Alternative Lead Joint

Repack the joint with oakum yarn, then seal with lead wool. Braid the wool into a rope, press into pipe hub and caulk with an iron, as for molten lead. This method eliminates the need to use molten lead, but it's costlier and more time-consuming.

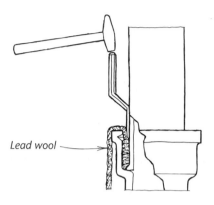

Lead wool

changing fittings or rerouting and extending hub-type cast-iron pipe, there's no need for the plumber's lead pot. As will be shown later, modern hubless cast-iron pipe eliminates the need for poured lead joints altogether. Unfortunately, not all local plumbing codes allow it.

Most of the time, a leaking joint is easily fixed by hammering on the lead gasket with a plumber's caulking iron to expand the soft metal tightly against the hub. Ideally, you'd use an inside iron first and then an outside iron to form the lead into the proper ridge. (The bevels on the edges of these are reversed.) If you can't borrow, rent or even find these tools, a cold chisel, prybar or length of steel bar will probably make a serviceable substitute.

Even if the joint is too loose to recaulk with an iron or if pieces of lead are actually missing, there's still no need to reform it with molten lead. With a chisel, remove the rest of the failed lead gasket to expose the underlying oakum yarning. This rope-like substance, when tightly packed, forms the actual waterproof seal—the lead gas-

ket just locks it in place and prevents the pipes from shifting or pulling apart. Replace any charred or rotted yarning or add new material to tighten up a loosely packed joint. The oakum is tightly packed with a blunt-edged yarning iron.

Seal the joint with lead wool. Braid the soft, heavy strands into a rope, press it into the hub and caulk it with an iron as for molten lead. The only reason lead wool isn't used by plumbers for all joints is that it costs about twice as much as ordinary lead and takes more time to work with. This isn't an issue if you're only repairing a joint or two.

If your local hardware store doesn't stock lead wool, use one of the water-based lead substitutes (Genova's Plastic Lead®, for example). Use a trowel to pack the hub with this putty-like compound, and don't run any water through the drain or allow the joint to flex until the compound is completely cured.

Settling can also cause the barrel of otherwise sound sections of pipe to crack. These cracks can range from minor hairlines to major abysses. Sometimes a small crack will become enlarged as its exposed edges corrode away.

The procedure for fixing a hairline crack in cast iron is similar to that for fixing splits in galvanized pipe. Drill a hole at each end of the crack to arrest further growth. Clean out debris and scaled rust with a wire brush or steel wool forced into the edges. Apply rust remover (naval jelly) and let it dry for several hours before rinsing the area with a wet paintbrush. When dry, spread plumber's epoxy patching compound (Epoxybond Plumber Paste®) over the crack with a putty knife, forcing it into the crack. The material is workable for 20 to 30 minutes at room temperature and cures permanently in three hours.

Wider cracks (up to 1 in. across) are patched with a stiffer epoxy putty (Epoxybond Plumber Seal®). Prepare the edges of the crack as before, chipping out any rusted edges. With your hands protected by disposable plastic gloves, work a ball of the putty into ³⁄₁₆-in. thick ropes about 6 in. or 8 in. long. Press the ropes firmly against the rough edges of the crack to form an anchor bead. Once this bead has set firm, close the crack by adding more layers of bead, keeping your hands moist to aid smoothing. The putty will set on a wet surface, which is useful if you can't stop the pipe from dripping.

Very large cracks or outright holes should be patched with fiberglass cloth, as in auto-body work. Coat the margins of the hole with the epoxy paste and embed the cloth patch in it, spreading more paste over the edges of the cloth. When the paste is dry, coat the rest of the cloth with paste and continue building up successive layers until the shape and thickness of the pipe is approximated.

Because naked cast iron is quickly attacked by rust, cast-iron pipe owes its longevity to the factory-applied asphalt-based coating, which normally doesn't wear off. Inferior grades of cast iron tend to corrode more readily. When struck with a hammer, corroded pipe makes a dull thunk instead of the sharp ring of sound pipe. Corrosion also presents itself as scaling patches of rust and ill-defined pits that crumble into ever larger holes when you try to clean them out for patching. Other than a small patch of rusted-out cast iron in an otherwise sound pipe, corroded pipe cannot be patched; it must be replaced.

If wholesale replacement is called for, switch over to ABS plastic, which is a lot cheaper, lighter and easier to work with. Remove the entire drain system up to the point where the sewer enters the foundation or disappears under the cellar slab. Adapters are available for mating plastic and cast iron (or just about any other combination of materials, if necessary). These are usually caulked to the joint with oakum and sealed with Plastic Lead®.

A stainless-steel clamp tightened over a neoprene gasket joins ABS plastic drainpipe to the stub end of a caulked cast-iron Y. Note the light-colored CPVC drain line, which is not allowed by some codes but is widely used by home plumbers.

Saddle Tap

Use where drain line is smaller in diameter than main drain.

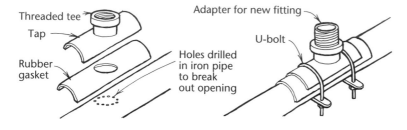

Adding a Drain-Line Extension to a Clean-Out Y

Remove and replace threaded section that holds plug. Screw bushing into opening and install new clean-out Y and elbow.

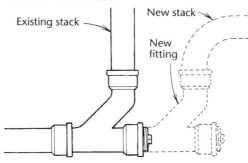

Other than repair work, the only other occasion you might have to take apart cast-iron drainpipes would be to install a tee or Y fitting for a drain-line extension to new fixtures.

Where the new drain line is smaller in diameter than the main drain, use a saddle tap instead of adding a tee, as shown in the top drawing above. Drill a circle of closely spaced holes in the face of the pipe and tap it until the circle breaks out. File down the rough edges, install the rubber gasket and clamp the saddle over the hole

by tightening down its U-bolts. Insert the appropriate adapter for connection to ABS pipe.

The brass plug that covers a clean-out Y is also an ideal place to add a drain-line extension. Installing an entirely new drain line could be preferable to taking apart an existing line. The added expense of the new pipe is offset by avoiding tearing up floors and walls and the possibility of damaging joints in the existing pipe as you work loose its upper sections. A bushing is screwed into the opening and a new clean-out Y and elbow installed for the added stack.

If you have no choice but to tap into the main stack or sewer line with a tee, at least try to run the extension into the horizontal sewer line in the cellar rather than the vertical stack in the walls. The sewer line is accessible, which is unlikely to be the case with the vent stack, unless a substantial chunk of wall covering, ceiling or flooring is removed first. Modern cast-iron pipe uses no-hub joints. The sections and fittings are joined together by neoprene rubber gaskets secured by an overlapping stainless-steel clamp. The no-hub system does away with caulking and lead sealers and makes assembly so fast and simple that anyone can do it.

To install a hubless fitting in an existing bell-and-spigot-type cast-iron line, cut out a section of pipe 1 in. longer than the length of the fitting to be installed. Slip the hubless connectors over the ends of the fitting, folding the rubber gasket back over on itself so that the fitting can be inserted between the stubs of the old pipe. The clamp is loosened so that it slides below the gasket. With the fitting in place, unfurl the rubber, position the clamp and tighten it down.

When removing a section of vertical pipe, make sure that the upper sections can't slide down. Wrap heavy steel pipe straps around one or two hubs and fasten them to the wall studs. Horizontal pipe should also be supported before cutting.

Cutting cast iron in place is a lot harder than cutting a section of pipe in the open. Since there probably won't be enough room to use a pipe cutter, you'll have to resign yourself to making the cut by hand. Make a cut completely around the pipe with a coarse blade (16 teeth per hacksaw, at least ¹⁄₁₆ in. deep). Gently hammer along this line with a cold chisel until the pipe breaks. If a jagged piece is left, don't use the chisel. Cut it off with the hacksaw instead. Getting to the back of the pipe with a hacksaw may prove challenging. If it is impossible, remove the entire section of pipe first by chiseling out its caulked lead joints. Tilt the section sideways to lift it out of the hub.

When local codes won't allow hubless pipe, a sisson fitting is needed to enable the new fitting to slip into the hubs of the existing pipe without raising it up. A section of pipe is cut and removed. The hubbed end is saved, cut to length and reinserted in the bell of the lower pipe. The sisson fitting is next, followed by the new hubbed fitting. Once everything is in place, the bell of the sisson fitting is expanded so that all the joints are tight and ready for caulking.

Leaks in plastic drain lines can be repaired with a plumber's poultice. Wrap alternating layers of cloth (an old bedsheet ripped into strips will do just fine) and wet plaster of Paris over the damaged area and allow it to set up. This bandage should last for years and be completely water-tight. If the drainpipe is dry, a small leak at a fitting can sometimes be stopped by coating the entire rim of the joist with a thick layer of joint cement. Scrape out as much of the edge of the fitting as you can before applying the cement.

The thin-walled chrome-plated brass tubing used for sink drains will leak either because a slip nut is too loose or cracked, or else because a washer is missing or defective. If simple tightening of the slip nuts doesn't solve the problem, take apart the joints and inspect the washers. Replace

Cast-Iron Connections

When using no-hub fittings to add a drain, make the two pipe cuts ½ in. farther apart than the length of the new fitting.

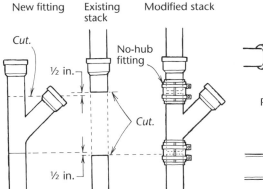

To connect plastic to cast-iron pipe, insert plastic spigot into cast-iron bell and seal with appropriate compound.

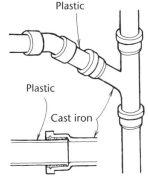

Where hubless pipe isn't allowed by code, add a drain using a sisson fitting. The sisson fitting, which requires that you caulk four joints, expands after it is in place.

Add stack fitting by lifting and tilting top portion of pipe, allowing it to protrude above the roof.

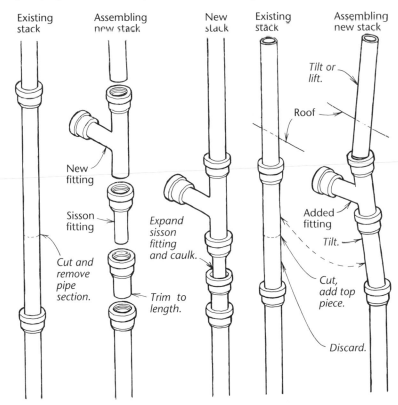

any frayed or cracked ones and retighten. Take care to align the pipes evenly, since misalignment is also a cause of leaks.

If the leak is in the pipe itself (usually at the bottom of the trap), the pipe has corroded or split. Water left to freeze in traps lacking a drain plug can split the pipe. These splits can be soldered, although it's easier to just replace the whole piece. A corroded pipe cannot be patched. It just falls apart. Brass will corrode when another kind of metal is in contact with it, as for example, if a nail or hairpin happens to fall into the sink and lodge in the bottom of the trap.

A cautionary tale

Routine remodeling operations have a way of turning into major plumbing problems. I remember remodeling a bathroom where I needed to remove the wall-mounted lavatory so I could install new drywall behind it. I disconnected the supply risers and loosened the slip nut between the drain extension and the trap. I discovered that the S-trap was corroded when half of it came with the sink as I lifted it off the wall. Replacing the trap would have been easy, except for the fact that the broken end was soldered into a short brass pipe that screwed into a galvanized steel elbow inside the former wall. To fit the slip-joint adapter for the new drain into this elbow, I had to remove the connector.

Undaunted, I set my pipe wrench on the brass nipple and gave it a tentative twist. Nothing budged. I pushed as hard as I dared on the wrench and still nothing moved. Luckily, there was enough room in the wall space so that I could conceivably unscrew the iron drainpipe instead and then safely disassemble the stubborn fitting. I placed my wrench on the pipe and pulled. There was an audible snap and suddenly the whole piece was very loose.

Now I was daunted. I'd managed to snap off the bottom of the pipe at a fitting. But when I pulled it up out of the floor, its threads were intact. I went down into the cellar to see what damage I'd done. I found that this section of the house was built over a crawl space, and the floor joists were only inches above the earth. There was barely enough room for a rat to crawl between them. I couldn't even see where the pipe was. Although my patience was wearing thin, my luck was still holding. As I needed to lay a new floor anyway, cutting an access hole through the old floor wouldn't be a problem.

This accomplished, I discovered that the galvanized pipe had been threaded into a cast-iron elbow, the remains of which were sticking up from the bell of a drain Y almost directly under the bathroom partition wall. About an hour and several skinned knuckles later, I'd managed to chisel out enough lead caulking to yank the shattered elbow out.

At the plumbing-supply shop, I discovered that it was a rather unusual elbow. One of the disadvantages of living in a rural area is that items like unusual cast-iron elbows are not routinely stocked by anybody within a 250-mile radius. Fortunately, the store did carry Plastic Lead®. Several hours later, I'd fitted a cobbed-up adapter into the bell of the old drain Y and run a new plastic drain line back up into the wall above. My simple five-minute operation had consumed the better part of a day and provided incontrovertible proof that old-house plumbing is governed by Murphy's Law.

Plumbing and Structural Changes

Because, as with electrical wiring, water-supply pipes and drainpipes are usually concealed within the walls, most plumbing renovation problems are really carpentry problems. How to find concealed pipes, gain access to walls with minimal damage, remove old and fit new piping into inaccessible places are just some of the difficulties you'll encounter.

As the number of rules in the code devoted to it suggests, proper venting of drain lines is very important for health reasons and for trouble-free operation. Depending on the location and types of fixtures and the local code requirements, adding a new bathroom can require raising floors, dropping ceilings and tearing out walls. Destruction and reconstruction can be minimized if you concentrate new plumbing in the same areas as the existing plumbing, by adding them back-to-back or one above the other. Then, at least, the supply pipes and the vent stack are already in place or near at hand. But if a new bathroom has to be installed at a great distance from the existing drain stack, it's usually a lot easier to run a new stack than to extend a new drain across a ceiling, as shown in the top drawing at right.

As with concealing electrical wiring, there are any number of ways to hide pipe under floors. Flooring can be taken up and the joists notched to receive the pipe. (Make sure not to nail through the pipe when putting the floor back down.) You could protect plastic and copper pipe where they cross joists with side pieces culled from steel electrical outlet boxes. Pipes, though, are a lot bigger than wires. Furthermore, because both drains and supply lines must pitch downward (¼ in. per ft. is required for drains), notching joists for anything larger than supply pipes will seriously compromise the strength of the framing (the notches get deeper as the run gets longer).

Installing a New Stack

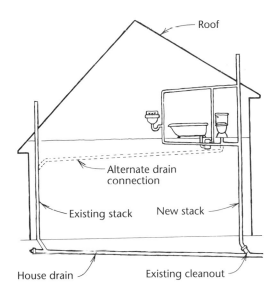

Notching Joists for Pipe

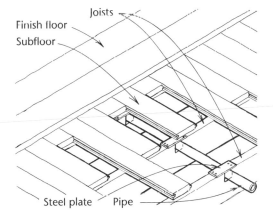

Concealing Large-Diameter Drain Lines

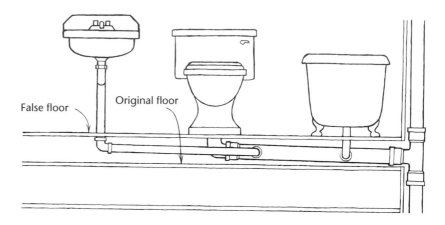

False floor   Original floor

Stiffening Notched Joints

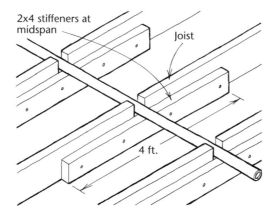

2x4 stiffeners at midspan

Joist

4 ft.

Where to Cut Joists to Avoid Structural Danger

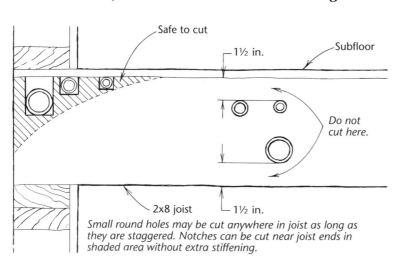

Safe to cut

1½ in.

Subfloor

Do not cut here.

2x8 joist   1½ in.

Small round holes may be cut anywhere in joist as long as they are staggered. Notches can be cut near joist ends in shaded area without extra stiffening.

If a step up into the bathroom is not objectionable, a high-ceilinged Victorian house has sufficient headroom to allow concealment of new drains under a false floor. This avoids dealing with structural problems entirely. Pipes can be run between floors without tearing into the walls by hiding them behind built-out corners and false walls, or even better, inside closets or the corners of built-in bookcases.

In the building trades, plumbers are even more renowned than electricians for their contributions to structural failure. It's one thing to bore a ¾-in. hole through a joist for a cable; it's quite another to hack out half a timber for a drain line. A cast-iron bath tub, filled with water and an average-sized person, can weigh as much as a ton. It seems obvious that if any floor joists have to be cut, notched or bored for drain lines, proper measures must be taken to ensure the safety of the floor framing. It's amazing how often the obvious is ignored and how both wall and floor frames have been indiscriminately hacked apart by heedless plumbers—amateur and professional alike.

Notched joists can be stiffened by nailing 2x4s alongside them. With old work (as opposed to new work), you won't often

Concealing Drain Lines between Joists

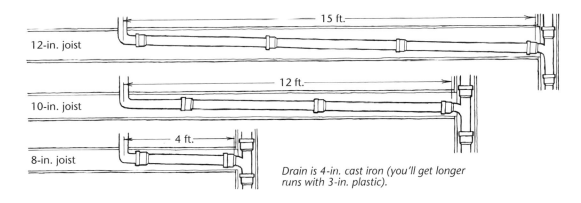

Drain is 4-in. cast iron (you'll get longer runs with 3-in. plastic).

have the luxury of exposed ceiling or floor framing. Thus, even though you can bore joists safely, you won't be able to slide full lengths of pipe through the holes. Sometimes you can use several short lengths, spliced together with couplers or other fittings. Otherwise, you'll have to notch the joists, drop ceilings or add false floors.

Depending on the depth of the joists, and the length of the drain run, a dropped ceiling may be needed to hide a toilet drain that runs parallel to the joists anyway. The drawing above shows the length of 4-in. drain that can be hidden between joists of varying widths at ¼-in. per ft. pitch.

If you can avoid running drain lines perpendicular to the joists whenever possible, you'll save yourself a lot of trouble. When this proves impossible, the cut joists must be supported by headers as for a stairwell opening. When it's the studs of a load-bearing wall that are notched, extra stiffening studs should be nailed flatwise alongside the cut ones, as shown in the drawing at right.

Strengthening Notched Load-Bearing Studs

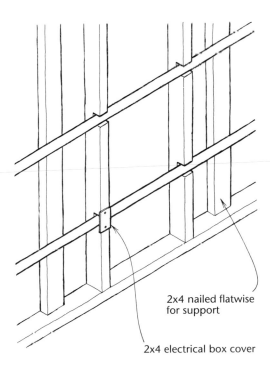

2x4 nailed flatwise for support

2x4 electrical box cover

Home Heating Systems

There's an old New England saying —"What with the high cost of heating, the average icicle on a roof costs about five dollars a foot."

—Eric Sloane, *A Reverence for Wood* (New York: Ballantine Books, 1965)

This modern high-efficiency gas boiler heats an entire two-story, 10-room house and occupies only a fraction of the space of the old furnace it replaced.

Although the installation of a new heating system is a job best left to a knowledgeable professional, it's still a good idea to understand how your home heating system works and to be familiar with its components. Too often we are at the mercy of the machines that are our slaves, and we live our lives surrounded by systems whose functioning is beyond our comprehension, leaving us feeling powerless and abused by forces outside our control. Our Colonial forebears, who made almost everything they needed with their own hands, would wonder at the state we've come to.

The deficiencies of heating a home by burning wood in a fireplace were so well known to the Colonists that the first of a long line of wood-burning stoves was introduced around the time of the Revolution. Despite the popular association of old houses with fireplaces and woodstoves, central heating was not a recent development. The first patent for a gravity hot-air heating system was taken out in 1815. With the growth of the factory system, reliable metal casting and a railway distribution system beginning in the 1830s, steam-heating systems came into wide use. Hot-water heat was the exotic new technology of 1876. By the close of World War I, the vast majority of urban homes and many rural homes were being heated by wood- or coal-fired hot-air, hot-water and steam systems.

As electric power became commonplace, blowers and pumps provided the forced circulation that soon replaced the inefficient gravity-driven systems of the past. A possible explanation for the persistence of woodstoves in rural areas is the relatively late arrival of electricity. (The REA program that was largely responsible for the electrification of farms began in the 1930s and continued well into the 1950s.) Since the homes of the rural aristocracy were often heated with coal and wood furnaces, poverty may also have played a part in prolonging the use of woodstoves.

Hot-Air Systems

Gravity-flow hot-air heating is simple in theory and inefficient in practice. A plenum (basically a sheet-metal box that sits on top of the furnace) collects air heated in a metal jacket surrounding the furnace firebox and channels it into ducts where, being lighter than ordinary air, it rises to circulate throughout the rooms of the house. Heavy cold air flows into floor ducts and falls into the cellar plenum.

To rise fast enough, plenum air has to be heated to high temperatures. Even so, the overall heat transfer rate is not very great. Unless it is full of moisture (which would be unlikely in an uninsulated, drafty old house, because of the relationship between relative humidity and outside infiltration), air is actually a poor heat-transfer medium. Some of the little heat it contains is also lost to radiation through the metal ducts as it rises to the upper stories. Cool air moving down walls and across the floor while hot air rises from floor ducts to the ceiling creates uncomfortable drafts. These same air currents probably circulate as much, if not more, household dust as heat.

The only thing a hot-air system has going for it is that it is cheap and simple. If it weren't for the addition of electrically powered blowers, which greatly increased the circulation rate and efficiency of the system (by pulling the cold air down into the plenum, not by forcing hot air out), hot-air heating would probably have become extinct. Today, forced hot-air systems are used whenever inexpensive and basically trouble-free heating is required. The draftiness still remains, together with the added drawback of a noisy blower.

Simple Forced-Hot-Air Heating System and Typical Maintenance Problems

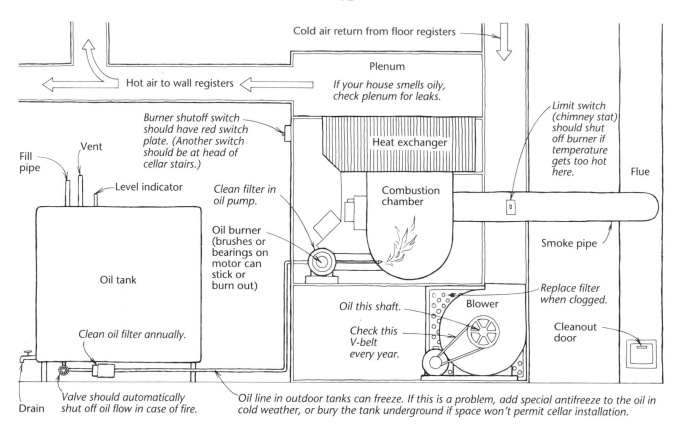

Cold air return from floor registers

Plenum

Hot air to wall registers

If your house smells oily, check plenum for leaks.

Heat exchanger

Limit switch (chimney stat) should shut off burner if temperature gets too hot here.

Flue

Burner shutoff switch should have red switch plate. (Another switch should be at head of cellar stairs.)

Combustion chamber

Vent

Fill pipe

Level indicator

Clean filter in oil pump.

Oil burner (brushes or bearings on motor can stick or burn out)

Smoke pipe

Oil tank

Oil this shaft.

Blower

Replace filter when clogged.

Cleanout door

Check this V-belt every year.

Clean oil filter annually.

Drain

Valve should automatically shut off oil flow in case of fire.

Oil line in outdoor tanks can freeze. If this is a problem, add special antifreeze to the oil in cold weather, or bury the tank underground if space won't permit cellar installation.

The drawing above shows the layout of a typical simple forced-hot-air furnace and fuel tank. Other than routine maintenance, such as oiling shafts, checking and replacing drive belts and filters, there isn't much else that can go wrong that the average home owner will be able to fix—other tasks are best left to the professionals who perform the annual fall tune-up. Cleaning and adjusting the burner orifices for maximum efficiency is precise work.

Steam-Heating Systems

Compared to gravity-flow hot-air heating, steam heat must have seemed like a godsend. The elegance of a naturally pressurized system, combined with the superior heat-transfer capacity of steam, raised home-heating systems to a heretofore unimaginable level of comfort and efficiency. Because steam (and hot water) heat by radiation rather than convection, drafts and dirt were now a thing of the past. Other than advances in controls and heating engineering, which improved safety, convenience and overall system responsiveness, the same two basic steam-heating systems developed back in the mid-19th century are still used today.

One-Pipe Steam System

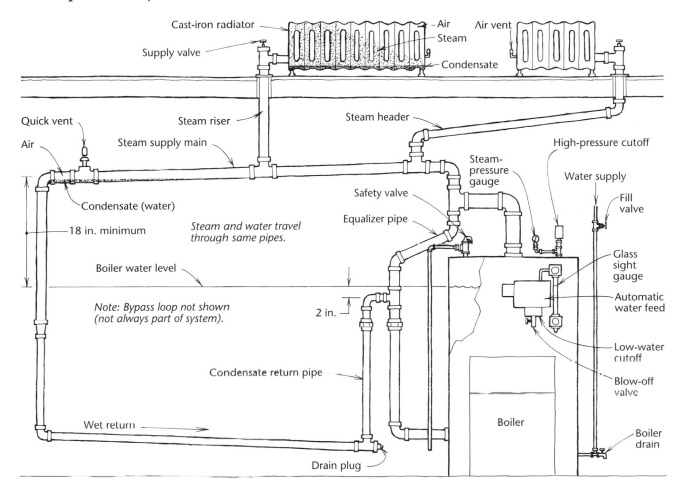

Cast-iron radiator
Supply valve
Air
Steam
Air vent
Condensate

Quick vent
Air
Steam riser
Steam supply main
Steam header
Condensate (water)
18 in. minimum
Steam and water travel through same pipes.
Safety valve
Equalizer pipe
Steam-pressure gauge
High-pressure cutoff
Water supply
Fill valve
Glass sight gauge
Automatic water feed
Low-water cutoff
Blow-off valve
Boiler water level
Note: Bypass loop not shown (not always part of system).
2 in.
Condensate return pipe
Wet return
Boiler
Drain plug
Boiler drain

The earliest and simplest system was the one-pipe system (see the drawing above). In this system, water is turned to steam in a boiler, expanding more than 1,000 times in volume as it does so. The hot steam rises up a pipe to a radiator, where it condenses back to water upon striking the cold metal and gives up its heat. The spent water (condensate) then flows back down the same pipe by gravity to the bottom of the boiler, where it is reheated to begin the cycle again. Because steam is ascending through the same pipe that water is descending, the one-pipe system requires fairly large-diameter pipes. Even so, a lot of heat is transferred to the cooled water by the counterflowing steam. The knocking sound traditionally associated with rising steam is caused as it pushes against pockets of water trapped in the pipes.

Two-Pipe Steam System

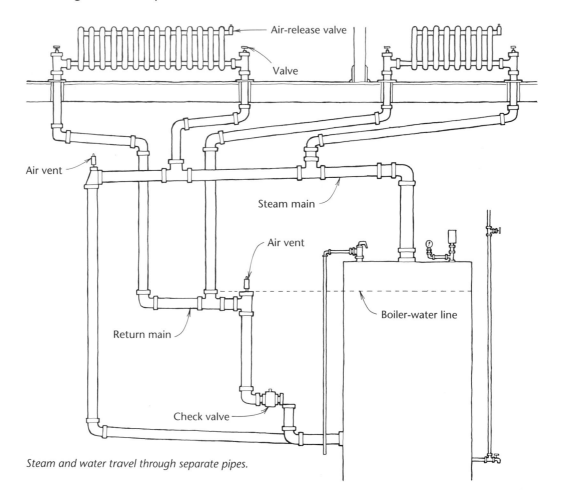

Steam and water travel through separate pipes.

The two-pipe steam system was developed to eliminate the drawbacks of the one-pipe system. In the two-pipe system, the steam rises to the radiators through one main and the condensate flows back down another. Smaller pipes can be used, knocking is eliminated and more heat is transferred to the radiators. But because it uses twice as much pipe (and labor), a two-pipe system is more expensive.

Venting

Before a radiator can fill with steam, the air it contains must be expelled through a vent on the side of the radiator. The venting rate determines how fast a radiator can heat up and how hot the room will get before the furnace shuts off. Besides a fully variable vent, steam vents are available in four speeds—very slow, slow, fast and very fast. Since the radiators farthest from the furnace will take the longest to heat, the system can be balanced by installing the appropriate vents along the circuit. If a variable vent is used in the room with the thermostat, the overall heat output for the entire system can be easily adjusted.

When the furnace shuts off and the radiators begin to cool down, the air that is drawn back into them cools them off even faster, and the thermostat soon calls for more heat. Thus, gravity steam heat tends to be uneven, with frequent cycles of hot and cold, rather than a steady heat output. If it hasn't already been done by a previous owner, the system should be converted to a vacuum flow. This requires nothing more complicated than replacing every vent, control valve and air valve throughout the system with vacuum vents and special "packless" (airtight) control valves. The vacuum vents allow air to escape but not re-enter as the system cools. In an airtight loop, the condensing steam creates a partial vacuum that draws more hot steam into the radiators, maintaining a more even temperature.

Maintenance and operation

Since the boiler feed water will always contain some air, which is released as it is heated, the oxygen in this air, plus the air drawn in by the radiators (in a nonvacuum system) causes a buildup of rust and scale throughout the system, especially in the boiler. These flakes of corrosion can interfere with the proper functioning of the safety and control valves and lead to premature boiler failure. Mineral buildup also reduces heat-transfer efficiency. Opening the blow-off valve (usually located on the automatic water feeder) once a month (a "blowdown") during the heating season to drain off these constantly accumulating sediments is a routine part of operating a steam-heating system. Drain the rusty water into a bucket until it runs clear.

Before purchasing an old house with an antique steam-heating system, give the boiler a test run. The most common maladies that afflict steam systems are usually easy to diagnose and cure. Unless the boil-

er and the steam mains have corroded to the point of no return, there's no compelling reason to replace the entire system.

A steam boiler has several important attachments that must be checked at frequent intervals for proper operation. These include: the glass sight gauge, the steam gauge and the safety valve; and in updated systems, the high-pressure limit switch, the low-water cut-off switch, the automatic water feed and the blow-off valve.

In the days before automatic water feeds, keeping the boiler filled with water was much more than just a bothersome chore. The safety of the house depended on constant attention to the boiler. Modern safety controls provide no security if they don't work. Not only should all the controls be checked at the beginning of each heating season, but the conscientious home owner will also get in the habit of glancing at the sight gauge every time he or she walks by the boiler. The water feed should be checked as part of the monthly blowdown.

Never fire up a boiler before checking the sight gauge, which is a vertical glass tube mounted on the side of the boiler that shows the water level inside the boiler. It should read about half full, slightly more when cold, slightly less when hot. If no water is showing, either the boiler is empty, the gauge is plugged or both. Don't turn the boiler on! Open the water feed and see if the gauge fills. If not, open the drain cock at its bottom end until the water runs clear. If the valve is still clogged, close its shut-off valves, unscrew the gauge retaining nuts and remove the sight glass for cleaning. Replace a nonfunctioning gauge. If the sight glass fills, the boiler is safe to turn on. Sometimes, a boiler is fitted with try-cocks instead of a sight gauge. These are two small faucets near the top of the boiler. Open the lower one carefully; water should stream out. With the boiler running, open the upper cock; steam should rush out, indicating that the water level is somewhere between the two try-cocks.

The steam gauge is a meter that shows the pressure (in psi) of the steam at the top of the boiler. Normal safe operating range for small domestic steam boilers is around 5 psi. Of course, the gauge for a vacuum system will have a negative scale. The danger zone begins above 12 psi. The boiler should also be equipped with a safety valve, similar to the pressure-relief valve required at the top of a water heater. The safety is preset to open at 15 psi, to prevent a runaway boiler from building up explosive force (at 50 psi, 30 gal. of water will blow the boiler and the house apart with the same force as a pound of nitroglycerine). Check the valve for proper operation yearly. With a long stick (to prevent scalding), gently lift up the release lever until steam escapes. Repeat until all debris is cleared out. If the lever has rusted shut, replace the entire unit after the boiler has cooled down.

Modern boilers are also equipped with backup safety controls that regulate the steam pressure in the boiler and determine its firing cycle. A small metal box connected to the burner controls by an electric cable contains the steam-pressure controls. Inside the twin unit are two lever-type switch contacts, with adjusting screws. The first set of contacts is marked "cut-in," and determines the steam pressure at which the burner will turn on when the thermostat calls for heat. The second switch, marked "differential," is adjusted to set the pressure at which the burner will shut down. This is a safety switch, since it will override any other control if pressure goes over the safe limit. Cut-in plus differential limit the normal operating range of the boiler. The switches are calibrated by fiddling with their adjustment screws until the desired cut-in and cut-out points match the reading on the steam pressure gauge. Normal cut-out pressure should not exceed 5 psi.

The same boiler that heats hot water for steam can also be used to heat it for domestic use in the summer. Since the thermostat is turned off, the cut-in switch won't work. Another control, the aquastat, responds to the water temperature inside the boiler. When it falls below the setting on the aquastat dial, it turns the boiler on until the water is heated a few degrees warmer than its upper setting, at which point the aquastat shuts the boiler off. The boiler heats water circulating through a heat exchanger to an external storage tank. Drinking water is never allowed to mix with boiler water, since the latter often contains chemical corrosion inhibitors.

The high-pressure limit switch is a safety device that automatically shuts off the boiler when the steam pressure exceeds 10 psi. An easy way to test its operation is to crank the thermostat up to the top of the dial and watch the steam-pressure gauge as the boiler struggles to answer the call. If the pressure goes over 10 psi and the boiler is still running, turn it off manually, using the red-colored emergency shut-off switch. Call a repair person.

The low-water cut-off switch is another safety device. This switch is usually part of the automatic water feed and blow-off system located on the side of the boiler. To test the switch, close the manual water feed so that the boiler cannot get more water. Open the blow-off valve with the boiler running. Just about when the water level drops below the bottom of the sight gauge, the boiler should shut off. If it doesn't, turn off the boiler immediately. Don't forget to reopen the feed valve so the boiler will fill back up. Call a repair person. If you must run the boiler in this potentially dangerous mode, check the sight gauge at least four times a day until the level switch is repaired.

In the unlikely event that your boiler is still supplied by a manual feed, don't use it before you have added an automatic water-feed control. This control looks like a cross between a circulating pump and a water meter, and is attached to a loop in the cold-water feed line so that its center is at the same level as the desired water level in the boiler. Like the float in a toilet tank, a control valve opens when the boiler water level drops and closes when it reaches the correct height. One cause of gurgling and knocking pipes is an overfilled boiler caused by a sticking automatic feed shutoff. The water is pushed up into the steam main from the top of the boiler and will eventually begin to dribble out the radiator vents. This turns your steam heat into a lukewarm water system, and the circulation must be fixed and the system drained back to the proper water level.

Test the automatic feed with the boiler off. First, make sure all the control valves are properly set—someone may have inadvertently shut down or partially opened one of the bypass valves. If the boiler water level reads too low, close the outfeed gate valve C (see the top drawing at right) and crack open union #2 just in front of it. Water should squirt out under pressure if the feeder's internal float valve is operating properly. If water doesn't squirt out, the float valve is probably stuck closed or clogged. If there's nothing wrong with the float, check the water line for blockage. If the water level is too high, close infeed gate valve A and open union #2 again.

If water continues to trickle out, the float is stuck open. Check the float action by trying to lift the float valve stem on the side of the feed control with a screwdriver blade (see the bottom drawing at right). If it won't move or holding it open doesn't flush the valve seat clean, take the control apart and replace the valve and all the gaskets. Bypass gate valve B allows water to flow into the boiler if you need to isolate the circulation loop (by closing valves A and C and opening B), as if, for example, you have to fix it during winter, when you don't want to shut down the system.

The only sound a properly operating steam-heating system should make is the hiss of steam escaping out the vent just after the radiator fills. If the hiss continues, the vent should be replaced. When water

Automatic Water-Feed System for Steam-Heat Boilers

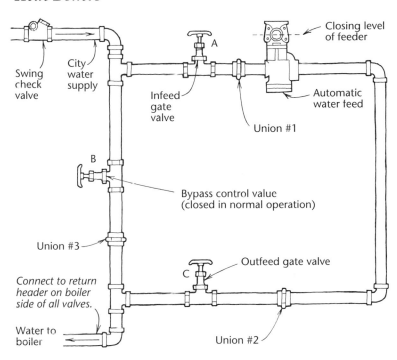

Testing and Cleaning the Float Valve Stem

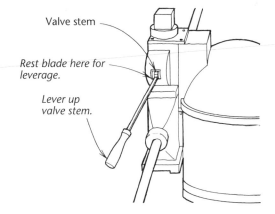

Causes of Water Hammer in Steam Pipes

Broken support

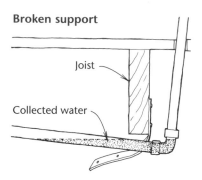

Joist

Collected water

When heat pipe drops and water collects, noise occurs when steam enters pipe.

Incorrect pipe installation

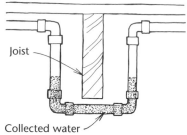

Joist

Collected water

Trapped water obstructs steam line. Pipes should go through or over obstructions.

or steam leaks out the radiator shut-off valve, the stem packing is worn out. With the system shut down, unscrew the valve stem and wrap new packing thread around the stem in the direction it turns down.

Gurgling, sloshing and thumping in the lines or radiators is caused by trapped water. Steam lines should always slope downward. Sometimes a broken pipe strap causes a section of steam pipe to drop, creating a water trap. Or an inexperienced home plumber may have run a steam line below an obstruction (like a joist); always route pipes over obstructions. Radiators should also slope toward the return line. If the floor has settled, a radiator can sometimes tilt in the wrong direction and trap water inside itself. Wood shims added under the feet on the low side will cure this problem.

For all practical purposes, the radiators used for steam and hot-water heat are identical, except for the vents. But finned baseboard heaters cannot be used for steam.

Finally, to reduce corrosion buildup, drain the boiler completely once a year to flush out sediment. Continue to refill and drain off until the water runs clear. Once the boiler is completely filled, add a corrosion-inhibiting compound through the safety-valve tap hole.

Hot-Water Heating Systems

The constant maintenance required to keep a steam-heat system in healthy condition, and the danger of explosion when these chores are ignored or a safety valve is rusted shut, is probably the reason why hot-water heat became so popular. Since water has a greater latent heat than steam, the radiators in a hot-water heating system will give off heat for a longer time. Hot-water heat is renowned for its gentle evenness. Unlike a steam system, it is almost impossible to run a hot-water boiler to dangerous pressures, since all the water in the lines and radiators would have to boil off before the boiler could become dangerously low. And as the water turned to steam, it would harmlessly vent out of the radiator air vents.

As with steam heat, the oldest hot-water heating systems were gravity flow. The drawing on the facing page shows a schematic of a simple gravity system. Basically, water is heated in a boiler, it rises up through a pipe to the radiator, gives up its heat and flows back down another pipe to the boiler. Since water expands when it is heated, the extra water rises up a pipe to an expansion tank somewhere up in the attic. This tank has an open drain, usually a pipe venting directly out onto the roof, to discharge any overflow.

At the same time that hot water is expanding, it gets lighter. The radiators above are filled with heavier cold water, which flows down the return pipes, pushing the lighter hot water up into the radiators. Because a gravity system is an open one, explosive pressure cannot build. The boiler could burn out, but it wouldn't blow up. But the constant loss of water via the expansion overflow is also a heat loss.

Simple Gravity Hot-Water System

Arrows show water flow.

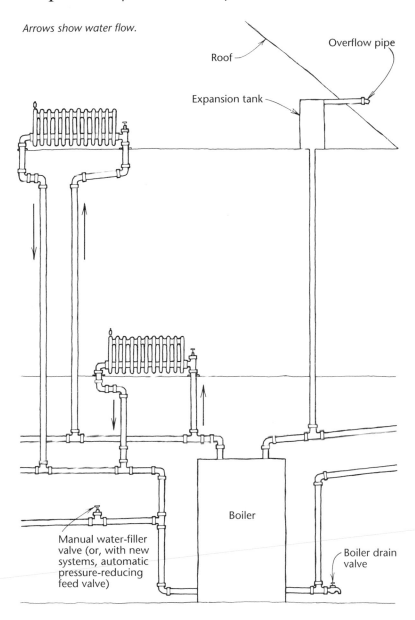

Since the difference between the hottest water (about 190°F) and the coolest water (170°F) is not great, the circulation and heat-transfer rate is slow, and large pipes are needed to overcome friction. The air brought into the system by the open expansion tank and the new replacement water also fosters relatively rapid corrosion.

The circulator pump is the heart of the modern forced-flow hot-water heating system. Forced circulation is much faster and more efficient than the earlier gravity-flow systems these pumps replaced.

The circulator pump is the heart of the modern forced-flow hot-water heating system. Forced circulation is much faster and more efficient than the earlier gravity-flow systems these pumps replaced.

Forced-flow systems

With the invention of small electric pumps, forced-flow (hydronic) hot-water heating systems were developed that eliminated the drawbacks of the gravity-flow systems. The pump circulates hot water at a rapid rate, greatly increasing the speed and efficiency of the heat transfer to the radiators and also allowing the use of much smaller pipes. Hydronic heat typically uses ¾-in. copper tubing instead of 2-in. black iron steam pipes. Forced systems are also closed systems. Since no water (or heat) is ever lost through the expansion tank, no new water need be added. Corrosion is reduced and system efficiency increased. Like the pressure tank of the water-supply system, the expansion tank should be drained yearly to prevent waterlogging. Since so little water is lost, automatic feeds and safety controls are not so critical.

One disadvantage of a heating system that depends on electric power is the potential havoc wrought by a power outage during the heating season. In the old days, when heating with a coal- or wood-fired furnace meant keeping the coal bin or wood shed full, there was no danger of losing the heat or of frozen pipes. Because it is a closed system, a modern hydronic sys-tem is no longer filled with water. Instead, a heat-transfer fluid (a nontoxic propylene-glycol-based antifreeze) circulates through the system and protects it both from corrosion and freezing.

The so-called single-pipe (or "loop") system, is the most economical and widely used hydronic installation. No hot-water system of any kind ever has just one pipe entering a radiator. This is one way to distinguish hot-water heat from steam heat. In a one-pipe hot-water system, both the radiator supply pipe (the "riser") and the return pipe are teed into a single pipe that makes a circuit of the house, returning to the circulator pump on the boiler. When the hot water enters a special directional, or "scoop," tee at the riser, a portion of its flow is diverted into the radiator. The more expensive two-pipe system uses a separate main feed and main return line. In the one-pipe system, the radiators closest to the boiler get the hottest water, and the ones at the end of the line get the coolest. The two-pipe system is more even, since the same-temperature water is equally available to every radiator.

It can be hard for the uninitiated to tell the difference between a two-pipe steam system and a hot-water heating system. Look at the radiator vents first. The bleeder valve on a hot-water system is tiny, whereas the air vent on a steam radiator is domed and fairly large. A steam boiler will often have the same general configuration as a hot-water boiler. But the hot-water boiler will never have a sight glass. It will have an altitude gauge as well as a temperature and pressure gauge. This indicates the height of the water in the topmost radiator. Open the bleeder valve to let out water and note the needle reading when that radiator is full. If it drops below that figure, the system is getting low on water.

The altitude gauge shows the level of water in the highest radiator of a hot-water system. Note the reading when that radiator is full. When the needle falls much below that level, it's time to add water to the boiler.

Maintenance and operation

Despite all their advantages, hot-water heating systems, like any mechanical arrangements, are subject to the infirmities of age. The most common problem with hot-water systems is a cold radiator. As with steam heat, in order to work, hot-water radiators must be purged of air. (Modern baseboard hot-water systems radiate heat through the fins attached to the water pipe—they don't contain any air.) Purge the radiators of air prior to the heating season, when the boiler is drained down and everything else is checked. Open the bleeder valve at the top of the radiator with a small socket wrench or radiator valve key until all the air is out and the water flows free of bubbles. Replace any valves that leak or don't drain. The radiators must also be purged of air whenever the system is drained down for repairs and refilled.

Forced-Flow Hot-Water Heating System

Single-pipe system

Pump circulates hot water around loop. Directional scoop tees direct water to each radiator.

(Domestic hot water [D.H.W.] circuit omitted for clarity.)

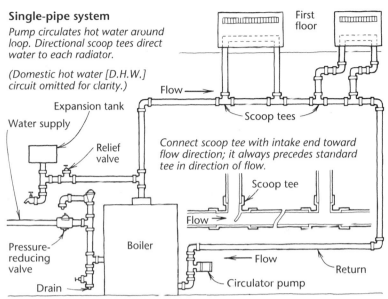

Two-pipe system

Each radiator has two pipes: one to the main feed and one to the main return.

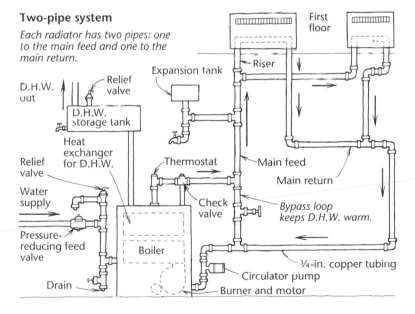

Radiators are also fitted with a control valve, which enables the radiator to be shut off or partially opened as needed to balance the system. These valves often require repacking. Suspect a partially closed zone valve if all the radiators on a line are too cold.

A hot-water system is equipped with a thermostat valve, similar to the one in a car radiator, installed in the hot-water output line coming from the boiler. This valve is designed to open at about 150°F, to prevent the circulator pump from forcing cold water into the radiators when the system first cycles up. If the furnace and the circulator both appear to be running and all the radiators are still cold, the thermostat may be stuck closed. Shut the system down and drain it. (Just about any repair of a hot-water boiler or its attached controls requires draining the system. Be sure to add boiler antifreeze when refilling.) Remove the thermostat. Set it in a pan of water and heat it on the stove. If the thermostat doesn't open long before the water boils, it's defective.

Another cause of cold radiators is a stuck check valve. This one-way valve is located right before the thermostat, and is supposed to prevent water from running backward through the system when the lever on its side is set in the "normal" position. In the "closed" position, the flow to the radiators is blocked so that the boiler can heat domestic hot water without heating the house in the summer. Use the "open" position, in which the water can flow either way, to drain the system.

If the circulator pump doesn't turn, hot water can't get to the radiators. A burned-out motor is unlikely to be the cause of the problem. Shut off the system and the furnace breaker and try to turn the pump with a pair of pliers. If it won't move or turns hard, someone has neglected to oil the pump bearing and it has run dry. Soak the frozen pump shaft with a silicone lubricant (such as WD-40®), and see if you can get it to turn. If not, drain the system, disassemble the pump and replace the shaft and bearing. The impellers may also be damaged. Replacement parts are usually available for most makes of circulator pumps. The spring-loaded coupling between the pump and the motor may also be broken; it, too, is easily replaced.

Your maintenance program should also include an annual furnace tune-up by a professional. But even running in top form, the average old boiler is only about 50% to 60% efficient. Boilers eventually wear out and need replacement. When the inevitable happens, installing a high-efficiency boiler will quickly pay for itself in reduced fuel costs. Modern boilers can attain efficiencies of 80% to 90%.

Adding and removing radiators

In the course of remodeling, it may be necessary to add or remove radiators. To add a radiator with steam heat, simply add a standard tee in the main at any point. For a two-pipe system, tap into the return main as well. To remove a radiator, replace the tee with a coupler or simply remove the riser, insert a short nipple into the existing tee and screw a cap onto it. If the radiator you wish to add happens to have been made for hot water, screw a plug into one of the unused openings and replace the bleeder valve with an air or vacuum vent. Insert a gate valve in the riser before the radiator.

You can even adapt a finned hot-water baseboard radiator for steam. Use a tapped elbow at one end to install the air vent and tilt the unit toward the feed pipe. As long as the vent is higher than the center tube of the radiator, it will work.

Adding a radiator to a hot-water system is basically the same as for a steam system. Add a scoop tee for the inlet and a standard tee for the outlet spaced so that the risers go straight up to the radiator. When cutting and capping the supply and return to remove the radiator in a one-pipe system, remove the scoop tee and install a coupler. The return tee can be capped. But don't leave sections of riser, which will trap steam, sticking up into the floor joists.

Finned copper radiators have a higher heat output than cast iron; and they work faster. But cast-iron heaters hold more water and thus give off heat for a longer time. They're also more suited to an old house. Because of the bulk and weight of cast-iron radiators, heating contractors may be glad to let you have them free for the carting when they're remodeling someone else's system.

Alternative Heating Systems

A lot of people who jumped onto the alternative energy bandwagon back in the 1970s become strangely reticent when the subject of solar panels or woodstoves comes up today. The crash of the tax credit scam brought down high-flying solar entrepreneurs along with the price of solar systems, and reduced the cost-effectiveness of complicated Rube Goldberg-like solar technologies. Likewise, the increased cost of firewood dampened the enthusiasm for new woodstoves even before strict new clean-air standards raised their cost to that of the average fossil-fuel heating plant.

Although no one seriously maintains anymore that our society is about to freeze in the dark, there are still good reasons to opt for strategies that minimize dependence on fossil fuels. It is still an inescapable fact that wood is a renewable resource and oil and gas aren't, that coal is too dirty, that present-day nuclear plants make messy garbage and that sunlight can be harvested in useful, if not terribly profitable, ways.

Out of the furor and often messianic fervor of the decade that made "crisis" a cliché, a few proven technologies emerged that enable individual home owners to play a part in reducing overall energy demand and the environmental degradation it fosters. What also emerged from the 1970s was a heightened awareness of the importance of conservation, its elevation to an ethical imperative. Whatever else

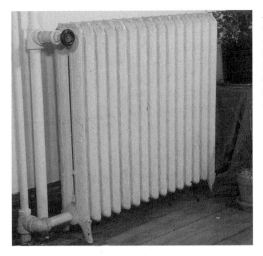

Although antique cast-iron radiators are not as quick to respond to heat demand as modern copper-finned radiators, they look more appropriate in an old house.

can be said about conservation, reducing consumption by conscious choice at the point of purchase, adequate home insulation, proper moisture control and upgraded heating-system efficiency creates comfort without mortgaging the future.

Now that an accessible methodology has been distilled from theory and experience, it's undeniable that simple, effective passive-solar techniques can supplement and reduce the burden on a fossil-fuel heating plant. Unfortunately, except for heating domestic water, the fancy gadgetry of active solar systems has been shown to be the expensive and cranky toy its critics always claimed it was. Likewise, at this point, the wide-scale use of photovoltaics is stymied by the economics of limited production and output.

But despite a depressed market, with the addition of newly developed catalytic converters that reduce smokestack pollution, wood-burning stoves are still a sensible way to help heat a house. In fact, with the continued development of systems that automatically feed pelletized wood (made from "waste" species), wood-fired central-heating systems are now coming onto the market that are competitive with conventional systems both in cost and convenience.

Wood-burning stoves

For the average owner of an old home, there are two ways to heat with wood. The typical one is to use a woodstove for occasional, one might say "ornamental," heating: The woodstove supplements the primary fossil-fuel system.

Because of its sporadic nature, backup wood heating sidesteps the very real problem of acquiring a large supply of firewood and finding a place to keep the bulky stuff dry and ready for use. The overall cost of heating (when the price of the wood is included) may not be any lower, but the fossil-fuel component is satisfyingly reduced. In a conventionally heated house, since all zones are roughly the same temperature, there is no place to go to get warm when you come in from the outside chilled to the bone. A woodstove provides a very definite place to warm up. And as your body warms, you move farther away from the stove—no thermostats, no motors or blowers, nothing but the relaxing massage of the stove. What could be simpler or more satisfying?

Since most people aren't dairy farmers (who can't leave home for very long), few would even think of using wood as their only heat source. No one wants to be tied to home or worry about frozen pipes. But for the home owner who has a woodlot or who lives where firewood is readily available, using wood as the primary fuel and a fossil-fuel system for backup makes sense. The backup function can be part of a multifuel boiler or furnace that takes over when the wood fire dies down. Or it could be a separate heating system that kicks in to smooth out the temperature swings that follow the ebb and flow of the woodstove fire.

If an existing heating plant is undersized or too inefficient, it may be cheaper in both the long and short term to add a woodstove instead of a new heating system. Likewise, when replacing a defunct system, consider the possibility of installing the smallest possible fossil-fuel plant that will keep the house from freezing, and depending on a high-efficiency woodstove to shoulder the day-to-day heating burden.

It is possible to heat a house entirely with wood. In my old house in Vermont, a woodstove preheated water circulating

Energy-efficiency, old-house style: The author's old house in Vermont was heated entirely with wood.

The brick wall behind this woodstove is more than decorative: It also stores heat that evens out the temperature swings typical of wood heating.

through a stainless-steel firebox coil (see the photo at right on the facing page). A black-painted galvanized steel tank stored the water and radiated heat into the room. When a tap was opened, the heated water flowed into an electric water heater installed directly above. A preheater tank prevented premature burnout of the electric-heater element because of excessively hot water. The brick wall behind the stove was hollow-cored with inlets and outlets to circulate heat to rooms on the other side of the wall. Together with a soapstone stove, it stored a great deal of heat, making for much more even room temperature than one would expect from a house heated entirely with wood.

A "dedicated" wood furnace makes up for what it lacks in convenience by being less expensive and more efficient than a multifuel furnace. Wood furnaces are also available as add-ons for conventional furnaces, where both systems utilize the existing ductwork or piping. The proper-sized furnace will heat any house quite comfortably. Without supplemental heat, the upper limit of a freestanding stove is somewhere around 10,000 cu. ft. to 12,000 cu. ft.—about the size of a traditional five-to-seven room, one-and-a-half story Cape-style farmhouse.

The success and comfort of "central" heating with a woodstove increases with the openness of the floor plan. This principle was embodied in the arrangement of a Colonial house around its massive central chimney. In the much larger farm and village houses of the 19th century, comfort for the outlying rooms was provided by the addition of separate stoves, typically vented into half-chimneys. Sometimes the stovepipe was routed through several rooms and walls before it joined the chimney. Heat radiating from the extended pipe would warm the rooms. Unfortunately, this alternative to ducted central heat was a serious fire hazard.

Another traditional heating conservation strategy is simply to close off the extraneous rooms (as long as there are no plumbing runs through the walls) and centralize the house around the stove. Since bedrooms are seldom used during daylight hours and many people prefer to sleep in cool rooms, a door left closed until nightfall may be all the zone control needed.

With a woodstove or furnace as the main heater, inexpensive to install but costly to operate electric baseboard heaters are cost-effective if used only to provide freeze protection or to take the chill off distant rooms. Electric blankets are also an excellent backup heating system for cold bedrooms. Another flexible and economical backup heating system, which could be used as an alternative to a central furnace, is a direct-vent gas heater. This type of unit mounts on a wall and vents through it to the outside. Direct-vent gas heaters are available with or without blowers, in sizes for heating a single room up to several rooms.

Passive solar heating

Many old-time builders had an intuitive understanding of the benefits of passive solar heating, as evidenced by the facades of old farmhouses that often faced due south. Old-timers also understood energy conservation. The windows of old houses were smaller than modern windows and less numerous on the north side of the house. Trees that blocked the winter winds and shaded the house from summer heat were planted close by. Although owners of old houses today may have a more sophisticated understanding of these principles, in most cases there is little more that they can do to implement them than the old-timers already did without doing serious harm to the integrity of the house.

Along with remuddling, the editors of *The Old-House Journal* warn against what they call "technological trashing," where in a singularly ill-conceived attempt to increase energy efficiency, the beauty of a house is destroyed by a passive-solar retro-

The Energy-Efficient Old House

There are many ways to increase the energy efficiency of an old house without retrofitting solar panels or other high-tech options.

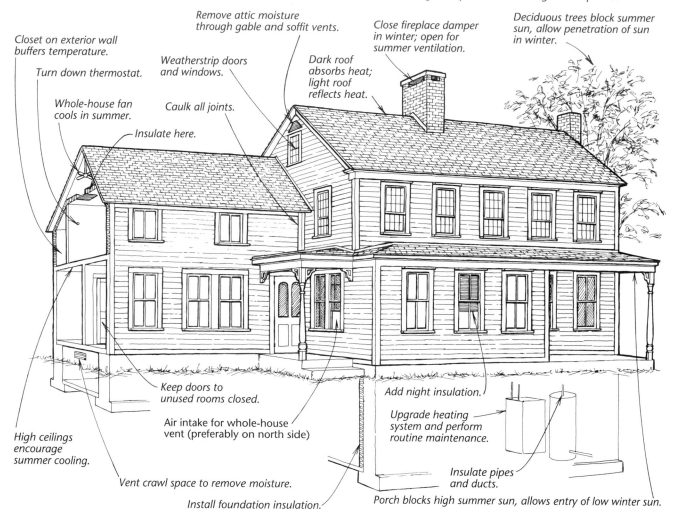

Closet on exterior wall buffers temperature.

Turn down thermostat.

Whole-house fan cools in summer.

Insulate here.

Remove attic moisture through gable and soffit vents.

Weatherstrip doors and windows.

Caulk all joints.

Close fireplace damper in winter; open for summer ventilation.

Dark roof absorbs heat; light roof reflects heat.

Deciduous trees block summer sun, allow penetration of sun in winter.

High ceilings encourage summer cooling.

Keep doors to unused rooms closed.

Air intake for whole-house vent (preferably on north side)

Vent crawl space to remove moisture.

Install foundation insulation.

Add night insulation.

Upgrade heating system and perform routine maintenance.

Insulate pipes and ducts.

Porch blocks high summer sun, allows entry of low winter sun.

fit. Other than the addition of solar panels flat against a sloping roof, where they will not be too obtrusive, foisting a solar-heating system upon an old house without destroying its character is almost impossible. I have seldom seen a felicitous mating of old and new. With attention to detail and a lot of money, a modern greenhouse could conceivably be integrated into a Victorian mansion (glass-walled conservatories were a traditional amenity of that era), but the sunspaces indiscriminately tacked onto farmhouses and townhouses alike are seldom harmonious. If energy efficiency is that important, build a new house, don't buy an old one.

Repairing and Restoring Chimneys

Combustion gases, whether from wood, coal, oil or gas, must be vented to the outside. A proper stovepipe installation and a workable chimney are crucial to the safety of the household as well as to the efficient functioning of the heating appliance. An unsafe chimney is a structural problem that must join foundation and roof problems as top-priority repairs.

The first chimneys were temporary expedients, built of sticks plastered with a mix of mortar and manure, as crude as the rough cabins they heated. These were soon replaced with more substantial stone or brick chimneys, whose flues were coated with refractory (heat-resistant) mortars. Clay flue liners did not come into use until the beginning of the 20th century. Because of their smooth surfaces, clay liners don't slow the ascending smoke as much as do rough masonry joints. The smoke doesn't cool as fast, creosote buildup is reduced, the chimney has a better draw and downdrafts are less frequent. There are fewer joints through which flue gases can leak into the rooms, and if a chimney fire does occur, it is usually contained safely within the flues. A fire in an unlined chimney could melt the mortar between bricks and burst out into the framing; before this happens, the bricks will become so hot that the surrounding wood catches fire. Flue liners are such a good idea that an unlined chimney should never be used.

An old chimney or fireplace should never be used before it is inspected. Hold up or dangle a light down the flue; use a mirror to find obstructions and offsets hidden behind walls and to inspect the brickwork for soundness. Chimneys and fireplaces that have been unused or covered for a long time are often clogged with fallen bricks, birds' nests and even dead birds, especially at the bottom slope of an offset or on the fireplace smokeshelf. Creosote buildup in these places can completely close off the flue.

Loosen a brick on the side of the offset by gently tapping along its mortar joints with a brick chisel. Remove another brick so that you can reach in and clean out the obstruction, bit by bit, or push it down the rest of the flue to the cleanout at the bottom of the chimney.

It often happens that in the course of renovations, an old unused fireplace or chimney will be found entrapped under the plaster. Some of these can be real treasures, well worth restoring. Old fireplaces can be reconstructed by a competent mason. (The original may have been covered because it smoked too much; early fireplace and chimney designs were sometimes flawed or incorrectly built by unskilled masons.) One common cure is to retrofit a smokeshelf and damper at the chimney throat.

If you decide to reopen a closed-off chimney, be sure that it hasn't been taken down below the roof and that openings weren't cut into it—old-timers weren't too fussy about running more than one stovepipe into a single flue. The presence of an old thimble (the opening in a flue for a stovepipe) behind a wall is indicated by a circular bulge in the wallpaper or plaster, or creosote stains on the wallpaper or woodwork and floors. Other than the vent from a gas or oil water heater, which can be teed into the furnace flue, modern fire codes prohibit the connection of more than one heating appliance per flue.

Relining a chimney

Chimneys can be relined with clay tiles, with a proprietary cementitious mix or with rigid or flexible stainless-steel chimney pipe. These materials are all expensive and/or time-consuming to install, and the work requires skills beyond those of the typical home owner. The choice of method depends on the type of chimney and the combustion products it will vent.

Coal and wood pose special problems. Coal flue gases are extremely corrosive, and although some manufacturers claim their products are corrosion-resistant, metal liners should never be used for a coal-burning system. Likewise, the stoke-and-starve cycle of wood burning encourages creosote formation, which often leads to chimney fires. Even clay flue liners can crack in a really bad chimney fire. A metal liner will burn through long before the flue gets hot enough to destroy flue tiles.

When wood is burned only sporadically, as in a fireplace, the likelihood of a chimney fire is low, and stainless-steel flue liners could be used. Even so, these liners won't last for more than 4 to 10 years when used in wood-burning chimneys. Although a cementitious or a standard clay liner might cost three or four times as much as a metal liner to install, it will last at least 50 years. Metal liners are only cost-efficient and safe with the relatively low flue-gas temperatures and clean burn of oil and gas fires.

Adding Clay Flue Tiles to an Unlined Chimney

2x4 block with offset hole — tilted block pinches against sides of flue while it is being lowered.

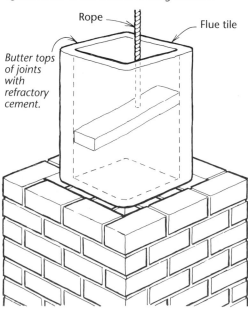

Rope

Flue tile

Butter tops of joints with refractory cement.

Overall, for reasons of safety and longevity, the best choice for relining a chimney is either with clay tiles or a cementitious mix. The latter is more expensive. In this patented process, which is available only through franchised dealers—National SUPA-FLU systems and the BPF (British Poured Flueliner) system are two of the better known—a special rubber form is inserted into the chimney and inflated to the desired diameter. Spacers keep the form from touching the walls of the chimney. A special mix of perlited refractory mortar is pumped into the space between the form and the chimney walls. After 10 to 12 hours, the form is deflated and extracted. The relined chimney can withstand temperatures of 2,000°F and has superior insulating qualities, which helps reduce heat loss and creosote buildup. But the process is not recommended for multi-flue chimneys.

The main disadvantage of clay liners is that it is usually necessary to tear out a face of the chimney at several points to slide the liner up or down in the flue. To gain access to the chimney, sections of walls must also be torn apart. Disposing of several tons of broken brick and crumbled mortar is a dirty, messy job. Wear a dust mask to avoid breathing in hazardous soot and creosote dust. Rebuild the brickwork before tearing out another section.

Flue tiles can be lowered down from the top of the chimney using a rope and a block of wood with an offset hole that allows the block to grab against the sides of the flue, as shown in the drawing at left. Butter the joints at the top of each section with refractory cement before lowering into place. You'll have only one chance to make sure it sets properly upon the previously installed tile without mashing the mortar. Use a mirror and light to inspect the joints. Wipe them smooth by gently lowering a sawdust-filled burlap bag down the flue.

When a chimney has an offset section, relining is much more complicated (and expensive), as it takes a skilled mason to remove enough of the offset so that the mitered flue liners can be inserted without collapsing the chimney. It is usually necessary to open up the offset even when using a poured liner to ensure that the form is properly positioned. Flexible steel liners can avoid this bottleneck, at least for gas or oil burners.

Repointing a chimney

The mortar joints between old brick were never intended to last as long as the brick itself. They need to be renewed occasionally by repointing (or "tucking"). With a cold chisel, rake out crumbling mortar to sound material, usually about 1 in. below the surface. This is painfully slow work. Don't be tempted to speed things up by cutting out the joints with a circular saw or power grinder—you'll ruin the edges of the bricks. Gently chip out and remove damaged bricks and replace them with used brick of similar size and (with luck) age. Be sure to place used brick weathered-side out, as the protected face will be much different in color and texture. Force new mortar into the joints with a narrow-bladed tuck-pointing trowel. Tool the joint with a joint raker to a concave profile, just inside the rounded-over edges of the old brick.

Antique "soft" mortars, in use up until about 1850, were formulated without the portland cement that is used in modern "hard" mortar. Traditional mortars used 2½ to 3 parts sand with 1 part hydrated (slaked) lime, with additives such as crushed oyster shells, pulverized brick or clay. A lime mortar is slightly flexible, allowing it to compress when bricks expand in hot weather and stretch when they contract in cold.

Portland-cement mortars remain rigid, and tend to spall the edges of bricks in hot weather or crack in cold. Whatever kind of mortar was used in the original chimney should be duplicated when repointing. A

This nicely corbeled chimney cap needs repointing before the bricks begin to get dangerously loose.

modified lime mortar that sets faster and is less mushy than pure lime mortars and still compatible with them uses 1 part portland cement to 3 parts lime and 12 to 20 parts sand, depending on the texture and strength needed.

It won't be possible to match the color of either replacement bricks or mortars exactly to the old. The materials weather at different rates in response to chemical composition and time. Some experts try to stain the mortar or brick with colorants of one kind or another (coffee grounds added to the mix are one suggestion), but these additives are only a temporary fix. The best solution is to match the mortar as closely as possible to the original, match the age of the bricks if you can, and let it all blend with time.

Rebuilding a chimney

When the masonry is badly decayed, it makes more sense to demolish the entire chimney than to repoint or reline it. In most cases, the portion that projects above the roof, having been exposed to the weather, will fall apart first and need rebuilding even if the rest of the chimney is sound. Rotted mortar is grainy, whiter and crumbles easily. Tap the bricks with the butt of your palm—if they move or can be lifted free of the mortar bed, ready the trowel. Continue removing the old bricks until a sound layer is reached, most likely a course or so below the roof line.

Sometimes a chimney will be so far gone that the decay does not stop below the roofline. If you can keep removing bricks by hand or with just the slightest tap of a hammer, you may find it necessary to demolish and rebuild the entire chimney.

The quality of old handmade brick was not always the best. Sometimes the bricks disintegrate even when not exposed to the weather. If you think an old chimney and fireplace might have historic value, consult a masonry-restoration specialist about possible approaches to preservation before you touch it. Even if the fireplace cannot be reconstructed using the original material, you may decide to leave it intact and unused, just to look at.

Examine the old bricks as you remove them. If they haven't spalled or become crumbly and brittle, they can be reused. Clean old brick by knocking off any adhering mortar with the point of a brick hammer. But don't strike the brick itself—it breaks easily. Remove loose scale, soot and mortar with a wire brush.

Soak the bricks in water prior to use, or they will suck the moisture out of the mortar and the bond will be weak. New brick will not match antique brick in either size or color, so don't try to mix the two where they will be seen together. If a chimney is to be concealed behind walls, a lot of time and expense is saved by using precast concrete chimney blocks instead of brick. The portion above the roof should be brick in any case. It looks and weathers better.

As with relining a flue, demolishing a brick chimney inside a house is messy work. Not only is there creosote, fossilized bird droppings and mortar dust to contend with, but plaster walls will have to be removed where the chimney is hidden behind them. Remember, creosote is a carcinogen: Wear a respirator, not a cheap paper dust mask. Also wear safety goggles.

Protect the rest of the house from an infusion of fine dust by enclosing the work area in plastic sheeting. Tape all but the flap of an access opening to the walls and floors. Cover the floors with several layers of cardboard to guard against damage by falling debris. Rosin-coated building paper (like the kind used between floorboards and subflooring) protects the walkways when you run your wheelbarrow through the house.

The amateur mason will discover that laying up a brick chimney is slow work. Begin in the cellar with a solid footing. A concrete pad at least 1 ft. deep and 3 ft. square will comfortably carry a single-flue chimney. Footings for larger chimneys must extend at least 6 in. on all sides beyond the chimney itself. Because of its tremendous weight (50 tons or more), the footings for a fieldstone chimney should be extra thick. Pour a rectangular 8-in. concrete wall 4 ft. deep and fill the enclosure with rocks and concrete. Cap it with a slab.

To locate the footing pad so that the chimney will go through the roof without striking beams or rafters, drop a plumb bob from the underside of the roof rafters through an opening cut in the floor(s) to mark one outside corner of the chimney, or plumb up from the cellar as necessary until the best location is found. Pour the pad. While it is still green, drive a nail into the concrete to mark a chimney corner and stretch a string up to the underside of the roof. Check once more for plumb and repeat for the other corners.

Cut the first flue tile for a clean-out door and set it in a bed of mortar. Lay the bricks level between each string up to the height of the first flue tile, butter its lip with refractory cement and set the next tile plumb. Continue laying brick and tile, checking for level across each course, varying the depth of the mortar bed slightly to compensate for any courses that start to run off. Don't lay more than 8 ft. in a day or the weight of the masonry will force the uncured mortar out of the lower joints. Don't fill the space between the flue liner and the bricks with mortar. The air gap is necessary to prevent heat from escaping through the bricks by conduction. Enough small blobs of mortar will inevitably fall from the brick joints to lock the flues in place.

Flue tiles are hard and brittle. The fastest and easiest way to cut them is with a masonry blade and circular saw. Make repeated scoring cuts at least halfway through the tile before tapping it with a hammer. To cut circular holes for thimbles, lay the tile on its side on a sand bed, pack it full of sand and use a carpenter's nailset to punch a series of closely spaced holes through the tile until you can knock the circle out. Don't worry if the cut isn't perfect; any gaps can be plugged with refractory cement.

Bricks are cut by striking repeatedly along the cut line with a 3-in. wide brick chisel. If you're lucky, the brick will actually break somewhere close to where you wanted it to. Chip off any extra or start on another brick if the piece can't be used.

If no other escape route is available, a chimney can be offset to fit around an obstruction such as a structural timber. In no case should the angle of the offset exceed 60°, nor should the centerline of the upper flue fall outside of the centerline of the lower chimney wall. The flue tiles are cut to the complement of the offset angle. The chimney is corbeled (extended outward) by projecting each course out beyond the lower one no more than 1 in. Corbeling is also used to finish chimney tops decoratively. It is occasionally used when it would be useful to add another flue for a second-story or attic stovepipe (see the drawing at right).

When a chimney passes through a floor or roof, maintain a minimum clearance of 2 in. between it and all combustibles. Stuff the gap in an attic ceiling with fiberglass insulation. Stop the ceiling finish or flooring 2 in. away from the chimney, and cover the gap with a metal trim

Chimney Offsets

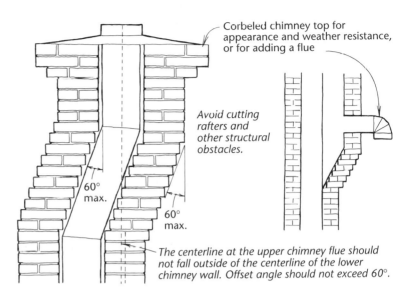

Corbeled chimney top for appearance and weather resistance, or for adding a flue

Avoid cutting rafters and other structural obstacles.

60° max.

60° max.

The centerline at the upper chimney flue should not fall outside of the centerline of the lower chimney wall. Offset angle should not exceed 60°.

collar that will dissipate heat quickly enough not to pose a fire hazard in the event of a chimney fire.

When a chimney cannot quite clear a beam, lay the last full course of brick up under the beam and, if they fit, the next courses on edge. If the chimney still cannot clear the beam with at least 1 in. of air space, then notch the beam out. Except under extreme (and unlikely) loads, an 8x8 beam can safely be notched up to one-quarter of its total width.

When the roof slope exceeds 5-in-12, a staging platform or some sort of saddle is needed to hold the bricks and mortar while you work. Ordinary roof brackets can support staging planks as long as they aren't loaded down with more than a few flue tiles and several dozen bricks at a time. For stronger support, build a pair of sturdy "chicken ladders" to carry the staging planks (see the drawing on p. 328). This setup works well as a base for pipe scaffolding when the top of the chimney is beyond your reach. Adjustable screw-type leg extensions are used to level the

Roof Scaffolding for Rebuilding a Chimney

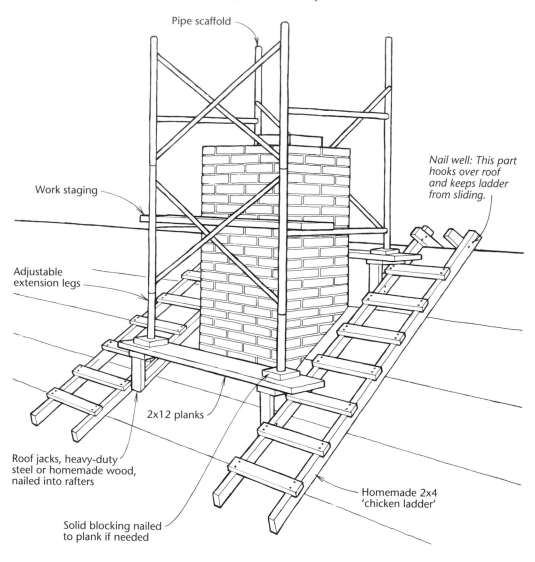

Pipe scaffold

Work staging

Adjustable
extension legs

2x12 planks

Roof jacks, heavy-duty
steel or homemade wood,
nailed into rafters

Solid blocking nailed
to plank if needed

Nail well: This part
hooks over roof
and keeps ladder
from sliding.

Homemade 2x4
'chicken ladder'

*Chimney caps offer an
opportunity to merge
whimsy and function.
This distinctive cap helps
reduce down-drafting
and keeps rain out.*

pipe scaffolding on the roof slope. A blunt-tipped ladder hook will not puncture old and delicate shingles when laid over the ridge.

The last flue tile should extend 4 in. to 6 in. above the last course of bricks. The opening is capped with a 2-in. layer of mortar, feathered to a thin edge to drain off water. Various decorative chimney caps and arches not only add a unique touch, but help reduce down-drafting and prevent rain from entering when the chimney is not in use. If the chimney penetrates the roof close to the eaves instead of the ridge and must therefore rise high above the roof, wrought-iron angle braces bedded into the mortar joints or attached to a band clamp will prevent it from blowing over.

Flashing a chimney

Because a masonry structure doesn't move much relative to the wood framing around it, counterflashing is used to create a watertight but flexible seal between the roofing shingles and the masonry. Counterflashing consists of two parts: a base flashing attached to the roof deck and a cap flashing inserted into the chimney mortar joints that overlaps the base. The overlap keeps out water (except at the back, where ice can build up and penetrate the seal, which is why crickets are used to divert water away from the back of chimneys). If the chimney were sealed directly to the roof deck with a single flashing instead of counter-flashed, the metal would tear out of the mortar joints or split if the roof sagged or the house settled.

Use lead or copper for flashing material. These metals are more expensive than galvanized steel or aluminum, but they will last at least as long as the brickwork and longer than the house frame. Use the more malleable lead when the metal must be formed to irregular stones. The drawing at right shows patterns for laying out base flashings for the roof deck. If you are more interested in getting the job done than doing it perfectly, trust Geocel® (acrylic copolymer caulk) and soft metal to fill in any small gaps in the corners. The flashing at the sides is either a single continuous piece as shown, which works well with metal or roll roofing, or individual pieces "stepped" into each course of shingles. Use 8-in. square pieces folded in half for the step flashings.

Base Flashing for a Chimney

Note: Step flashings can be substituted for continuous base flashings at sides of chimney.

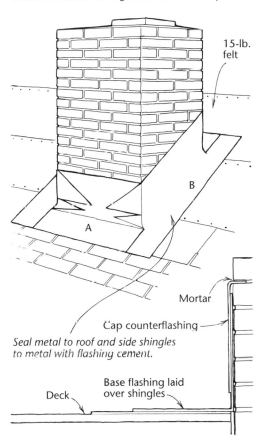

15-lb. felt

B

A

Mortar

Cap counterflashing

Seal metal to roof and side shingles to metal with flashing cement.

Base flashing laid over shingles

Deck

Pattern A: Top and bottom

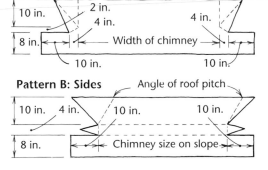

10 in.   2 in.   4 in.   4 in.

8 in.   Width of chimney

10 in.   10 in.

Pattern B: Sides   Angle of roof pitch

10 in.   4 in.   10 in.   10 in.

8 in.   Chimney size on slope

To avoid mortar-spattered shingles and cleanup problems, counterflashing should ideally be installed into the brickwork before the roof is shingled. It is bent upward out of the way while the base flashings are fitted to the shingles.

Old flashing is seldom reusable. It also seems that few masons knew the first thing about proper flashing or bothered to take the time to make a counterflashing. Usually, it's easier to tear out the old flashing and replace it with new metal than to try to fix it. Clean out the joints in the brickwork with a cold chisel. Better still, the narrow cut made by a circular saw equipped with a masonry blade is perfect for holding new flashing, especially if it runs diagonally across the masonry. Make the cut about 1 in. deep and run a bead of "cement-patch" caulking in the notch. Fold the end of lead flashing metal over itself and gently force it into the crack with a blunt chisel so that the folded edge locks the metal into the groove. Finish the joint with another bead of caulk, tooled to a concave profile.

Chimney draw

The top of the chimney should project at least 2 ft. above the ridgeline of the house or any other ridgeline that is within 10 ft. (horizontally) of the chimney. If the chimney is not centered on the ridge, it should extend at least 2½ ft. above it. A chimney draws because of a difference in temperature between hot air at the fire and cooler outside air. Air moving rapidly across the lip of the flue also creates a partial vacuum, which helps the chimney draw, especially when it is cold and the fire newly kindled. Under the right conditions, with a large enough temperature difference, cold air can be drawn down into the chimney at the same time hot air is rushing up. The effect of this phenomenon is the familiar sudden puff of smoke that bursts from the stove—the down draft.

Chimney draw is also directly related to height. To draw at all, the outlet of a chimney should be at least 15 ft. above the inlet of the thimble. A single-story house with a low roof does not allow for a chimney tall enough to produce a decent draft. If the air currents at the chimney top are obstructed by ridgelines, an adjacent building wall or large overhanging trees, which cause air turbulence and eddies, poor draw and down-drafting will result.

Fissures between the bricks of an unlined chimney act to shorten its effective length, which is why a lot of tired old chimneys smoke. There is also a definite relationship between flue height and flue volume. The wider the chimney, the less friction between its walls and the rising smoke, which is the rationale for the rounded corners of flue tiles. Round flues are even better, but they have a smaller cross-sectional area. But after a certain point, an increase in flue diameter only slows down the velocity of the rising smoke, increasing cooling and creosote condensation, and decreasing draw.

Excessive cooling is also the reason why a chimney and fireplace built against an outside wall will often draw poorly. The bricks are so much colder that they chill the smoke, which also increases creosote deposition. By the time they do warm up, the fire has gone out, so heat loss is much greater. The central-fireplace Colonial floor plan used this radiant heat loss to warm the house.

A Few Thoughts about Fireplaces

In the canons of energy conservation, the fireplace is anathema. So much has been written about the inefficiency of fireplaces as a heat source that nothing more need be said, except that in the age of central heating no one actually tries to heat with a fireplace anymore.

No amount of reasoned analysis can change the persistent notion that a house is not a home without a fireplace. In the dim and smoky womb of a rock cave, the first humans huddled around the glowing embers, warm and well fed, while the night creatures howled outside the magic circle. These ancestral memories reverberate in the common origin of the words hearth, home and heart, and their association with centering. When someone is asked to draw an image of home, invariably a fireplace is included. The fire is frequently described as "cheerful" or "cozy." When our presidents address the nation with their words of assurance, they are frequently seated beside the flickering grate. Although wolves no longer prowl outside the door, the memory lingers. As one stares into the flames, visions dance, and old feelings, like coals under the grate, are stirred. The room softens and draws closer, dreams shimmer beyond the sphere of sight. For a moment, the mind's clutch slips.

The construction of a masonry fireplace is a precise art. Count Benjamin Thomas Rumford, an 18th-century American expatriate, spent years studying the smoky, constantly down-drafting and poorly heating fireplaces of his time. The improvements he recommends in his treatise on fireplace design, based on sound theory and minute observations, are irrefutably validated by experience. The "Rumford fireplace" has such a shallow, sloping firebox, the fire almost seems to sit out in the room. It radiates a good deal more heat than traditional designs and always draws perfectly.

As Rumford's ruminations suggest, an improperly proportioned fireplace is a frequent cause of a poorly drawing chimney. An experienced mason or chimney sweep can diagnose fireplace ills and suggest modifications to improve performance. Most carpentry and masonry handbooks also contain charts for standard chimney and fireplace dimensions derived from Rumford's observations. Kitchen fireplaces, used for cooking, have quite different dimensions than sitting-room fireplaces used for heating. Their backs are vertical so that cooking pots could be hung at different heights above the fire. The lintel was set so high that a person could actually step into the firebox recess. To prevent smoke from drifting out into the room, the firebox was extended quite a way up behind the lintel. The opening for a heating fireplace is nowhere near as

high. In fact, good proportion and good draw require that the lintel for a 3-ft. wide opening be set only 30 in. above the hearth.

If you hire a mason to rebuild an old fireplace or even to build a new one, insist that he or she follow the designs and dimensions given in the plans exactly. Country masons are noted for their stubbornness and distrust of "fancy flatlander architect booklearning," and will not hesitate to change the design to fit "the way I always done it." Remember, a lot of traditional smoky chimneys were built by traditional masons.

Finally, any fireplace renovation should include the installation of a tight-fitting pair of glass doors. This addition will prevent excessive heat loss when the fireplace is not in use. If the fireplace is to be out of use for any length of time, stuff a batt of insulation into the throat and close the damper.

This fireplace is literally the high point of the house. All the walls and floors have settled away from it.

Afterword

I've often thought that if it were possible to choose another life, in another time, I would be a master builder of a medieval cathedral. In the Middle Ages, builders coordinated an undertaking that involved the spiritual and financial resources of an entire community for generations. In our age, only the devotion of the military-industrial complex to the myth of the Cold War has come close to that shared undertaking. For us, tradition has disintegrated like the mortar of an old chimney: The moral order has been replaced by the technical order, intuitions by institutions, beauty by bureaucracy. Left only with the shards of private mythologies, we build our cathedrals in our backyards and find transcendence in vegetable gardens and remodeled kitchens.

After a day of hard work, sleep is welcome, deep and dreamless. Sitting by the woodstove on a winter's evening, a peace settles over me like an old quilt. At this moment it seems possible to live like a pebble on a stream bottom, worn smooth and rounded by the flow—the rough edges, the bad dreams, forgotten. "I could be bounded in a nutshell/And count myself king of infinite space." (Shakespeare, *Hamlet* II:2)

But there is a danger inherent in individualism that is untempered by a sense of community. Individualism without the recognition that we all live downstream from someone else is the root of the rapacity that is poisoning our planet. If we are all one, what we do as individuals reverberates forever.

How does all this relate to the renovator of old houses on a mundane level? What we feed our family dog each year could support a family in Bangladesh: Does that mean that we shouldn't keep dogs? I don't think so. But it might mean that you shouldn't use aluminum or vinyl siding to refurbish your dwelling. There seems to be a direct relationship between the cost of a material and the damage done to the earth to produce it. Many highly processed building materials consume nonrenewable resources, require prodigious amount of energy to produce and pollute the environment in every step of their production and distribution.

Wood is renewable. To use it gently requires patience and skill; the reward is a house that lives in harmony with its materials. Feel a piece of wood, absorb its grain and texture. Now meditate on a piece of vinyl or aluminum. These materials, like white flour, have had the life ground out of them. They give nothing back to the craftsman. Without any exchange, there is no joy.

The choices you make affect the flow of energy. No one will manufacture what no one uses. The conscious builder has a responsibility not to contribute to further destruction. Use natural, native materials —wood, stone, brick, earth, adobe, bamboo. Use synthetics as a last resort, where nothing else will fit the function as well. Whenever possible, use processed materials that are low on the energy scale— asphalt shingles, steel roofing, gypsum drywall, fiberglass insulation instead of urethane foam, real boards instead of textured plywood. Because natural materials pulse with life, the structures they shape share this vitality. Compare a real Christmas tree to an artificial one. If you can't see the difference, you probably shouldn't be living in an old house.

The perception of a built form as beautiful or satisfying seems related to the organic content of the materials used in its construction, and its familiar and well-worn human-scale proportions. So much of grand architecture is only momentarily satisfying, a game of ego and display, like the latest fashions, soon out of style and funny looking to future ages. Why is it that the lines of old houses, like the music of Mozart, grow more timeless and pleasing with every passing decade? Why is it that very little built in the last 50 years has that feeling?

In *House Form and Culture* (Englewood Cliffs, N.J.: Prentice Hall, 1969), Amos Rapoport writes: "If a man does, in fact, have certain inborn rhythms, biological rhythms, biological needs and responses, which are unchanging, a complete relativism becomes impossible and the built environment of the past may still be valid." The house forms of the past are vessels of accumulated sensibilities derived from the constraints of the environment and the technology of the time. The forms of old houses grow from this creative tension. They recapitulate the trees from which their bones were hewn, an image of the cathedral, an interface between earth and sky, the play of light in the lofty vaulting of the leaves and the soaring trunk thrusting out of the earth, lifting the sap and spirit far above gravity's dark embrace. Such a house is linear only in the narrow sense that wood has a grain, a linear direction unlike the oceanic roundness of earth and stone. Wood framing balances the fastness of the earth with that which drives the tree beyond it. As the tree tires, it returns to earth. The old houses slowly incline toward the horizontal. A state of pleasing decay, the slow music of return, strikes in us the twin chords of our own mortality and our eternal connection to past and future.

Pir Vilayat, a Sufi sage, could have easily been speaking of a love affair with old houses when he wrote in his book *Toward the One:*

We carry within us dim and shifting intuitions of greater perfections beyond those normally seen or experienced on Earth. We try to grasp them while remaining in our everyday con-

sciousness and attribute our failure to the assumption that they must have been pure conjecture, astral fantasy, or wishful thinking and suffer for want of giving them expression in ourselves, for they are knocking at our door, offering to fertilize us with their bounty, and our feeling of slipping failure is nature's way of reminding us of the urgency of fulfilling this imperative human need.

What is it about old houses, anyway?

Bibliography

A lot of books have been written about renovating, restoring and remodeling old houses. No single volume could possibly cover every aspect of the subject, but a lot of books on the market don't even do justice to the basics, and some are so utterly lacking in any sensitivity to the special character of old houses that no one should ever read them. Unless they have some other merit, my suggested reading list won't include books that tell you to look for another house at the first sign of a crack in the foundation or worms in the woodwork—if you could afford a perfectly restored old house, you probably wouldn't be reading this book in the first place. But the listing does include various handbooks for skills associated with renovation that are by necessity only touched upon in this book.

For those whose interests range beyond the mere how-to, I've listed some background readings in the historical, architectural and philosophical aspects of the subject. The reasons for building new houses are fairly obvious; rebuilding old houses involves a peculiar form of masochism and dedication that is worthy of further exploration. Good luck!

Building History and Architectural Styles

American Building: Materials and Techniques from the First Colonial Settlements to the Present
Carl W. Condit (Chicago: University of Chicago Press, 1968)
The title says it all—a comprehensive history of American building.

Big House, Little House, Back House, Barn: The Connected Farm Buildings of New England
Thomas C. Hubka (Hanover, N.H.: University Press Of New England, 1984)
An engaging architectural and social history of a style of building that is unique to northern New England.

Building Early America
Carpenters' Company of the City and County of Philadelphia, eds. (Radnor, Pa.: Chilton Book Co., 1976)
Articles on the development of central heating, masonry methods, house framing, early roofing materials and window glass.

Early American Homes for Today
Herbert Wheaton Congdon (Dublin, N.H.: William L. Bauhan, 1985)
A reprint of the original 1963 edition, this book is a practical restoration manual, an architectural history and a sourcebook of decorative details, written by the son of the famous Gothic Revival architect, himself a practicing architect and lover of old Vermont country houses.

Early Domestic Architecture of Connecticut
John Frederick Kelly (New York: Dover Publications, 1963)
A reprint of a classic work, full of details and lore about 17th- and 18th-century timber-framed houses. An excellent companion to the Congdon volume.

A Field Guide to American Houses
Virginia and Lee McAlester (New York: Knopf, 1984)
An encyclopedic taxonomy of American housing from the 17th century to the present.

Remodeled Farmhouses
Mary H. Northead (Boston: Little, Brown & Co., 1915)
If you can find this book in your library, you'll enjoy hours of fascinating reading with these case studies of the remodeling of 22 farmhouses back before electricity and pumped water systems were considered standard. Contains a lot of practical old-time information and decorative details, as well as a fascinating perspective on how the craftsmen of an earlier era dealt with renovation problems.

Conservation Methods and Philosophy

Historic Preservation
National Trust for Historic Preservation (Washington, D.C.)
Nontechnical preservation journal, good for professional contractors.

The Impecunious House Restorer
John T. Kirk (New York: Alfred A. Knopf, 1984)
An essay in attitude adjustment designed to foster reverence for old homes. Good on researching and documenting the age of a house.

The Restoration Manual
Orin Bullock, Jr. (Norwalk, Conn.: Silvermine Publishers, 1966)
A book for the conservationist, devoted to ferreting out the original beauty of antique buildings and rescuing them from the ravages of modernization. Written by a sensitive architect.

Buying, Inspecting and Evaluating Old Houses

Don't Go Buy Appearances
George C. Hoffman (Westminster, Md.: Ballantine Books, 1972)
Tells you what to look for when inspecting a house and how to evaluate it.

Finding and Buying Your Place in the Country
Les Scher (Riverside, N.J.: Collier Books, 1974)
Written by a lawyer, this book tells you how to do exactly what the title says with a minimum of hassle and expense.

Home: A Short History of an Idea
Witold Rybczynski (New York: Viking Penguin, 1986)
A study of the development of the idea of comfort, which answers part of the question, "What makes a house a home?" By an architect who also happens to be a fine writer.

How to Inspect a House
George C. Hoffman (New York: Addison-Wesley Publishing Co., 1985)
Good on checklists, bug problems, bargaining to get the best price.

Hands-On Renovation

The Apple Corps Guide to the Well-Built House
Jim Locke (Boston, Mass.: Houghton Mifflin, 1988)
A beginner's guide to the care and feeding of your contractor. This book presents a wealth of experience and good practical details.

How to Rehabilitate An Abandoned Building
Donald R. Brann (Briarcliff Manor, N.Y.: Easi-Bild Pattern Co., 1974)
A good book for the urban renovator, as it addresses problems rural home owners seldom encounter.

New Houses from Old
R.R. Hawkins and C.H. Abbe (New York: McGraw-Hill Book Co., 1948)
This out-of-print volume was intended as a guide for modernizing the old houses of an earlier generation. It is a treasury of obsolete details and techniques one is likely to encounter in today's old houses.

New Life for Old Houses
George Stephen (Washington, D.C.: The Preservation Press, 1989)
An update of his 1973 volume, *Remodeling Old Houses Without Destroying Their Character* (New York: Knopf). Good on design and planning, with a thoughtful and sensitive appreciation for the spirit of old houses. Stresses nondestructive remodeling. Good information on restoring brownstones as well as wood-frame buildings.

Old American Houses: How to Restore, Remodel and Reproduce Them
Henry L. and Ottalie K. Williams (New York: Coward-McCann, 1957)
This is one of the earliest books written with the home owner in mind. A bit thin on real solid how-to, even in the updated versions.

The Old House
Time-Life Books staff (Alexandria, Va.: Time-Life, 1980)
As with all the volumes in the *Home Repair and Improvement* series, this book has excellent drawings and good how-to information. Strictly for amateurs, *The Old House* covers all the basics, with one or two hints that even an experienced professional might find useful.

The Old-House Doctor
Christopher Evers (Woodstock, N.Y.: The
Overlook Press, 1986)
I like this guy—we think alike. I can't tell how
many ideas he borrowed from me, and I'm sure
he can't tell how many I've borrowed from him,
but the diagnostic approach and the historical
asides, coupled with generally solid techniques
based on his experiences, make this an invaluable
book.

The Old-House Journal Compendium
Clem Labine and staff of *The Old-House
Journal*, eds. (New York: Overlook Press, 1980)

The Old-House Journal New Compendium
Patricia Poore and Clem Labine, eds. (New
York: Doubleday/Dolphin Books, 1983).
These two books are compilations of articles that
previously appeared in *The Old-House Journal*
(Brooklyn, N.Y.). I can't recommend this monthly newsletter enough for its reader-written historical, anecdotal and eminently practical advice on
all phases of restoration. Also publishers of the
annual *Old-House Journal Catalog*, which is an
indispensable sourcebook for all kinds of hard-
to-find hardware, fixtures and fittings for old
houses. No one in the old-house business should
be without at least one of these volumes.

Renovation: A Complete Guide
Michael W. Litchfield (New York: John Wiley
and Sons, 1982)
A comprehensive volume on residential renova-
tion by the founding editor of Taunton Press's
Fine Homebuilding magazine.

*The Timber-Frame House: Design,
Construction, Finishing*
Tedd Benson (Newtown, Conn.: Taunton
Press, 1988)
An indispensable book on modern timber-frame
construction.

Catalogs of Materials

The Brand New Old-House Catalog
Warner Books (New York: Warner Books,
1980)
A superb sourcebook.

*The Complete Illustrated Guide to Everything
Sold in Hardware Stores*
Tom Philbin and Steve Ettlinger (New York:
Macmillan Publishing Co., 1988)
This book tells you the names of all those wid-
gets and fittings that you'll need to ask for at the
hardware store.

*This Old House Guide to Building and
Remodeling Materials*
Bob Vila, with Norm Abrams, Stewart Byrnes
and Larry Stains (New York: Warner Books,
1986)
An encyclopedia of building materials, very useful for nonprofessionals to learn how to choose
the right materials for the job.

Carpentry Skills

*Basic Building Data: 10,000 Timeless
Construction Facts*
Don Graf (New York: Van Nostrand Reinhold,
1949)
Although some building practices aren't timeless,
it's amazing how little the building industry has
changed in the last half-century.

Carpentry
Leonard Koel (Homewood, Ill.: American
Technical Pubs., 1985)
A good textbook for residential and commercial
work.

*Carpentry: Some Tricks of the Trade from an
Old-Style Carpenter*
Bob Syvanen (Chester, Conn.: The Globe
Pequot Press, 1982)
Tells you how to take those shortcuts that every
experienced carpenter knows.

Modern Carpentry
Willis H. Wagner (South Holland, Ill.:
Goodheart-Wilcox Co, 1983)
This vocational textbook is a bible of modern
residential carpentry methods. A lot of builders,
myself included, got started with this book. A
little basic knowledge of carpentry goes a long
way, even in an old house.

*The Reader's Digest Complete Do-it-Yourself
Manual*
(Pleasantville, N.Y.: Reader's Digest, 1973 and
other editions)
This manual is handy for just about anything
around the house, from adjusting a furnace to
fixing a washing machine.

Simplified Carpentry Estimating
J. Douglas Wilson and Clell M. Rogers (New
York: Simmons-Boardman Books, 1962)
Although wages and prices have gone up, the
shortcuts builders use to price a job haven't
changed.

Subtrade Handbooks

In general, the older the edition of a guide-book, the more pertinent the information will be to old-house work. You'll know how and why the old-timers did what nobody does anymore. Temper this information with what you learn from modern guide-books, since some of the materials and methods the old-timers recommend are bound to be inferior or completely irrelevant. There's no sense romanticizing the mistakes of the past. What do you think a Colonial carpenter would have done with his broadax if you gave him a power planer and a circular saw to use? Following is a list of some guidebooks that cover the subtrades that arc an inseparable part of old-house remodeling. It usually takes browsing through two or three of them before you get the idea. There's always more than one way to do a job.

Audel's Carpenters and Builders Library
Frank D. Graham, ed. (New York: Theodore Audel & Co., 1948)

Audel's Complete Roofing Handbook
James E. Brunbaugh (New York: Theodore Audel & Co., 1986)
Good on slate, tiles, hex-tab shingles, but has nothing on corrugated steel roofing.

Audel's Guide to Domestic Water Supply and Sewage Disposal
Edwin P. Anderson (New York: Theodore Audel & Co.,1960)
Good on springs and wells.

Audel's Masons and Builders Library Vols I & II
Louis M. Dezettel (New York: Theodore Audel & Co., 1978)
Good on stucco, concrete block, tile and ornamental concrete finishes. The earlier editions (1924) are good for old-time masonry techniques.

Audel's Painting and Decorating Manual
Harold J. Highland (New York: Theodore Audel & Co., 1965)

Audel's Plumbers and Pipefitters Library
Jules Oravetz, Sr. (New York: Theodore Audel & Co.,1966)
Good on cast-iron piping.

Audel's Plumbers and Steamfitters Guide
(New York: Theodore Audel & Co., 1948)

The Bricklayer's Bible
Charles R. Self (Blue Ridge Summit, Pa.: TAB Books Inc., 1980)
TAB "bibles" explore all the basic materials and techniques of the trades they cover. Older editions are especially useful for renovators.

Clean and Decent
Lawrence Wright (Buffalo, N.Y.: University of Toronto Press, 1960)
An engaging history of the bathroom. Insights into cultural attitudes towards bodily functions, sewerage systems and plumbing.

DeChristoforo's Complete Book of Power Tools, Both Stationary and Portable
R.J. DeChristoforo (New York: Harper & Row, 1972)
Everything you always wanted to know about your radial-arm saw and table saw.

Do-It-Yourself Plumbing
Max Alth (New York: Sterling Publishing Co., 1987)
One of the best books on plumbing, especially good on how systems work and how to fix them when they don't.

Do-It-Yourself Wiring Handbook
Sears Roebuck and Co.
This pamphlet, which can be ordered through the Sears Catalog, is a clear, concise guide.

The Forgotten Art of Building a Good Fireplace
Vrest Orton (Dublin, N.H.: Yankee Books, 1969)

Heating Your Home with Wood
Neil Soderstrom (New York: Harper & Row, Publishers, 1978)
A very complete guide to installing woodstoves and furnaces, with good advice on chain-saw use, cutting and seasoning wood.

Home Guide to Plumbing, Heating and Air-Conditioning
George Daniels (New York: Harper & Row, Publishers, 1973)
Good on plastic pipes.

How To Design and Install Plumbing
A.J. Matthias, Jr. (Chicago: American Technical Society, 1940)
Old plumbing books are great for explaining how to work with cast iron and other long-gone materials. The ATS also publishes handbooks in other fields.

How to Do Your Own Home Insulating
L. Donald Meyers (New York: Harper & Row, Publishers, 1978)
One of the titles in the *Popular Science Skill Book* series. All the volumes are basic, with solid information and clear explanations and drawings.

How to Do Your Own Painting and Wallpapering
Jackson Hand (New York: Harper & Row, Publishers, 1976)
Also includes a chapter on floor finishing.

How to Work with Concrete and Masonry
Darrell Huff (New York: Harper & Row, Publishers, 1976)

How to Work with Tools and Wood
Robert Campbell (New York: Simon & Schuster, 1952)
Originally published by Stanley Tools, this small book is a classic.

In the Bank or Up the Chimney
U.S. Dept. of Housing and Urban Development (Radnor, Pa.: Chilton Book Co., 1976)
This popular pamphlet is one of the best on how to insulate a house and on home energy conservation in general.

Painted Ladies: San Francisco's Resplendent Victorians
M. Baer, E. Pomada and M. Larsen (New York: Dutton, 1978)
With the rediscovery of authentic Victorian painting colors and schemes, this book celebrates, inspires and informs.

The Passive Solar Construction Handbook
Steven Winter Associates. (Emmaus, Pa.: Rodale Press, 1983)
Lots of schematic drawings and rules of thumb, mostly for new construction, but also useful for retrofitting greenhouses and sunspaces.

Practical Electrical Wiring
H.P. Richter (New York: McGraw-Hill Book Co., 1972)
This book has been in print since 1939 and is updated every few years. It's an eminently practical exegesis of the NEC filled with solid how-to techniques. Good for amateurs and professionals alike.

Residential Heating Operations and Troubleshooting
John E. Traister (Englewood Cliffs, N.J.: Prentice-Hall, 1985)
An outline of modern heating-plant design and operating theory.

Stone Masonry
Ken Kern, Steve Magers and Lou Penfield (Oakhurst, Calif.: Owner-Builder Publications, 1976)
For those who want to rebuild their stone foundation the right way.

The Toilet Papers
Sym Van der Ryn (Santa Barbara, Calif.: Capra Press, 1978)
Thoughts on the culture of waste and many designs for composting toilets, mostly for warm climates.

Wood-Inhabiting Insects and Houses: Their Identification, Biology, Prevention and Control
Harry B. Moore (Washington, D.C.: Government Printing Office, 1979)
If you really feel like crawling into the woodwork, this is your travel guide.

The Woodburner's Encyclopedia
Jay Shelton and Andrew Shapiro (Waitsfield, Vt.: Crossroads Press, 1976)
Shelton is the foremost expert on all aspects of wood heat, efficiency and performance.

Index

A

Additions:
  preservation guidelines
    for, 39
  of sheds and garages,
    214-15
  of stories, 55
Air infiltration:
  explained, 227
  and heat loss, 173-74
  reducing, 174-76
  See also Caulk. Insulation.
    Weatherstripping.
Air-vapor barriers:
  explained, 227-29
  using, 192, 229, 233
Architects: need for,
  debated, 63
Asphalt:
  applying, to foundation,
    93
  See also Roofing.
Attics:
  conversion of, 52-54
  evaluating, 36-37
  insulated roofs for, 215
  roof pitch of, and floor
    space, 53
  ventilation in, necessity
    of, 194

B

Backhoes:
  directing, 71-72
  for wall straightening,
    129
Basements: See Cellars.
Bathrooms:
  fixtures in, saving, 38
  See also Plumbing.
Beams:
  added, finish for, 238
  cleaning, 253
  for jacking, 82, 85-86
  load-carrying, adding,
    238
  steel,
    adding, 240-41
    types of, 240
  See also Framing.

Beetles: damage from,
  evaluating, 20
Bibliography: annotated,
  334-38
Blockwork:
  fasteners for, 240
  surface-bonded, 80, 89
Brickwork:
  framing attachment to,
    240
  stained, cleaner for, 205
  stripping, 205
  as wall insulation, 19
Builders: See Workers.
Builder's paper: use of,
  discouraged, 192
Bulkheads:
  evaluating, 35
  See also Cellars.
Bulldozers:
  traxcavator, 96
  utilizing, 94
  winches with, using, 129

C

Carpenter ants: damage
  from, evaluating, 20
Carpenters: See Workers.
Caulk:
  applying, 174-75
  choosing, 174
  removable, 176
  for thresholds, 185
  translucent wood-
    appearing, 252
Ceilings:
  drywall for, 253
  evaluating, 37
  lowering, disadvised,
    256-57
  subfloor, painting, 253
  texturing, 255
  T&G boards for, 254, 256,
    257
  tin, installing, 255-56
  treatments for, 252-57
  wooden, coved, 257

Cellars:
  adding, 95-97
  alongside, house moved
    over, 97-98
  entrances of,
    evaluating, 35
    footings for, 92
  evaluating, 27-30
  floors for,
    drains in, 99
    pouring, 98-101
  foundations for, 92
  repairing, 50
  sump pits for, 99
  walls for, pouring, 50
Chalk lines: with wood
  shingles, 160, 199
Chimneys:
  caps for, 328-29
  codes on, 323-24
  crickets of, flashing, 146
  evaluating, 21-22, 37-38,
    323
  excavating around, 96-97
  flashing for, 329-30
  flue widths for, 330
  framing clearances for,
    327
  half-, problems from, 129
  heights for, 330
  inauthentic, ugliness of,
    172
  mortar for, old vs. new,
    325
  obstructions in,
    removing, 323
  offsets in, building, 327
  rebuilding, 325-29
  relining, 323-25
  repointing, 325
Clapboards: See Siding.
Come-alongs:
  using, 125-26, 129
  See also Turnbuckles.
Concrete:
  amounts of, calculating,
    90
  curing time for, 89
  delivering, to far corners,
    100
  framing attachment to,
    240

  nails for, hardened, 240
  reinforcement mesh for,
    99-100
  strengths of, 90-91
  water in, 91
Condensation:
  explained, 227-29
  See also Air infiltration.
    Air-vapor barriers.
Contractors:
  acting as, 60, 61
  contracts with, 60-61
  dealings with, 60-61
  hiring, 60
  See also Workers.
Cornices:
  returns of,
    repairing, 194
    rotted, 31
Cracks:
  repairing, 122-23
  serious vs. natural, 121-22

D

Design:
  developing, 46-49
  timeless, 332-33
Designers: need for,
  debated, 63
Doors:
  evaluating, 25
  hanging, 187-89
  hinges for, placement of,
    188
  inauthentic, ugliness of,
    172
  jambs for, 187
  moisture-proofing, 185
  problems with, 28, 186
  recycling, 187
  repairing, 185-96
  replacement, choosing,
    186
  screen, installing, 189
  stops for, 188
  storm, installing, 189
  thresholds for, 189
    replacing, 184-85
  weatherstripping, 188
Dormers: adding, 52-54, 219

Drywall:
  between ceiling beams, 254-55
  installing, 246-48
  over plaster, 226
  as plaster patch, 223
  taping, 248-49
Dumpsters: renting, 149

E

Eaves:
  adding, after gutter removal, 196
  protecting, 164-65
Electricity:
  explained, 263
  See also Wiring.
Ells: defined, 215
End grain: sealing, 193, 209
Excavation: preservation guidelines for, 38

F

Finances:
  considering, 39-42
  moral dimension to, 41-42
Fireplaces:
  design of, 331
  doors for, 331
  drama of, 330-31
Flashing:
  for chimneys, 329-30
  eaves drip-edge, 145
  failed, 141
  for metal roofing, 161-62
  nails for, 157
  old, care with, 145
  for porch roofs, 208, 213
  between siding and sills, 192
  step, adding, 146
  for television antennas, 146-47
  of thresholds, 184
  valley,
    corroded, 23
    exposure rule for, 144
    installing, 156-58
  for wood shingles, 159
Floors:
  cellar, with sleepers, 98
  concrete,
    pouring, 98-101
    reinforcement mesh for, 99-100
  evaluating, 29, 37-38

finishes for, 259-61
holes in, patching, 238-39
level check for, with string, 117
linoleum on, removing, 258
patches in, color matching for, 238
porch, rot susceptibility of, 208
preservation guidelines for, 39
renovating, 51
repairing, 259
rotted, replacing, 119-20
sagging, repairing, 116-20
sanding, 260-61
strip, removing, 259
strip vs. wide, 258-59
Footings:
  aligning, with raised sills, 86-87
  digging, 86
  forms for, 87
  leveling, 87
  pouring, 78, 87
  rebar in, 87
  width of, 86
Forms:
  books on, 90
  bracing, 91
  building, 90
  manufactured, 88
  service chases in, 92
Foundations:
  backfilling to, 80, 93
  blockwork, 73, 74
    vs. poured, 88, 92-93
    cap for, 88-89
  buttresses against, pouring, 68-69
  problems of, 21, 111
  drainage systems for, installing, 67-70
  nonfunctional, 68
  evaluating, 15, 18-19, 26, 37, 66-68
    from cellar, 27-30
  forms for, manufactured, 88
  and hydrostatic pressure, effects of, 65-66, 68
  leveling, 115
  moving house onto, 55
  owner-poured vs. contractor-poured, 87-88
  repairing, 70-71, 106-11
    costs of, 18-19
  replacing, 71-93
  wall-slab leaks in, fixing, 68

waterproofing,
    exterior, 69, 93
    interior, 68
  See also Forms. House raising. Window wells.
Framing:
  balloon, history of, 105
  braces in, adding, 127
  plank-house, explained, 104
  studs in,
    repairing, 111, 120
    shimming, 114-15
  for staircases, 242-43
  with steel beams, 241
  stick, advantages of, 105-107
  See also Beams. Ceilings. Doors. Girts. Joists. Knee braces. Plates. Posts. Roofs. Timber framing. Windows.
Furnaces:
  excavating around, 96
  See also Heating systems.

G

Garages: blending, 215
Girders: See Girts.
Girts:
  defined, 74
  jacking, 85
  sagging, correcting, 116-18
  scarf joint for, 123
  stiffening, 118-19
  tenons in, replacing, 123
  See also Sills.
Grading: with bulldozer, 94
Gutters:
  aluminum,
    considering, 168
    installing, 169
  built-in, relining, 166
  copper, 169
  downspouts for, sizing, 168
  pitch for, 169
  for porches, 208
  problems of, 165
  repairing, 166-67
  sizing, 168
  vinyl, caveats against, 168
  wooden,
    protecting, 167
    rebuilding, 167
    removing, 167-68
    replacing, 168
  and soffit vents, 196
Yankee, 165-66, 167

H

Heat loss:
  explained, 227
  See also Air infiltration. Condensation.
Heating systems:
  alternative, 319-20
  evaluating, 34
  history of, 307
  hot-air, forced, 307-308
  hot-water,
    gravity-flow, 314-15
    maintenance of, 316-18
    trouble-shooting, 318
    types of, 316
  preservation guidelines for, 39
  radiators for,
    adding, 318-19
    finned, for steam, 318
  solar, 321-23
  steam,
    maintenance of, 311, 313-14
    manual-feed, replacing, 312-13
    one-pipe, 309
    safety mechanisms for, 311-13
    two-pipe, 310
    vacuum-flow, 311
    venting, 310-11
  wood, 320-21
House holding: blockwork allowances in, 88-89
House raising:
  advantages of, 73
  chronicle of, 77-81
  cribbing for, 73, 79, 80, 81, 82, 85
  expert help with, 73
  vs. house holding, 73
  jacks for, 82-83
  load analysis for, 74-76
  process of, 84-86
  rules for, 83-84
  sequence of, 106-109
  timbers for, 82, 85-86
  See also House holding.

I

Insulation:
adding,
to attic roofs, 215
priorities for, 231-32
over sheathing, 192
characteristics of, charted,
230-31
and condensation, 22-23,
228-29
evaluating, 36
exterior foundation,
protecting, 80, 93-94
retrofitting, 93-94
fiberglass, 227
covering, 234
faced vs. unfaced,
232-33
foam perimeter,
installing, 93-94
installing, 232-34
with plaster walls, adding,
225
rules for, 233
R-values of, 229-30
See also Air infiltration.

J

Jacks.
pump, using, 148
roof,
placement of, 156
slopes for, 147
using, 82-83, 129,
208-209
Joinery:
mortise-and-tenon,
joist-to-wall, 5
repairing, 123
scarf, tension, 123
Joists:
hangers for, 119, 122
insulation between,
233-34
lag screws for, 122
notching, for pipes, 303,
304-305
porch,
ground clearance for,
210
pitch for, 209
repairing, 210
preservation guidelines
for, 39
repairing, 111
rim, replacing, 114
stiffening, 118-19
support, for sill repair,
110, 111, 114

K

Knee braces:
problems with, 125
reinforcing, 191-92
Kneewalls: adding, 128

L

Ladders: aluminum vs.
wood, 148
Legalities:
book on, 42
considering, 42

M

Masonry:
framing attachment to,
240
pointing, 70
preservation guidelines
for, 38
stuccoing, 68, 70
See also Chimneys.
Fireplaces.
Metal connectors:
joist-hanger, custom, 119
plate, types of, 122
Moisture:
wall problems from,
22-23, 293
See also Condensation.
Moldings:
matching, 193
for shiplapped siding, 202
Mortise-and-tenon:
See Joinery.

N

Nails:
for flashing, 157
hardened, 240
for metal roofing, 163
powder-actuated, 240,
241

P

Paint:
alligatoring, causes of,
203
applying, temperatures
for, 203
asphalt fiber-reinforced,
144, 207
blistering, causes of, 203
over calcimine, 224
for ceilings, 255
chalking, dealing with,
203
crazing of, causes of, 203

failures of, diagnosing,
22-23, 202-203
latex vs. oil, 204-205
mildewed, dealing with,
202
and moisture problems,
203-204
for plastered ceilings, 226
for porch floors, 209
preservation guidelines
for, 39
stain, 205
stripping, 204, 258
vapor-barrier, 204, 225
wrinkles in, causes of, 203
Paneling:
in ceiling, 254
history of, 249
installing, 250-52
scribing for, 252
Pantograph: making, 252
Plaster:
applying, 223
calcimine on, painting,
223-24
between ceiling beams,
254
over drywall, 255
evaluating, 37-38
finishes for, 226-27
patching, 221-23
preservation guidelines
for, 38-39, 39
removing, 224-25
over Rocklath®, 226
sagging, repairing, 222
texturing, 255
tin ceilings over, 255
wallpaper on, removing,
222
Plates: replacing, 124
Plumbing:
chases for,
in floors, 303, 304-305
in forms, 92
codes on, 281
dealing with, in house
raising, 73, 74
designing, 289-90
evaluating, 32-33
freeze-proofing, 288-90
leaks in, repairing, 293-95

pipes for,
ABS, 282
cast-iron, additions to,
300
cast-iron, cutting, 301
cast-iron, repairs to,
297-99
cast-iron, replacing,
299
copper, 283
copper, repairing,
295-97
CPVC, dangers of, 282
plastic, repairing, 301
polybutylene, 282-83
polyethylene, 282
sink, repairing, 301-302
supply-line, repairs to,
292-97
pump systems for,
artesian, 285-86
evaluating, 33
gravity, 34, 285
jet, 286, 288
low-well piston, 286,
288
repair of, 286-88
shallow-well, 286
submersible, 286
from source to pump, 284
stacks for, installing, 303
traps for, 290
typical, diagram of, 289
vents for, 290
See also Waste disposal
systems. Water.
Porches:
advantages of, 206-207
columns of,
repairing, 210
venting, 210
drainage for, 212
evaluating, 26-27
floors of,
end-grain protection
for, 209
painting, 209
repairing, 209
foundations for, 212
lattice panels of, dealing
with, 210-11
problems with, 26-27
railings of,
repairing, 210
supports for, 210
repairing, jacks for, 208-
209
replacing, 50, 211-12
roofs for, 207-208
See also Stoops.

Posts:
  adding, 118
  bearing for, 118
  bracing systems around, 113
  load-bearing, supporting, 111, 113
  repairing, 115-18
  replacing, 115, 118
  tenons in, replacing, 123
Preservation:
  defined, 4-7
  guidelines for, 38-39

R

Rafters:
  collar ties on,
    adding, 127
    lack of, problems from, 125
  evaluating, 36
  gussets for, adding, 127-28
  plate under, replacing, 124
  preservation guidelines for, 39
  stiffening, 128
  straightening, with 2x4s, 121
  undersized, problems from, 125
Remodeling: defined, 8-9
Renovation:
  checklist for, 43, 47
  costs of, considering, 39-42
  defined, 6-10, 13
  degrees of, 4, 8-9
  morality of, 41-42, 332-33
  photostudy of, 50-52
  priorities for, setting, 44-49, 55-59
  whys of, 3-4
Restoration: defined, 6
Ridge caps: for wooden shingles, 159
Ridge vents: commercial, recommended, 171

Roofing:
  asphalt-shingle, 134-36
    application techniques for, 155-56
  architect, 136
  bundles of, lifting, 152
  corrugated, 137
  estimating, 153
  evaluating, 23
  fiberglass-based, 136
  giant, 136
  ground cloth for, 148-49
  hex-lock, 135
  horizontal layout for, 154-55
  installing, 152-56
  jet, 136
    applying, 158
  lock-tab, 136, 137
    applying, 158
  removing, 147-50
    scaffolding for, 147-49
  repairing, 139-40
  replacing, at eaves, 167
  reroofing with, 144-59
  ridge-cap,
    applying, 156
    repairing, 140
  vertical layout for, 153-54
  weight of, figuring, 144
  built-up, repairing, 138-39
  cement, 133
  cement-asbestos, 133
    repairing, 142
  for eave protection, 164-65
  emergency, 150
  evaluating, 22-23
  fiber-reinforced coating for, 144, 207
  metal, 132
    applying, 161-63
    cutting, 163
    evaluating, 23
    nailing, 163
    painting, 163
    repairing, 143-44
  pitch-limit table for, 134
  for porches, 207-208
  roll, 134, 135
    applying, 158-59
    as under-roofing, 150, 151

  slate, 131
    evaluating, 23
    repairing, 140-42
    supply source for, 141
  terne, 132-33
  tile, 133-34
    repairing, 142-43
  under-, installing, 150
  wood-shingle, 131
    applying, 159-60
    evaluating, 23
    repairing, 143
  See also Flashing.
Roofs:
  cold,
    building, 170-71
    retrofitting, 215-16
    ridge vents for, 171
    soffit vents in, 195
  evaluating, 22-23, 36
  as indicators, 16, 17
  insulation for, adding, 215
  leaks in, 137-38
  not-level, diagnosing, 125
  plates in, ventilation through, 196
  rebuilding, 54, 55
  removing, 216-18
  replacing, 218-19
  roofing weights and, 144
  See also Flashing. Jacks. Ladders. Ridge vents. Scaffolding. Sheathing.
Rot: damage from, evaluating, 20-21
R-values:
  explained, 229-30
  of walls, 229

S

Sanity: preserving, with house, 55-59
Scaffolding:
  pipe, using, 148
  roof, for chimney work, 329
Screws: holes for, repairing, 186
Septic systems: See Waste-disposal systems.

Sheathing:
  air-vapor barrier over, 192
  flashing for, at sills, 192
  plywood over, 151
  repairing, 151, 191
  rotted, causes of, 151
  shimming, 114-15
Sheds:
  attached, evaluating, 26-27, 214-15
Shims: using, 115
Siding:
  aluminum as, discouraged, 190-91
  asphalt-impregnated fiber, problems with, 202
  board-and-batten,
    described, 200
    installing, 201
  cement-asbestos, cautions for, 24
  clapboard,
    exposure for, 196
    grades of, 196
    installing, 196-99
  against concrete, flashing for, 192
  evaluating, 24
  history of, 189
  as indicator, 18, 20
  new-into-old, weaving, 183-84
  novelty, installing, 201
  replacing, 190, 191
  shiplapped, installing, 201-202
  vinyl as, discouraged, 190-91
  wood, weathering of, 173, 189
  wood-shingle,
    exposure for, 199
    installing, 199-200
  See also Paint.
Sills:
  beveling, for insulation, 93
  evaluating, 15, 17, 20-21, 30
  replacing, 50, 79, 80, 90, 108, 109-15
  rot in, explained, 103
  vertical shims with, 80
  See also Girts.

Soffits: vents for,
   retrofitting, 194-96
Stains:
   dilute, for ceilings, 254
   discussed, 205
Staircases:
   designing, 241-43
   evaluating, 37-38
   repairing, 243-45
   schematic of, 244
   stringers for, 243
   See also Steps. Stoops.
Steps: porch, repairing, 211
Stoops: rebuilding, 213
Stucco:
   over exterior insulation,
      80, 93-94
   over old masonry, 68, 70
   surface-bonding, 80
Studs: See Framing.

T
Tar paper:
   installing, 150
Termites: damage from,
   evaluating, 20
Timber framing:
   history of, 103-105
   insulation for, 234
   schematic of, 75
   stiffening, 191-92
   straightening, 56
   See also Beams. Girts.
      Posts. Sills.
Trim:
   and drywall, 226
      extension molding for,
         225, 226
   exterior, problems with,
      24-25
   importance of, 8-9
   natural, deciding on,
      257-58
   oak, caveats for, 258
   preservation guidelines
      for, 39
   removing, 258
   repairing, 193
   replacing, 193-94
   See also Cornices.
      Moldings.
Turnbuckles: using, 126-27

V
Ventilation:
   attic, importance of, 151
   through soffits,
      providing, 194-96
   See also Air infiltration.

W
Waferboard: nail-holding
   ability of, 215
Wallpaper:
   recommended, 226
   removing, 222
Walls:
   and addition, joining,
      51, 52
   bearing, removing,
      237-39
   crooked, siding and, 197
   evaluating, 15, 17-18, 19,
      28, 31, 37
   foundations under,
      adding, 51
   heat loss through, 227
   interior finishes for,
      245-46
   with large stud spaces,
      insulating, 234
   moisture in, combatting,
      203-204
   nonbearing, removing,
      234-37
   off-plumb, correcting,
      125-29
   partition, adding, 239-41
   preservation guidelines
      for, 39
   R-values of, 229
   straightening, 86-87, 108,
      109
   turnbuckle support for,
      127
   See also Knee walls.
Waste-disposal systems:
   evaluating, 30-33
   health codes on, 32
   percolation tests for, 32,
      291
   septic tanks for, 291
      alternatives to, 291
      cautions for, 292
      locating, 292
      problems with,
         garbage-disposal
         caused, 292
      problems with,
         treating, 291-92
   traps for, 290
   vents for, 290

Water:
   sources for,
      evaluating, 33-34
      spring, 33, 283-84
      well, 33, 284
Water heaters: evaluating,
   34, 35
Weatherstripping:
   for doors, 188
   EPDM, 175
   spring-metal, 176
   to-be-avoided, 175
   vinyl, 175
Windows:
   adding,
      considerations for, 181
      heights for, 182
      larger, 182-83
   bay, foundation for, 51
   casings of, insulation
      under, 192
   double-glazing, 177
   drip caps for, 191
   evaluating, 24-25
      cellar, 36
   filling in, 183-84
   glazing, 179
   inauthentic, ugliness of,
      172, 177
   rebuilding, 177-80
   removing, 178
   replacement,
      commercial authentic,
         177
      to-be-avoided, 181
   sash cords in, 179
   sills, of replacing, 180-81
   storm, aluminum vs.
      wood, 177
   weatherstripping, 175,
      180
   See also Dormers.
Window wells:
   insulation for, 67
   louvers for, ventilating,
      67
   moisture problems from,
      solving, 67-68
Wings: defined, 215
Wiring:
   aluminum, dangers of,
      266
   boxes in, extension
      collars for, 225, 226

   chases for,
      baseboard, 275
      in ceilings, 253-54
      in forms, 92
      in wainscotings, 275-76
   circuits of,
      designing, 267-68
      surface-mounting, 269
   codes on, 264-65, 267,
      272, 275
   color codes for, 264, 276
   connections in, chart for,
      276, 277-79
   evaluating, 34-35, 264-67
   explained, 263-64
   between floors, installing,
      273-75
   freeing, in wall removal,
      235-36
   ground-fault interrupters
      in, 267
   lightning arresters for,
      286
   minimum-service, 266-67
   outlet boxes for,
      installing, 269-73
      special-purpose,
         269-71, 272
   protecting, 275
   rerouting, 236-37
   switches for, installing,
      272-73
   tools for, 268
Wood:
   rot in, discussed, 103
   See also various wooden
      components.
Workers: owner dealings
   with, 61-62

Z
Zoning: and building
   footprint, 49

Editor: Laura Tringali
Designer: Steve Hunter
Layout artist: Catherine Cassidy
Copy editor: Carlo Codato
Production editor: Peter Chapman
Illustrator: Lee Hov
Photographers: George Nash, Jane Waterman

Typeface: ITC Stone
Paper: Warren Patina Matte, 70 lb., neutral pH
Printer and binder: Arcata Graphics/Hawkins, New Canton, Tennessee